THE LAW AS A CONVERSATION AMONG EQUALS

In a time of disenchantment with democracy, massive social protests, and the "erosion" of the system of checks and balances, this book proposes to reflect upon the main problems of our constitutional democracies from a particular regulative ideal: that of the conversation among equals. It examines the structural character of the current democratic crisis and the way in which, from its origins, constitutions were built around a "discomfort with democracy." In this sense, the book critically explores the creation of different restraints upon majority rule and collective debate: constitutional rights that are presented as limits to (and not, fundamentally, as a product of) democratic debate; an elitist system of judicial review; a checks and balances scheme that discourages, rather than promotes, dialogue between the different branches of power; etc. Finally, the book proposes a dignified constitutional democracy aimed at enabling fraternal conversation within the framework of a community of equals.

ROBERTO GARGARELLA is Professor of Constitutional Law at the University of Buenos Aires and a senior researcher at the National Scientific and Technical Research Council (CONICET). He has published numerous books and articles, including *The Legal Foundations of Inequality* (2010), *Latin American Constitutionalism* (2013), *The Latin American Casebook: Courts, Constitutions, and Rights* (with J. F. Gonzalez-Bertomeu, 2016), and *Constituent Assemblies* (with J. Elster et al., 2018).

CAMBRIDGE STUDIES IN CONSTITUTIONAL LAW

The aim of this series is to produce leading monographs in constitutional law. All areas of constitutional law and public law fall within the ambit of the series, including human rights and civil liberties law, administrative law, as well as constitutional theory and the history of constitutional law. A wide variety of scholarly approaches is encouraged, with the governing criterion being simply that the work is of interest to an international audience. Thus, works concerned with only one jurisdiction will be included in the series as appropriate, while, at the same time, the series will include works which are explicitly comparative or theoretical - or both. The series editors likewise welcome proposals that work at the intersection of constitutional and international law, or that seek to bridge the gaps between civil law systems, the US, and the common law jurisdictions of the Commonwealth.

Books in the series

The Law As a Conversation among Equals
Roberto Gargarella

Micronations and the Search for Sovereignty
Harry Hobbs and George Williams

Fundamental Rights and the Legal Obligations of Business
David Bilchitz

Courting Constitutionalism: The Politics of Public Law and Judicial Review in Pakistan
Moeen Cheema

Ruling by Cheating: Governance in Illiberal Democracy
András Sajó

Local Meanings of Proportionality
Afroditi Marketou

Property Rights and Social Justice: Progressive Property in Action
Rachael Walsh

Carl Schmitt's Early Legal-Theoretical Writings: Statute and Judgment and the Value of the State and the Significance of the Individual
Lars Vinx and Samuel Garrett Zeitlin

Remedies for Human Rights Violations: A Two-Track Approach to Supra-national and National Law
Kent Roach

Europe's Second Constitution: Crisis, Courts and Community
Markus W. Gehring

A.V. Dicey and the Common Law Constitutional Tradition: A Legal Turn of Mind
Mark D. Walters

Administrative Competence: Reimagining Administrative Law
Elizabeth Fisher and Sidney A. Shapiro

Legal Sabotage: Ernst Fraenkel in Hitler's Germany
Douglas Morris

Proportionality in Action: Comparative and Empirical Perspectives on the Judicial Practice
Edited by Mordechai Kremnitzer, Tayla Steiner and Andrej Lang

Constitutional Dialogue: Democracy, Rights, Institutions
Edited by Geoffrey Sigalet, Grégoire Webber and Rosalind Dixon

The Veiled Sceptre: Reserve Powers of Heads of State in Westminster Systems
Anne Twomey

Vigilance and Restraint in the Common Law of Judicial Review
Dean Knight

The Alchemists: Questioning Our Faith in Courts as Democracy-Builders
Tom Gerald Daly

Australia's Constitution after Whitlam
Brendan Lim

Building the Constitution: The Practice of Constitutional Interpretation in Post-Apartheid South Africa
James Fowkes

Dimensions of Dignity: The Theory and Practice of Modern Constitutional Law
Jacob Weinrib

Reason of State: Law, Prerogative, Empire
Thomas Poole

Bills of Rights in the Common Law
Robert Leckey

The Guardian of the Constitution: Hans Kelsen and Carl Schmitt on the Limits of Constitutional Law
Translated by Lars Vinx, with an introduction and notes by Lars Vinx

Parliamentary Bills of Rights: The Experiences of New Zealand and the United Kingdom
Janet L. Hiebert and James B. Kelly

Lawyering for the Rule of Law: Government Lawyers and the Rise of Judicial Power in Israel
Yoav Dotan

Balancing Constitutional Rights: The Origins and Meanings of Postwar Legal Discourse
Jacco Bomhoff

Judges on Trial: The Independence and Accountability of the English Judiciary
Shimon Shetreet and Sophie Turenne

Proportionality and Constitutional Culture
Moshe Cohen-Eliya and Iddo Porat

The Politics of Principle: The First South African Constitutional Court, 1995–2005
Theunis Roux

The New Commonwealth Model of Constitutionalism: Theory and Practice
Stephen Gardbaum

Searching for the State in British Legal Thought: Competing Conceptions of the Public Sphere
Janet McLean

Judging Social Rights
Jeff King

Proportionality: Constitutional Rights and their Limitations
Aharon Barak

Parliamentary Sovereignty: Contemporary Debates
Jeffrey Goldsworthy

THE LAW AS A CONVERSATION AMONG EQUALS

ROBERTO GARGARELLA
Senior Researcher at the National Research Center (CONICET, Argentina)

CAMBRIDGE
UNIVERSITY PRESS

The silver lining of the generally dark and worrying panorama that drove me to write this book involves a number of recent phenomena that allowed me to recognize and assert the feasibility of my ideal of law as conversation among equals. These manifestations negate the traditional retort that such an ideal for social structure is no more than a utopian abstraction or illusion that can only work in the scenario of meetings held behind closed doors. We have now seen (and will later examine) examples of deliberative assemblies that have taken place in many Western countries. These include (which is even more relevant for my argument) inclusive, thorough public debates over controversial topics (such as abortion in Catholic countries like Ireland and Argentina). These examples reveal, for starters, the value, meaning, and importance of democratic dialogue – even in societies divided by political convictions or beliefs – around questions related to basic rights (a possibility that predominant political and legal theory, with its insistence on separating questions related to rights from democratic debates, has rejected). However, the significance of these examples goes further, for they also demonstrate that such experiments can produce real results. They show that public discussion is not only possible but can even prove effective in heterogenous, institutionally deficient societies.

In early October 2019, having wrapped up my classes and most of my other professional obligations for the year, I left for the United States. There I encountered supportive scholars with whom I could converse whenever necessary plus a network of excellent libraries where I could work for hours on end. Three in particular, the libraries at the University of Columbia (when I was uptown), at New York University (when I was downtown), and the New York Public Library (near Grand Central), made my stay one of austere yet intense happiness.

To my surprise, after a few weeks of working long hours that flew by, I finished the first draft of the book. Unexpectedly, long before planned, and as if the book had written itself, or as if someone had dictated it to me. I had not had to struggle with my ideas to disentangle my thoughts and make the arguments clear. (During those days in the US, Jon Elster confessed to me that it also happened to him sometimes: writing "downhill" - that is, sliding quietly. And he suggested me to stop writing when the exercise turned "uphill" - when writing became dificult or unpleasant). It was as if someone was reading the book to me and I was trying so hard to keep up that I entered into a sort of trance.

One last clarification about the book. This is a book aimed at discussing ideas, in which I present thoughts and arguments that I have been maturing – with more or less fortune – for decades. To facilitate my writing and your reading, I decided not to burden it with scholarly quotes, references, and footnotes. This choice greatly facilitated my writing, making it – I believe – more fluid and lighter. I hope it also helps your reading and engagement with the discussions I present.

ACKNOWLEDGMENTS

At this point, and only at this point, I would like to express my gratitude to several of the people who helped me. I thank Carlos Díaz and Caty Galdeano for the friendly support that made the book possible. I thank Martin Abregú and Mirna Goransky for putting me up without asking anything in return. My thanks to Vicky Murillo and family, for always being there for me. I would like to thank the friends who kept me company during my stay: Christian Courtis, Jorge Contesse, César Rodriguez Garavito, Sergio Chejfec, Roberto de Michele, Patricio Navia, David Sekiguchi. I would like to thank Sebastian Guidi, Fernando Bracaccini, Patricio Kenny, and Emiliano Catán for their help. I would like to thank the scholars who met with me: Adam Przeworski, Jon Elster, Owen Fiss, Robert Post, Helene Landemore, Lewis Kornhauser, Joseph Raz, and Jeremy Waldron. Very special thanks to David Dyzenhaus, for his immense generosity and for the great opportunity of teaching a seminar on the book with him for the University of Toronto. I would also like to thank Leonardo Filippini for encouraging me to pursue this idea and to my friend Siri Gloppen, for her support and encouragement. Thanks so much Brad Hayes for a wonderful, "active," and "participatory" translation! And thanks to Vanina Domizzi for the corrections. I would like to thank my friends in Argentina who give everything meaning to me. Thanks Paula for her curiosity. Thanks to my parents, my brothers and sisters, my extended family, and my nephew Juan. Thank you all.

This book is dedicated to the memory of my father, Nicola, an Italian immigrant

1

Constitutionalism and Democracy

An Institutional Problem of Structural Nature

I am writing this book during difficult political times (and I am writing it at this particular moment largely because of them). We live in the era of the "Arab Spring," "Black Lives Matter" in the United States, and the rise of *Syriza* in Greece and *Podemos* in Spain, not to mention the "They all must go" movement in Argentina ("*Que se vayan todos*"). It is a time of massive demonstrations and protest against current authorities in Catalonia and Ecuador, a time when millions have descended to the streets to demand President Piñera's resignation in Chile. Many of our constitutional democracies seem haunted by the same specter, that of "democratic fatigue" or "discontent." Citizens seem fed up with their government institutions and tired of those who represent them in it. The notion of "democratic fatigue" and the related sense that democracy is being "eroded from within" to the point of being hollowed out are commonplace in the current social science literature. No longer are we as worried by the prospect of democracies "dying in a single blow" as was typical in the recent postcolonial era of military coups and dictatorships. Rather, we now talk about the "slow death" of our democracies through a gradual "dismantling" of their institutions by leaders who have consolidated their power in a series of arguably legal moves.

The outcome of progressive degradation in the government system is familiar (and is what generates the "fatigue"). There is a tendency to move from a government "of the people, by the people, for the people" to a government "of a few people, controlled by a minority, at the service of the privileged." Our institutional system (and I say "our" with the constitutional model in mind that has been adopted in most Western nations since the end of the eighteenth century) resembles a system that has been "captured."[1] Utterly perplexing stories are told all over of authorities who

[1] As will be seen, this work is largely comparative. The "heart" and center of the comparative analysis is American constitutionalism (American as in from North and South America, not only the United States) yet the ramifications of the analysis, to the degree I am able, will be traced beyond the Western hemisphere.

behave simply and unabashedly however they want, as if the rules they have to follow have been suspended, as if the boundaries on their power did not exist – authorities who proudly wear constitutional robes and democratic trappings while spouting human rights discourse. Moreover, they go unflinchingly about their business in a bureaucratically efficient manner, with an eye on best practices, proper attire, and the requisite array of erudite legal references.

I am writing this book in the face of a disheartening landscape and am trying to facilitate critical reflection on the situation in which we find ourselves – a reflection that is meant to help clarify our ideas and reexamine the settled truths we unthinkingly repeat. I am particularly interested in pushing back against a tendency coming from the social sciences to relate the democratic crisis underway with the actions of some reckless leader currently in power (say Jair Bolsonaro, Nicolás Maduro, Daniel Ortega, Viktor Orban, or Recep Erdogan) or with the breakdown of an institutional system that has been corrupted (as in Argentina, Colombia, Mexico, or Peru where dozens of parliamentarians and political leaders have been convicted). This kind of approach – which I will argue is mistaken – leads many prominent authors in the current generation of social scientists to focus their efforts on bringing about a change of leader (Impeach Trump!), adjusting the "old model" (to restore checks and balances, recuperate effective controls, or reestablish institutional "escape valves"). Or they focus their efforts on reinvigorating the sense of civic responsibility and duty in order to resolve, more or less definitively, the political "dramas" of our times.

I will argue that these efforts are useless for several reasons that will be subjected to a fairly meticulous examination over the course of this book. Above all, I will argue that it is mistaken to blame the apathy, indifference, or distaste of "people in general" (to the degree that the population's views can be generalized) toward politics on a lack of engagement or desire to participate in political decision-making. Rather, I hold, the apparent indifference should be understood as an endogenous product of the institutional system itself; that is, something about the way the system is arranged produces or at least aggravates it. The protests and demonstrations that take place on a daily basis from Seattle to Washington, DC belie the notion of generalized political apathy as it is traditionally understood in the United States – and so did the thousands of volunteers who went from neighborhood to neighborhood knocking on doors to support Barack Obama's presidential campaigns. Whether or not these examples are convincing, what can be observed is not a population disinterested in politics, but an institutional system that currently represents the only effective channel of democratic participation and yet discourages regular voting. Similarly, the hollowness of the notion of "apathy" that was used for decades to describe the political context in countries like Brazil or Argentina has also been revealed by frequent, massive demonstrations by sectors of the population actively demanding respect for their rights. These demonstrations take place despite the limitations imposed by very restrictive institutional systems that characterize the region (the most restrictive of which being the Chilean model put in place by the dictator Augusto Pinochet forty years ago that remains intact today). Again, if citizen engagement is lacking, the cause has to do with the institutional arrangements that discourage or prevent it.

This is why I emphasize so strongly the importance of avoiding *the conflation of democratic and constitutional problems* – something that, I believe, we continue to do. The type of crisis we are facing has more to do with a *democratic deficit* (the way our institutions resist and block citizen control and decision-making power) than with the specific processes within the constitutional system by which each branch of the government checks and balances the others. I do not deny that this internal system is being undermined, but the recent impairments are rooted in deeper problems that date back from long ago.

The problems we are facing go well beyond personal ambitions and political circumstances. We need to look past the current political situation and leaders. I would like to show that changing the leadership or making "technical adjustments" to the current system will not enable us to regain what we lost or eliminate what causes our revulsion and fatigue. I would like to focus on structural factors related to the institutions we have. Among those institutions, I will center my examination on those that are germane to constitutional democracy, not because I take the "constitutional bases" as necessarily our most important institutions, but rather because I feel that they deserve special attention and careful study, which they have largely failed to attract.[2]

[2] Part of the problem is that much of political theory and legal sciences neglects the theoretical and philosophical examination of the institutions that create law. That is why Jeremy Waldron begins his most recent book by addressing this area of reflection. The book starts with a criticism of Isaiah Berlin's political philosophy that ignored the role of institutions (in the Anglo-Saxon world, particularly England, Waldron observes, political theory is studied as a branch of ethics instead of a discipline that normatively examines institutional structures), and ends by praising Hannah Arendt's constitutional politics (Waldron, 2016).

In this regard, throughout this work I will repeatedly return to the idea that the original institutional system has been completely overwhelmed (to give a sense of the environment in which I am writing this book, at the moment extraordinary demonstrations are rocking Chile, Ecuador, Bolivia, and Spain). The institutional scheme no longer appears capable of carrying out even a portion of what it promised at its foundational moment – the promise on which its legitimacy stands.[3] To make sure my point is clear, not even were the current institutional system functioning perfectly could it

[3] Let me clarify, and give some more precise content, to the idea of the "broken promises" of modern constitutionalism that I just mentioned. I will do so by mentioning, albeit briefly, three interrelated arguments: one historical, another constitutional, and the other sociological. First of all, I believe that my basic claim finds significant historical support – at least, clearly, in the history of the Americas, which is at the center of my study. In the struggle for independence, in the Americas, the revolutionary leaders used to raise very radical ideals, such as the ideal of self-government. Undoubtedly, they needed to endow their struggles with popular support and social legitimacy. The fact is, however, that after their victory they could not sustain their claims – something that generated early social tensions. As Gordon Wood put it (quoting Fisher Ames), shortly after the end of the Independence Revolution, "the people [began to turn] against their teachers the doctrines which were inculcated in order to effect the late revolution" (Wood 1969, 397; see also Wood 1991). In Wood's words, the Revolution had "shattered traditional structures of authority, and common people increasingly discovered that they no longer had to accept the old distinctions that had separated them from the upper ranks of the gentry. Ordinary farmers, tradesmen, and artisans began to think they were as good as any gentleman and that they actually counted for something in the movements of events. Not only were the people being equated with God, but half-literate plowmen were being told even by aristocrats like Thomas Jefferson that they had as much common or moral sense as learned professors" (Wood 2002, 131). I found support to similar claims, concerning Latin America's history, in Gargarella 2010 and 2013.

In addition, the first constitutions that were written, after independence, tended to strengthen this critical, tense situation. All the new constitutions appealed to great principles (freedom, equality, etc.) and many among them used a radicalized rhetoric, of the Rousseauian type (in Latin America, this was something very common in many of the first constitutional documents, such as those we find in Venezuela, Uruguay, and Mexico). Again, then, there was a break between what the law said and what the actual political practice offered. The break between constitutional rhetoric and practice was, in a way, inevitable: the new constitutions tried to establish the foundation of a new political-institutional order, and this objective seemed incompatible with (something like) the maintenance of a permanent deliberative state in the society. It is also true, however, that in the unfair social context that prevailed in many of these countries – a context that was characterized by the presence of deep and unjustified inequalities – the elites that drafted the new constitutions took advantage of the situation to consolidate their privileges or shield them from possible attacks. The concentration of power that continues to prevail in so many countries, or the discouragement of political participation, are clearly the product of that situation. In the end, as expected, the prevailing political-economic inequality was translated into constitutional inequality. (This was my argument in Gargarella 2010.)

make good on its early ambitious promises. I am referring to its inclusive promise – "full representation"; to its promise of respect for the rights of overlooked minorities; and its promise to recognize the sovereignty of the people's voice. As we will see, countless changes have taken place since the foundational moment – changes in circumstances and in thinking. These changes have been so profound that we should not be surprised that the situation we face is dramatically expressed in terms of overwhelmed institutions and an alienated society. The institutions are no longer capable of meeting the expectations of their initial aspirations and promises while the society increasingly sees them as alien, distant, and removed.

1.1 The Democratic Objection is Still There

"When he woke up, the dinosaur was still there."

– Augusto Monterroso

The concrete institutional problems that I identified as characteristic of our time are rooted in causes that transcend both our current dilemma and the cast of political actors currently on stage. For that reason, I hope you will allow me to take a few steps back. My approach in this book requires a certain distance for the sake of perspective and a thorough analysis.

Practically speaking, constitutional democracy as we know it has displayed certain traits from its outset – over two centuries ago – that should concern us. These traits threaten to make our worst fears reality. The risk is that constitutionalism, instead of reinforcing freedom – both personal and collective – may be used to broaden the liberty of some at the expense of the liberty of others. This is the type of problem to which we refer when we speak of the *tension between constitutionalism and democracy.*

As will be shown, the first problem of our constitutional legal tradition is that, from its outset, its framers have been reticent, if not unwilling, to grant the general populace a protagonist role in civic matters. Instead, they sought to limit, not foster what Thomas Jefferson called the "direct

Finally, I would mention a sociological argument that is bound to appear repeatedly in this book: what I will call the "dissonance" argument. The point (presented decades ago, in a different version, by Samuel Huntington) refers to the political and institutional tensions that are generated when societies change in depth (e.g., in their number, social composition, heterogeneity, expectations) while the institutions that govern them remain basically the same after centuries (Crozier et al. 1975; Huntington 1983). The current tension between social expectations and institutions, as I understand it, is based in part, and in part reinforces, the preexisting social tensions that marked the life of regional constitutionalism.

and constant control by the citizens."[4] Our constitutional legal tradition was thus marked by *distrust* of the common citizens' capacity for political virtue – what Michael Sandel would call "democracy's discontent."[5]

This distrust can be detected in the notion that only certain people have the ability to recognize what comprises the "public interest" that law should serve (the "representatives" of the people rather than the people themselves; trained "judges" rather than ordinary citizens). Such elitist presumptions were characteristic of the predominant discourse at the "founding moments" of modern constitutionalism, yet they neither disappeared over time nor grew obsolete, like laws passed in a bygone era that we simply forget. The initial "distrust" was translated, from the outset and ever since, into a system of institutions that remains intact. In some cases, the framers expressed anti-majoritarian intentions unabashedly. A severe case is that of Jaime Guzmán, the juridical architect of Pinochet in Chile, whose 1980 constitution was explicitly devised to prevent the conservative minority's adversaries from dislodging them from power – reducing constitutionalism to a small cage to keep democracy under control.[6] We live by mechanisms for governance designed upon these types of premises, premises that justify the democratic objections of today and yesteryear against the scheme in place: the *democratic objection* that arose alongside constitutionalism has never dissipated, while constitutionalism itself has been consolidated.

[4] Jefferson to John Taylor, May 28, 1816, in Jefferson 1999, 208.

[5] This state of affairs is alarming because the first promise of law itself is that it will serve each and every one of us inasmuch as we stand as equal citizens before it. Law rises above other rules because its rules are written collectively for everyone and in everyone's name, with the ultimate aim of improving conditions for everyone. That is precisely where the beauty of law lies: to acquire its respectability, legitimacy, and support – the consent of everyone – law must be written in universal terms (i.e., "everyone has the right to" express themselves freely, acquire property, and so forth) which every single citizen can invoke. Universality is what makes it possible for everyone to recognize the law and accept it. Notwithstanding, depending on when, where, and by whom the law is written, respect for this criterion may falter or even vanish. To take an example from the founding moment of the United States Constitution, we could cite the framers' decision to exclude the problem of slavery, such that the institution was allowed to continue hidden from the face of the law. Similarly, including numerous clauses in the constitution that protect the right to property and market values increases the risk that the law be used to bolster an unjust and unequal system because its language is facially neutral and nondiscriminatory.

[6] At that time, Guzmán himself asserted: "The Constitution must ensure that if [our] adversaries come to rule, they are constrained to follow an action not so different from what one would yearn for, [so that] the range of [available alternatives become] sufficiently reduced" (Guzmán 1979).

What is worse, the constitutional system of checks and balances has not mitigated the democratic deficit over time. Instead, the problem has deepened, which only reinforces the validity of the democratic objection. Matters have worsened, as we will see, in at least two important ways. To begin with, the institutional situation is much worse, because the societies in which we live have evolved so much since the days of the framers. The societies that the "founding fathers" had in the backs of their minds when they drew up the original constitutions differ starkly in terms of composition, looming dangers, internal conflicts, and the divisions upon which social identities are formed. Secondly, and this point is more relevant to my argument in this book, we are coming off the "victory" of democracy as the dominant paradigm over communism, when more than ever people subscribe to its values. Never before has the citizenry been as "empowered," following the current jargon, to intervene and participate capably in decisions on public matters that concern it. What I am trying to say is that the institutions designed on the basis of distrust toward the masses now clash with a citizenry that demands trust, one that will no longer lower its voice, bow its head, and go sit and wait at home. Addressing the discrepancy between what the institutions were designed to do, what they promised to deliver, and what society expects of them has thus become imperative. The gravity of the situation is compounded by the unfortunate circumstance – the circumstance that, in a way, drove me to write this book – that the most heralded theorists within the constitutional tradition, the ones that recognize the democratic "fatigue" or "erosion" afflicting us, nevertheless superimpose the issue of democratic deficit on questions of constitutionalism. The resulting theory thus proposes constitutional solutions ("tightening screws" in the "engine room" of the constitutional system) for problems whose root is of another order – the nature of our democracy itself. As a result, even in the best of cases, the democratic deficit causing our anguish goes on, untouched and intact.

After more than two hundred years, the democratic objection to the original constitutional framework remains, without doubt, as strong as it ever was. Like the dinosaur in Monterroso's short story (often considered the shortest story ever told), we have woken up but the "democratic objection" has not left. Despite decades upon decades spent in debates and refutations, the simple, even obvious objection still stands, right where it has been from the start. For that reason alone, we have the right to ask ourselves why the decisions on the matters that are most important to us are left to others to make, in our name, and in spite of our disagreements with them. We argue and haggle until we can shout no more, so we take a break, and when we start up again, the democratic objection is right where we left it.

1.2 Of History and Ideas

What I have been describing, in terms of the institutional limitations that beleaguer us, points to an issue that is especially relevant for my argument in this book. I am referring to the "mismatch" between our institutions and the expectations and demands that the citizenry has of and places on them. We will delve into this issue in more detail in the next chapter, but to put it briefly, the institutions of which we currently dispose do not respond very well to our needs or our expectations. The mismatch is likely produced by many factors but, for the purpose of this work, I will emphasize two in particular: causes rooted in the historical paths our nations have followed and ideological reasons; that is, reasons related to ideas about objectives and regulation. Without going into them deeply at this point, I would like to provide some preliminary considerations.

1.2.1 "History"

Regarding the historical reasons for the discrepancy that concerns us here, among the many explanations for the choice of constitutional institutions with which we find ourselves, one in particular focuses on the history of constitutionalism itself. Many of our most important institutions were created in response to the specific problems our ancestors confronted during an era or historic moment. At the time, they may have represented the best response available, considering the circumstances in which they were deemed necessary, but that does not mean that they would necessarily continue to be adequate for the new problems to come brought by changing times.

In my opinion, the Argentine jurist Juan Bautista Alberdi wrote brilliantly about these matters. He recognized the importance of designing constitutions that addressed the problems – the "dramas" or "tragedies" – facing society at the time. In this regard, the starting point for his reflection on constitutionalism differed significantly from that of many other jurists of his time, for whom constitutionalism represented a long-term project. For them, the idea was to elaborate a constitution that would crystallize society along the lines it established and, for that reason, it made sense to elaborate a "rigid" charter to make changes or reforms more difficult. Against that predominant vision, Alberdi proposed an understanding of constitutionalism in terms of the "dramas" of the time. Different eras faced different dramas, thus requiring different constitutional responses. For different, perhaps even more interesting reasons (related to collective self-government), Thomas Jefferson would also adopt a vision of constitutionalism much more grounded in the immediate context. Jefferson went as far as suggesting that the constitution be modified every nineteen years, the period that according to his calculations corresponded to generational turnover. Each generation, he maintained, should have its own constitution. Similarly, Article 28 of the Declaration of the Rights of Man and of the Citizen adopted by France in 1793 established that "A people has always the right to review, to reform, and to alter its constitution. One generation cannot subject to its law the future generations."

Alberdi's thinking followed a comparable, sympathetic, and ultimately similar line. He praised the constitutional theorists who had preceded him in America, theorists whom many of his contemporaries criticized. Alberdi extolled his predecessors for correctly conceptualizing the problem: they had recognized that constitutions are born of and in response to the "dramas" of the moment, and the constitutions they produced had done just that.[7] Alberdi asked himself:

> All the Constitutions enacted in South America during the war of independence were complete expressions of the needs that dominated their time. That need consisted in putting an end to the political power exercised by Europe in America, which began during the conquest and continued during the time of colonialism … Independence and external freedom were the vital interests that concerned the legislators of the time. They were right: they understood the needs of their time, and they knew what to do.
>
> (Alberdi 1981, 26)

In other words, Alberdi praised the first American constitutionalists because they understood the need for, first and foremost, independence. Body and soul, they devoted themselves to consolidating independence through a constitutional framework. With this understanding in mind, it should not be hard to anticipate the question he posed to the jurists of his own generation. He asked his contemporaries to consider the needs of

[7] As Brinks and Blass have argued, "las Constituciones son catálogos de esperanzas y temores, antes que afirmaciones de certeza o manifiestos" ("Constitutions are catalogs of hopes and fears, rather tan affirmations of certainty or manifestos") (Brinks & Blass 2018).

the new era, the "dramas" that they needed to resolve. Naturally, he also offered an answer. Alberdi declared:

> At that time, what was required was to consolidate independence through the material and moral enhancement of our peoples. The main goals of that time were political goals: today we need to concern ourselves with the economic goals.
>
> (Alberdi 1981, 123)

What was needed, therefore – in his personal opinion – was populating the country in order to confront – as he would famously argue – the drama of the "desert." This involved promoting immigration to provide an adequate labor force, developing commerce with other nations, and establishing legal frameworks for contractual obligations that, together, would lead to economic development. All of these required a completely new and distinct constitutional ordering. Above all, I want to draw attention to the aspect of Alberdi's reasoning that is most relevant to this work, and I want to do it in an "Alberdian" way. I want to focus on the "mismatch" that Alberdi implicitly identified between the original constitution of Argentina and the "dramas" facing his generation in order to shed light on our own dilemma. Part of the institutional problem we are facing is related to a central aspect of Alberdi's intuition. It is possible that our institutional arrangement has become obsolete, but not for the simple reason that it was created hundreds of years ago, or because so much has happened since then. Rather, it is simply not equipped to recognize and address the urgent, even dire "dramas" that mark the present day. We must answer for ourselves the question Alberdi posed to his contemporaries: What are the distinctive aspects of our era, the demands, needs, expectations, and calamities, that should be identified and addressed by the highest law of the land – constitutional law? Is it time for us to pay serious attention, finally (and through constitutional means), to the "drama" of inequality in which we have long been mired?

1.2.2 "Ideas"

In addition to foreshadowing some of the crucial historical factors behind our current dilemma that this book explores, I also want to give an indication of the ideological terrain to be covered, for the heart of this book is especially centered on the ideas (or principles and promises, if ideas is too vague) upon which modern constitutions rest. I am going to argue that modern constitutions are the fruit of a certain way of conceptualizing and understanding the world, which itself was the product of premises and principles from times long past (the times when those original constitutions were written). I would like to emphasize a specific problem related to what I have described above in terms of a "mismatch." Our constitutions were conceived at a particular moment in our histories when power over the Americas passed from metropolitan European elites to colonial American ones. Yet they were still written by local elites whose thoughts and actions squared harmoniously within an elitist paradigm. In saying this, I am not giving credence to any conspiracy theories regarding the intentions of our founding fathers, or drawing on explanations that are either far-fetched or anachronous. It has long been established by respected scholars of many stripes that our "constitutional fathers" – almost without exception – shared a sense of, as I will refer to it repeatedly, "democratic distrust." They distrusted the common citizens' capacity for self-government; they distrusted their ability to exercise self-restraint out of respect for minorities; and they distrusted their aptitude for resisting the temptation of impulsive behavior.

This shared understanding was expressed in hundreds of "founding" documents and speeches. Its breadth and depth preclude any attempt to reduce it "anecdotally" to, for example, "the way people used to talk" – but no longer do, having long understood, once and for all, how preposterous that kind of elitist rhetoric is. I am interested in showing how our constitutions feed on those elitist premises and principles, and how the latter have shaped our current institutions. In other words, "democratic distrust" – the fear of being subjected to majority rule and the consequent counter-majoritarian bias that motivated our founding fathers – did not "evaporate" as society evolved to some higher awareness. It was incrusted in concrete institutional arrangements that still form the nucleus of our constitutions. Allow me to provide a few familiar examples to illustrate my point (examples that represent a central part of the analysis to come). Our current organizational model for the judiciary, for instance, is based on the hypothesis that impartiality is better served by entrusting adjudication to highly trained individuals than to democratic or collective reflection. Similarly, the "distance" or "gap" that we currently observe between electors and the elected derives in large part from a model chosen in order to insulate elected representatives as much as possible from the passions or irrationality of the masses. Hence the highly reduced number of institutional channels for communication with and control over our representatives – which for most people extend no further than voting in periodic elections. This feature is not an anomaly or oversight of the system; rather it reflects that the conviction could and should operate with little citizen participation or engagement. The idea of democratic distrust is of first-order importance in the explanations for all of these crucial decisions in our constitutional structure.

Because of this ideological landscape characterized by distrust of the citizens, resistance against civic engagement, and fear of democratic rule, a rift between constitutionalism and democracy has emerged. Moreover, for reasons I will discuss, the rift has become much more radical of late. Constitutional institutions are no longer conceived as centrally devoted to recognizing, expressing, or facilitating the formulation of the citizens' collective will. The opposite is closer to the truth: democratic rule has been confined to narrow spaces under the care and control of the leading elites. That is why some of the most renowned studies of democracy and constitutionalism of our time ask, as Robert Dahl did in one of his most well-known books, *How Democratic Is the American Constitution?* (2013) or even assert that is not, as Sanford Levinson did in the title of his renowned book, *Our Undemocratic Constitution* (2008).

The spirit that animates this present work, however, is contributing to rebuilding the ties, now long destroyed, between democracy and constitutionalism. The task does not involve repairing what has broken, nor resuscitating practices from distant times and places. The chore we face is rebuilding the link between constitutionalism and democracy through the most honorable and respectable means: through conversation among equals.

1.3 Three Clarifications

Before continuing, I would like to make three clarifications in order to preclude possible misunderstandings of what I have already presented, as these clarifications will take on greater relevance in the pages that follow.

1.3.1 Rights

Above all, I must insist that giving democratic deliberation back its central place in constitutional self-government does not imply in any way making concern for rights secondary or peripheral, or adopting, as some do, an attitude inspired by Jeremy Bentham's dismissal of rights as "nonsense upon stilts."[8] Such a misunderstanding is made possible by the error of believing that there exists only one way to protect rights – by explicitly enumerating the rights to be strictly protected by "traditional" legal means. I am referring to the misunderstanding that expresses itself in the idea that only counter-majoritarian institutions are capable of guaranteeing rights. This assumption implies, conversely, that the only way to take rights seriously is by undermining, in one form or another, the democratic caliber of constitutionalism. In fact, there are various ways to protect rights, and not all of them require abandoning or compromising our basic democratic demands. We can keep democratic dialogue in the center of the process of government decision-making without abandoning our commitment to procedures that help us ensure effective rights. Mechanisms to reinforce limits on power without negating majority rule, for example the abandoned practice of "resending" questionable laws to the legislature for revision, come to mind. Similarly, in the past, forms of legislative "insistence" were conceived to require broader majorities in certain circumstances. Another possibility, one that is regaining attention, is instituting judicial review that is more deferential to the legislature. In other words, the courts are asked to show greater consideration for the democratic caliber of the laws that come before them. As will be shown, strict adherence to democratic principles does not require aversion to rights.

1.3.2 Democracy

The second clarification I would like to make is the following: My repeated insistence on the centrality of the democratic nature of the dilemma before us in no way implicates an overly simplistic notion of democracy essentially limited to its most direct and spectacular expression – making decisions through votes. The contrary is more accurate: in this work, I defend a notion of democracy that is somewhat peculiar. It is in line with the *regulative ideal* that arises and takes shape with reflection on law as a *conversation among equals*. That ideal involves a more demanding and complex notion of democracy. It is one that puts special importance on requirements such as equality (equal status for every participant); making sure all groups affected by a decision have been heard; and a prolonged period for debate (which increases the need for information, transparency,

[8] He stated: "Natural rights is simple nonsense: natural and imprescriptible rights, rhetorical nonsense, nonsense upon stilts." See *The Collected Works of Jeremy Bentham* (2002, 328).

and public discussions where proposals can be mutually presented, challenged, and revised). From this ideal point of view – that of a conversation among equals – the plebiscitary option (in its least interesting yet most familiar form) is seen as the exception (one that must be strictly regulated in order to be acceptable), rather than as the rule. The referendums we have recently seen (from the Brexit vote in England to the referendum for the peace agreement in Colombia) seem to be, from this perspective, more indicative of the problem than a solution to it. Contemporary plebiscites are less "conversations among equals" than the final blow of the gavel in a ceremony organized by a central power who knows how to leverage its increasingly vertical integration to its advantage when organizing the referendum.

1.3.3 Utopian Fantasies?

The third concern that I would like to address at the outset relates to the apparently utopian character (meaning far removed from reality and the law) of the model of democracy I am defending. Far too often, whenever someone suggests alternatives involving democratic deliberation or dialogue, the immediate energetic and even arrogant response is the "realist" critique that usually takes the form of "that all sounds great, but in this world it simply is not possible." These detractors suggest that we must return to reality – the reality that they understand better than anyone else. Fortunately, reality has finally come in line with the vision defended by those in favor of democratic dialogue, such that we now have marvelous examples that refute this kind of criticism. Truth be told, the present political moment of humankind, however dark and complex it is, does have something interesting to show us. It relates to the recent emergence of numerous experiences that illustrate, in practice, the possibility and effectiveness of what we mean when we speak of "democratic dialogue" or "collective conversation." What we are talking about, ultimately, are extensive and inclusive debates in which "all those affected" participate. I am particularly interested in examining collective, open, and frank collective public discussions such as the one that took place in Ireland on the topic of abortion (or, on the same topic, even in Argentina, although the process there was subjected to more "top-down control"). Other instances include the "deliberative assemblies" that have been popping up across the western world since the beginning of the twenty-first century: from Australia to Canada; from Iceland to Chile or France. Examples such as those cited (we will explore several others in the pages to come) enable us to negate without fuss the widespread "realist refutation." We are talking about discussions in which people of all ages – from teenagers to the elderly – took part. Some were highly trained professionals, others practically uneducated. The discussions took place in a wide range of social settings and seem to have (accidentally and unexpectedly) created the conditions necessary for people of apparently firm and even biased convictions to change or significantly modify their positions after debating them with others. Who would expect, for example, that a Catholic agrarian society where the Church is as powerful as in Ireland would open itself to discussions that led a majority to adopt a position in favor of legal abortion? We will look more closely at what occurred when I examine the new forms of collective dialogue.

To put it bluntly, it is possible to protect rights without a counter-majoritarian institutional system and constitutionalism does not require sacrificing democracy.

2

The Law As Conversation among Equals

In this chapter, I will try to clarify what I mean every time I speak of "the law as conversation among equals." To do so, I will start with an imaginary example that I hope will help us recognize the distinctive elements of what a conversation among equals should imply. Similarly, I will try to show the repercussions of an example as simple as mine for the routine constitutional practices in which we are immersed. These elements will allow us to describe the ideal form that a conversation among equals could take as a *regulative ideal*. We will turn back to this ideal throughout this work to provide a reference point for the critical analysis of the institutions and practices currently in place.

2.1 Immigrants in the "Promised Land"

The hypothetical I propose is the following. We are part of a group of immigrants making our way towards the "promised land."[1] We received an attractive offer from a country on the other side of the Atlantic Ocean. The country will give us a large tract of land in exchange for our promise to work and live there. The offer is not only promising, it is practically impossible for us to turn down because of the conditions in our homeland – the aftermath of war, widespread poverty. Many of us knew each other back home while others of us met during the long journey across the sea.[2]

[1] In chapter V of *The Concept of Law*, legal philosopher Herbert Hart explored the emergence of "primary" and "secondary" rules through the example of a primitive, imaginary community. He said: "It is, of course, possible to imagine a society without a legislature, courts, or officials of any kind. Indeed, there are many studies of primitive communities which not only claim that this possibility is realized but depict in detail the life of a society where the only means of social control is that general attitude of the group towards its own standard modes of behavior in terms of which we have characterized rules of obligation" (Hart 1961, 91). Herein, I want to employ a similar thought experiment in order to start reflecting upon the difficult problems involved in writing and interpretating a constitution.

[2] Historically speaking, I understand that this example may be somehow related to the "Mayflower Compact" (the "Agreement Between the Settlers of New Plymouth") that the

Our excitement and the long wait largely explained why we spent so much time in lively conversation about the lives that awaited us in our unknown destination. How would we organize ourselves? How would we make a living? How should we select people for the positions needed for collective labor and distribute the benefits reaped from it? The conversations are animated, full of fresh ideas. The number of hard questions that come up is so dizzying that we realize the need for a few basic principles or rules around which we might build the future for which we hope. We come together around the idea of "building a better world." Maria digs out an old notebook she has held onto since her school days, one that is still mostly blank. We choose the person among us with the best penmanship to take notes. Don Vincenzo, who is the oldest person in the group, and who has accumulated wisdom through years of hardship, participates with an enthusiasm that belies his years. We agree that everyone will work from sunup to sundown, six days a week, leaving Sunday for rest. We also agree, on Juan's request, that the produce will be divided equally. By now we are friends, or at least acquaintances, and we respect each other. Even though we are aware of the differences in our skills and capacities, we see each other as equals – no one matters more than anyone else does. José, the most confrontational among us – the person with whom we argue the most – asks us to include another rule: that no one be prevented from voicing their complaints before everyone else. All right, we say, and assent.

After the long crossing, exhausted from more than two weeks at sea and a few days of travel over land, we arrive at our long-awaited destination. The land is solid and fertile, and stretches further than the eye can see. The first days are tough, full of fear and outbursts of emotion. Little by little, we settle in and eventually feel like the genuine owners of the land. As we feel more and more comfortable, differences of opinion and conflicts begin to arise. Most are minor, insignificant, but others are complicated. For example, one Saturday, not too long after we arrived, Nicola asks if it would be all right for him to work on Sundays as well. Several of us are surprised, not only by his untiring will to work but, especially, by his asking permission. "Of course!" we emphatically respond, "how could we order you not to work as much as you want, on any day that you wish?" He candidly answers: "Since you had written

passengers of the Mayflower (who were fleeing from religious prosecution by King James I of England) signed, aboard their ship, in November 1620. I see it, however, more in line with Gerald Cohen's "camping trip" example (Cohen 2009).

that we were not to work on Sundays, I thought I should ask." Not long afterwards, Francesco tells us he cannot work the fields during the cold winters. We know he has respiratory problems because of his coughing every night. It is so bad that we fear for his health and future well-being. He asks, "Would it be all right if I stayed behind to help in the kitchen and chop firewood?" adding, "Does kitchen work qualify as 'work'?" We have known Francesco for a long time and do not doubt his good faith. We feel bad about his dilemma, so we respond without hesitation: "Of course you can stay behind and cook. Someone has to do it and it is also work!" These are a couple examples of the simple, minor conflicts we had to deal with in the early days, but there were also more complicated situations that we needed to resolve.[3]

One Sunday, over coffee after the siesta, Aida, whom we do not know very well, reluctantly confesses that Saturday is the day of rest ordained by her religion. She goes on, "here the written rules say that we can only rest on Sundays, and I do not know what to do about it." José checks the notebook. "It's true," he confirms, "it is written that we rest on Sundays." Someone tells Aida, "What a shame we cannot allow you to rest on Saturdays, since we never work on Sundays here." Someone else stands up in protest, asking "What are you saying? What kind of argument is that? Just because we do not work on Sundays now, does that mean we will never do so?" Someone else raises her hand, adding, "I am sorry, but the problem is that we have written the rule so it is established and cannot be changed." Many of us are left speechless, perplexed. We look to each other, silently thinking and nodding our heads, until Juan, known for his common sense, speaks up. "What is the real problem? We wrote the rule this way because we were unaware of our different beliefs. But we did not write the rules to be slaves to them, we wrote them to improve our organization. For that reason, if we all agree, we should correct what we wrote in the notebook, and the problem will be solved." As we all did in fact agree – we very much respected Aida and knew how religious she was – we amended that part of the notebook, making clear that whoever needed to take their weekly day of rest on a day other than Sunday, whether for religious or personal reasons, was entitled to do so. In the end, solving the problem was not so difficult after all![4]

3 About the practice of mutual justification see, for example, Forst 2013.

4 Am I assuming here that people are reasonable, kind, and always willing to change their minds (in the face of the force of the best argument)? Not at all (neither am I assuming that people offer, or need to offer, only public reasons, when discussing public matters). I do assume, yes, that the conversation takes place under certain conditions (of equality), which

I could draw my hypothetical out further, even infinitely, with more difficult situations and complex cases. I believe, however, that I have gone far enough already for the reader to understand what I mean, fundamentally, when I speak of "conversation among equals."[5] I mean precisely the dialogue that we could and should have with those around us about the way we wish to live and the principles and rules that will define and organize our social lives. There is nothing mysterious or unusual about it. It is elemental, basic, and obvious: when differences among us arise, when conflicts appear, we attempt to find agreement by discussing possible solutions. Why would that seem exotic? What is so strange about it? Should not this be the normal way to go about resolving differences? Apparently not. Apparently, this "conversation among equals" model implicitly requires some intricate, drawn-out justification. The way I see it, it is any alternative model that would need to provide convincing arguments for departing from it!

help us to minimize the role of force and violence in our interactions. Then, of course, sharp conflicts, intractable differences, and deep disagreements can ensue. These confrontations, as we shall see, must then be processed by the institutions that – from this egalitarian starting point – we design.

5 We could continue this story, to imagine how "secondary rules" (following Hart's terminology) emerge. One possible continuation of the story would be the following. After some time, our community of immigrants becomes well-known and admired by foreigners, and new people begin to ask us authorization to participate in our community. Little by little, the number of our members increases, and it becomes more and more difficult to solve our conflicts informally, or all together in a common assembly. So – let's say – after five years, we select a group of us, "The Delegates," who will be in charge of solving our most fundamental conflicts concerning our common rules, which have also grown in number (say, we have rules concerning how to spend our resources; how to distribute the food we produce in common; etc.). Now, it is important to notice that we did not designate "The Delegates" under the assumption that only they know what the rules of the community are, or how those rules should be understood (we will later explore this point in more detail, in order to discuss legal interpretation). By contrast, our common assumption still is (and has always been) that we are all equal and that we are committed to solving our conflicts together, talking to each other. Simply, the fact is that today we do not have sufficient time and space to solve all our important conflicts together, as we use to do. As a result of these assumptions, if one day one of "The Delegates" came to us and proclaimed: "now I shall tell all of you how to properly understand the common rules," we would remain astonished: that claim would be completely foreign to the spirit of our community. The idea has always been that we created those rules in order to live together, that we are the "owners" of those rules, and that we solve our conflicts by talking to each other. Similarly, if one of "The Delegates" tell us that the rules have to be interpreted according to what was said in Year One of our living together, or according to what our "founding fathers" (i.e., Don Vincenzo, in our example) said, we would also be shocked. It is clear to all of us that this view has little to do with our common understanding. The idea is not to remember or find out what the first, original community said or could have said about the point in conflict, but rather think collectively about the problem and decide how we want to deal with it.

Another very important observation can be drawn from my hypothetical example. The "conversation among equals" centers on the development of rules to organize collective life. Disagreements over the rules arise, and solutions to those disagreements are sought dialogically, that is, put simply, the way people who take one another as equals tend to do. This is because they respect each other despite their differences and because they assume no one has a natural right to "command" the others, imposing their vision of what the rules should be "because I say so."

In any case, I understand that the scenario presented by the example is not extremely common and can provoke resistance, which I find misguided. The example, as I will argue, only idealizes situations with which we are already familiar. Still, in my head, I hear certain repeated objections: "What a hoax! Everyone in the example knows each other!"; "Absurd! They are all friends!"; "Incorrect! We are not colonists in a foreign land!"; or even "It's such a small community – how can you compare it to our real lives in today's world?"

I know these claims (I have heard them already), but I don't think they present decisive obstacles to my proposed example. The purpose of a simplified, ideal hypothetical is precisely that: in order to focus attention on the most relevant aspects of the situation we want to discuss, it is useful to choose an example that minimizes the number of external variables. It is also the function that a *regulative ideal* is meant to perform. For the moment, I would just add the following. First of all, I understand the objection about the "scale" of the example (is such an example useful, to think about the modes of conflict resolution in a society of millions of people?). In this regard, I would just add two things. On the one hand, the idea of the example is to reflect on the criteria and guiding principles suggested by the ideal of a "conversation among equals." On the other hand, I would point out that some institutional practices that we are going to examine towards the end of this book (i.e., those related to the new "citizen assemblies") suggest, at least, that the ideal of the "inclusive conversation" is not simply utopian. Of course, I will not present such practices as "the realized utopia." I only emphasize that those recent practices allow us to resist the objection that democratic dialogue is impossible in modern societies. In other words, it is possible to imagine new institutional designs that help us promote an inclusive conversation in an interesting and plausible way. Finally, I would add a small comment about the "friendship" or the "deep mutual knowledge" that characterized the common life among our "immigrants" (features that would not be present in the complex and anonymous social life of our time). The question that I would like to address is this: Is it that the difference between "ideal" and "reality" (say, friendship versus anonymity) confirms the impossibility of approaching the "conversation between equals"? I would say no. On the one hand, and returning to what has been said: we have practical examples that – at least – suggest the opposite: extending the democratic conversation is possible (even without "civic friendship"). Second (as Madison said, and as we will analyze in a moment), it is possible (and imaginable) to do a lot, and improve a lot our institutional design, without even assuming the existence of "civic virtue" among participants and officials. Third, I would add *contra* Madison that it would be desirable (if possible, as I think it is) to promote institutional practices that encourage a more "virtuous" behavior among members of our public life (i.e., through decentralization, the development of smaller communities, the opening of new public spaces for social meetings, etc.). Finally (and this is only a hypothesis about the "endogenous formation of character," to which I will return) I consider that the same participation in civic assemblies could help us shape our civic character differently, and in a (democratically) more fruitful way.

Having reached this point, and in order to better understand the meaning of our proposed "conversation among equals," I will now return to my hypothetical, refining it in order to identify the salient points that will be the object of our analysis.

2.2 Six Basic Elements of a Conversation among Equals

Using as a starting point the hypothetical example, I will attempt to illustrate certain fundamental theoretical questions posed by the regulative ideal of the "conversation among equals." These questions will enable us to recognize its essential defining characteristics.

Equality. The essential aspect of the example that stands out before all the others is related to the idea of equality. Equality among the members of the group appears to be the starting point for the example, independently of the obvious fact that, in the example as in reality, we are all "different." Nicola works the hardest; Aida is the most religious; José the most insightful; and Maria the most studious; and so on – but none of those differences negate the fundamental equality that they all share. In terms of moral dignity, each shares the same worth; no one matters more than the people beside them. That is why they try to find agreement in cases of conflict and discuss as a group the rules to implement and then how to interpret them. It is the idea that in the modern era we have summed up in one steadfast principle, that of "one person, one vote." Belief in the basic equality shared by all people (like the immigrants in my hypothetical) rejects the idea that some people, for some unjustified reason, be permitted to "impose" their authority over the others, as if such authority were "natural" (e.g., based on race, gender, ethnicity, age) or "proper" (following the patriarchal model of the father's dominion over his family, which assumes that all matters affecting the family should be left exclusively to his judgment).

Disagreement. Another central aspect of the hypothetical, one which explains to a large degree the conversational dynamic in our group of immigrants, involves the repeated "disagreements" that arise among them: over what rules to put down in writing in the notebook; which to leave out; how to read them; and how, when the time comes, to change them. There is no reason to believe such disagreements will ever disappear in diverse societies (societies that John Rawls described as marked by "the fact of reasonable pluralism" in 1991). They constitute one of the most distinctive elements of modernity – the element that Jeremy Waldron considered central to the "political circumstances" of our times (Waldron, 1999).

Inclusiveness. The conversations in our imaginary example were completely "inclusive" in the sense that they were carried out in the presence of all those "potentially affected" by their conclusions (using the famous formulation of Habermas from 1996). In our example, everyone ("all those potentially affected") participated in the discussions of their future on "solid land"; just as everyone had the opportunity to intervene in the debates over the rules that would govern life at their destination, and again when questions over the proper interpretation of the established rules arose. The basis on which I rely to affirm the importance of effective participation of everyone affected in the public discussions is related to the principle (derived from the work of John Stuart Mill in his monumental *On Liberty*) that each adult ought to be treated – for the purposes of making decisions – as the proper judge of his or her own interests.[6] Mill justified his affirmation with the argument that no one other than the person in question is more interested in that person's well-being (Mill, 2003). He was sensitive to the genuine concern that people feel for the fate of others, to the point of intervening in their affairs, yet, inevitably, they would encounter

[6] For Mill: "with respect to his own feelings and circumstances, the most ordinary man or woman has means of knowledge immeasurably surpassing those that can be possessed by any one else" (Mill 2003, 64). More recently, Robert Dahl similarly argued that, "in making individual or collective decisions each adult ought to be treated . . . as the proper judge of his or her own interests" (Dahl 1989, 100).

unsurmountable obstacles when it came to accurately understanding and balancing the interests of the person affected. However hard we try, even when making great effort to identify and respect the points of view of the others, it is often difficult to understand the way others process the circumstances and how much weight they ascribe to the problems they face, to the solutions they see, and to the objectives that drive them.[7]

Before moving on, I would like to reaffirm this point more strongly. In the "conversation among equals" model, the privation of one person's perspective – of any single person – should be considered a fundamental, irreparable "loss" – a serious problem – that will end up harming the impartiality of the decision-making process. If, in our example, Aida, the only person of another religious faith, had not been present during the deliberations, all the others would have ended up making a wrong decision (and moreover, one that would have embarrassed them) by failing to recognizing a nonconformist point of view. On their own, they probably would not have even realized that not everyone shared their religious practices, or that the failure to show respect and care for the members of the group who followed a different faith could cause them significant harm. This is why, as we will see, I tend to favor public debates that are as inclusive as possible, because the value of incorporating as many diverse perspectives as possible outweighs the potential drawbacks.

Deliberation. As we saw in our imagined conversation among equals, allowing everyone "potentially affected" by a decision to intervene was crucial to arriving at satisfactory agreements. Just as crucial for the effectiveness of the discussions was giving time for mutual criticism and the genuine exchange of ideas and arguments. "Debate" in this context is not merely an interesting phenomenon of collective life – a luxury in which we might indulge or abstain from depending on our mood. The exchange of ideas and the effort spent helping each other refine and formulate them clearly and accurately work to the betterment of all. The process improves the chances of reaching impartial decisions, ones that best respect everyone's interests. In our hypothetical, the decision to make Sunday the weekly day of rest illustrated a process of mutual correction. At first, the immigrants happily agreed to the principle

[7] What else explains why, for decades and decades, parliaments composed almost entirely of men displayed so much resistance or indifference to take up issues of interest to women (marital violence, access to public positions, political rights for women, matters of reproductive health, etc.)? It has not always been the case that the congresses were consciously sexist. In many cases, the legislators had well-meaning intentions and acted in good faith, yet they simply failed to perceive the relevance of women's demands, interests, and needs.

without thinking too hard about the concrete implications of the decision. Once their project of collective living began, however, they realized that the decision seriously affected one of the group's members. As a result, they took up the question of what to do about it (which was complicated by the fact that they had consecrated the principle as a written rule). They evaluated the worthiness of the arguments for and against the rule and decided, in the end, after expressing doubts, posing questions, and correcting each other's statements, and found an acceptable solution compatible with the interests of all.

The Debates Focus on Topics of Public Interest. Another important and difficult point central in the hypothetical presented is that the discussions of the immigrants overwhelmingly concerned matters of common interest – public issues or, as Carlos Nino would call them, questions of "intersubjective morality." It is important to distinguish these issues from matters of personal or private morality, which are "self-referential." To explain the distinction using examples from our hypothetical, the immigrants do not question whether Aida should or should not follow her faith, nor do they question Nicola's desire to work on Sundays. Doing so would imply questioning someone's life project. What they discuss are shared problems: from the rules that govern collective life (how much each person must work, which days, how to share the earnings from it) to the interpretations of the rules and the limits of individual rights. There is an important difference, one that is sometimes hard to distinguish, between establishing the rules organizing coexistence and questioning the personal life projects of Aida and Nicola. As I have tried to express, one of my presumptions is that in matters that pertain to an individual's personal life, that is, those areas where someone's decisions do not present significant risk of harm to others, "everyone is sovereign" – the master of their own life. My presumption here is related to what John Stuart Mill called the "harm principle" (which he felt provided the organizing foundation for state use of coercive power). This principle requires protecting individuals from harm caused by "third parties" and finds its basis in the idea that each person be considered "sovereign over oneself, over one's own mind and body" (Mill 2003, 18).[8]

Open, Continuous, and Ongoing Dialogue. The discussions among our group of immigrants in the hypothetical are open, continuous, and ongoing.

[8] In both its commitment to "dialogue" and "neutrality," the "conversational" approach that I here advance may have some resemblance with the view that was once proposed by Bruce Ackerman, in his book *Social Justice in the Liberal State* (Ackerman 1980). We do not share, however, the same understanding of "dialogue," its formalities and its requirements.

They begin during the voyage at sea, continue when they reach their destination, and are renewed once they are settled and deeper fissures among them begin to appear. Our immigrants do not expect any "finish" to them, and they do not subscribe to the notion that establishing the rules in written form puts all questions to rest, for they realize there is still a need to discuss future disagreements and the proper interpretation of the established rules. Ideally, as in the example of the immigrants, each discussion will close with unanimous agreement, for a unanimous agreement – which we all know is hard to reach – maximizes the chances of having found the most appropriate solution, the most impartial of all. Notwithstanding (as we saw in the hypothetical), unanimous agreements can still lead to unjust or biased decisions when the group fails to consider some of the potential implications of the agreement at the time. But such instances do not pose insurmountable obstacles. As Juan argued, we control the rules, not the other way around. We can thus rethink agreements, resume the discussion over them as a group, reach a revised, unanimous agreement, and change the rules accordingly.

We have just distilled some of the fundamental elements of a *dialogue among equals*. Of course – we are still talking about a regulative ideal – I understand that we rarely encounter such ideal situations in practice. In real life, we usually speak of dire, adverse conditions – in social, political, economic, and institutional terms – when discussing the prospects of carrying out dialogue where all parties have equal standing. There are a multitude of communities divided by strong tensions. Asymmetries in power effectively give some groups more capacity to exert influence than others. At an individual level, people possess differing competences, degrees of authority, and levels of persuasive and rhetoric skill. Time constraints usually preclude the discussion of everything we would like or even need to cover (especially if reaching unanimity is the goal). This is all well-known, and obvious. Yet none of these factors negates the validity of conversation among equals as a regulative ideal. I must insist that the purpose of this regulative ideal is not to portray reality accurately, like a photograph. The purpose of the ideal is to provide a perspective from which we can subject reality to critical analysis and tools with which we can better evaluate it.

2.3 "Constitutional Moments" As Collective Conversation

I started this work with an idealized example of what a dialogue among equals might look like: a conversation among acquaintances (colonists, immigrants) regarding the rules that these same people establish (to organize their collective labor in the "promised land"). Allow me to offer a few less idealized examples that bear a stronger relation to present day practices, *examples that do not perfectly match the requirements of our ideal type but are not overcome by the adverse conditions either.*

I would like to demonstrate how, even in the very difficult social and institutional conditions before us, constitutional dialogue takes place in interesting ways. Valuable constitutional discussions have emerged that – even from our demanding idealized perspective – have very positive results in democratic terms. This is not always the case, nor is it even common, but the possibility is real, even in the critical conditions confronting us.

Bruce Ackerman, one of the most notable constitutional scholars of the twentieth century, has explored a related idea for decades (Ackerman 1991). In his view, the constitutional practice of many countries, such as the United States (which is the primary focus of his analysis), usually follows two different tracks. He calls the first track that of *normal politics.* It is on this level that we find the worst and most common version of democratic politics, the one that leaves people indifferent if not apathetic, because it is so removed from their private lives. In normal politics, politicians are virtually free to follow their inclination, making decisions according to their own discretion. Law after law is passed, sometimes in a matter of minutes or in the middle of the night, without attracting anyone's attention and without regard for the possible consequences.

However, Ackerman adds, on exceptional occasions the circumstances change, and another type of situation emerges. Ackerman defines these extraordinary situations in terms of "constitutional politics" or *constitutional moments.* It is up to each country and society to recognize the constitutional moments in its history. During these moments, "normal politics" gives way to rising political activism. Normally the process is gradual even though the trigger for these rare occasions is often a crisis or deep conflict. Citizens begin to demonstrate concern for fundamental matters of public life (e.g., rising economic difficulties, racial discrimination, or some other manifestation of deep social injustice), matters that had previously been largely ignored or tolerated. Sometimes at the instigation of political leaders, citizens decide to "take a stand" in these situations. They mobilize, march, protest, make demands, denounce the authorities, and hold discussions and debates. The political parties react to these developments by choosing a side. Government officials propose policy changes and new legislation. Judges become anxious and waver in doubt; some simply choose to look to the past and declare (conservatively) that the new proposals do not align with established rules, while others devote special attention to the brewing changes. The dispute continues, social conflict intensifies, and tensions between the branches of government appear. This goes on until, finally, everyone realizes a new phase has been reached, a phase in which the law governing the community has changed. The constitution (whether or not it has been modified through formal procedures) is no longer the same; this is when the people can affirm that a *constitutional moment* has come to pass.

This account might seem exaggeratedly spectacular and melodramatic, but that is how Ackerman describes some of the "constitutional moments" that have occurred in the history of the United States. The New Deal is Ackerman's clearest and favorite example. The tale starts in the early twentieth century, following an economic crisis that has affected much of the Western world. The economic crisis is so deep that it leads to social and political crises. That is when the first semblance of an interventionist state appears. The reigning legal and constitutional paradigm, however, remains the dogma of the "invisible hand" and free markets. The US Constitution seems to condone that paradigm because, according to many scholars, it implicitly repudiated government regulation of the economy. It is during these years of crisis that one of the first significant government regulations is implemented (an economic measure meant to regulate the workweek). In 1905, however, the Supreme Court hands down its infamous decision in *Lochner* v. *New York* overturning that regulation. The justices emphatically insist that it contradicts the Constitution although nothing in the constitutional text seems to support their conclusion. Following *Lochner*, the Supreme Court digs in against the "new" interventionist State. It declares the new regulations unconstitutional in over two hundred cases. The executive power, however, refuses to back down. President Roosevelt, who will become famously known as the "father" of the New Deal, continues to pass new laws and implement regulatory policies, with the support of the legislature. Roosevelt holds a series of "fireside chats" on the radio, in which he asks for the people's support and encourages them to mobilize. Demonstrations are organized to defend the President and Congress. The Court holds firm, and the President doubles down. Thirty-two years after *Lochner* and a very drawn-out battle, he announces his plan to pack the Court by increasing its size so he can nominate sympathetic justices to it. Only when the tension reaches a point where it seems ready to explode does the Court back down. In its 1937 decision *West Coast Hotel* v. *Parrish*, the US

Supreme Court took a step back by upholding a state minimum wage law, validating the type of regulation that, until then, it had systematically, time after time, declared unconstitutional.

Seen from up close, this example illustrates the chaos of government branches facing off against each other. We see disobedience, aggressive behavior, mobilization, resentment, and resistance. If we take a few steps back, however, we perceive something more interesting. In Ackerman's terms, we see *the gestation and development of a new constitutional moment*. Following a process that unfolded over many years, one that involved bitter disputes and mass demonstrations, the law of the land changed, Ackerman would argue, even though the US Constitution underwent no formal modification during this period. This phase began with an economic crisis at the end of the nineteenth century that ran up against a legal establishment opposed to economic regulations and prepared to invalidate them. It ended decades later with an active regulatory policy bolstered by widespread popular support and, finally, a *renovated constitutional interpretation* that validated the legality of the economic regulations previously rejected. This shift thus definitively marked the arrival of a new *constitutional policy*.

We might reasonably describe that process, taken in context with the tools that we possess, as a *constitutional dialogue*. Although its form was much more complex and conflictual than our ideal example, what we find is essentially the same: challenges and conflicts, disagreements, disputes, and intervention by the affected parties that communicate with one another, and, after a long back-and-forth process, consensus that leads to a new agreement.

In the end, we can assert with confidence that, at least on occasion and even in the framework of a deficient constitutional structure coupled with tense political, social, and economic situations, dialogue that does not include just words, but also actions, pacts, emotions, angry conflicts can lead to new agreements that are democratically legitimate and valid. The theoretical tools that we already possess and those that we are in the process of developing help us evaluate the benefits of what has been achieved. They also help us imagine what might be done going forward to remove or reduce the burden of the institutional obstructions that currently weigh us down. We must do what we can to ensure the necessary conditions for constitutional dialogue to be not only possible, but probable, so it is no longer confined to exceptional situations – those of "high politics" in contrast to "normal politics" – that Ackerman identifies as constitutional moments.

2.4 Autonomy, Self-Government, Rights, and Democracy in the Conversation of Equals

At the close of this chapter, which is meant to clarify with precision the notion that serves as connecting thread for the whole work – the notion of *conversation among equals* – I would like to pause one last time. I would like to demonstrate the bond between the idea of dialogue and the two fundamental pillars of modern constitutionalism: rights and democratic rule.

This is because whenever we approach the essential core of what a conversation among equals entails, we encounter a strong commitment to *two principles that occupy a central role in any study of democratic constitutionalism: the ideals of personal autonomy (personal freedom) and collective self-government (democracy).* Allow me to clarify how they relate to the "dialogue among equals."

2.5 Autonomy and Self-Government

Let us begin with the question of individual autonomy, which I relate to the freedom of each person to live their life according to their convictions (as Nino put it, the liberty to choose and carry out their own life project). In our example, concern with the ideal of autonomy can be seen when the immigrants recognize the obligation to respect everyone's religious convictions, when they emphasize the particular importance of respecting differences (and the public expression of those differences), and when they recognize that everyone has the right to live their life as they wish – such as Nicola's decision to work on Sundays. The ideal of collective self-government also appears repeatedly in various forms: the decision to organize collective life around rules, for example. The commitment to the principle of self-government also comes up at crucial moments that arise once the common rules have been defined. More generally, it can be seen in the inclination of the immigrants to discuss, as a group, the rules to establish. It comes up more specifically in the conversations that follow after the rules are set. It is made apparent by the openness demonstrated by the group as a whole to discuss the deeper meaning and intent of the rules that were inscribed in the notebook (which leads them to change the original scheme to allow Aida and anyone like her to honor her religious convictions in an appropriate manner). It is also evident in the very decision to allow discussion of matters related to individual rights (again, when deciding how to regulate collectively the expression of an individual's religious beliefs).

2.6 Rights and Democracy

With regard to this issue, allow me to draw attention to the intimate relation between the principles just discussed and the explicit, essential, and fundamental aspects of any constitutional text. To begin, respect for the principle of individual autonomy usually explains – in decisive terms – our constitutional attachment to a list of (individual) rights. In other words, the *declarations of rights* present in every constitution should be seen as an attempt to protect the basic interests we share in terms of individual freedoms (our autonomy). The idea (to which I will return) is the following: keeping in mind our historical knowledge and our knowledge of basic human nature, we can easily expect situations where temptations and impulses drive people to put their interests over the freedom of others. That explains the purpose (as Madison famously argued) behind the construction of a "wall of separation" to protect our most basic freedoms, a wall represented by a list of rights (the "bricks" of the protective wall). Rights, in this sense, must be understood as the result of the intent to construct a protective wall for individual freedoms.

That said about rights, allow me to turn to democracy. The very idea of *democracy* – specifically, the idea of majority rule – conveys our commitment to the idea of *collective self-government*. The commitment to self-government/democracy is typically reflected in the other crucial element of nearly every constitution; that is, the section devoted to the *organization of power*. This is the part of the constitution that defines how the "democratic mechanisms" are to operate, and how to keep them running. To synthesize, constitutions combine our preoccupation for personal freedoms and our desire for collective self-government. That is why they incorporate into their text both a list of fundamental rights (meant to protect personal freedoms) and a set of rules for the processes of collective deliberation and decision-making.

In our hypothetical, the immigrants gave a lot of thought to the rights to be protected and, at the same time, the conversations were horizontal, democratic, in that no-one's voice mattered more than the others and they sought complete agreement. Both preoccupations (for personal freedom and for collective decision-making, along with the rules to make them possible) came up repeatedly from the start. They also, it should be noted and remembered, democratically debated what the substance, reach, and limits of those rights should be (something that, as we will see, not everyone accepts nowadays, for instance those who argue that "rights are not open for discussion or voted on" – a position that I reject).

3

"Democratic Dissonance"

Elitism Translated into Institutions

3.1 Three Great Jurists from the Age of Revolutions: Madison, Alberdi, and Bello

I would like to start this chapter by briefly referring to three stories related to the trajectories of three of the most remarkable legal minds of the Americas: the North American James Madison, the Argentine Juan Bautista Alberdi, and the Venezuelan Andrés Bello. They lived at around the same time (Madison died in 1836, Alberdi in 1884, and Bello in 1865) and all directly participated in and decisively influenced the "founding moment" of American constitutionalism (which took place roughly between 1776 and 1787 in the United States and between 1850 and 1890 in South America). Madison was the "father" of the 1787 US Constitution, Alberdi of the 1853 Argentine Constitution, and Bello, to large degree, of the 1833 Chilean Constitution (where the Venezuelan spent much of his life). Through these stories, my hope is to bring out the most important aspects of the American constitutional tradition. I will thus be talking about more than the three individuals. I will be discussing the work of an entire generation of great regional jurists, jurists emblematic of an era.

In the few lines I devote to each of the three constitutional theorists, I will emphasize two aspects of each. First, I want to demonstrate the impact of their work, which in each case was centered in their homeland but spread far beyond it. Second, I would like to identify a common thread that ties together all of these authors' extraordinary work: *a disposition of "democratic distrust" that motivated them.* I realize that the oeuvre of these three men is vast, extremely important, rich, and diverse, and that concentrating on their "democratic distrust" might therefore seem inappropriate. My intention is not to treat the men unfairly, however, by evaluating them using current standards. My intent is, in the first place (although not exclusively), descriptive rather than evaluative. I want to draw attention to the "distrust" – which traverses American constitutionalism – because I believe that (i) recognizing the "democratic distrust" that was predominant in their time enables us to understand better and more critically the current state of constitutionalism and because (ii) we tend to neglect the importance and the ongoing impact of that aspect of our constitutional tradition present from the outset on law how it is conceived and practiced today, which is curious and, I argue, incorrect.

With that in mind, what follows are three brief biographies of these three authors who "fathered" American constitutionalism.

3.2 Madison

James Madison was born in Virginia on March 16, 1751, and is largely considered the "father of the United States Constitution." The fragile institutional organization implemented immediately following the Revolutionary War dissatisfied him and he criticized the model of government adopted by many states (dominated, according to Madison, by uncontrolled legislatures). He was very involved in designing his country's legal system. His "Virginia Plan" provided the basis for the Constitutional Convention (which produced the 1787 Constitution). Madison was the primary intellectual and ideologue behind the new constitution and served as secretary of the Convention, which was held behind closed doors (which Thomas Jefferson denounced as an "abominable antecedent"). Madison took copious notes during the Convention, which were published decades later and continue to serve as our main source of the rich debates that took place. Moreover, Madison played a decisive role in the constitution's ratification (because it had been formulated behind locked doors, the final text was sent to each state for consideration and approval). Madison began publishing newspaper articles, together with Alexander Hamilton and John Jay, in order to enlist the necessary support the text would need to be approved. This series of articles itself, compiled and published under the title of "The Federalist Papers," has become simply indispensable for anyone who wants to understand the true meaning of the 1787 Constitution.

Once the constitution was ratified, Madison was elected to the House of Representatives, and then became an advisor to George Washington. He also played a decisive role in passing the Bill of Rights. His aversion to the economic policies of his former colleague Alexander Hamilton – who had become the Secretary of the Treasury – led him to found, together with Thomas Jefferson, the Democrat-Republican Party that opposed Hamilton's Federalist Party. In 1800, Jefferson (who was a personal friend with whom Madison disagreed strongly on many constitutional matters) won the presidential election and Madison became his Secretary of State. Madison would then succeed Jefferson as President following the 1808 election.

Of the immense public service Madison devoted to his country, what stands out most, without any doubt, is the legacy he left in constitutional matters. His contribution is simply extraordinary. To a large degree, I am tempted to say, the history of constitutionalism as we know it took a noticeable turn because of it and his writings. The notion of checks and balances is largely a product of his creation. He also played an important role in the dispute over religious freedom and in the ratification process. Not only was Madison the primary theorist of the US Constitution, he was also an adept political advocate for its acceptance by the states.

Madison's constitutional legacy – for the United States and modern civilization – is marked by clear-cut liberalism committed to the most basic rights and structured to prevent abuse of power. In those difficult times, abuse of power and social conflict were common, at one point reaching the verge of civil war. Madison played a central role in defining the emergent constitutional theory in terms of "a system of government that permits neither tyranny nor anarchy." This maxim is revealing and extremely important.

At this point, it should be noted that Madisonian liberalism was unlike what we consider a democratic system nowadays. Like most political leaders of the time, Madison distrusted democracy, the political participation of the masses, assemblies, and the "tumult" of town meetings. Although he took greater care with his language than many of his peers and was known as extremely conciliatory in his demands (which is one reason, I add, that he became one of the greatest politicians of his generation), Madison expressed his true elitist feelings in unmistakable terms on many occasions. In the Federalist Papers No. 63, for example, he admitted that the representative system he had helped create was meant for "the total exclusion of the people in their collective capacity." In No. 48, he described democracy as where "a multitude of people exercise in person the legislative functions, and are continually exposed, by their incapacity for regular deliberation and concerted measures." In No. 55, he argued – as if it were a scientific principle – that, unerringly, "in all very numerous assemblies ... passion never fails to wrest the sceptre from reason."

Madison's contribution to modern constitutionalism was decisive. It was marked by the predominant liberal theory of his time, which is reflected as much in the "balance" that he proposed to organize power as in its emphasis on fundamental rights, which are defined through declarations of rights. *Democratic distrust* is present in the entire constitutional structure he advocated.

3.3 Alberdi

The great Argentine jurist Juan Bautista Alberdi was born in Tucumán on August 29, 1810 – the year of Argentine independence. He moved to Buenos Aires after receiving a scholarship to pursue his studies in the capital. During his youth, Alberdi studied law – in Buenos Aires, Córdoba, and Montevideo – and music, for which he had a special inclination. He composed several musical works and music was the subject of his first book (*The Spirit of Music*). In 1835, once more back in Buenos Aires, he became interested in politics. He began to frequent the "Literary Salon" where he grew close to many of the intellectuals who would make up the famous "Generation of '37" along with him. In November 1838, after he refused to present an oath of allegiance to Juan Manuel de Rosas, the governor of the province who had consolidated his power by violently persecuting those who opposed him, Alberdi went into exile. Alberdi spent the rest of his life, excepting a brief period from 1879 to 1880, in voluntary and involuntary exile. When he died in 1884, he had spent forty-five of his seventy-three years of life abroad.

Alberdi was living in Chile when Juan Manuel de Rosas was defeated on February 3, 1852. The jurist realized that an opportunity for national political reorganization had come. In only two weeks he wrote a book that would bring him great intellectual renown and provide the basis for the Argentina national constitution that largely remains intact today. The title of Alberdi's book, published in May 1852 by El Mercurio in Valparaíso, Chile, leaves little room to doubt its purpose: *Bases and Starting Points for the Political Organization of Argentina*. The book's critical precision and acuity helped change the course of Latin American constitutionalism. Moreover, its exercise of comparative constitutional analysis is matchless. How Alberdi, given the incredible distances and limited means of communication available to him, was able to take account of, comprehend, and analyze law in a comparative framework as well as he did, simply put, defies the imagination.

Not long afterwards, after the Argentine Constitution had been passed and ratified in 1854, Alberdi published another important book, again in Valparaiso, although this one has attracted much less attention than the earlier one. Under the title *Sistema económico y rentístico de la Confederación Argentina según su Constitución de 1853* ["The Economic and Rentier System of the Argentine Confederation to its 1853 Constitution"], this work is also rich in recommendations and the criteria that guided the author. In what is perhaps the most cited paragraph of the book, Alberdi argued that:

> I stay away from the fanaticism that naively, when not hypocritically, demands full political freedoms for people who only know how to use them to create their own tyrants. Yet I do wish for unlimited and abundant civil liberties for our peoples, among which belong the economic freedom to acquire, dispose of, ship, trade, transfer, and exercise any industry.

The declaration is particularly interesting coming from whom it does and when it was expressed. Alberdi, the great ideologue of the Argentine Constitution and one of the greatest jurists of his generation, at a crucial moment in the development of Latin American constitutionalism, made clear his skepticism of the citizens' capacity for self-government – which was to come at a later point. This moment (in the mid-nineteenth century) did not seem right for "political freedoms." Universal suffrage and democratic participation had to wait; now was the time to lay the concrete foundations to make democracy possible in the future. According to Alberdi, the times called for restricted political freedoms, yes, but also, and especially "unlimited and abundant" civil (economic) liberties (Alberdi 1920, vol. xiv, 64–65).

3.4 Bello

Andrés Bello, a contemporary of Alberdi's, was the other great jurist of Latin America. Born in Venezuela in 1781, for a short time he taught Simón Bolívar, the "Liberator," and was active in the struggle for independence of his country. Like Alberdi, however, he would spend much of his life outside his native country. Between 1810 and 1820 he lived (in difficult conditions) in England, where he had gone with Bolivar on a diplomatic mission to obtain the economic support needed by the independence movement for success. In 1820, he moved his family to Chile, where he was contracted by the authoritarian administration of

Diego Portales. In a very short time, he became a senator (which is especially curious and unusual given his foreign status) and a professor. He directed several local newspapers and cofounded the University of Chile. Above all, however, Bello became a great legal writer in Chile, and it was there that he composed the most important parts of his extensive and extraordinary oeuvre. Among his works, all of which were influential, the Chilean Civil Code stands out (for several reasons) together with his contribution to the 1833 Chilean Constitution, which, in the twentieth century, would become the most stable constitution in the entire region. The 1833 Chilean Constitution was eventually esteemed as the only celebrated example of a "successful constitution" in Latin America because of its durability.

While reflecting on his legal work and the significance of the 1833 Constitution, Bello made the following observation:

> People are less zealous about the conservation of their political liberties than about the conservation of their civil rights. The ability to participate in public affairs is infinitely less important than the ability to secure life . . . Rare is the man who is so free of selfishness that he will prefer the exercise of political rights granted by the Constitution, to the care and conservation of his own interests. He would be (less) hurt when arbitrarily deprived of the right to vote than when violently deprived of his property.
>
> (Jaksic 2001, 212)

Bello conveyed in these lines what he considered an indisputable claim that, moreover, is crucial to his entire juridical work and the principles that guide it. Like Alberdi, Bellow believed that "political freedoms" were not, for the time being, very important, and could wait. Bello also went a bit further. Alberdi proposed vehement action regardless of the citizenry that did not appear ready for self-government: their time would come. Bello, however, based the same conclusion (postponing "political freedoms" while affirming "economic freedoms") on another reason. For Bello, waiting was the preference of the common citizens themselves, even if they had not expressed it. The expression for Bello lay in the facts "Nor could it be otherwise!" as Bello emphatically put it. What truly interests people is something else: the fate of their families, business, and property. Men are, Bello added, "egoists" above all else: "Rare is the man so devoid of egoism that he prefers the exercise of any of the political rights . . . to the conservations of his interests and existence." Rare is he who feels "more injured" when dispossessed "of the right to vote than when he is violently dispossessed of his goods." They are much more concerned with their belongings than their right to vote![1]

3.5 Elitist Discourse in an Exclusive Framework: Constitutions Conceived for Another Time

The transcendent importance of these three jurists is undeniable. They helped consolidate, at the end of the eighteenth century in the United States and France and in the mid-nineteenth century in South America, the primary foundations of constitutionalism that remain intact in its current form. In those days, at its origin, the basic structure of modern constitutions was molded with great care. To a large degree, the constitutions of most nations today display identical traits – more than two centuries later. Today we still find power organized in terms of three primary branches – the legislature, judiciary, and executive, whose powers are distinct and separate in order to create checks and balances among them – and enumerated rights. That these aspects have remained largely intact is nearly as remarkable as the low degree of modification they have undergone. As Adam Przeworski has argued, our *lack of institutional imagination* is shocking in that, since those days, the basic scheme of our institutions appears to be paralyzed by utter inertia.

This inertia is worrying, especially now, because *the basic structure of the constitutions we hold to today were conceived in a completely different context.* This statement might seem trivial, even tautological, for every constitution – especially old ones – were born of circumstances and conditions that are not our own. Notwithstanding, allow me to underscore an aspect that is not at all trivial. *The constitutions that we hold to*

[1] In similar fashion, in Colombia, the liberal intellectual José María Samper, one of the principal figures together with Miguel Antonio Caro behind that country's 1886 Constitution, advocated for the new constitution despite the limitations it placed on rights: "The Colombian people," Samper said, "undoubtedly wanted organization and a government that ensured peace and national unity; one that guaranteed proper freedom, dignity, and the independence of religion and the Church, without prejudice towards the dignity and independence of the Republic; one that recognized and made effectual a set of necessary public freedoms and limited yet clear and effective civil and political rights; one that suppressed anarchy and all the elements of the constant disruption of order engrained in almost all the institutions since 1858 . . . one that suppresses the irresponsible constitutional despotism of the legislative bodies . . . one that returns freedom to the vote, scientific regularity, dignity and truth, as a fair and lucid expression of the national conscience" (Valencia Villa 1992, 154–155).

today were conceived in terms of political sociology and institutional philosophy that are foreign to us today.

3.6 Political Sociology

To begin with, briefly, the "founding fathers" of American constitutionalism conceived the constitution for a different political sociology. They assumed – rightly or wrongly (I believe wrongly, even then) – that the societies in which they lived were relatively simple, far from complex, and basically divided into two groups (rich and poor, landowning or not, creditors or debtors, majority and minority). These groups were considered *internally homogenous* and comprised of individuals *motivated fundamentally by self-interest.* These assumptions allowed them to conclude, then, that incorporating a few representatives of each group into the institutional system (something they believed completely feasible through mechanisms such as direct or indirect elections or specific requirements for different positions), would make it possible for everyone's interests to be adequately represented and defended within the government. This is clearly, as we will see, a depiction of reality that cannot be defended any longer. Our societies today are unmistakably pluralist, multicultural, divided into enormous range of diverse groups, many of which are themselves internally heterogeneous – even individuals today can be considered a "world" onto themselves, with all the contradictions and tensions that entails. We cannot simply define a person by their profession, their wealth, or their gender (topics we will return to further on).

Moreover, this political sociology came with a particular reading of social dynamics, conflicts, and interaction. Basically, as we will see, it was assumed that a good deal of society did not participate and/or was not adequately informed to participate in political decision-making. The data in this respect are straightforward, objective, and can be verified with a simple glance at the distribution of political rights in each country (the high percentage of the population that was barred from participating in elections, several types of restrictions on voting rights, among other restrictions on political participation) and the high level of state repression deployed to counter any type of protest.

3.6.1 Institutional Philosophy

This political sociology was partly a product of the exclusionary character of the predominant attitudes of the time, and partly of a set of ideas and hypotheses that reinforced exclusionary attitudes. It was, above all, fueled by and expressed through an elitist political philosophy that has become more and more entrenched ever since. The theoretical arguments of the jurists of the time, including the ones cited above, were used to justify the incipient institutional arrangement, in whose design they were directly involved. As we will see, the constitutional design that emerged was founded on corollaries of the principles of (democratic) "distrust." These include the principles that played a part in determining political priorities ("establishing the material foundations of the country"). They include principles that determined the need for a low level of political participation ("the population is not yet sufficiently educated and competent for active political involvement"). They include the principles used to justify, temporarily yet somehow still today, the dominance of exclusionary policies ("the time for political freedom is yet to come").

3.7 Elitism Translated into Principles and Institutions

In response to the representation of the origins of "democratic distrust" in the last few pages, one might say (as in fact many do seem to presume, rather uncritically): "Let's ignore the beliefs and discourse that dominated intellectual circles during the founding era and concentrate on the institutions that the 'fathers of constitutionalism' left us." In other words, why insist on incisively and scornfully pointing to old-fashioned elitism – that "sign of the times" – when our intellectual energy could be better spent in other endeavors, like constitutional or institutional design? That "old-fashioned stuff" (surly debates, derogatory statements, ill-treatment of commoners, elitist and arrogant discourse) "went away centuries ago." Such aggressive rhetoric is dead and gone and what is left is a unique, vibrant set of institutions. Now we live in constitutional democracies that are the direct heirs of that age. What, then, is the problem?

For my part, I understand and share a similar attitude, with an important exception that I will try to explain now. The way I understand it, it is true that elitist discourse has (almost) completely vanished from public discourse. The reasons for its disappearance may have been good or may have been bad. It might have been because of matters of principle or ones of convenience (to a large degree, as Jon Elster might say, because of the "civilizing force of hypocrisy" or reflecting the celebrated maxim of La Rochefoucauld, who said, "hypocrisy is the tribute that vice pays to virtue"). Yet the fact that we no longer hear, at least as frequently or as alarmingly, leaders express the same kind of opinions as our elitist ancestors, does not negate the impact that those political views had on the design of the institutions that we continue to inhabit. What I mean is, that elitism was not simply rhetoric. The rhetoric is indeed "a thing of the past." We have forgotten or forgiven it. The problem is the part that is not gone. *The problem is the way we view the elitist discourse that ended up in our constitutions as somehow innocuous. More specifically, the problem is that elitist assumptions and principles, relics of the predominant public discourse among leaders more than two centuries ago, were entrenched, and still are, in our primary institutions.*

In an effort to support the claims just made, I will illustrate, first, *how the elitist discourse was reflected in the assumptions and principles elaborated at the time and, then, how they were translated into institutions.*

3.8 Assumptions, Principles, Institutions

Moving on from the (elitist) discourse that belonged to a past age, I would like to focus on some of the assumptions that fueled it, the principles derived from it, and the institutional translations that grew out of it. What interests us here, then, is observing *how assumptions became principles and how the principles were translated into institutions.*

Assumptions. In regard to the predominant assumptions of constitutionalism's "founding period," I would start with the idea that individuals reflecting in isolation, or perhaps a few well-educated or technically prepared individuals, constitutes the best way to arrive at correct or impartial decisions in public matters. This is what Professor Morton White aptly called the "epistemic elitism" shared by most "Federalists" at the time (White 1987). That assumption – "epistemic elitism" – arises, then as it does today, in opposition to the idea that *collective reflection* represents the best path to reaching impartial decisions (the latter being the idea that, in our times, the German philosopher Jürgen Habermas famously defended or, more recently, the Argentine philosopher Carlos Nino, who used it in his "epistemic conception of democracy"). We should note the significant differences between those two postures. In the first, which was predominant during the founding moments of constitutionalism, the more voices that are incorporated into public discussion, the greater the diversity of the voices heard, the richer the public discussion is (this is the idea of "the wisdom of crowds" of which Aristotle spoke and to which we will return). In the opposing vision, however, the greater the number of voices that participate, the more quickly public discussion breaks down and the less productive it becomes.

This assumption goes hand in hand with others, for instance, related to a conception of equality that distinguishes between our natural state ("we are all born free and equal") and how we develop over time. As we will see, Alexander Hamilton defended, in the Federalist Paper No. 31, an idea expressed by John Locke regarding the equal capacity of individuals to know "fundamental" or "primary" truths. However, this is quickly followed up by a corollary notion that radically qualifies the principle of equality: most people, it turns out, whether because of "defect or disorder" in the "perceptive organs" or because of the particular influence of interests or passions, end up unable to recognize what these truths are.

Now it is possible to see how assumptions related to human motives, to rational and irrational behavior, also influenced thinkers of the time. I recall, for example, the assumption that people are *rational egoists* – the notion on which Adam Smith relies to defend his theory of the "invisible hand" – or the notion made popular by David Hume that reason tends to become a "slave of passion." Deeply influenced by such notions, most of the North American Federalists assumed, without much discussion, that different social groups (particularly among the majority of the population) were primarily motivated by passions and disposed to blindly imposing their interests over anyone else's. The last assumption I will focus on is the supposedly pure irrationality of mass political behavior. This assumption, related to the irrationality of which the people were habitually characterized, prevailed in Latin America as well during the foundational phase. The vast majority of liberals and conservatives in the region (the parties whose political agreement gave rise to the constitutions whose structure is still maintained relatively intact today) largely shared it. The priest Bartolomé Herrera, perhaps the most relevant figure among Peruvian conservatives in the mid-nineteenth century, expressed a particularly staunch version of this view (and I choose this exaggerated or highly visible example only to demonstrate how widespread it was). Herrera believed that the people – the sum of all individuals regardless of age or condition – did not have the capacity nor the right to make laws. For Herrera, the law was based on eternal principles based on nature, principles that could not be clearly perceived without the knowledge formed through mastering the difficulty of mental work and disciplined scientific reasoning (Basadre 1949, 217–218).

Principles. Having pointed out some of the prevailing theoretical assumptions shared by the political leadership during the "foundational" years of constitutionalism, allow me to turn, briefly as well, to ways these assumptions were quickly translated into "institutional principles" – principles that serve as maxims to guide the design of institutions.

For example, among much of the North American leadership, it was generally held that "the more numerous an assembly was" (an assembly charged with taking decisions), "the greater the risk that it would end up dominated by passions," the more susceptible it would be to rhetorical arguments (subject to "demagoguery"), or the more likely the majorities would give in to their crudest urges. This type of judgment led Madison to affirm – as we saw – the unequivocal principle (that he presented as scientific truth) that "all numerous assemblies," regardless the manner of their composition, would end up, inevitably, following passion over reason.

Similarly, the notion that all people were created equal was accepted as a valid presumption by most leaders during the period that concerns us. Many of them, however, developed the notion in ways that enabled them to deduce principles that significantly differentiated individuals. Simón Bolívar, for example, emphatically declared that everyone was born "equal with equal rights," yet he immediately went on to clarify how that did not exclusively or necessarily imply that everyone deserved equal treatment. Bolívar argued that "real differences exist, and can be observed among individuals, even in the most liberal societies" (Bolívar 1951, v. 1, 182).

Likewise, as we will see, the "egoism" or "self-interestedness" assumed to lie at the center of an individual's motivation, ultimately justified crucial aspects of institutional organization. Madison used it to arrive at a principle that would play a definitive role in his institutional reasoning, the principle being that "ambition must be made to counteract ambition." This idea is based on the same logic as that of the "invisible hand" and lay behind some of his most innovative and influential institutional proposals. A very similar way of thinking – involving similar assumptions and principles – traversed Latin America from one end to the other. Alberdi was one of the intellectuals of the time who most strongly defended the premise of self-interestedness and who also translated it into a principle. This principle – still common today – of "inaction" or "nonintervention" was meant to liberate or allow space for the creative faculties of individuals to develop. Alberdi argued,

> present-day society owes the progress of its civilization to the individual understood as such ... It is not the liberties of the Homeland that has

> made modern nations great, but rather the individual liberties that allowed man to create and toil for his own personal greatness, the elemental factor behind the strength of the truly great and free nations, which are those of the North in both hemispheres.

Institutions. As indicated, the "founding fathers" took certain assumptions for granted, from which they elaborated principles that guided institutional design. One could argue that each one of the institutional arrangements created during this period derived from assumptions and principles related to those just described. In other words, the political views that we know through the writings and rhetoric they left did not simply "evaporate" into the air over time. Instead, as might be imagined, they were embedded in institutions. Allow me to provide a few examples.

To begin with important, acknowledged cases, let us look at the way the assumption relating impartiality to "isolated reflection" ("epistemic elitism") that found expression in the beliefs that majoritarian institutions tended to function poorly wound up translated into an entire complex of institutional arrangements. An especially visible example is the decision to assign "the last word" on institutional behavior to judges (who reflect individually or in small groups in conditions that supposedly isolate them from or ensure their independence from outside influence, and who possess high technical training). This decision directly stems from the assumption that the rumination of technically trained individuals is more likely to result in impartial decisions. Similarly, the place and the powers conceded to the executive branch also reflects this type of reasoning. As was argued in the constitutional debates prior to the formation of the United States, "one single person," isolated and well-prepared, would be able to resist urges and the irrational, biased demands of majorities motivated by local interests. The conception even reaches the design of Congress, where the premise can be seen in everything from executive veto power over the laws it passes to the creation of the Senate itself as well as the particular competences assigned to it. It can also be seen in electoral systems where, for many decades and in some instances still today, indirect elections are reserved for choosing the organs to oversee elections and making the most important decisions. From the beginning, for example, it is the President and the Senate (whose members were indirectly elected) who were in charge of appointing judges and ambassadors and subjects related to foreign relations.

Likewise, the principle elaborated by Madison – pointed out earlier – to leverage "ambition" as a means of "counterbalancing ambition" became the key notion behind the system of *checks and balances*. In effect, the entire logic of the system is based on the rationale of the "invisible hand." As Madison argued in the Federalist Paper No. 51, "personal motivations" should be conjugated with the "institutional opportunities" allocated in accordance with a system for internal control. In other words, doing so would make it possible to orient or channel institutionally the basest of civic motivations towards the common good: egoism or ambition could sustain or activate the whole system of internal control through checks and balances.

In addition, the assumption of Hamilton regarding the "truths cognizable by all" that are ultimately "distorted" by majority rule (through "defects or disorder," passions, or interests) is operative in the defense he made for a scheme that severely restricted democratic participation by concentrating power in the executive and entrusting judges with the "final" intervention in case of conflicts.

Assumptions and principles such as those described, finally, did not only have an impact on the choice of basic institutions as in the examples just offered. These assumptions were also operative in the decisions to abstain from adopting certain institutions, to reject certain others, to suppress still others. Consider a few of the numerous ones that had sparked imaginations during the post-revolutionary and pre-Convention period of the United States (1776–1785), institutions that disappeared from the stage of public opinion and imagination after the Constitution was adopted: town meetings, which at a certain point seemed an established practice; "mandatory instructions" and, by consequence, the right to recall, which was implemented in many states; annual elections ("when annual elections end," it was argued at the time, "slavery begins"); mandatory rotation in important positions; brief mandates; among others (Gargarella 1995).

What I am trying to emphasize here, however briefly, is the arc that travels "from" elitist discourse and rhetoric "to" principles that undergird a particular model of constitutionalism that, in its basic aspects, we continue to maintain.

3.9 What Has Stayed the Same and What Changed in Constitutional Terms: The "Fact of Democracy"

Looking back at all that has occurred in terms of constitutional development since the founding moments of modern constitutionalism – more than two hundred years ago – to the present day offers important lessons about the evolutions of our institutions. Here I would simply like to draw attention to two crucial facets of that enormously rich panorama, to which I have partially alluded previously. One of the facets concerns the aspects of our constitutional tradition that have remained and the other concerns ones that are no longer part of life in our constitutional democracies.

I have already pointed out aspects that have stayed with us – the most important ones. The basic structure for the organization of power, above all, remains intact in our current constitutions. In this aspect, no meaningful changes have taken place. More specifically, there have been meaningful amendments to the two main parts of every constitution – the part regarding the organization of power and the part enumerating rights – but, since the beginning of the twentieth century, they have overwhelmingly concentrated, as we will see, on the part regarding rights. The declarations of rights have tended to expand, often much more than might have been expected (in many cases we have gone from a short list of "classic liberal rights" to ones that also include social, economic, cultural, and multicultural rights). Meanwhile, with regard to the organization of power, almost everything remains as it was: three primary branches of government that are separated by a system of checks and balances; a legislature comprised of a Senate that tends to be conservative and a lower house that tends to be relatively diverse; a judiciary that retains the "last word" on constitutional matters; an executive concentrated in a single, very powerful figure; and some form of federalism.

This general system which has prevailed is very much a "product of its time" in the sense that its characteristics were defined by the assumptions and guiding principles that were widely accepted then, characteristics that comprise a doctrine that could be qualified in terms of its "anti-popular sensibility."[2] Among contemporary scholars, no one more clearly expressed those traits of our institutional system than Roberto Unger when he coined the phrase, "the dirty little secret of contemporary jurisprudence." In Unger's opinion, the secret is the dissatisfaction of law with democracy, which is the primary theme of the next chapter in this work.

So, what has changed? Just as I focused on one sole aspect of what has remained the same in our constitutional tradition since its founding

[2] However, I would not consider most of these elitist institutional systems as "wicked legal systems," this is to say – according to David Dyzenhaus' view – legal systems whose laws have been made the instrument of a repugnant moral ideology (Dyzenhaus 2010).

moment (the structure of the organization of power), I will only focus on only one aspect of what has changed. That aspect, however, is a crucial one: context. I made reference above to the rather crude yet influential political sociology of the time that conceived society in simple terms: one with a relatively low population comprised of a few internally homogenous social groups. I brought up political sociology while arguing that the institutional system under development at the time (between the end of the eighteenth century and middle of the nineteenth) was designed with this predominant notion of the sociological framework in mind. The design of the constitutional structures was thus motivated by the concern for equilibrium – to prevent abuse of power – and was very "constricted" – meant to operate in relatively exclusionary societies where the conditions for democratic participation were limited.

If anything has changed since the foundational period, it is precisely the social context out of which constitutionalism grew. If the political sociology that prevailed during the foundational period was crude then, today it is completely unthinkable. Our present-day societies are absolutely distinct in key respects. Not only are our respective populations incomparably greater, the degree of complexity has increased exponentially. Our societies now comprise individuals from many different cultures along with countless internally heterogeneous social groups. Even more importantly, today we face mobilized societies that are politically active, "empowered," critical of their representatives, and avid for democratic participation. These qualifiers – that for the sake of simplicity I have decided to treat as an operative assumption of our times – indicate a paradigmatic change in democratic terms. We might refer to that change as the fact of democracy (in alignment with John Rawls' notion of the "fact of pluralism" or Jeremy Waldron's "fact of disagreement").

What I am trying to express is my belief that the way politics is thought and lived today in public life is completely different from the way it was thought and lived a couple centuries ago. Let me try to express my belief clearly. I am not trying to argue that, at present, people have acquired some "civic virtue" previously lacking or that every individual is now eager to participate actively in public decision-making. Not at all. What I believe has changed is something else. What I believe has changed is that now we all believe that it is our right to participate in the political process (whenever we want and decisively). We now assume the right to intervene, monitor, audit, hold accountable, make demands or impose requirements, and weigh in before and after decisions are made. We may choose to exercise these rights on some occasions and cede them on others; regardless the level of our individual engagement, we hold onto the option to exercise these rights as always ours, and that is the manner by which we manifest them. We live in the times of the *indignados* – the indignant – and our indignity arises from the offense felt when others – our political leaders – act improperly. They act improperly when they act in our name without consulting us. They act improperly when they make decisions that affect us without even notifying us ahead of time. We feel outrage because we believe they lack the authority for such action, because we believe it is our interests that they should pursue (not partisan or personal interests).

3.10 "Democratic Dissonance" and the Tight-Fitting Suit of Constitutionalism

Keeping in mind both what has essentially stayed the same in our constitutional democracies and what has changed since their "foundational moments," the crucial difficulty facing us – the difficulty we might consider as the challenge of our time – becomes apparent. I am referring to the problem that comes up throughout this book and gives it much of its meaning: the problem of *democratic dissonance*. I employ the term "democratic dissonance" to refer to the rupture between political practices and our expectations of them, a gap produced by institutions erected on the basis of a social model that no longer adequately reflects real conditions. Allow to explain in more detail.

To begin, (i) the prevailing constitutional system was created in relation to and in light of a social model that was fundamentally exclusionary. This exclusionary character was not only expressed through economic and social marginalization but also through restrictions, which are more relevant to the argument of this work, on political rights and political participation. In other words, the original constitutional system was set up to operate within a very restricted social structure. Over time, however (ii) greater political rights were won, such as universal suffrage and space for popular political participation, and civic activism and protests became commonplace. At the time considered an "overload" of democratic demands, the social context on which the original institutional scheme rested changed radically, with the foreseeable outcome that (iii) the institutional system became detached from the political sociology for which it was designed. To put it more graphically, a constitutional suit was tailored for a slim body politic that changed significantly over the past two hundred years. It bursts at the seams when we try to wear it today, so we have simply stopped trying to put it on.

The central institutions of our constitutional traditions have remained basically intact from their creation to the present day, while "we," as a society, have radically changed ("we" meaning both who we are as a society and, above all, the "we" that the founding fathers had in mind in particular). Here is where the dissonance lies. It is in the mismatch between what our institutions help us or allow us to do and what "we" the citizens – the People – now reasonably expect and demand of them. The mismatch has expanded to the breaking point between the institutions and practices of our constitutional structure on one side and what we consider reasonable democratic expectations and demands on the other. We are confronted by the *dissonance between constitutional structure and democratic aspirations.*[3] There is deep

[3] Although a long time has passed, I see that there are certain resemblances between my view on "democratic dissonances," and what Samuel Huntington and other experts maintained, decades ago. In fact, during the 1960s, Samuel Huntington, together with Michael Crozier and others, published the famous *Trilateral Commission's Report on the Governability of Democracies*, where they described the emergence of an increasing gulf between social expectations and demands and the capacity of the institutional system for satisfying those claims. The political system – they maintained – had become "overloaded" by demands from the citizenry. In their view, a "democratic surge" in the 1960s raised the level of popular expectations and demands on the government, which tended to undermine the governmental authority and put the whole democratic system in crisis (Crozier et al. 1975; Huntington 1983). Curiously or not, most of those studies concluded by suggesting the need of limiting democracy as the only reasonable "cure" to the problem of an "overloaded" institutional system (Crozier et al. 1975; Dahl 1956; Huntington 1983; Lechner 1991; Schumpeter 2008). Schumpeter, as we know, proposed what was deemed an "elitist" model of democracy in which citizens voted for the purpose of selecting competing elites. This was, for him, the only reasonable response to be offered in the face of a popular opinion that was, for him, easily manipulated or manufactured – in the face of citizens that seemed unable to make intelligent political decisions. Similarly, Huntington and his colleagues urged moderation in the level of demands. For them, "the effective operation of a democratic political system" required "some measure of apathy and noninvolvement on the part of some individuals or groups" (Crozier et al. 1975). Herein, and mainly focusing our attention on constitutional matters, I shall argue for opposite solutions, which I shall base on opposite foundations (mainly, on confidence rather than distrust of democracy). More specifically, I shall advocate for the adoption of profound constitutional changes, which would be required in order to honor our shared democratic commitments. The point is that, in spite of the substantive changes that emerged in the last decades, in terms of democratic conscience/awareness, our Constitutions remained basically untouched in what concerns their organization of powers, and most counter-majoritarian devices are still in place.

tension between most current constitutions and widely shared basic democratic ideals.[4]

To a large degree, the rest of this book will be devoted to the examination of this "rupture" or decisive "fissure" facing constitutionalism today. It is a fissure that represents, simultaneously, a mortal wound for current forms of public life and possible hope for a solution (as Leonard Cohen might say, "there is a crack in everything . . . that's how the light gets in"). Finding that light, showing how constitutionalism might be realigned with and at the service of our democratic demands and expectations, is the main objective of this book.

In the next chapter, we will start to explore, part by part, the "keys" of modern constitutionalism designed or conceived more than two centuries ago: the notion of "representation" that was adopted at the time; the conception of "minorities"; the structure of "separation of powers" and checks and balances; the "internal" control system (through which one branch of government controls the others); and so on. That examination will enable us to gauge the dimensions of the problems we are facing, as well as understand the limits and potential of the institutional developments that have occurred since the founding period. This critical understanding is absolutely necessary – I believe – for the collective construction of an alternative democratic system.

[4] I do not feel the need to specify what those democratic ideals are for the moment, especially if the distance between the present-day basic understanding of democracy and the basic understanding that prevailed among those who designed our constitutional institutions more than two centuries ago is recognized. Even those with a modest idea of democracy should appreciate the difference clearly enough to see my point.

4

A Constitution Marked by a "Discomfort with Democracy"

In this chapter, we will begin to examine in more detail the "construction" of "counter-majoritarian" constitutions or, to use the terms employed by the Brazilian jurist Roberto Mangabeira Unger, constitutions constructed around a "discomfort with democracy." This discomfort is conveyed, as Unger famously described it, through a "ceaseless identification of restraints upon majority rule, rather than of restraints upon the power of dominant minorities, as the overriding responsibility of judged and jurists; in the consequent hypertrophy of countermajoritarian practices and arrangements, in the opposition to all institutional reforms, particularly those designed to heighten the level of popular political engagement, as threats to a regime of rights ..." (Unger 1996, 72–73). We will approach the subject through the most important "doorway" – the one that, in my opinion, played a defining role and as such affords a view and understanding of the whole structure (the "Aleph" of American constitutionalism). This "doorway" is provided by the discourse surrounding "factions."

4.1 Madison and "Factions"

The volume we know as "The Federalist Papers" consists of eighty-five essays written by James Madison, Alexander Hamilton, and John Jay (fifty-one by Hamilton, twenty-nine by Madison, and five by Jay) published under the pseudonym "Publius" between 1787 and 1788 (most between October 1787 and April 1788). This was during the ratification period of the new constitutional text drafted at the Philadelphia Convention and the purpose of the essays was to convince citizens to vote in its favor. The essays are simply exceptional for many reasons: they are short, well thought out, focused on public arguments, and written in language easy for anyone to understand. They were published in local newspapers, the three most important of which were the *Independent Journal*, the *New York Packet*, and *The Daily Advertiser*. The primary value of the essays involves the public argumentation offered by three of the most prominent figures in the Convention debates, three figures representing different positions on the political spectrum. Hamilton was the most conservative, and Madison was the most liberal. Together they took it upon themselves to explain and justify each of the central principles and institutions that the new Constitution put in motion: the separation of powers, the independent judiciary, the system of checks and balances, judicial review, and so on. For these reasons it represents a unique reference that is still consulted today, in the United States and beyond, even at the highest levels (the US Supreme Court) when discussing our institutions. I say "our" institutions because these texts provide the basis for the institutional system that, as a "whole" and in its details, was implemented in an enormous range of countries following the ratification of the US Constitution. That is another reason for the level of interest in and ongoing study of the Federalist Papers, both within the United States and abroad.

Of the eighty-five essays, the best known and most renowned is No. 10, written by James Madison. The essay stands out for the level of care and almost mathematical precision with which it is written and argued. The topic that Hamilton focuses on lies at the heart of the Constitution: factions. Hamilton makes it clear in the essay that *his primary motive for writing the constitution was confronting, through institutions, the concerted activity of factions.* To briefly summarize a very long story that is extremely complex and has been told a thousand times: following the War of Independence that ended in 1776, conditions in the newly independent colonies did not immediately or significantly improve for most of the people living in them. The country was in a state of "disorder" because the various states were only bound by a weak agreement – the Articles of Confederation – that did not establish any foundation for solid cooperation and organization. Much worse – and here is where factions come into play – different groups of citizens, usually formed of people who had fallen into debt during or after the Revolutionary War (or lost their property during the conflict) began demanding relief in several states. Some of these groups of debtors managed to gain control of local legislatures, which began passing laws that favored them, neglecting or to the detriment to – the story goes – the common interest.

In a piece written before the Constitutional Convention in Philadelphia (one to which we will return in somewhat more detail), "Vices of the Political System in the US," Madison expressed horror at the behavior of local assemblies, which seemed beyond anyone's control. He listed as the three principal vices of the institutional system: the "multiplicity," "mutability," and "injustice" that characterized state legislation. In light of this assessment, the constitution that would be drafted later that year can largely be interpreted as a direct response to the "tragedy" of the day: out of control legislatures captured by partisan groups – factions – in order to impose their particular interests on the entire community. That would explain why the US Constitution emphasizes so heavily institutional controls on power and, especially, the power of legislature.

Returning to the subject of our concern now, related to factions, Madison believed they represented the "motor" that caused the whole problem. Factions had set in motion the oppressive procedures that now needed to be stopped or at least contained. That is why factions are at the center of his most important essay in the Federalist Papers. At the beginning of No. 10, Madison defines with unique clarity the concept of "faction" around which all his attention and reasoning revolved.

With the precision of a surgeon, Madison offered this definition:

> By a faction, I understand a number of citizens, whether amounting to a majority or a minority of the whole, who are united and actuated by some common impulse of passion, or of interest, contrary to the rights of other citizens, or to the permanent and aggregate interests of the community.

One could devote an entire book to tracing the implications of the definition offered by Madison. It incorporates many of the most influential beliefs of his age. Madison affirms these extremely relevant notions lucidly, controversially, politically, and astutely. Without going into exhaustive detail, it is worth taking a closer look at his definition of factions, concentrating on the way it touches on four main themes:

1 Direct democracy,
2 Personal motivations,
3 Rights violations, and
4 The tensions between majorities and minorities.

4.2 Direct Democracy

In the first place, underlying Madison's definition are his objections to the democratic political system associated with Ancient Greece. Madison would in fact dedicate several pages in this essay and others in the Federalist Papers to criticizing direct democracy as it was practiced in Athens. Clearly, however, by criticizing a form of government so distant, removed, and in a way forgotten, Madison took advantage of the opportunity to take objection to, indirectly, the behavior of state assemblies in neighboring states (such as Pennsylvania, Vermont, and Rhode Island) that he characterized as controlled by uncontained, violent factions with majority support. Note, for example, the following paragraph that Madison devoted, a few lines after providing his definition of "faction," to the problem. Here Madison is speaking about direct democracy in small communities:

> Hence it is that such democracies have ever been spectacles of turbulence and contention; have ever been found incompatible with personal security or the rights of property; and have in general been as short in their lives as they have been violent in their deaths. Theoretic politicians, who have patronized this species of government, have erroneously supposed that by reducing mankind to a perfect equality in their political rights, they would, at the same time, be perfectly equalized and assimilated in their possessions, their opinions, and their passions.

Factions, as we will ascertain next, may arise as a result of behavior or action by groups in the minority or the majority, as Madison notes in the first part of his definition. The ones that caused him real concern, however (as we will soon see that he goes on to affirm), were those with majority support – the legislative behavior of assemblies that stayed within the proper bounds of "direct democracy."

4.3 Motivations

The second especially relevant position of Madison that is reflected in his short definition of factions involves *personal motivations*. Madison's position seems influenced by Scottish philosophy, which from Adam Smith to David Hume was extremely prominent at the time. A "number of citizens" – individuals – "are united and actuated by some common impulse of passion, or of interest, adverse to the rights of other citizens." In other words, personal or collective interests, and emotions (passions), tend to "take the place of reason." As Madison would say later in No. 55: "In all very numerous assemblies, of whatever characters composed, passion never fails to wrest the sceptre from reason." I will set aside this controversial point to be addressed in another chapter, in order to point out a third consideration or theme that is central in Madison's definition of factions.

4.4 Violations of Rights

In his definition, Madison suggests that factions, moved by a common passion or interest, tend to work against "the *rights of other citizens*, or to the permanent and aggregate interests of the community" (italics added). Still, we might ask ourselves what lies behind this affirmation (and in that respect, taking a look at Bernard Manin's great 1997 book, *The Principles of Representative Government*, might be in order). This part of the definition is particularly controversial (although for our purposes, analyzing the uncomfortable generalization is unnecessary) because Madison was talking about the need to protect, above all, "the rights of other citizens." As it so happened, the main problem facing the country at the time in terms of rights violations was without a doubt the violation of the rights of a large group of the "noncitizens": the slaves. Madison (in the Federalist Papers) and part of the political leadership at the time spoke of "persons" when referring to slaves, not "citizens," as they represented one of the classes of people excluded from citizenship (it is also worth clarifying that many of the Constitutional Convention participants were themselves slave-owners). This is why, when Madison identified the principal objective of the Constitution as confronting the problem of factions in Federalist Paper No. 10, and described the problems caused by factions and the rights endangered by them, the problem of slavery was nowhere to be seen. What I am saying is that, from the moment of its creation, it was always clear that the drafters of the US Constitution were not interested in addressing the problem of slavery, which was "swept under the rug" of the text. Notwithstanding, as might be expected, I do not want to get stuck on the details surrounding this problem – a grave problem indeed yet also rooted in the historical context of the period. I will devote some more attention, however, to another problem, the fourth problem raised by Madison's definition: the tension between majorities and minorities.

4.5 Majorities and Minorities: The Construction of a Counter-Majoritarian Constitution

Given the relevance of this theme to the argument of this work, I would like to dedicate a special section to the question of majorities and minorities, which is also central in Madison's definition of factions.

Majorities versus Minorities. The problem to which I refer has special importance because it allows us to perceive how, bit by bit, a counter-majoritarian Constitution was put together. To give an idea of the angle I am taking, let us start with the beginning of Madison's definition of factions. Madison makes it clear that he understood factions as a certain "number of citizens, whether amounting to a majority or a minority" whose behavior goes against the rights of other citizens or the interests of the community. Yet let us pause where Madison refers to a "majority or minority." The reference is of interest because the author seeks to convey explicitly, from the start, the honesty of his approach to the question. What I mean is that he recognizes from the get-go that any type of social group is liable to violate the rights of others. To express it in terms from Madison's historical context, ones Madison himself uses in No. 10, he speaks of "debtors" (majorities) and "creditors" (minorities) or, in a similar sense, of "those who hold and those who are without property." As I see it, it was very important for Madison to make clear then, as people have been emphasizing ever since, that serious violations of rights were a risk whenever any social group, indistinctly of the group's identity, formed a faction. Still . . .

We have already seen one way Madison limited the scope of the problem. He made it clear that he was not talking about the rights of slaves (by only mentioning the rights of citizens). The main rights violation committed by the "minority" of "creditors" and "landowners" was thus by definition removed from the scope of analysis. Yet there is a second reframing that I would also like to point out, one just as serious as the first. Madison emphasizes in the same essay that, *although theoretically prepared to consider rights violations by either minority or majority factions, in truth what he is only interested in addressing the risk posed by ones in the majority*. In Madison's words:

> *If a faction consists of less than a majority, relief is supplied by the republican principle*, which enables the majority to defeat its sinister views by regular vote. It may clog the administration, it may convulse the society; but it will be unable to execute and mask its violence under the forms of the Constitution. When a majority is included in a faction, the form of popular government, on the other hand, enables it to sacrifice to its ruling passion or interest both the public good and the rights of other citizens. To secure the public good and private rights against the danger of such a faction, and at the same time to preserve the spirit and the form of popular government, is then the great object to which our inquiries are directed. (italics added)

Note the importance of Madison's observation: while true that rights violations may theoretically be committed by groups in the majority or minority, *we do not need constitutional protection against the risk of the latter because the majority can block those legislative initiatives through the vote*. That is what Madison means when he says that if a group "consists of less than a majority," then there is an easy solution at hand, for "relief is supplied by the republican principle" – voting by majority rule. He goes on to clarity that it "enables the majority to defeat [the minority's] sinister views by regular vote." In other words, if a minority of politicians seeks to silence its critics, and to do so they present a bill in Congress suppressing critical political expression and persecuting dissidents . . . there is an easy solution! We vote against the bill!

At least in my eyes, Madison's facile arrangement is enormously unattractive. Furthermore (without even going into his failure to take into account one of the greatest violation of rights in the institution of slavery), Madison reduces the fractious behavior of minorities to the misbehavior of factions of representatives *in Congress*. Naturally, framed in this way, the solution truly is "supplied by the republican principle." The problem, however, one that Robert Dahl masterfully shows in his analysis of Madisonian democracy in the classic work, *A Preface to Democratic Theory* published in 1956, is that the risk of rights violations usually stems from pressure and activity by minorities operating outside of Congress. Hence, Madison has (once again) reframed the issue in a way that leaves a monumental problem outside the confines of analysis.

In any case, the point – of enormous importance for our analysis – can be summarized as follows: If (i) the major problem requiring a constitutional solution consists of factions and (ii) factions are defined as groups indeterminate of majority or minority status but (iii) the problem of minority factions is not actually important (since we can deal with it the "republican" way), then (iv) *the real problem for which we need a constitutional remedy is the one represented by factious majorities; that is, the problem of majority rule itself, or simply democracy.*

4.6 A Constitution Made to Protect Minorities

The constitutional model that took form in the United States, one that Madison more than anyone else theorized and molded, thus presented a clear counter-majoritarian imprint. The objective of the Constitution turned out to be confronting the potential of majoritarian factions. More specifically, the Constitution has been dedicated from its start to managing what was considered the great institutional problem of the time by much of the political class: the problem of local legislatures that come under the control of (biased) majorities that end up, as might be expected, imposing their (sinister) agendas on the other citizens. In other words, the Constitution was devoted, from the outset, to solving a serious, widespread problem, the problem of majority groups that threatened the rights of minorities. Beyond the limits and reframing of Madison's representation of the problem, there is an evident defect in it, and that is that the problem actually calls for some other legal treatment (among which a much more thought-out constitutional remedy could be included). It is also important to note that, without diminishing the relevance of the considerations I have just laid out, it is perfectly sensible for a constitution to take as one of its fundamental objections the special protection of minorities.

Still, to continue along the line we have been following, it is worth pointing out that the constitutional model emphasizing the protection of minorities – for as much sense as it makes – does not represent the only model available. It is simply untrue that the only function or the most important function of constitutions is protecting minorities. In fact, as is well-known, an alternative model saw the light of day around the same time in France, one that differed substantially from the US Constitution. I am referring to the *majoritarian constitutional model* that emerged following the French Revolution. Put another way, the constitution implemented in France around the same time as the United States Constitution was fundamentally devoted to the opposite problem; that is, rather than primarily aimed at offering special protection to threatened minorities, it was especially designed to favor the decision-making and expressive power of the groups that had majority support. In France, to summarize, effort was made to conceive of – at least in the early years of the revolutionary period – a constitution capable of honoring the principle of *popular sovereignty*, a constitution that would favor the expression of the *general will*. In the United States, that model seems to have been anticipated in some of the state legislatures, many of which, perhaps prematurely and rudimentarily, experimented with constitutional arrangements after independence that ensured special expression for majority rule. (As we have seen, on different occasions Madison attacked and ridiculed many of the forms such legislatures took by likening them to the schemes – which he found unacceptable – of direct democracy associated with Ancient Greece.)

For the time being, what is important to retain is that: the United States constitutional model, which is the one that was later adopted everywhere in Latin America, was designed with a particular project in mind, that of offering special protection to minorities – without doubt, a plausible constitutional purpose, at least in principle. Doing so, however, meant setting aside an alternative model, for instance the one adopted in France following its revolution, according to which the fundamental mission of the constitution is facilitating the formation and expression of the general will through majority rule.

I will close this section with a few additional comments. First, I would like to observe that, regardless of the model followed (for instance, the one adopted in France or the one in the United States), constitutional frameworks may be of greater or lesser quality; their institutional design more or less effective. Yet nothing inherently, I will argue, dooms certain constitutional models to failure or guarantees the success of others ("success" and "failure" being terms that also require definition beyond simple associations with notions like "stability" and "instability").

Second, I would like to emphasize that the model chosen for protecting minorities adopted by the United States Constitution was primarily, and this should be remembered, *anti-majoritarian*. What I mean is that the drafters decided to establish minority protections by undermining the decision-making power and control of majorities. This bears repeating because other means of affording special protection for minorities within an essentially majoritarian system do exist. The 1776 Pennsylvania state constitution inspired by Thomas Paine's ideas and written under the direction of Benjamin Franklin, for example, incorporated at an early, exploratory phase some such mechanisms.[1] In any case, what I am interested in pointing out at the moment is the existence of different institutional means to ensure minority protection within a decisively majoritarian constitutional framework. *In other words, handicapping the majoritarian component of a constitution is not the only way to extend protection to the most vulnerable social groups.*

Now I would like to draw attention to another problematic issue that derives from the United States model's counter-majoritarian defense of minorities: the connotations of the notion of minorities during this period.

4.7 Exactly Which of the Minorities Warrant Protection?

As we just saw in the previous section, the decision to orient a constitution towards the protection of minorities is both reasonable and feasible. The "majoritarian" model that was devised during the early

[1] Paine had the idea, for example, of having the legislature elect judges. He also thought of having a Council of Censors, which would be in charge of assessing the constitutionality of legislation and whose members would be chosen through direct elections (!). Similarly, in the face of critical comments his project received, Paine proposed a mechanism for the legislative revision of laws that involved choosing a committee of representatives from the one-chamber legislature by lottery. The lottery would ensure the distribution of the power among different factions without compromising the democratic legitimacy of the committee (we will return to this example).

days of the French Revolution appears, for many of us, more attractive in principle, but this does not negate the importance of the model followed by the United States. We also noted in the previous section that the quality and success of a particular constitution depends on factors other than the model chosen, which include the measures taken to protect minorities as well as the mode by which these "minorities" are qualified. Respecting the type of measures chosen, as will be shown, what was done in the US Constitution to bolster the strength of minorities, or to ensure them protection, turned out – I will argue – to be unacceptable as it offends our democratic propensities. Regarding the manner by which minorities are identified, this turns out to be important because we can define them in very different ways, not all of which are particularly apt for the functions we want the constitution to perform.

Vulnerability. One possible criterion for the definition of minorities could be the "weakness" of the group, understood as the degree to which it is "disadvantaged" and its member fragile. From this perspective, for example, the social group comprising women would receive minority treatment because the criterion of vulnerability is more important than the number of people in the group. In fact, in certain cases, women may represent a majority in that they outnumber men but still qualify as a minority in terms of legal treatment in accordance with this definition.

Strict Percentage. A second possible criterion would be to define minorities strictly in terms of their reduced size, which places them at the mercy of the majority. Using this criterion, women would no longer comprise a minority group, but immigrants would, as would African- and Hispanic Americans in the United States. This definition of minority would also qualify as a minority the "rich and powerful" individuals in society, whereas using the first criterion of vulnerability would not.

Class? The "founding fathers" of US constitutionalism, as I understand it, often used the term "minorities" – along with other terms – loosely. This allowed them to play with general connotations that evoke, for example, disadvantaged minorities when they usually had another minority – property holders – in mind. In fact, many of the "founding fathers" habitually employed terms like "creditors," "large landowners," "rich," "well-born," and "minorities" synonymously (the same way they used interchangeably terms like "debtors," "the poor," and "majorities"). Madison, for example, during the Constitutional Convention, described the Senate as an institution meant to protect the opulent minority from the majority (Farrand 1937, v. 1, 431).

As Robert Dahl would argue, "Madison wished to erect a political system that would guarantee the liberties of certain minorities whose advantages of status, power, and wealth would, he thought, probably not be tolerated indefinitely by a constitutionally untrammeled majority" (Dahl 1956, 31).

Decisively, whether or not the "Federalists" intentionally played upon the ambiguities surrounding the term "minorities," what they usually had in mind was a very restricted notion of the term, one which basically associated minorities with one minority in particular – the "minority of the powerful." This is one reason why we might conclude that the decision to orient the constitution towards the protection of minorities would have been more convincing if a broader conception of the term, or one emphasizing powerless groups, had been employed. Instead, the frequent association of the term with the "rich and well-born" had the effect of diminishing the attraction of Madison's proposed model.

For our purposes, it is important to insist once again that the legacy of the 1787 US Constitution goes beyond the borders of that nation and that it is not purely rhetorical. The US Constitution left an institutional legacy that we cannot dismiss the way we might excuse or overlook the "elitist" or perhaps simply cunning use of the term "minorities." In the end, there is no point in belaboring the rhetoric used over two hundred years ago, unless of course it turns out that the "elitist" conception of what constitutes a minority actually did inform the constitutional structure still in place today. We will soon see that it did, and in which ways.

4.8 So, What to Do About Majority Factions? (Another) Counter-Majoritarian Response

Let us concede, at least provisionally, Madison's motive to structure the constitution for the protection of minorities. Let us even assume a broad, inclusive definition of minorities (in contrast to the narrow, partial sense employed by the framers of the US model). From this perspective of Madison's commitment, what does No. 10 propose to contain the danger posed by factions? As we will see, what Madison suggested was, since it was impossible to prevent them from forming, one should limit the harm they could do – the effects of their actions. In his words: "There are two methods of curing the mischiefs of faction: the one, by removing its causes; the other, by controlling its effects." As we will see, Madison ruled out the first option, which he considered either absurd or impossible, in favor of the second. He laid out his reasoning in No. 10, in a passage that has since gained renown as one of his "argumentative jewels." Let us have a look.

Attack the Causes? Absurd or Impossible. In ruling out the possibility of confronting the causes of factions, Madison maintained: "There are again two methods of removing the causes of faction: the one, by destroying the liberty which is essential to its existence; the other, by giving to every citizen the same opinions, the same passions, and the same interests." He immediately went on to clarify, however, that he rejected the first option of "attacking the causes" of factions. He put it this way:

> It could never be more truly said than of the first remedy, that it was worse than the disease. Liberty is to faction what air is to fire, an aliment without which it instantly expires. But it could not be less folly to abolish liberty, which is essential to political life, because it nourishes faction, than it would be to wish the annihilation of air, which is essential to animal life, because it imparts to fire its destructive agency.
>
> The second expedient is as impracticable as the first would be unwise. As long as the reason of man continues fallible, and he is at liberty to exercise it, different opinions will be formed. As long as the connection subsists between his reason and his self-love, his opinions and his passions will have a reciprocal influence on each other; and the former will be objects to which the latter will attach themselves. The diversity in the faculties of men, from which the rights of property originate, is not less an insuperable obstacle to a uniformity of interests. The protection of these faculties is the first object of government.

In other words, the two conceivable means for attacking the causes of factions must be dismissed: attacking the liberty that allows factions to form would be "absurd" – a cure "worse than the disease" itself. The second conceivable means, meanwhile – striving to ensure everyone enjoys the same conditions – is considered impractical. This argumentation bridges the assumption that the "causes of factions" lie in the "nature of man" to the suggestion that fighting the causes be abandoned in order to concentrate on attacking the "effects" of factions.

Attacking Effects and the Counter-Majoritarian Option. Madison's starting point for this argument is the conclusion of his previous claim: "The inference to which we are brought is, that the causes of faction cannot be removed, and that relief is only to be sought in the means of controlling its effects." In pondering the manner through which such effects should be countered, as we saw, Madison was specifically interested in limiting the power of factions with majority support (for, as shown, factions without majority support could be simply voted down).

In the face of oppressive majorities, Madison proposed that the Constitution ought to: "Secure the public good and private rights against the danger of such a faction, and at the same time to preserve the spirit and the form of popular government."

How? Here Madison came up with another two-alternative scenario of which only one, once again, seemed practical. He maintained that, referring to the objective of containing the effects of factions, either measures could be taken to prevent passions or interests that "blind" people from taking hold or, if such dangerous passions have already attained majority support, the faction must be incapacitated to prevent it from carrying out its "plans of oppression." The faction would be incapacitated by ensuring that the (oppressive) "inclination" did not coincide with any "opportunity" (to oppress).[2]

This strategy of using gateways and veto points – like dikes – to prevent the coincidence of "inclination and opportunity" has been incorporated into our constitutions ever since. If a (majority) group demonstrated any oppressive inclination (naturally present in all groups), constitutional mechanisms should be in place to eliminate any "opportunity" for the group to realize it. This is why Madison concluded that "pure" or direct forms of democracy had to be avoided. Madison considered, based on his knowledge of history, direct democracy (and he had a very expansive understanding of what qualified as direct democracy) to be the worst institutional arrangement of all. He therefore dismissed a more robust democratic solution, which he described in these terms:

> From this view of the subject it may be concluded that a pure democracy, by which I mean a society consisting of a small number of citizens, who assemble and administer the government in person, can admit of no cure for the mischiefs of faction. A common passion or interest will, in almost every case, be felt by a majority of the whole; a communication and concert result from the form of government itself; and there is nothing to check the inducements to sacrifice the weaker party or an obnoxious individual.

[2] In Madison's words: "By what means is this object attainable? Evidently by one of two only. Either the existence of the same passion or interest in a majority at the same time must be prevented, or the majority, having such coexistent passion or interest, must be rendered, by their number and local situation, unable to concert and carry into effect schemes of oppression. If the impulse and the opportunity be suffered to coincide, we well know that neither moral nor religious motives can be relied on as an adequate control. They are not found to be such on the injustice and violence of individuals, and lose their efficacy in proportion to the number combined together, that is, in proportion as their efficacy becomes needful."

Faced with the option that Madison considered unacceptable, "pure democracy," the only plausible alternative he found was the one he deemed "republican," although what he was really talking about was the system we now define as *representative government*. He argued that "a republic, by which I mean a government in which the scheme of representation takes place, opens a different prospect, and promises the cure for which we are seeking." This is where Madison clarified the distinction between representative government and "pure" democracy, and his clarification reveals important aspects of his counter-majoritarian approach to the matter. Madison distinguished two factors of representative government that enabled it to contain the danger of factions and made it preferable to "pure" democracy. To understand the contrast, the "enemy" or counter-model he was arguing against should be kept in mind: (essentially inexistent) situations where, in small communities, the people are in direct control of the government or situations in which the government is closely related to or identified with a group that has majority support. Madison did consider the latter case relevant, evidenced by his identification of "rebel" states like Pennsylvania, Vermont, and Rhode Island as examples of this situation (even if in his argumentation he concentrated on the danger of "pure" democracy in Ancient Greece for illustration).

The two major differences between, as I will call them, representative and majoritarian governments that Madison identified are foreseeably related to the two traits that Madison attributed to dangerous "pure" democracies: *the reduced size of the communities and the direct control of government by citizens*. Regarding the former, Madison argued that representative government was less dangerous or worrisome because republican government could administer larger, more populated territories. The larger size would make such governments less sensitive to "factious combinations."[3]

However, I am much more interested – as was Madison – in the other differentiating factor between "pure" democracy and representative government. This is the "refinement" or "filtering" of the public's voice that is ensured by the representative system. The precise paragraph is very important (and we will return to it when discussing representation).

[3] In Madison's words: "the greater number of citizens and extent of territory which may be brought within the compass of republican than of democratic government; and it is this circumstance principally which renders factious combinations less to be dreaded in the former than in the latter."

Madison argued that representative government, unlike the alternative, "pure" democracy:

> to refine and enlarge the public views, by passing them through the medium of a chosen body of citizens, whose wisdom may best discern the true interest of their country, and whose patriotism and love of justice will be least likely to sacrifice it to temporary or partial considerations. Under such a regulation, it may well happen that the public voice, pronounced by the representatives of the people, will be more consonant to the public good than if pronounced by the people themselves, convened for the purpose.

Although we will return to this issue soon, I would like to emphasize certain aspects of this influential and striking characterization of representative government immediately. Madison advances a very particular reading of representation: (i) the representatives are "separated" from the citizenry; (ii) the representatives take the place of the citizenry, replacing it; (iii) the representatives comprise a group of individuals with special qualities (in both the sense that they are "chosen" and that they are "select" or special); and, especially controversially, (iv) the representatives tend to make better decisions than the citizenry. For these reasons, Madison concludes, the representative system is "better" than any system of direct democracy. *Representative government is not presented as a "necessary evil" or as a "second-best option," but instead as the preferred choice.*

The counter-majoritarian bias of Madison's characterization, in my view, is wholly evident in this perspective of the representative system, a perspective that permeates the entire US Constitution. The Constitution was devised to limit citizen participation in politics, to "separate" citizens from their representatives, to prevent them from imposing their opinions on legislators, to make sure electors cannot force their representatives to favor the particular interests of their locality over the general interests of the nation, and so on. From this characterization and line of reasoning began counter-majoritarian constitutionalism.

5

Motivations and Institutions: "If Men Were Angels"

If men were angels, no government would be necessary. If angels were to govern men, neither external nor internal controls on government would be necessary.

(The Federalist Papers n. 51)

From "The Federalist Papers," a remarkable work both in its day and in ours, three essays are particularly relevant for the argument presented in this book. No. 10 represents the heart or nucleus of the constitutional project it advocated (for in it the Constitution is described as an instrument to contain "factions"). No. 78 is especially important because it discusses the principles and directives behind the design of the judiciary. Lastly, No. 51, which I will address now, warrants attention for two reasons. First, because it justifies the model of "checks and balances" that the Constitution implemented. Second, and perhaps more importantly, it provides the keys to understanding how the framers understood citizens and their basic motivations during the founding period. There is a paragraph in No. 51, which was written by James Madison, that stands out:

> Ambition must be made to counteract ambition. The interest of the man must be connected with the constitutional rights of the place. It may be a reflection on human nature, that such devices should be necessary to control the abuses of government. But what is government itself, but the greatest of all reflections on human nature? *If men were angels, no government would be necessary. If angels were to govern men, neither external nor internal controls on government would be necessary.* In framing a government which is to be administered by men over men, the great difficulty lies in this: you must first enable the government to control the governed; and in the next place oblige it to control itself. A dependence on the people is, no doubt, the primary control on the government; but experience has taught mankind the necessity of auxiliary precautions.
>
> (italics added)

Every affirmation in this paragraph is important, but I will concentrate on the lines in italics. Madison sought to emphasize that people are not "angels" (and not because he was prone to rhetorical flourish). Why? And why is this affirmation so important to make at this historical moment?

Many different concurrent discussions are picked up in "The Federalist Papers," and this essay is no different. Madison addresses several different interlocutors in the same piece. One of his main foils was the radical republicans, the American democrats inspired by Rousseau. This discussion pitted him against Thomas Jefferson and his allies over the issue of *civic virtues*. At one point, Madison shared their republican interest in public virtue. As John Adams put it, everyone at the time could be considered republican (all, or at least the vast majority, of the framers, after all, had opposed the English Crown). Moreover, many of them published texts proclaiming the value and importance of a "virtuous" and committed citizenry involved in public affairs.

Notwithstanding, there were some – the most determined, well-prepared, and daring republicans – whose declarations and proposals worried Madison and other leaders. These republicans seemed persuaded by the French revolutionaries who took "civic virtue" not as decorative rhetoric, but rather as an *indispensable quality of character* that the State needed to cultivate for its very survival. Without civically virtuous citizens, the Republic could not maintain stability, the radical republicans believed, and would collapse. Madison was not only uncomfortable with the emphasis on the qualities that could be required of citizens, but more so with requiring such qualities from government officials. Why, he asked, require so much, when through much more modest means as much or more could be attained? However, and especially, the premise underlying such a high requirement seemed too demanding and was difficult to accept. For the radical republicans, "cultivating virtue" went beyond simple discourse and propaganda. Civic virtue – commitment to community – required robust egalitarianism, small societies, and institutions open to public participation.

Such demands appeared to vex Madison and many of his contemporaries. Their discomfort with the importance the republicans put on these values often led them to depict their rivals as "naïve," as if they did not understand the real purpose of the institutional system, and much less the type of behavior one could expect from those charged with running them. When Madison says, "If men were angels," he is not engaging in some rhetorical exercise. His main goal is to hit back against the theory opposing his, in this case that of the radical republicans, by arguing that they did not seem to understand the reason for the institutions being created. He seemed to be telling them: "You are making a mistake by insisting on civic virtues and political engagement! We cannot treat an ideal or desire as our basic assumption! If we could (if 'civic virtue' were a reliable fact), why would we even need a constitution with controls and limitations on government?" It was precisely because people were not by nature or predictably "angels" – politically committed, virtuous individuals – that a system of mutual control was necessary. It was for that very reason that the Constitution was written! It was thus sheer naivety to believe the contrary (that people were politically motivated, of virtuous character, and so on).

Yet there is another side to Madison's affirmations that is also important, which could be seen as the flip side of his criticism of the republican ideals that comes out in his recommendations for the creation of institutions. He was basically making the case that institutions should be designed under the assumption that all public officials would behave like demons. If the institutional system was capable to discipline a band of demons, then it could, in principle, be considered well-planned. Again, Madison might ask, if public officials presumably behaved for the most part like angels, why would controls be necessary? Why would we even need government? We set up institutions because we cannot count on virtue, commitment, and honesty.

Although we will go right into the limitations and problems of Madison's scheme, I do not want to close this introductory section without emphasizing its relevance in light of the quality of public life and the models of institutional design that predominate in many of our countries. In truth, many of the institutions in countries like ours are actually designed as if they were run by "angels." Take for example the hyper-presidentialism so common in Latin America (or the rise of "imperial presidency" that Bruce Ackerman describes with the United States in mind). These should not be seen pathologically – as anomalies that occur as a result of bad or corrupt officials combined with unfortunate circumstances. On the contrary, hyper-presidentialism is certainly the result of mistakes made in the institutional design. Moreover, it is what Madison said so clearly that makes this conclusion evident: we have in place a system that appears to depend, crucially, on the chances of electing a President who is decent, progressive, energetic – and able to sustain these qualities for the entire duration of his or her mandate. In other words, the current system depends on finding a "President-angel" who is capable of and willing to demonstrate the qualities of his or her character throughout the term of her administration. When the miracle occurs, the system functions wonderfully: the President will be able to carry out all their magnificent projects with little resistance or external control. If, on the contrary, the person elected President does not turn out to be up to the job, or is susceptible to pressure and influence, or takes offense at criticism from society and begins acting in an authoritarian or abusive manner, then the bare reality of the institutional system is revealed. We realize that the system is a total failure, utterly incapable of performing the one function it was meant for. When this happens, we see that the system, in truth, is incapable of imposing firm control, that it allows abuse to continue, and that it is vulnerable to authoritarian manipulation. In these circumstances, we are able to see that the institutional design is not only defective, it could not be any worse in terms of the purpose of and guiding principles behind it.

Now I would like to review three issues related to what has been discussed; that is, the premises that served as guiding principles for the institutional design of modern constitutionalism. I would like to highlight (i) the attractive traits of the republican model criticized by Madison, (ii) the defects of Madison's interesting proposal, and (iii) the "moral" compromises inherent in any institutional project. Then I will close the chapter with an aside reflecting on the "material preconditions of political self-government."

5.1 How Far Off Were the Radical Republicans?

It is undeniable (as was noted in the previous aside on hyper-presidentialist systems) that many countries ended up adopting inadequate institutional designs – fundamentally vulnerable or fragile – that were apparently construed with "angelical" leaders in mind. That is precisely why "Madison's advice" (to choose a system capable of carrying out its function even administered by "demons") has historically been considered reasonable, even lucid. Similarly, much of Madison's criticism of his republican colleagues deserves attention. It seems clear that many of his adversaries conceived of politics as if they were living the myth of virtuous citizens associated with Ancient Greece. Up to this point, it is hard to find fault with Madison. I would like to examine in a bit more detail, however, the views of his rivals, because I believe there is much more of interest and much less naivety than Madison and his generation presumed. If we consider the best version of the republicans' proposals, we see that rather than ingenuousness, what lies behind them is an alternative conception of the institutional design.

To summarize in broad strokes the model that many of the republicans seemed to have in mind, I would describe their alternative in terms of the following traits. In the first place, their regulative ideal, their ultimate objective was neither individual autonomy nor personal liberty. It was *collective self-government.* This ideal (as we will see) informs the rest of their proposals for the organization of government. Secondly, for the republicans, attaining collective self-government depended on the *civic virtue* of the citizens. It required citizens willing to stand up in defense of the nation, the homeland, the community, and common interest. Thomas Jefferson, for example, once observed that the foundations of "republican government" were "not in the constitution, but merely in the spirit of our people." That spirit, he concluded, would force even a "despot" to govern democratically (Jefferson 1999, 212). In any case, it seems clear that no one rises to defend their community – no one willingly puts their life and property on the line (as many French and North Americans did during their revolutions) – without strong and deep motivation. For the successful defense of the community, *certain moral qualities and strong character are expected (and needed) from the citizens.* To elicit such qualities, whether in reference to an individual's identification with their community or their commitment to the ideals of their nation, the citizens must feel a close bond with the rest of the citizenry, for the project fails if anyone, in this context, feels detached from the common interest.

This brings us to the most interesting point concerning the "naivety" or "realism" of many of these republicans. If, after reading the description of what collective self-government requires in the preceding paragraph, you take a look up at your surroundings, it might be natural for you to exclaim like Madison, "How naïve these republicans are! Where are these special humans who put the community above themselves?" The way I understand it, however, the republicans did not take such selflessness as a fact of human nature – or even as request, demand, or preference regarding the way they expected everyone to behave.

In my opinion, the republicans did not assume that people were "virtuous angels." They simply recognized that one precondition for self-government was civic virtue (a quality of character that institutions could help develop), and *from there they immediately turned to the material and institutional conditions that were necessary for that moral disposition to emerge.* One relevant example we might refer to is the emblematic author of the "republicanism of virtues," Jean-Jacques Rousseau.

Rousseau paradigmatically conceived of the "general will" not as the "mere" sum of the desires of all the individuals in a collective. Rather, he considered it to be the expression of the *collective's particular interest*: the common good. Rousseau did not assume, however, that "virtue" and civic engagement naturally followed from the general will, or that such dispositions could be simply "demanded" from individuals. Rousseau's confidence in collective self-government – government that resulted from and expressed the general will – stemmed from the relation he saw between those virtues and material, institutional, and personal conditions that he felt were perfectly possible or attainable in the framework of societies such as the one in Geneva. As for the conditions in his surroundings that led to his confidence, to begin with, Geneva was one of small dimensions. It also represented a small community, one with a history of government and institutions that facilitated the practice. Furthermore, Genevan society was relatively egalitarian in economic terms. These conditions were anything but common, but they were desirable, in addition to imaginable, possible, and realistic. They provided a (realistic) framework in which an institutional arrangement could be conceived in terms of "civic virtue," republican commitment, a strong group identity with a corollary concern for the fate of others, "self-government," and "general will."

It was in this context, and only in this context – the republicans assumed – that virtue could be "cultivated." To be specific, this virtue included commitment to public values, the strength of character needed for a republic, a group identity of the community as a whole, the sense of belonging, and, finally, the necessary moral dispositions for self-government. It did not require rhetoric or enthusiastic calls to action ("the time has come for all to rise together for the nation!"), but instead certain *social, economic, political, and institutional conditions that had to be put in place.* This awareness of the work to be done explains why I fail to see naivety or ineptitude in the republican proposals. They called for imperative changes that would be demanding and costly.

With this clarified, we can move to the second point, which involved the fundamental attraction of the Madisonian project. As we have seen, Madison argued for his model to a large degree by arguing, somewhat unfairly and definitely exaggeratedly, against the republican one.

5.2 Egoism As "Fuel" for and the "Endogenous Product" of the Institutional System

I am going to focus now on the Madisonian model, drawing special attention to his manner of conceiving human motives and the relation of this conception to the form and operation of institutions. As was mentioned, in No. 51 of "The Federalist Papers," Madison argued, correctly, that an institutional system should not be drawn up on the premise that the officials and administrators that ran it, or the common citizens it served, for that matter, would be "angelical." Such a vision – he might say – involves a pale and ultimately inaccurate portrait of the world we live in. We cannot base our actions on those presuppositions, then, if our intention is constructing institutions for the world we do live in, here and now. A more accurate foundation, one that is more grounded in the reality of the here and now, requires a current assessment of the human behavior in our surroundings. Does anyone have the impression that everyone around them is virtuous, committed in solidarity, ready to make sacrifices for the community's well-being? I hazard that it is much more common to cross paths with people who are generally selfish, politically disinterested, and detached from their communities – people who do not worry much about the common good or even the fate of those outside their immediate circles and family members. Although it is certain that not everyone we bump into falls into this category (which could be considered that of "demons" in comparison with the archetype of republican "angels"), many probably are. Chances are we even know more people in the "demon" category than that of "angels," especially if we know a lot of people who work in government.

The axioms regarding human motivation on which Madison based his arguments were widely accepted at the time, and he relied on them as pillars justifying all his reasoning and institutional proposals. They center around the idea – present in the paragraph cited at the beginning of this chapter – that "ambition must be made to counteract ambition" (an idea that I will return to later in more detail because of its importance). This idea is extremely revealing, for it supposes that (i) self-interest is the primary motor of human behavior (at least for government officials) and (ii) it is possible to obtain positive results by combining base motivations (by pairing the "egoism" or "ambition" of some people in tension with the "egoism" or "ambition" of others).

It is worth noting the debt Madison's ideas of personal motivation, self-interest, institutions, and the common good owe to Scottish moral philosophy (White 1987). This school of thought combines the visions of thinkers like David Hume and Adam Smith. From Hume, Madison adopts the notion that "passions" often "cloud" one's "reason" (or as Hume famously put it, that reason is the "slave of the passions"). Madison habitually refers to this axiom to explain the irrational demands of groups that allow their "passions" to overcome their reason. In The

Federalist No. 55, as we know, Madison went so far as to write that "in all very numerous assemblies, of whatever character composed, passion never fails to wrest the sceptre from reason." Yet even in No. 10, Madison had already revealed the central place he assigned to this premise (when speaking of the *common passion, or interest averse to the rights of others* or to the permanent interests of the community as a whole that moved factions).

In order to understand better the centrality of egoism and self-interest in Madison's thinking, it is also worth mentioning the theory of the "invisible hand" proposed by Adam Smith and the Manchester school of economic liberalism. According to the "invisible hand" model described by Smith, rational self-interested individuals could in concert contribute to the common good when institutions were established to provide the proper incentive. You could not expect John would get his daily "bread" from the generosity of Mary the "baker," but if Mary made a reasonable profit by baking bread, certainly bread would be available to John to buy every day. This kind of scheme does not require – Adam Smith argued – generosity, solidarity, or "angelic" behavior. The metaphor is meant to convey the idea that, through adequate institutions and appropriate incentives, everyone can obtain what they wish, even when they behave (and because they behave) selfishly.

The institutional scheme proposed by Madison is in essence identical to the bread metaphor. We do not need "angels" or "virtuous" citizens for good governance where no group oppresses another. We can simply build upon the "egoism" or "ambition" of all to reach that objective. All that is needed are the right institutional incentives for government officials (checking "ambition" with "ambition"). *Egoism or self-interest becomes, in this way, the fuel that powers the whole mechanic of government.*

Still, this scheme, based on a realistic, feet-on-the-ground, anything-but-naïve assessment of human motivation, has several problems of its own, problems that it makes sense to look at before simply reaffirming the impact that the model has had on our present-day institutions. I would like to bring up three questions that are worth keeping in mind when defending or assessing it.

(i) In the first place, arranging political institutions to use egoism as "fuel" rather than some other principle, for example solidarity, is at first glance itself problematic. A similar move would be organizing the judiciary around the principle of deception rather than truth. The problem is not merely that lying is bad in itself, but also that it implies using something for support that runs counter to the objectives of the judicial process. If the judicial system arranged this way somehow finally arrived at the "truth" (from some combination of "lie" versus "lie," let's say), the "truth" obtained would only be a possible subproduct that could be displaced each time the main actors in the judicial process felt it convenient to do so. The "truth" would not be obtained by virtue of the convictions or moral principles of the actors in the legal conflict, but rather through the indirect, more haphazard mechanism devised. In the political system, the risk is even clearer. Since, in the Madisonian model, none of the political actors are bound to serve the common good and the system itself is designed to incentivize egoistic behavior, it should come as no surprise that political officials often neglect the common good when presented with an opportunity to further their own interest without making any important concessions (such as supporting a reform that only benefits them while undermining the common good by, for example, passing a law that restricts the majority political decision-making power). What I mean is that in such a scheme, representatives are bound by no commitment at all (or are incentivized to favor) the public good (later on I will return to this point).

(ii) A second difficulty Madison's presentation of the problem. It gives insufficient attention to the fact that *this kind of selfish motivation results to a great extent from the structure of the proposed scheme: it is an endogenous product of the institutional system under debate.* This is very important, in my opinion, because it challenges the largely unquestioned premise that self-interest is the common baseline within the framework of individual motivation. I must insist that simply granting the "natural" character of self-interest is problematic. It implies that a selfish moral disposition is not to a large degree culturally constructed – that it is not an endogenous product of the institutional system upon which the system also largely relies.

When we become aware of this dynamic – the at least partial responsibility of the institutional system for the egoism of those who carry out its functions – it makes sense to ask how far we want to promote, encourage, develop, and foster it, given its tension with our ultimate objective regarding the institutions we design (the common good).

(iii) This second problems leads us to the third issue I would like to bring up. This problem was mentioned in the previous section about the value and attraction of the republican alternative to the Madisonian model. One of the conclusions reached was that the model of "civic virtue" defended by the republicans was not simply a naïve, abstract ideal. It involved an ideal scenario that was anything but common at the time (and is not common today either), but it still represented a scenario that was *desirable*, *imaginable*, and *possible*. If this is so, if "civic virtue republicanism" does not merely consist of utopian fantasy, then it makes sense to ask, when (re)designing an institutional system (especially during "foundational moments"), whether it would make sense to orient the system such that egoism or self-interest are less central to its operation. Why not choose incentives that align with or encourage motives we value or need (solidarity, honesty, decency – "civic virtues")?

5.3 No System Is "Neutral"

Having called attention to the defects of the Madisonian model, I would like to turn to a particular criticism of alternative models, like the republican one, that emerges from the Madisonian perspective. This is the objection that holds republicanism to be a "comprehensive" doctrine; that is, a robust conception imposed on citizens by the State. For liberal positions (like the one present behind the Madisonian model), this notion is wrapped up in the idea that equal respect for individuals and their life plans requires a "neutral" State, one that does not impose or promote a certain vision of how people should or should not behave – or what qualities of character are better than others. The State, therefore, must not engage in "cultivating virtue" or promoting personal values. It must remain neutral in that respect. Each person should live their life according to their beliefs, and the State must avoid reproaching anyone for choices rightfully made.

In principle, I do not see any problem with that perspective, provided we add some precision to it. On one side, respect for the life choices of each individual is indeed a very important value. The State must therefore make great effort to remain "neutral" with regard to personal choices. From another side, it is also true that the policy advanced by the republican model presents definite "risks." As the contemporary philosopher Michael Sandel has written, the republicans seem to have embarked on a "risky" social and institutional project. The idea that the State could use the powers in its control (economic resources, coercive measures) to define and "impose" certain character traits deemed appropriate (by the current administration or career bureaucrats, for example) is particularly scary. That objection (and the fear of its implications) is understandable, but they lead to at least two more questions that warrant examination.

In the first place, republicanism does not necessarily imply promoting initiatives that can be in the end useless or directly counterproductive, for example, propaganda campaigns favoring certain values ("show solidarity!"). Indoctrination, in the best of scenarios, might end up influencing people to adopt certain behaviors, but it will be because they have been indoctrinated rather than genuinely convinced of the value of the behaviors in question. What I am trying to say is that republicanism does not need an iron-fisted approach to attain (badly) what can be encouraged through better means. A few examples follow. Mandatory voting as it exists in several countries might represent an important and relatively economical incentive to encourage political participation (a republican value). Normally the cost of not voting is low in those countries, and the options of voting for no one or having one's vote annulled also exist. Similarly, implementing egalitarian policies might help instill respect for the government among the populace, or even a greater sense of engagement with their fellow citizens. Although it does not need saying, economic egalitarianism has absolutely nothing to do with the frightening policies (of imposing values or brain-washing) that liberals might like to impute to republicanism. There are many means through which republicans can encourage civic commitment without employing "social engineering" or authoritarian measures.

In the second place, it might be worth looking at the feasibility of implementing an effectively "neutral" political system in terms of its relation to the life plans of individuals. First, I would like to recognize that, regardless of the difficulty or feasibility of attaining genuine "neutrality" (which I will ask about next), the ideal is one that the State should make maximal effort to respect with regard to personal choices. To put it another way, the State should make maximal effort to ensure everyone's individual autonomy. I want to come back to the other point, however: every institutional system has an impact on individual character and behavior. Whatever system it is, it will incentivize certain types of civic behavior over others (that we could characterize as better or worse, or as more or less convenient). This affirmation does not reject the existence or the value of neutrality or embrace permissive relativism (the attitude that ultimately nothing really matters). The State may be more or less respectful of personal choices and from the perspective that I suggest, the State must (I insist) make the greatest effort to respect individual autonomy. In doing so, however, the State must acknowledge that any "basic structure," any political and economic organization, makes commitments to varying degrees, in various ways, and more or less openly, to certain values. It promotes certain principles and resists others.

As we are already aware, some of the explicit goals of republicanism – through the model of government it proposed – were political participation, public engagement, and communitarian virtues. Conservatism, also explicitly, put the state apparatus (and even the coercive means it controls) at the service of the values (e.g., religious) that it deemed appropriate.[1] Yet even liberalism, despite its devotion to the "cause" of state neutrality, was also always committed to a particular moral hierarchy. By constructing a counter-majoritarian political and juridical system (i.e., by creating a judiciary that has "the last word"), it clearly takes a position in favor of more passive citizenship. By advancing a representative system as its preferred option (and not merely as a "necessary evil"), liberalism does the same. When the list of rights enshrines property, free trade, and the freedom of contract over political rights or social safeguards that might enable all people to "play the democratic game," it once again sides with a model that is not especially participatory.

5.4 The Economic Preconditions of Political Self-Government

The idea that individual behaviors should, to a great extent, be considered endogenous to the institutional system has been lost over time, but it was once considered a rock-hard truth. It represented a direct assumption shared without discussion by the original constitutional theorists. In this regard, I would like to draw attention to the link – once again, one that

[1] In the Latin American history of the nineteenth century, for example, a very strong version of conservatism tended to predominate, which attempted to write its values into the constitution and explicitly commit the institutional system to its goals (to name two extreme examples, the 1823 Chilean Constitution, written by Juan Egana, was implemented along with a Moral Code that contained hundreds of articles governing the smallest details of the "moral" life of the people, and the 1869 Constitution of Ecuador promulgated by President Gabriel García with severe authoritarian policies that included moral policing, which was referred to as the "Letter of Slavery to the Vatican").

was clearly recognized by our predecessors yet forgotten in our time – between self-government and "material conditions." More specifically, the link is between the economic system, politics, and personal character. The continuity seen between those spheres – the economic, the political, and the personal – was so clear that Juan Bautista Alberdi went directly from writing his masterful comparative study of constitutionalism (*Las bases intelectuales del constitucionalismo argentino*) to the publication only a few months later, as if the logical suite of the very same train of thought, his book on economics and profit-seeking (*Sistema económico y rentístico*). In an even stronger sense, the true character of republicanism stands out. As a counterexample, take the work of Thomas Paine, who after having shaken America with his pamphlet *Common Sense* in 1776 (advocating a break with England), and immediately following *Rights of Man* (in defense of the French Revolution and in response to the criticism of Edmund Burke), published another extraordinary pamphlet, *Agrarian Justice*, also a natural continuation of his previous reflections, which promoted what we call today universal basic income. For Paine, it was simply obvious that political independence and self-government needed to be based on egalitarian economic foundations. In a similar way, take the case of another public figure closely linked to Thomas Paine. I am referring to Thomas Jefferson, who closely followed Paine's political activism and his numerous constitutional writings and their economic corollaries for *agrarian democracy* – which can be attested in Jefferson's *Notes on the State of Virginia*. Later on, the Republican Party promise (in the southern states recently defeated in the Civil War) of "forty acres and a mule" for the liberated slaves would be based on this tradition.

In addition to these antecedents, I have two remarks on what we could consider the legacy of republican thought that demonstrate the lucidity – more than naivety – of republican thought. The republicans, I will argue, offered (despite what Madison and others like him imputed) a richer and more complex vision of human motivation.

Economy and Character. The first remark in this regard is intended to underline the *impact of economic foundations on qualities of character*. Such was the certainty of the republicans in this regard that many of their most notable figures set about rethinking the institutional structure of their community on the basis, in the first place, of the impact of the economic organization on the type of character it would encourage. Paying attention to their reflections is worthwhile, for the germ of their reasoning directly questions and ultimately reverses the assumptions we tend to hold today. Indeed, today we not only tend to think of the political and the economic as separate spheres, but we also think of the economic system as a "choice" without any concern whatsoever for the potential impact of that "choice" on personal matters. During the "founding" moment of constitutionalism, by contrast, the republicans' reasoning was simply the opposite. This is so not only because of the way in which the three spheres (economy, politics, and personal morality) were seen as interconnected, but also, and above all, because of the way in which, *thinking about the character traits that they wanted to cultivate, they came to their decisions regarding the economic program that best favored the development of such traits.* Typically, they started from the need for virtuous citizens committed to public affairs and concerned with the destiny of their community. From there they reflected on the type of economic organization that could best serve the purpose of promoting such moral dispositions. For example, it was very common then for republicans to reject, in the face of economic dilemma before them (the choice between a commercial economy or one based on small agrarian communities), a "commercial" orientation because of their certainty that such an economic structure would lead to "corrupt" and "vicious" citizens who cared little for their peers. In this sense, the Antifederalist George Mason claimed that virtue was essential to the life of the republic and "cannot exist without frugality, probity, and rigor in morals" (Sandel 1996, 126). Authorities such as John Adams and Benjamin Franklin expressed themselves in the same way. No one went as far as Benjamin Franklin when it came to obsession over character (who used to train daily to cultivate his own civic virtues). He clearly believed that "only a virtuous people is capable of attaining liberty. When a nation becomes corrupt and vicious, then it becomes necessary for someone to dominate it" (Sandel 1996, 126).

Economy and Politics. My second remark involves the clarity with which the republicans recognized, in their day, the impact of economic equality and inequality on political egalitarianism. It was based on the certainty of the close connection of these two spheres that Jefferson tended to affirm the value of small, egalitarian, homogenous communities. A similar economic base seemed indispensable to forge a new political system. Indeed, for Jefferson, without arrangements that take this into account, the people's ties to the political system, which they would see as distant from their own affairs, would be weakened. According to the Virginia statesman, social organization in small, homogenous communities would make "true democracy" possible, one where everyone would be concerned with the issues closest and most important to them. For the rest, this activism at the local level would favor civic control over decisions made at higher representative levels. Thus organized, Jefferson maintained, citizens would be able to "break, in a peaceful and periodic way, the usurpations of their less trustworthy representatives, rescuing them from the horrible necessity of having to do it in an insurrectionary way" (Jefferson 1999, 219).

I will conclude these remarks with a short but interesting story that illustrates how we have forgotten the importance, recognized by our republican predecessors, of a democratized economy to ensure democratic politics. In 1847, there was no universal suffrage in Colombia. Instead, there was what was called the "census" or "restricted" vote (typically along economic criteria: those who did not possess economic resources were excluded from participating in elections). The radical politician Murillo Toro then presented a constitutional reform project aimed at eliminating the census vote that had been enshrined in all the constitutions up to then – the ones promulgated in 1821, 1830, 1832, and 1843. He emphatically proposed replacing the existing restrictions (at the time, citizenship was only extended to literate men over twenty-one years of age who owned land) with a model based on universal suffrage. Murillo's initiative was ultimately defeated by two votes, but it permanently changed the discussion. The radical politician became the first and best advocate for the extended vote against the opposition of a good part of the political leadership, including some of his fellow activists. A few years later, through Colombia's 1853 Liberal constitution, an extensive model of suffrage was enshrined.

After the initial euphoria, however, the spirit of the defenders of extended suffrage quickly changed. In the first elections held under the new constitution, the most progressive groups suffered resounding defeat. The reasons were various, including the dominance exercised by large landowners over the poorest workers who depended on them. The conservatives thus prevailed, and many of those who had long stood by Murillo Toro turned against him, indignantly blaming him for the turn of events.

Murillo Toro, who even back then boasted of "always looking at politics from the economic angle," reacted vehemently to his new adversaries, asking them:

> What does direct and universal suffrage mean in a society where [the enormous majority of voters] lack any ensured means of subsistence but

> depend on a single man for it? What does federation mean every federal district must depend, in the most demanding conditions, on one, two, or three individuals who have a monopoly on industry and therefore knowledge?
>
> (Murillo Toro 1979, 70)

Murillo Toro then proposed combining his political reform with a profound economic reform aimed at changing, above all, the organization of land ownership. Reaffirming the economic measures he had taken as Minister of Finance (which limited the amount of land that could be accumulated), he asserted that "land property" is the "permanent and incontestable cause of this social inequality; the cause of this systematic exploitation of the greatest number in favor of the smallest, against whose effects the selfish will uselessly oppose all imaginable political forms" (Murillo Toro 1979, 72).

The lesson was clear: it was not a matter of reversing the political reforms undertaken, which had been blocked by a state of affairs marked by extreme economic inequality. On the contrary – and in a distinctive and defining way of the original republican thinking – Murillo proposed to do the opposite; that is, to radicalize the reforms, extending them to the economic sphere. The certainty upon which his proposal rested was once again that *only an egalitarian economic base would make possible the realization of a political life among equals.*

6

The Structural Difficulties of Representation

In this chapter, I am going to concentrate on the analysis of the representative system that occupies the center of the political organization of all of our countries. I will say, in particular, that it currently faces difficulties that will be very hard to overcome if we want to achieve the goals that the founders set for themselves and gave our democratic projects meaning. In particular, the mechanisms chosen to attain "full representation" of the community currently face extraordinary structural obstacles that force us to reflect on, rethink, and reorganize the institutional arrangement in order to meet the original, explicit representational ambitions. To introduce this discussion, I focus first on the famous "Bristol debates" of the mid-eighteenth century, which represented a sort of democratic "Big Bang" that provoked discussions across the globe, discussions that we must recuperate and renew among ourselves.

6.1 The Bristol Debates

Some of the most important debates in the history of contemporary politics took place in 1774, when two politicians debated their conflicting views on representation in the city of Bristol, England. Edmund Burke was an author who has marked the modern history of conservative thought, while Henry Cruger was a merchant who at that time defended a "radical" view of representation. Burke and Cruger's opinions differed greatly about the nature of the bond that should exist between citizens and their representatives.

In these "Bristol debates," Burke argued that, once elected, representatives should have the freedom to think, act, and decide on their own, regardless of the will of their constituents. Cruger defended the exact opposite position. In his view, the representatives should be considered mere "delegates" appointed by their constituents – delegated in the sense that the elected representatives should respect and follow their electors' main demands. In this sense (and this point was a central question in the debate), Cruger spoke out in favor of allowing citizens to stipulate instructions that compelled their elected representatives to pursue a certain course of action, whereas Burke considered this position totally unacceptable.

Through these contrasting visions the two men developed their opposing understandings of representation. The first of these visions, represented by Burke's position, sees the representative as a trustee or fiduciary, that is, as an agent who guides himself according to his own criteria for the best action to pursue in each case. The opposite view was put forward by Cruger, in which the representative appears as a delegate, ambassador, or advocate for the interests of the citizens. Understood in this way, the delegate is someone who can be removed by voters at will and at any time. For example, a president could be removed if electors felt that he or she acted in breach of the commitments made just as any of us could do with a lawyer who failed to meet our expectations, or as countries do with appointed ambassadors (the underlying assumption being that appointed agents only deserve to remain in their position insofar as we perceive their performance as serving our interests).

These two opposing viewpoints offer us notable criteria that, even today, should be considered when we think about representation. Both conceptions alerted us, in effect, to specific, particularly concerning risks, and suggested opposing alternatives to mitigate them. Although in tension, both alternatives are worthy of consideration.

What was important about Burke's position? He called our attention to what was at stake when designing a representative system by alerting us to dangerous risks that would predictably arise in the process. He stressed that representatives must be given the authority to think on their own. They could not remain confined by what the voters of their localities said one day, for it is possible that electors may want, or need, to modify their initial opinion. Most importantly, representatives must be able to change their opinions if, in debate with the representatives of other localities or in the face of fresh ideas, they encounter consideration that better serve the common good. Indeed, Burke added, once elected representatives are no longer to be considered the representative of their small, separate constituencies, but of the national interest. All these affirmations are absolutely relevant, especially because of the way that Burke skillfully framed them within a genuine commitment to public deliberation (to the point that his writings in this regard have become an obligatory reference for all of us who defend the ideal of deliberative democracy). In a crucial section of his presentation in Bristol, Burke declared:

> Parliament is not a Congress of Ambassadors from different and hostile interests ... Parliament is the deliberative Assembly of one Nation, with one Interest, that of the whole; where, not local Purposes, not local Prejudices ought to guide, but the general Good, resulting from the general Reason of the whole. You choose a Member of Parliament.[1]

All Burke's considerations are of extraordinary interest although, as should and will soon be pointed out, they were founded on a clearly elitist vision of democracy. In short, for Burke the representatives should enjoy the higher level of autonomy that he attributed to them because, to a large extent and for several reasons, the representatives were better than the common citizens themselves at discovering what their interests were. Burke illustrated this (epistemically) elitist view with a simple metaphor, one that compared the relationship between representatives and citizens to the relationship between doctors and their patients. Thus, the representative was to listen to the citizens (like the doctor to his patients) and citizens were to inform representatives of their problems (just as patients describe their ailments to doctors). Yet in the end it was the representatives and not the citizens (the doctor rather than the patients) who were to determine a solution for the complaints (or ailments) of the citizens (or patients). In Burke's terms, what should always prevail was the "judgment" of the representatives over the mere "opinions" of the citizens.

In response to the valuable insights of the conservative Burke, his "radical" opponent, Henry Cruger, added worthy comments of his own. Cruger made a point of emphasizing his view that the voters did indeed have the right to "instruct" their representatives (i.e., to give representatives "commandments" that they were then to execute from their seats in parliament), because – in Cruger's mind – it was the duty of Congress to follow guidelines defined by the "advice" and "instructions" of the citizens.

[1] Burke 1999 [1774], 16–17 http://oll-resources.s3.amazonaws.com/titles/659/Burke_0005-04_EBk_v6.0.pdf).

German professor Hanna Pitkin referred to the Bristol debates in her famous book on "the concept of representation" – arguably the most influential book ever published on the idea of political representation (Pitkin 1972). Pitkin wrote that Burke's conception of representation rested on the existence of few, fixed, clearly defined, and fundamentally economic interests.

Underlying Cruger's position were two absolutely crucial matters which ran contrary to what Burke suggested and were linked to two risks deserving careful attention by anyone with an interest in cultivating public life. In the first place, Cruger referred to the question of political knowledge in a very unique way: while Burke appeared to assume the existence of "objective truths" that could only be reached through the "judgment" of the most enlightened minds, for Cruger – as for many past and present thinkers – the implicit assumption contrasted starkly in that everyone is perceived as having something relevant to say, depending on how each individual is affected by general or public decisions and what can be done to modify those decisions. (Moreover, the radically elitist bias that is evident in the "doctors and patients" metaphor is clear: whereas the natural sciences revolve around the "truth" in terms of the identifiable origin of our ailments, constitutional values and commitments – including freedom of expression and social rights – are open to disagreement even among the most reasonable and disciplined thinkers, none of whom has the right to decide or impose their vision over the rest.) This important assumption about the nature of knowledge explains Cruger's keen interest in minimizing a very serious risk that is neglected or underestimated in Burke's reasoning: the risk that representatives, once elected, begin to act on their own wholly independently from the needs and demands of their electors, thus losing contact with the surrounding reality that justified their obtaining their posts. The second crucial issue that distinguishes Cruger's viewpoint from Burke's is related to the use of power. The disconnection that grows between citizens and representatives (based on schemes such as the one suggested by Burke, which is now predominant) not only aggravates the risk that representatives gradually lose contact with the surrounding reality (and therefore cease to recognize or respond to the main claims of their electors). Such a disconnection also, and above all, creates a tremendous risk that representatives will begin to develop their own interests, and work in their pursuit rather than in favor of the interests of the society as a whole.

Of course, Cruger's position, and in particular his defense of the right to "instruct" representatives (and therefore to "revoke" mandates in case of noncompliance) was vulnerable to many objections – including those that Burke advanced. Representatives must be allowed to think beyond local interests. It is important that they be able to act on or change their mind on the basis of what they learn from their discussions with other representatives. Representatives should not be reduced to "talking dolls" that repeat like automatons the demands of their constituents (Sunstein

1993, ch. 1). It is not clear, however, that these valid points outweigh the merits of Cruger's position, nor is it clear that all the criticisms directed towards his position were as valid. In particular, the most common criticism that accountability tools such as "instructions" for representatives reduced them to mere "talking dolls" was highly debatable. "Mandatory instructions" (e.g., telling your representatives to vote for or against abortion), does not imply that you believe they should abstain from thinking "freely" in other areas (e.g., what economic policy to promote or which social policies to encourage). Giving representatives such an instruction does not even preclude the representatives from using their judgment and discernment in relation to the issue in question (abortion). In effect, the "mandated" representative could end up voting in favor of what was decided by his electors (say, an abortion law) but doing so may have been compatible with a number of options involving different means and remedies (e.g., absolute prohibition, criminalization, prohibition in some cases, prohibition without criminalization). In short, there exists a margin in which a stricter relationship between representatives and represented can be defended without falling into absurd statements or generalizations (i.e., "the representative cannot think on his own").

As I understand it, both positions – symbolized by the arguments of Burke and Cruger – address important issues despite the differences between them. At the same time, it is also immediately evident that the consolidation of either of these alternatives involved important risks, which each contender denounced in the rival position. Burke reminded us of the value of representatives able to think freely, change their minds, and remain attentive to the interest of the whole. His position, however, increases the risk of a ruling class that eventually becomes disconnected from the will of the citizenry and becomes preoccupied with its own interests. Cruger, meanwhile, emphasized the value of representatives who respect the will of their constituents. His proposal, however, increases the risk that a different type of ruling class might emerge, one for which looking beyond the interests of local voters is extremely difficult.

Finally, as we shall see, the position that ended up prevailing – the conception of representation that eventually gathered more support – was quite similar to the one advocated by Burke: in most democratic systems, representatives enjoy wide margins for maneuver and are subject to relatively weak controls (elections held every several years). They include incentives for representatives to use their competencies and authority for their own benefit, even at the expense of the voters' will.

Someone might add, in light of what has been said: "the representatives will not tend to act at their discretion (or in defense of their own interests) because they fear the sanction of their voters in the next election" (some authors bring this notion up in reference to the "retrospective" nature of the elections, see for example Przeworski et al. 1999). However, and as we know, the potential strength of this mechanism and by extension the argument is quite restricted. The ability of the vote to sanction, discipline or (re)direct the actions of the representatives – the ability, ultimately, to "threaten" or intimidate representatives with future electoral loss – is severely limited (we will return to this point). Indeed, when voting, the elector must take too many things into account (the message she wants to convey, who she wants to reward and to what degree, who she wants to discourage or sanction and to what degree), and her ability to convey such complexity is almost null with a single vote. (What do you do if you want to punish a certain party, except one of its members; or punish the majority, but not all; or punish only one candidate, but at the same time reward them for some of their actions, or to discourage them from persisting in a certain stance, but at the same time encouraging them to stand firm in all the others?) Hence, representatives are able to carry out their own plans, during their mandate, in relative comfort: they know very well that the ability of the voter to "select" or sanction candidates for any "misconduct" is extremely limited (sometimes, getting reelected is almost as simple as assuming such a low profile so as to go unnoticed by voters during their term).[2]

6.2 Do We Need to "Filter" the Citizen Voice?

The vision of the representative system defended by Edmund Burke, who prioritized the "independence" of the representatives in relation to the immediate and localized demands of their electors, gained strength and stability with the passage of time, and became entrenched in Great Britain and its colonies, from where it went on to spread to a good part of the Western world.

[2] Of course, many variables come into play, especially the type of electoral system in place. For example, in "uninominal" systems where a single candidate is chosen (or in "strike-through" systems, where a particular candidate can be identified), the possibility of awarding or sanctioning the representative is obviously greater than in proportional systems, where the representatives are elected *en bloc*, in proportion to the number of votes received by their party (even if uninominal and strikethrough systems possess other disadvantages, especially in relation to the representation of minority groups).

In the United States, this conception of representation gained early prestige, especially the version advanced by the "federalist" politicians, who held a majority within the Constitutional Convention of 1787. James Madison, in particular, articulated it very carefully – as was his custom – in a way that, at least in appearance, rendered it devoid of the elitist features that largely defined the version proposed by Edmund Burke.

In a key paragraph of his most influential piece – Federalist No. 10 – Madison defended the representative system (which he called "republican" at the time), differentiating it from others closer to those he considered typical of Ancient Greece – direct democracy. After establishing the distinction, Madison maintained:

> [representative system helps to] refine and enlarge the public views, by passing them through the medium of a chosen body of citizens, whose wisdom may best discern the true interest of their country, and whose patriotism and love of justice will be least likely to sacrifice it to temporary or partial considerations. Under such a regulation, it may well happen that the public voice, pronounced by the representatives of the people, will be more consonant to the public good than if pronounced by the people themselves, convened for the purpose.

The vision proposed by Madison, which would eventually prevail in the Constitution of the United States and spread from there to all of Latin America, was as interesting as it was problematic. In paragraphs like those cited, Madison took care to avoid, or to obscure as much as possible, the elitist biases of Burke's position: there was nothing "natural" about the political class that set representatives in a privileged position above the rest (in "epistemic" terms). In principle, Madison's position was compatible with the idea that anyone could attain, in principle, the knowledge of politically important truths (this was the position that John Locke had defended in his time, as we will see in more detail later). However, in this and other writings, Madison made an effort to show that, for "functional" reasons (the time they could afford to devote to reflecting on public affairs, their education, their experience, etc.), public officials were in a position to *make decisions "more consonant to the public good than if pronounced by the people themselves, convened for the purpose"* (!) This is also why Madison emphasized the idea of putting the voice of the people "through a sieve" or filter (which otherwise would apparently be filled with "impurities") and used the idea of a "select group" (linked to the notion, common at the time, of the "select few") which, ambiguously, could refer both to the "elected" character of the representatives or to their status as members, assumedly, of the prevailing elites at the time rather than "ordinary" citizens – Madison played with language this way to convey different messages to each of his different audiences (Manin 1997). Finally, his greatest concern, in this case as in others, was with "runaway majorities," which he associated with the "factional" movements that were typical of his time.

The truly dangerous factions, Madison thought, were those with majority support, and the great risk they posed was falling prey to the irrational, passionate impulses of local groups. On the other hand, if the faction was a minority – declared the Virginian, again holding some important cards close to his chest – then "the republican remedy" of voting them down was sufficient for their control. Hence the need to "separate" electors from the elected through the "filter" of representation. For Madison, the more direct the people's control over government, the greater the threat of a factional rule.

Despite the effort, typical of Madison, made to strike a chord of moderation, balance, and conciliation between the parties, he clearly defended a very problematic notion of representation: representation as a "first option," that is, representation in a sense that political representation did not simply comprise a necessary resource, one required in societies composed of hundreds of thousands or millions of people, but ultimately undesirable. No. For Madison, representation was a "good," in that it was always preferable to direct decision-making by the citizens. This Madisonian vision of representation was undoubtedly very different from the one defended by many of his contemporaries, such as Thomas Paine or Thomas Jefferson. Jefferson, in fact, portrayed representation as a "necessary evil" or "second best" option which became necessary in the context of very populous societies.

The option for a representative model understood as a "first option" or "desired objective" went hand in hand with many other institutional choices – that were equally worrisome, I would add. One of them, especially relevant for our purposes, was the discouragement or non-promotion of citizen intervention in politics. It seems clear that if representation is desirable, rather than a "necessary evil," then representative decision-making must be defended and preferred over direct decision-making by the people. On the other hand, when one accepts – resignedly, if need be – representative decision-making for the simple reason that collective self-government in a society of millions of people is materially impossible, then one must seek and celebrate any possibility of expanding the framework of participation in public decisions whenever possible. It is in the difference between these two attitudes that we find the traces of these two different theoretical worlds, which ultimately stem from two different approaches to democracy, and which, in the end, imply very different institutional designs.

6.3 The Problems of the Predominant Model: Isolation, "Capture," Ignorance

The model of "political representation" that has become entrenched in modern times was born with the marks of those initial features and assumptions: the assumption that representatives had better access to knowledge ("political truths") that, in principle, was denied to common citizens (elitism); and the conviction that the people's voice must be "sifted" through the "filter" of a "chosen group" (democratic distrust). These traits defined the profile that the representative system gradually took on as it reached its form as we know it today, whether we are referring to the perceived need to "distance" representatives from the represented; the degree of "independence" we grant them; or the fear of undue influence of "passions" or "impulses" that the electorate might exercise over them.

Much of the justification for adopting that model remains relevant (the value of greater reflection; the expectation of less impulsive debates; the commitment to experience; confidence in the specialized expertise of the political class; etc.). However, it is also clear that many of the problems latent in the criteria that became dominant also continue to accompany us. I am referring to the fact that both of the disputed positions on representation promised benefits and entailed problems from the beginning: each was formulated in reaction to and in dialogue with the opposite position, lauding its own virtues while underscoring the defects inherent to the rival position on representation. Today, hundreds of years after the affirmation of a particular model, we have grounds for celebrating what has been achieved in terms of representation, but we must also take careful note of the difficulties that have been reaffirmed as well, and that they were, in most cases, foreseeable from the outset. Surely, if the alternative model had become predominant, today we would be talking about the evils derived from the risks that are typical of this alternative position and were foreseeable from its original moments. Nonetheless, what we must urgently address are the risks currently affecting us – those derived from the idea of representation as "separation" or "independence" – risks that are, I would add, extraordinarily serious.

The serious risks to which I allude include the danger that, through seeking to ensure the ability of our representatives to think freely and independently, those representatives gradually lose the connection with their constituents, and begin to ignore or misunderstand what is needed or demanded of them. Hannah Arendt – quoting Jefferson's view – made a similar point. For her,

> because of the way the government of the union was constituted, with its division and separation of powers, with controls, checks and balances, built into its very center-it was highly unlikely ... that a tyranny could arise out of it. What could happen, and what indeed has happened over and over again since, was that "the representative organs should become corrupt and perverted."
>
> (Arendt 2006, 243)[3]

And then there is also the risk that, seeking to isolate representatives from majority pressures, they lose their "fear" of the sanction by voters or their responsibility to them (accountability); or the risk that the representatives begin to develop a separate group identity with its own interests, separated from the rest of society (the "iron law of the oligarchy" of which Robert Michels spoke); or, finally, the possibility that, because of the isolation, lack of controls, and pursuit of self-interests, corrupt and other noxious practices by representatives become more common. Going back to Arendt I would state: "Paradoxical as it may sound, it was in fact under the impact of the Revolution that the revolutionary spirit in (American) began to wither away, and *it was the Constitution itself, this greatest achievement of the American people,* which eventually cheated them of their proudest possession" (Arendt 2006, 231, italics added).

6.4 From "Virtual" Representation to Representation As "Mirror": Representation and "Presence"

Faced with the kind of scenarios described above where the "separateness" or "independence" of the citizens' representatives is problematic, what can be done? The first line of response that jumps to mind is that of the "alternative" models against which the elitist proposal of Burke and the Madisonian model of representative "distance" and "filter" were erected.

Some of these proposals sought to "bridle" the representatives strictly using "mandates" imposed by the citizens. These "mandates" aimed to prevent representatives from "becoming independent" or breaking the ties

[3] Arendt is quoting Jefferson's famous letter to Samuel Kercheval, from September 5, 1816.

between them and their voters. The "mandatory instructions" that Cruger defended in his debate against Burke were clearly directed in this sense: to prevent the formation of a "class" of representatives with its own interests, unconcerned with citizen demands, the capacity to act on their own, and little fear of any sanction for any act contrary to the will of their voters. We will examine this type of control over representatives later, when we examine the external and internal forms of oversight (or accountability), but now I will focus on other responses to the problem of "separation" between electors and elected, which also garnered significant attention and influence during the foundational period of constitutionalism.

In fact, and as I understand it, the most common alternative advanced by the adversaries of the United States "Federalists" (many of them grouped under the broad umbrella of "Antifederalism") was a model for representation oriented to reproduce or "mirror" society itself, in political bodies. The underlying idea behind this notion of "mirror" representation was that no group was qualified to speak, in any political debate, on behalf of the interests of any group absent from those deliberations (Przeworski et al. 1999). A strand of that debate had begun before the independence of the United States, when the members of the British Parliament maintained that they "virtually" represented the interests of the colonists, even though no colonists had a seat in the English forum. The Americans rejected that claim, believing that their interests were not genuinely represented under the scheme. Hence the American demand, crucial in the struggle for independence, for "no taxation without representation." The logic behind the revolutionaries' position in that dispute made the idea of "specular" representation more and more popular in the North American sphere. Following this notion of representation, each section of society had to be able to speak on behalf of its own interests. It therefore required an especially numerous and diverse Congress, one capable of reflecting the increasing number of different interests in society, rather than attempting to represent the many with very few. For example, the Antifederalist Richard Henry Lee, writing under the pseudonym of "A Federal Farmer," defended the idea of Congress as a "mirror of society." In this regard, he maintained that "the wisest and most respectable assemblies of which we are aware have been those consisting of several hundred members," and that "the most numerous state assemblies and conventions, universally, have discovered a greater wisdom, and they have shown to have as much order, as the less numerous" (Storing 1981, vol. 2, 284).

More contemporaneously (and whether accepting the impossibility of representing all the different groups existing in society or prioritizing the need or urgency to represent some particular interests), different groups have begun to fight for the effective "presence" of some of its members in the organs of political representation. Women, indigenous groups, and linguistic minorities have all typically struggled to obtain "presence" in Congress. This undertaking is not so much due, for example, to any expectation that the "presence" of some women in the assembly would "guarantee" adequate or full representation of their interests within the decision-making bodies, but from the conviction that the systematic or effective "absence" of their voice "maximized" the risks of inadequate attention to their claims and views (Phillips 1995, Kymlicka 1996). The assumption that lies at the heart of the demand for effective "presence" is the same that led the American revolutionaries to reject the notion of "virtual" representation. No matter how much good faith and empathy the representatives show and no matter how enthusiastically they take up the interests of those not present, the risks of their not recognizing, not understanding, or not properly processing (i.e., with the requisite commitment) the interests of those absent are too high. A solid empirical example can be seen in the tremendous difficulty, which has gone on for centuries, of parliaments comprised only of men in assuming or appropriately addressing the demands of women.

The association that we have intuitively established in practice between representation and "presence" is extraordinarily powerful: we have seemingly assumed, for a long time now, that the "absence" of certain relevant voices from representative bodies directly threatens their claim of impartiality. It seems clear to us that an assembly composed only of white people in South Africa, or one without indigenous voices in Guatemala, represents a serious fault that implicates a very poorly representative body.

I would go further: the association that we have drawn between representation and "presence" is even stronger than has been suggested. The association extends to the point that we often assume – usually in silence, with an effort to conceal our thoughts or at least avoid explicitly admitting it – that even nonrepresentative bodies, such as judicial bodies, ought to be representative. Thus, although legal academics sometimes proclaim that judges only reach decisions by following the written letter of the law, the truth is that we assume that the "correct" legal decision requires much more than (merely) reading and applying the law. What explains, elsewise, why (to take a relevant case) one judge from each member country sits on the European Court of Human Rights? What explains the arrangement is the conviction of all the member states that impartiality requires much more than properly "reading" the law, and that the "absence" of a judge "representative" of the country itself would greatly increase the chances that the Court fails to properly weigh the interests of the country in question. The same principle applies, in a different way, to the (less numerous) Inter-American Court of Human Rights, on which no more than one judge from the same country can sit, the idea being that over-representation of one country's perspective in the judicial organ would lead to undue bias towards the interests of that country. For an even more remarkable and intriguing exercise: what would we say if the United States Supreme Court (a nonrepresentative body par excellence) returned at some point to an all-white or all-male composition? We would consider it scandalous, even if we later repeated – as is our custom – that judges ought only abide by the letter of the law, or that all we truly care about is their impartiality.

6.5 The Structural Difficulty of Representation

If we grant the validity of the observations made so far in this chapter, they leave us in a good position to, at the very least, recognize the imposing dimension of the serious representational problems that we face. Basically, we have for decades intuitively demanded stronger representation, requiring the direct "presence" of agents of different groups in representative bodies (even in proclaimed nonrepresentative bodies). At the same time, we have grown increasingly aware of the inability of our institutional system to ensure minimally acceptable forms of representation. Indeed, anyone who reflects for more than a moment on the representative system within which she lives should be able recognize defects in its delivery of adequate representation. Those defects are even more apparent when that system prioritizes the "separation" or "autonomy" of the representatives and weakens or "loosens" democratic controls over them. Furthermore, we also know that, unfortunately, all the "vices" or "evils" that might foreseeably spring from the chosen representation model ended up, to a large extent, occurring. A "class" or "caste" of representatives has formed, one with a distinct set of interests; a good part of the political class devotes significant energy and resources to practices generally considered corrupt; the most weakly represented groups feel their interests have been abandoned; and so on.

In my opinion, the most worrying sign in terms of political representation in the context described is that, even where we would predict that the predominant model of representation would work best (I mean places free of political corruption, where representatives are honestly "committed" to their tasks and dutifully perform the functions of their office), this system would not work well. This is due to the *structural difficulty* of the system to represent the wealth and diversity of interests, points of view, and demands that are present in society. The difficulty involves a variety of factors, of which I will content myself for now to mention only a few.

In the first place, I would bring up the *multicultural character* of our societies, which exposes the imperfect, crude, or incomplete political sociology that prevailed in the founding moments of constitutionalism. At that time, as we know, authors like Madison spoke of a simple society, one basically divided into two large groups: "creditors and debtors," "wealthy" groups and groups with "minor interests," or "owners and nonowners." In short, his majorities and minorities. The purpose was ensuring that those primary or fundamental interests were built into the decision-making process: in this way, public decisions would incorporate and reflect the interest of the whole.[4] The suspicion that Madison and others like him may have deliberately described eighteenth-century North American society in an overly simple (if not directly misleading) fashion is difficult to dismiss. However, for our purposes, such a historical discussion is, in principle, irrelevant. The fact is that it is now clearly the case that all of our societies – marked, as John Rawls would say, by the "fact of pluralism" – are fragmented into countless groups with diverse and comprehensible interests: from religious, ethnic, and sexual, to ideological minorities, and so on. By consequence, undertaking today what the "founding fathers" of constitutionalism attempted to do; that is, ensuring adequate representation of the main factions or groups present in society would require somehow giving it to groups whose defining criteria are completely foreign to the current representative system, groups that the system is poorly suited to recognize, "capture" or "incorporate" in any relevant way.

Second, I would mention the *heterogeneous nature* of the different groups existing in society. That is to say: not only do we find ourselves today facing a reality comprised of a multiplicity of relevant groups that were not taken into account when the representational system was designed (women, indigenous peoples, migrants, religious minorities,

[4] That purpose was based, of course, on other crucial assumptions involving, for example, the proper (or natural) degree of each individual's regard for "self-interest" – a controversial assumption that is open to discussion.

etc.), but also, there is no reason at present – if at all there ever was – to presume that the different groups are internally homogeneous. In the origins of constitutionalism, homogeneity seemed to be assumed, which allowed the conclusion that, by including in the political system representatives of the main groups in society (e.g., by designing the system so large landowners, merchants, and manual workers are all represented in Congress) the whole of society could be represented.

In societies like ours, each individual must be conceptualized and recognized as a multidimensional subject. I mean that it is no longer possible to say seriously – again, if it ever was – that someone is fundamentally and essentially a "debtor," an "owner," or a "worker." Any one of us might be, at the same time, an owner, a worker, a woman, a lesbian, a Jew, a communist, etc. Each and every one of these identities is highly relevant for the self-identity of the individual in question, yet none, taken alone, sufficiently captures it. Hence the enormous structural or formalistic difficulty (if not impossibility) for any system that aspires, at present, to provide adequate representation for the relevant dimensions of individual self-identity necessary to achieve effective representation of the collective.

Finally, I would highlight the fact that, in the early days of constitutionalism, it could be assumed, with some justification, that institutional means that ensured or at least favored the representation of intended sectors actually existed. In particular, tools such as "direct" or "indirect elections" seemed conducive for the inclusion of one social sector over another in the government system. Typically, it could be assumed at the time, "direct" elections favored candidates positioned closer to popular interests and, in the same way, the further an election was removed from the people – the more indirect it was – the more it favored "exclusive," "minority," or "privileged" candidates. Hence, for the positions that were considered more relevant or delicate, more indirect election systems were chosen: the selection of judges or ambassadors, for example, was generally left to the executive branch (indirectly elected) and the Senate (also indirectly elected) to decide on together. This connection between indirect elections and the selection of members from privileged sectors of society became clear during the United States constitutional convention debates. Madison said in this regard, for example, that indirect elections were more "judicious" in that they avoided the selection of demagogues (Farrand 1937, vol. 3, 330).

At present, none of the previous conditions and assumptions seem to hold: we cannot speak of societies divided into only two or three groups;

nor of homogeneous groups; nor of one-dimensional individuals. Neither can we rely any longer on simple methods such as direct versus indirect elections to ensure adequate representation of members from this or that group. We could restrict certain choices to certain groups; or reserve special seats for some of them in parliament, as a way of ensuring that at least certain number of relevant groups have a "presence" in it. However, once again – and without disparaging the value of initiatives such as quotas to ensure some "presence" – the overarching question remains open: What are the appropriate institutional modes of representation in multicultural societies made up of people who define themselves by many qualities at once (gender, religion, sexual identity, ideology, etc.)? Which dimensions should be privileged in order to ensure the "full" representation (or, at least, the "fullest possible" representation) of society? (Gargarella 1998).

The fact is that there are innumerable groups and voices to represent; too many personal "dimensions" to consider; and countless institutional difficulties that stand in the way of recognizing, incorporating, and giving voice to all the voices that need to speak in the current systems that do not make direct government possible. In such conditions, the representative systems we know – those that prevail in our countries – remain exaggeratedly "small": they are "tight-fitting suits" that restrict the free movement of our growing, developing political body, preventing it from adequately reacting to the changing world around it. Not even when they are working well and fully will our representative institutions be able to provide us with what we need and expect from them. There is too much "political life" outside of our institutional schemes that they are not structurally tooled to recognize, incorporate, and express.

7

The Rise and Fall of Popular Control

"We may say with truth and meaning that governments are more or less republican as they have more or less of the element of popular election and control in their composition."

Letter from Thomas Jefferson to John Taylor, 1816.

7.1 Citizens and Representatives

In his work *Notes on the State of Virginia*, considered the most important book written in the United States before 1800, Thomas Jefferson gave an account of his vision of society and institutional design, taking as an example the state where he was born – Virginia. Among other issues, his *Notes* make particular reference to the Constitution, controls on the government, and the role of the public in this task. In those parts, the Virginian politician spoke out in defense of popular or "exogenous" controls, even – or in particular – to check possible violations of the Constitution. Every time it was necessary to alter or correct "breaches" of the constitution" – Jefferson argued – a new "convention" should be called for the purpose.

Jefferson's point was as extreme as it was, in the end, logical, at least for those like him who understood that the ultimate source of democratic sovereignty resided in the people. In fact, Jefferson had written *Notes* during his long stay in Paris, France, which explains both his absence from the United States Constitutional Convention and his somewhat radicalized or "Rousseauian" vision of political life.

For those who lived in the United States during the "foundational moment," these works of Jefferson could be difficult to accept. At the time, the apparent national "drama" was – finally – the country's political stabilization following independence and the turbulent years of the Confederation. In a time when the priority seemed moving to an institutional scheme favorable to negotiation and social peace, proposals like

Jefferson's were seen as threatening. Jefferson's friend and colleague, James Madison, let him know as much in a letter "To the People of the State of New York" – Federalist No. 49 – which he wrote directly and specifically in response to Jefferson's *Notes*. Madison began by praising the intelligence of the "author of the *Notes*." Madison then proceeded, however, to critique sharply Jefferson's proposal (to call a special convention whenever the constitution was breached) with three main arguments. Allow me to examine them, because they shed light on *two opposing worldviews regarding the relationship between citizens and government, and how to conceptualize the idea of (popular) controls over government power.*

The first argument presented by Madison referred precisely to the "risk of disturbing the public tranquility" through strong appeals to "public passions." Madison understood Jefferson's proposal as implicating the "unduly interested" citizenry in public affairs, thereby stoking public passions which in turn generated greater risk that the desired objectives for social peace and political stability would not be met. The second argument referred to the fact that "appeals to the people" implicitly undermined the authority of the government in office, depriving it of the "veneration" needed for the proper exercise of its functions. Finally, Madison argued that recourse to popular consultation to solve government problems would bias the mechanism for balancing power in favor of the legislative branch. The legislature was the branch of power closest to the people, so if they were consulted about tension between, say, the executive's preferred course of action and that of Congress, the people's response would tend to align with, logically, the organ that reflected its inclinations more closely – that is, it would favor the legislature.

This debate between two colleagues and friends – Madison and Jefferson – who held opposing positions on many issues (in particular, I would highlight, the way they thought about democracy), suggested the existence of larger and more socially widespread disagreements. One of the disagreements that brewed between them, as we will see throughout this chapter, was a very important debate about how to understand the mechanisms of control over power. The disagreement can be summarized, first of all, as variance over the proper locus of the controls on government power. Jefferson seemed to defend "external," "exogenous," "popular" controls; that is, controls of the citizenry over the rulers. Madison, instead, defended "internal" or "endogenous" controls: a system of "checks and balances" that mainly involved controls of the different branches of government among themselves.

Before going into them, I would like to conclude this introduction by pointing out that, for those of us who defend a "strong" notion of democracy, arguments such as those presented by Madison at the time, ones that argued against systems that emphasized "popular" controls, were and are not particularly attractive or forceful. It was not obvious then (and it is much less so now) that citizens would tend to identify more with Congress than with the executive. For example, recall the cases of George Washington, Andrew Jackson, or Jefferson in the United States; or consider experiences such as those that took place more recently in Peru, where citizens repeatedly supported initiatives by the President to "close" the Congress when the two branches clashed. Nor is it clear that the government in power will lose its needed "veneration" if the people are consulted in cases of serious institutional conflicts (in any case, it would be the serious conflict that would deprive it of veneration). Finally, and most importantly, Madison's habitual argument regarding the risk of "igniting" popular passions is typical of those who defend very narrow, elitist or "minimalist" views of democracy. In general, those who hold such controversial positions seem to prefer stability over democratic legitimacy, in addition to apparently basing their arguments on highly debatable assumptions regarding the irrationality or lack of reflective capacity of citizens (citizens are passionate and out of control, citizens are blind to reason, and so on – all defects that at the very least are neither obvious nor limited to factions that have majority support).

7.2 On Institutions Sensitive to Popular Will in Radical English Thought

The discussion around the value of "external" or "popular" controls on power has run through constitutional thought since the beginning of the modern era. Debates such as the aforementioned one that took place in the United States landed in America from Europe, influenced both by French revolutionary thought and from the radical movements that emerged in Great Britain. In the wake of the political scandals that had erupted in England around the mid-eighteenth century (I am thinking of the issues that exploded around the 1769 Middlesex election affair), many political thinkers and activists began considering and formulating proposals for the adoption of far-reaching political reforms aimed at ensuring a central role for citizens in public affairs.

Thus, for example, in an influential book published in 1774 – *Political Disquisitions* – James Burgh defended the urgency of restoring the democratic spirit of the Constitution, primarily through three political measures: annual elections to Parliament; purging the House of Commons; and reforms to attain adequate political representation. The work represented an important first step to reform the established institutional system to render it more sensitive to popular demands. Additionally, Burgh defended two tools that went on to gain significant acceptance in Anglo-Saxon political life: mandatory rotation in office and the right to write mandatory instructions for representatives. In line with Burgh's influential claims, two great public figures in British life at the time, Joseph Priestley and Richard Price, also enlisted in the proposal for major political reforms. In his "General Introduction and Supplement" to *Two Tracts on Civil Liberty*, Price defended limited government and the obligation of public officials to act as "public servants" of the citizenry. Similarly, in his work *Observations on the Nature of Civil Liberty, the Principles of Government, and the Justice and Policy of the War with America*, Price declared that representatives should be held accountable by the public for their acts. In these works, he staked out the idea that citizens should maintain strict control over the actions of those who represented them.

Meanwhile, Joseph Priestley, who would rise to fame because of a sermon he gave in defense of the revolutionary movements in France, would also defend "frequent exchange" between the citizens and their representatives as a way of honoring his sense of the ideals of self-government (Priestley 1791, 257). John Cartwright, meanwhile – another exceptional figure in the eighteenth-century British radical movement – also advanced proposals for institutional reform in his work *Take Your Choice*.

The other great figure who should be included in the discussion of the radicals' reform proposals of the time is Thomas Paine. Paine represents a singular figure who serves as the perfect bridge between radical thought of English origin and the more "democratic" currents that picked up in the United States during the early days of independence. Born in Great Britain, Paine helped clarify and put in order many of the ideas in favor of self-government circulating in Europe that caught on in America. Through various works, especially beginning with his book *The Rights of Man*, Paine spoke out strongly in favor of the right to self-government. In particular, his unpublished 1776 pamphlet "Common Sense" circulated widely in the United States (the popularity of Paine's writing was such that John Adams said that without "the Paine's pen" in "Common Sense," Washington's sword "would have been raised in vain"). Invited to the United States through an arrangement set up by Benjamin Franklin, Paine ended up living in the country for many years (before settling in France in the late eighteenth century where he became an ardent defender of the French Revolution).

In the United States, Paine's prestige and influence reached their climax after an initial stage when he was relatively unknown in his home country. Not only did the aforementioned pamphlet – "Common Sense" – unleash a "fever" in the United States, but Paine became actively involved in local politics, where he was largely responsible for the drafting of the remarkable Constitution of Pennsylvania of 1776. The Constitution of Pennsylvania symbolized, from its appearance, the birth of "radical" or "radicalized" constitutionalism in the United States. As we shall see, the Constitution of the United States would be formulated in reaction to the early radicalized experiments of the first state legislatures of the independent colonies.

7.3 Instructions, Rotation in Positions, Annual Elections: Different Forms of "Popular" Control

After the War of Independence, the moment seemed right for redesigning local political institutions to make them more inclusive and open to the demands of the citizenry. First of all, after years of struggle for independence, the idea that the government belonged to the people had taken shape, as had the idea that the people had the right to create and modify their own institutions at will (the historian Gordon Wood speaks of the citizenry using the same slogans and "sovereignty of the people" principle against the young country's leadership that the revolutionaries had used to drum up support for the war). Hence, for example, the Pennsylvania Constitution established, in Article III of its declaration of rights, that only the people possessed the right to govern. Also, in Article V of that declaration, the Pennsylvania Constitution written by Paine enshrined the "undoubted and inalienable" right of the people to "alter, reform, or abolish the government," however they found conducive to their well-being.

In practice, responding to the particular political and social moment that the country was going through, several states opened up to new initiatives for institutional change. A wide variety of constitutional reforms were thrown into discussion, many of which showed "radical" imprints. In many cases, tools were eventually established at the constitutional level that either favored local self-government or facilitated "external" or "exogenous" political control by citizens. In the process, the system of "communal assemblies" or "town meetings" gained strength. This system offered citizens themselves the opportunity to directly discuss and make decisions regarding public affairs of their interest.

The most innovative tools of "popular control" adopted at the time had the potential to bolster the weight of the public's voice in common affairs, but at the same time they attracted various sorts of criticism. We are already aware of some and of the debates they caused. *Mandatory instructions*, for example, were one instrument commonly adopted at the time to control representatives. These instructions were usually accompanied by the *right to revoke mandates*, which provided for the removal of representatives who did not comply with their instructions. This type of mechanism generated enthusiasm for its capacity to ensure that representatives remained attentive to and respectful of the interests of their electors. However, as we know, many resisted such instruments because they were seen as leaving no space for the representatives' free discernment and prevented them from changing their minds.

Annual elections represented another way to ensure steady popular control over the representatives. A repeated saying at the time was "when annual elections end, there slavery begins" (a quote attributed to future United States President John Adams). Annual elections were seen as a means to maintain strict control over the representatives, and prevent them from acting on their own accord. However, many attacked – then, as today – these initiatives under the belief that this permanent mode of control would impede any public policy from reaching consolidation. Rather, it was thought they put in place incentives that would result in "permanent change," dramatically undermining the stability of any government program.

Mandatory rotation was yet another tool typically favored by the most radical activists. It was meant to boost the participation of ordinary citizens in public offices, prevent the formation of political "castes" or oligarchies, and "oxygenate" governing bodies. Here, many denounced the proposal, feeling that permanent rotation would amount to too much waste, both in terms of the experience gained by sitting representatives and the time "newcomers" would be forced to spend trying to familiarize themselves with the mechanisms of public administration.

These tools and others like them were not simply abstract mental exercises. On the contrary, they were incorporated into the constitutional texts and practices of many states. Among the institutional tools effectively adopted at the state level, I would point out in particular the unicameral design (i.e., by the original state constitutions) of the legislatures in Pennsylvania, Georgia, and Vermont, the election of the head of the executive branch by the legislature in nine of the eighteen state constitutions adopted after independence, the lack of executive veto power, a constitutional council directly elected by citizens that evaluated compliance with the constitution (Pennsylvania, Vermont), direct election of most government positions, direct elections for the Senate (in all state constitutions except Maryland), mandatory rotation of senators (in New York, Delaware, and Virginia), and rotation in the highest government posts (in Delaware, Georgia, Pennsylvania, Maryland, North Carolina, and Virginia) (Lutz 1988, 104–105).

For those of us who value the political participation of ordinary citizens and place special emphasis on the importance of placing controls on government power, the objections mentioned simply call for greater refinement of the tools chosen. The criticisms leveled against them do not put in question the principles that organize them and give them meaning.

7.4 The Gradual Elimination of "Popular" Controls

The proposals meant to establish broader, more intensive "exogenous" controls such as those described in the previous section did not prevail during the initial, critical period of constitutionalism. The political philosophy that generally prevailed was distinct in that it assumed that "too much" public interest in public affairs tended to "overheat" the institutional system, giving "passions" the edge over "reasons" in political decision-making, favoring decisions that oppressed or disregarded the rights of minorities, and, finally, jeopardizing the very stability of the institutional system. These judgments were based on incomplete empirical premises and unfounded prejudices, yet they still permeated a significant portion of the ruling class, even some of the most enlightened. The great "drama" of the time – the "paper money crisis" – had led to confrontation between opposing social groups (usually debtors versus creditors), sometimes violently (Shays' Rebellion being the most famous uprising), as well as questionable legislative initiatives to provide debtor relief. In this context, a good part of the leadership of the time accepted as valid empirical premises that, in other circumstances, would have been recognized as mere prejudices.

In this atmosphere of social effervescence and political violence, the first – so-called – "radical [state] constitutions" became the center of attention of the public opinion and were blamed by the political elite of the time for the "irrationality" and "excesses" that occurred. In Madison's influential description of the malfunction of state political systems (a description that he presented in his text "Vices of the Political System of the United States," a manuscript that appeared right before he began his work advocating a national constitution) he spoke of the "multiplicity," "mutability," and "injustices" that had come to characterize the normative production of state legislatures. The objective was to put an end to the disorder that he believed was a direct product of severely flawed state constitutional systems by implementing one at the national level.

To return to the example of the Pennsylvania Constitution, according to its critics, that state's constitution was apparently responsible for all the problems afflicting the state at the time. In particular, the explanation of the political crisis that exploded after the Revolutionary War was found in the structure it consecrated. The Constitution set forth, according to its adversaries, an institutional scheme that opened the path for the expansive ambitions of the legislature (which, it was assumed, would encroach upon the remaining branches of government until it had brought them under its control). By consequence, the Constitution allowed the "oppression" of one social sector by others and that was completely incapable of "filtering," moderating, or restraining in any way the transitory passions of the majority and nothing, according to Madison's prediction, prevented the majority from erecting as law everything it sought.

Looking at the facts, it was not at all obvious that Pennsylvania's 1776 Constitution had malfunctioned – although it is true that significant economic measures were taken within its framework, including the expropriation of land – or that the constitution was not equipped to "moderate" the decision-making process, as claimed by its critics (the Constitution enshrined principles of transparency, publicity, and openness to the public more than any other constitution of the time). However, its opponents frequently spoke out against the institutional design that it put in place, especially against its unicameral legislature. For John Adams, this Constitution was "too democratic," and unduly enshrined a "simple democracy." For Rufus King, meanwhile, it represented what he called "the madness of democracy." Theophilus Parsons, for his part, stated that such legislatures were frequently influenced by the "vices, follies, passions and prejudices of individuals."

Paine – the ideologue responsible for the design of the Pennsylvania Constitution – rejected the barrage of criticism, suggesting some changes be made to the system in response to those who insisted that the system was incapable of tempering the decision-making system. He proposed using some sort of lottery to divide the single representative body into two or three sections. Proposed rules would be successively discussed in each section before all the parties would reunite in a single room for a final debate and make a decision. Notably, Paine wanted to demonstrate that he was not against more "sedate" deliberation, that the unicameral system was not incompatible with it, and, above all, that resorting to mechanisms such as a Senate was not necessary to improve the quality of legislative deliberation. Creating a Senate was precisely what the majority of the constitution's critics proposed, which for Paine implied reverting to an aristocratic mechanism that put the majoritarian democratic character of the constitution he had formulated in jeopardy.

In any case, the truth is that, just as the Pennsylvania Constitution came to symbolize the apex of a "radical" constitution with its emphasis on "exogenous" controls, it went on to serve as the example of what a constitution ought not to do. To a large extent, it could be argued that *the serious imperfections attributed by critics to "radical" constitutions such as that of Pennsylvania explain many of the central elements that went on to become distinctive of the United States Constitution.* Whereas constitutions such as Pennsylvania's were blamed for lacking mechanisms to "check" government action and for the weakness of its internal controls, the one in the United States is often characterized in terms of its "checks and balances." Whereas the former had an overabundance of "popular" controls, the US Constitution is notorious for its preference for "endogenous" ones. If the Pennsylvania Constitution could be described as "majoritarian," the national one should be considered counter-majoritarian.

In general terms, the constitutional model that – starting with the 1787 United States Constitution – began to spread to other countries until it became the prevailing model, places strong emphasis on "internal" over "external" controls; presents a certain bias against democratic participation; and contains many restrictions on the power of the majority. These traits developed, in a very special way, in dialogue with and in reaction against an original, alternative model, which seemed to insist on values in tension with those that became dominant (constitutions that placed great importance on majority rule, democratic participation, and "popular" controls). In this way (through the exclusion of citizens, the absence of significant popular controls, the concentration of power in a few, etc.) the institutional system began to favor the development of what Jeremy Bentham named "the sinister interests" of those in power. In other words, the ruling elite was thus allowed to work primarily for its own interest (Bentham spoke at the time of the "sinister" interest in "money," "power," "reputation," and "occasionally revenge," Bentham 1843, 19).

In the face of such severe institutional difficulties, the low degree of constitutional imagination that we have shown is actually striking (Bentham, instead, suggested numerous institutional reforms, aimed at "opening" the institutional system to more vigorous forms of citizen participation, including annual vote, secret ballot, radical expansion of political rights, etc.). Unfortunately, since the moment in which the Constitution of 1787 was consolidated as the preferred option, we have tended to reproduce the American, "federalist," Madisonian model, one that very specifically responded to problems, needs, prejudices, and assumptions typical of the eighteenth century. And this is unfortunate, I submit, because the alternative, Jeffersonian model would have probably helped us avoid many of the institutional problems that we suffer today, while at the same time favoring the emergence of benefits that we lack today. And this is so because "whether Jefferson knew it or not . . . no one could be called happy without his share in public happiness . . . no one could be called free without his experience in public freedom, and . . . no one could be called either happy or free without participating, and having a share, in public affairs" (Arendt 2006, 247).

8

The Periodic Vote, or "Electoral Extortion"

8.1 Regular Voting As the Only Bridge Standing between Citizens and Representatives

The adoption of the North American Constitution of 1787 largely signified the death of the alternative constitutional organization model – the model of "exogenous" controls – which had prevailed for a decade during the "paper money crisis," that is, from 1776 (the year the United States became independent from England) until the consecration of the 1787 Constitution.

With the implementation of the national constitution, the schematic emphasis on "exogenous" controls came to an abrupt end. This affirmation, however, does not mean that the new constitutional organization adopted lacked any "popular" controls, nor does it imply that it only involved the novel scheme of checks and balances. Yes, the new system was organized around the axis of "checks and balances," but it did preserve a type of "external" or "popular" control. In effect, the only institutional channel to ensure democratic oversight of the government boiled down to the periodic vote.

Because of this winnowing, the periodic vote took on extraordinary responsibility for the mediation of the relationship between citizens and government. Qualifying it as an "extraordinary responsibility" makes sense because this mediation had originally been distributed among several institutions or channels. In the first stage of democratic constitutionalism, in effect, the periodic vote was complemented by various other instruments that facilitated the task of maintaining a fluid, direct, and productive link between citizens and representatives. Allow me to put it like this: mandatory rotation in the positions meant many ordinary citizens had direct experience with government functions; organizing government through citizen assemblies or town meetings delegated a good part of decision-making directly to citizens that the periodic vote subsequently had to assume; and annual elections reduced the momentous import of each electoral cycle. When all these "electoral supplements" are lost and the democratic tools originally conceived lose their centrality, the periodic vote takes on enormous weight: public decision-making begins to depend on it, and to depend on it exclusively. Elections must now perform all the tasks that were previously carried out through a variety of tools. It is not only that the elections assume greater importance – which is true – but also that a multiplicity of different tasks were concentrated into this single mechanism, which it was expected to carry out simultaneously, threatening the very effectiveness of the mechanism. As a result, the expectations for and the consequences of elections are magnified (since other means of public participation in decision-making within the institutional scheme are not apparent). The messages elections must convey and the decisions they are supposed to affect multiply and diversify while their real scope of influence remains unchanged. In short, the vote is required to fulfill multiple tasks (that are often contradictory or in tension with each other) while tools capable of providing separate channels for them are removed. Under these conditions, periodic elections will always disappoint the expectations put in them: given their limited power and influence, they are simply unable to satisfy the requirements. That we continue to place very high expectations in the power of the vote, despite the enormous degree of dissatisfaction in their results should come as no surprise. The truth is that, even when carried out in conditions close to ideal, periodic elections cannot meet all the expectations of democratic self-government – they are simply insufficient. In what follows, I will shore up these claims around the demands placed on periodic elections and the limitations of elections that make the demands impossible to meet.

8.2 "Electoral Extortion"

I would like to start with the multiple and contradictory tasks that we assign to periodic elections. From that exaggerated or irresponsible initial step taken to focus virtually all popular control into this mechanism, I derive, on the one hand, the objective difficulties of elections to satisfy all the expectations and demands placed on them and, on the other hand, the social frustration that is exacerbated by the malfunction of the system.

Past and Future. Both the *retrospective* and the *prospective* nature of elections have been discussed, and rightly so (Przeworski et al. 1999). Elections are supposed, simultaneously, to provide voters with a means of addressing past complaints and stake out their position regarding decisions that must be taken in the near or distant future. This might seem reasonable, in principle. On the one hand, we use our votes to endorse or disapprove of the government currently in power and, at the same time, to convey a message about what the government that wins the election should do in the future. These are the most obvious purposes that we can reasonably assign to the vote with hope that it will be able to achieve them. They are, moreover, tasks that could once have been assigned to different tools. For example, the practice of revoking mandates fundamentally served, long ago, the first of these tasks. It enabled citizens to sanction representatives for improper use of the political responsibility that had been assigned to them. Today, however, voting in elections is the only communicative tool at our disposal to weigh in on both past and future decisions. These are different tasks that often involve demands that are contradictory or simply in tension, yet for which we only have one response: periodic elections.

This can be easily illustrated with a hypothetical example. For instance, we could, after reflection, decide that we want to reward the current government for its general performance up to the present, but also voice our concern regarding an aspect of its behavior that we find particularly relevant for future action (e.g., that it address, once and for all, some issues that have been neglected). Imagine, for example, that after a period of authoritarian rule, we vote for a government committed to democracy, which enables us to climb out of the authoritarian abyss where we had fallen. The present government has largely satisfied our expectations – we are no longer trapped in an authoritarian system that does not leave any room for democratic decision-making! – but nonetheless we would like our government to correct, urgently in the near future, its economic policy. We trust this government, we clearly and emphatically prefer it to the previous government, and also to the alternatives among which we may choose at present. But we desperately want to signal our conviction that it must urgently change the orientation of its economic program (or, in a different scenario, we might want to convey our sentiment that the government should, once and for all, legislatively deal with the issue of abortion, which we consider urgent yet has gone completely neglected). In either of these scenarios, we begin to realize our dilemma: we only have one tool – a single vote – that makes it impossible to send that simple (although not unambiguous) message. Worse yet, what seemed at first a reasonable expectation (that we would be able to convey the opinion to the current government that its democratic caliber satisfies us, but that it must, in the future, depending on the scenario, either change its economic approach or resolve the legality of abortion), becomes impossible or, worse, risky, even threatening. When we congratulate the government of the day for what it has done in the past, requesting a single change for future action, we enter very dangerous terrain. After all, in the end all we wanted was to endorse its performance along with making a small but relevant correction in its course. Reasonably, however, voting against the government (intended to emphasize what it still "owes") could be read as irremediable, unconditional, and complete chastisement. It could be interpreted as an emphatic affirmation of precisely what we were denying with conviction: "The election results represent a resounding rejection demanding that the current government leave and never return!" – some pundits might proclaim, and no one could counter them. To put it another way, we are in a predicament that we could call *electoral* or *democratic extortion*: to affirm what we want most, we may be forced to approve, through that same means (the vote), what we most reject. The sole tool that we have – the one that promises us power and freedom – in reality seems to control us by allowing us to pass a single message that might be interpreted in multiple senses. In this way, it opens up the possibility (not only that our message is misunderstood but also) that our message means the opposite of what we intended. In our example, by affirming through the vote our desired future course of action ("improve social policy"), we can easily end up approving what we most rejected ("that the current government leave, never to return").

Multiple Policies. A problem similar to the one described in the previous paragraph regarding "past and future" decisions arises in relation to the multiple policies that governments – any government – adopt. In order to simplify the problem, we will focus on the simple case of a government that carries out two fundamental policies (without taking into account the fact that any government, anywhere, constantly, is developing and implementing dozens of policies). Let us imagine that the government has only started its administration a short time ago, and is promoting an active social policy to aid the most vulnerable groups while hardening measures to counter its opponents. In terms of freedom of expression, we will assume that the government begins to exercise fierce censorship against those who dare to question its procedures. As is obvious from this "ambiguous" (and easily imaginable) policy by the government, we will encounter many people who strongly support the government's action in one of the areas mentioned (say, the social policy promoted), while emphatically rejecting what the government does in the other (persecuting opponents). Hypothetically, many people will want to sanction the government for its strong authoritarian bias, although they would also like to reward it for its active policies in social matters. The fact is, again, that each of these people has only one vote. Allow me to underscore once again what is obvious: by oversimplifying the scenarios that occur in reality, we are left with the simple situation of a government with only two major measures in operation. Even in this crude, simple schematic, relying solely on elections places us in a dilemma without exit: how do we manifest our opinion? If we vote in favor of the government because of its valuable social policies, it can be taken as a vote of full confidence: our decision will be interpreted as accepting the government's treatment of its opponents, or at least as being unconcerned about the very serious implications of such policies. We would actually reward the government for them! In the same way, if we vote against the government in order to make clear our anger towards its policy on freedom of expression, it will seem that we also reject its policy on social matters, which we actually find worthy of the highest praise. This is what we would like to reward the government for! In short, even in this oversimplified scheme, by which we only take into account two of the multiple policies that any government implements, only having one vote once again backs us into a corner: we are confronted, once again, with "electoral extortion."

I would like to emphasize that although our exercise involves two policies that elicit mixed reactions from voters (favorable to one, against the other), a similar dynamic can occur, and identical extortion, within the framework of a single policy. Examples are easy to imagine. Take a single, significant proactive policy through which the government favors certain relevant social interests (say, the "Family Grant" programs in certain Latin American countries that provide modest food subsidies to the poorest in order to promote school attendance and preventive healthcare). It may well be that the policy, which we support in principle because of its egalitarian aims, generates serious doubt that finally leads us to reject the program out of the fear that it provides cover for or institutionalizes corrupt practices (I do not think it is necessary for me to clarify that this hypothetical is related to actual cases involving certain Latin American governments at the beginning of the twenty-first century – they are abundant and do not need to be listed). For example, the government may take advantage of the enormous size of the program's budget (the budget for social programs), in order to obtain improper benefits from suppliers, or it may propose costly reforms in order to augment the budgetary allocation to the program, which officials then use for illegitimate enrichment. In any of these and similar scenarios, we are faced with a single social policy that pulls us in opposite directions: we have, at the same time, strong reasons to support and promote it and, at the same time, good reasons to reject it and denounce it. What should our proper response be, given the tension in which this situation places us (and disregarding for the moment our assessment of all the other public policies that the government has been implementing)?

Notice, again, that the dilemma we are dealing with is not merely a question of doubts over whether to support or not an especially attractive policy. Rather, it is the common situation in which we have strong reasons to reject and to endorse the very same policy based on different reasons pertaining to different aspects of it. As a result, we may want, emphatically, to vote for it and against it at the same time, but we only have a single vote. Only having a single expressive mechanism, one that is at the same time extremely rudimentary, puts us in an uncomfortable political position. Rather than adequately expressing our will in the public sphere, the vote might obscure or even completely distort the message we mean to convey. Does it even make sense to vote in these conditions?

Choosing among Candidates. Now let us take one more step to add an additional dimension of complexity to the scenario already presented. We already know that voting places us in dilemmatic situations ("electoral extortion"), both in terms of how to convey our position regarding past and future decisions and how to convey it regarding separate policies (or different features of the same policy). What to say then, regarding not the politics but the actual candidates who appear on the ballot? When we vote, we are given lists of candidates. We naturally evaluate them in terms of policies and platforms, the way we evaluate management in general, taken together with our consideration of what the future holds (with all the extraordinary complications of which we are already aware). But what about the candidates themselves? Here we clearly confront another dilemma very similar in structure to those already mentioned.

In the first place (and depending on the electoral system where we vote) it is possible to expect several candidates aligned with the same government or party on the list (remembering that my country, Argentina, along with many others, currently uses proportional voting systems with closed lists). It is foreseeable that, in any given election, some will excite us more than others. The situation just described does not seem serious enough to elicit real concern, at least not yet, but the question that interests us is already evident. I am referring again to the question hanging over the vote's expressive capacity; that is, the instrument's communicative power. Does the vote in this situation help to convey praise or complaints? For example, take the common practice by which a government or party "hides" certain candidates (who for some reason are "controversial" or less attractive) by burying their names in the middle or at the end of lists of more popular candidates.[1] In such situations, the citizen faces the same type of dilemma already seen: how to convey clearly, through the vote, strong adherence to one candidate on the list while strongly expressing rejection of another from the same party. It is clearly difficult if not impossible to do so the way elections are currently run and in the absence of other mechanisms. The vote, once again, places us in a bind comparable to "democratic extortion." Should we vote for any candidate if our vote might be reasonably interpreted as signifying the opposite of what we intend? Today we know that there are institutional means to overcome this difficulty, including single-member districts and disqualification systems, among others. In other words, in certain contexts, mechanisms have been devised to dismantle some of these dilemmas (disregarding the serious defects associated with each of these remedies). Yet even so, the root of the problem remains. This can be verified by giving our problem one last twist, one that mirrors the path that we followed when discussing the problem of staking out a nuanced position on diverse policies through the vote. We noted that the problem did not boil down to the presence of policies in tension with each other, but was rather enhanced when we found the same policy could combine attractive and unacceptable features. The same problem occurs when we consider candidates instead of policies.

Indeed, it is not uncommon to encounter candidates who although they can boast of significant achievements – say, for example, allocating part of their budget for the construction of social housing – have also been involved in some scandal (perhaps part of the funds allocated to social housing unduly went to supporters). A decent political system should obviously allow us to discriminate between the two actions: it should authorize us to encourage the candidate for the achievement – assuming you agree with the program – while enabling us to reproach the same candidate for any improper behavior. "Naturally!" – we might

[1] Translator's note: this is the first instance where the word "popular" is used in the more common English sense of "well-liked" as opposed to "of the people."

instinctively respond – "that's obvious!" Part of our duty as engaged citizens is helping candidates orient themselves in the shifting landscape of popular sentiment, and warn them against repeating missteps; it is that simple. But here again, unique reliance on a single vote forces us to take the risk of being understood as saying the opposite of what we intend. If we vote in the hypothetical candidate's favor to signal our approbation of the work done to advance social justice, we might be understood as not caring about or – worse still – condoning corrupt behavior. If we vote against the candidate to punish the corrupt behavior, it may be understood that we do not care or – worse still – that we reject the candidate's stand for solidarity. The single vote, again, places us in a situation where the most sensible thing to do is to reject it: as decent voters we may prefer not voting at all than risking that our vote be interpreted as the opposite of what we intend.

8.3 Elections from the Representative's Point of View: Voting and Interpreting the Vote

What has been said so far may help us to assess the seriousness of the problems that surround periodic voting today. It still might make sense to reinforce the arguments laid out above with some additional notes. In the first place, we must not lose sight of the fact that the problems that we have been dissecting separately are in truth problems that come together and are intertwined. I mean, faced with almost any choice, we are routinely faced with a multiplicity of tragic dilemmas. It is reasonable to expect our representatives to understand when we applaud the government or specific leaders for certain actions and disapprove of failure to take other actions or take ones we consider unacceptable. We should be able to expect to be able to convey our insistence that the government follow through on one set of policies while pleading that it give up others. We should be able to communicate to our representatives that some decision was excellent (like the measure to legalize abortion in certain conditions in Argentina) and express abhorrence for another (like treating a hostile prosecutor as an enemy of the state). We should be able to express our support for some of the candidates presented by a party as well as the horror that others inspire. We should be able to vote for a candidate (say, the first candidate from a new party we like who has ever run for the Senate), encourage that candidate to stand firm on a position that we applaud (like their past work for social justice), and discourage them from engaging in other behavior (that might lead to corruption scandals like the ones with which they were once associated), all in the same election. These nuanced sentiments are common in almost every election, and we have not considered many other factors that complicate the choice even more. Yet we only possess one avenue of communication to express them, which is why no one always understands, in the end, why we voted or what we were trying to say by doing so. Or, what is worse, and unfortunately frequent, our vote may be interpreted as directly in favor of (or against) what we actually rejected (or approved).

Reflections like these focus our attention on the difficulties citizens encounter when attempting to express themselves politically through voting; that is, through the primary institutional channel designed to maintain the relationship between electors and elected. Still, the situation is even more worrying than what we have just indicated. This becomes clear when we ask what the representatives themselves – the most interested observers of the electoral process – can do or tend to do in the context of the difficulties just described.

If their position is at stake, representatives who are familiar with the way elections unfold and are run have several strategies and answers at their disposition. If candidates have already been elected, through a "closed" list because of their ties to the party leadership (e.g., because they are "disciplined" politicians who respect the mandate of their "superiors" in the party), they might adopt as the main strategy to remain in office that of "not making waves" – doing what they can to avoid the attention of the electorate – while concentrating on ingratiating or strengthening their relationships with the party leadership. Their position, after all, ultimately depends on their alignment with the political body to which they pertain, and what the leadership of those bodies usually demands are discipline and obedience. The result is not good.

In the context of other types of electoral systems, such as single-member constituencies, where candidates are often more easily identifiable, it is not clear that the representative should feel very concerned either. Candidates in these systems know that most of their weaknesses and missteps, sometimes even very serious ones, can be obscured by emphasizing more notable and appreciated acts. What I mean is that representatives can predict, fairly accurately, that voters face an extraordinary difficulty in discriminating, with a single vote, between their laudable and reprehensible actions. There is little reason, then, to distress over serious faults if, a year later, no one will remember them, or if they will be buried under all the events that transpire in the meantime (which may include some act that puts them in a much better situation).

Thinkers who highlight the "retrospective" nature of the elections seem to assume that the representatives fear electoral sanctions, and that they reorient their behavior taking into account the reactions and expectations of the voters. However, we already know that all these solid predictions and calculations fade into thin air: depending on the electoral system in question, the representatives can often jump on the coattails of other more attractive representatives, fall in line with party leaders in complete disregard of popular demands, or calmly place their trust in the inability of the vote to express the true intent of voters. Voters are "trapped" and unable to sanction representatives for some particular fault (even if it is serious) if the representatives know how to compensate for their defects with some positive act (which is easier still when they are running against an even less attractive political alternative).

These dynamics that we have been examining, moreover, have been reinforced with the passage of time. In the long-forgotten context of "annual elections," representatives might genuinely fear in the threat of sanction by voters. But in the context of elections held every two, three, four, or more years, what grounds remain for fear? The representatives know all too well now that their voters are unable to react promptly to "failures" or serious errors. They can rely on the passage of time for oblivion to set in before any reckoning. Voters do not usually think about what scandalized them years ago when they go to the voting booths. Moreover, along with the advantage of the passage of time, representatives know that voters have little chance of clarifying or qualifying their vote in any significant way. They know voters are "trapped" with their single vote, and will have a hard time if they try to punish them for a particular reprehensible act if they are capable of following it up with some action worthy of praise. The result, again, is simply bad.

It goes without saying that those in power (and, in a special but by no means exclusive way, those who hold political power over those in power) are the ultimate readers and interpreters of election results. Their voice is particularly salient in this interpretative step, for it is the political leadership that is charged with reacting concretely to elections. The tragedy, then, is not only that "they" impose interpretations that are not true or, more accurately, are adjusted to bring the reality most of us voters wanted to express with their priorities. The tragedy is also that, on a regular basis, we want to convey multiple messages in elections, but we only have one opportunity to say anything, which someone else will then interpret and characterize. What the group has said can be reconstructed by anyone in their own way, and no one will be in a position to refute the reconstruction. Each of us, surely, will have wanted to say many things with our single vote, but the results will portray a cacophony of mixed voices superimposed among themselves – full of background noise with popping here and there: pure confusion. This cacophony, however, is not followed by silence. Someone is going to speak, someone is going to respond, and politicians are going to act accordingly. The reconstruction, how elections are read, then, is what matters most, but nothing prevents them from interpreting the results almost as they please, or that they knowingly present interpretations that are wholly whimsical manipulations as objectively good. After the election, then, almost anything can happen.

8.4 From the Agora to the Dark Booth: The Absence of Dialogue

There are some common chords that run through all the above considerations and can largely help us understand them better. I will only mention two for now, of which I will only hold on to one. The first note that resonates throughout is the absence of the collective dimension, or the reduction of the vote to an individual, isolated act. The heart of politics moved from the public meeting place of Ancient Greece – the agora – where citizens came together, looked into each other's eyes, and let loose their excitement or anger – to a dark booth. In this booth, we are supposed to confer only with ourselves, consider only our own interests, and conceive politics only in terms of how it relates to each of us, and each of us to it, as if no one else existed, or had nothing important to add, or were simply not necessary. In the dark booth, political decisions become an isolated, individual act, separate from everything and everybody else. In the dark booth – what a metaphor – the distinctive, defining aspect of politics is the absence of the gaze of others and the reduction of politics to the private domain (the time will soon come when we vote from our bedrooms; we will not even have to go to schools or other public buildings to cast a ballot, and politics will have been completely privatized).

However, the absent gaze of others was not the distinctive note I wanted to focus on. I am interested in reflecting, above all, on a second chord that rings through all our earlier observations: the absence of dialogue. The absence is noticeable even if we paid minimal attention to the observations with which this chapter began. If others can – reasonably, and without bad faith – interpret our votes in any direction, or however they want, this is because, among other reasons, we do not talk to each other about our votes. When making our decisions on the course we would like political leaders to take, we are prevented from talking to others. We are forced to vote in isolation, without any recourse to advice, dialogue, or even the presence of other people to clarify confusion or provide help.

If, instead, when making crucial policy decisions, we could talk with others – assuming and only if we were so motivated – then the situation would be quite different. First of all, faced with an erroneous, abusive, or deceitful interpretation of what we have said or wanted to say, we could simply raise our hands and comment to those around us, or to those who have misinterpreted us: "That was not what I wanted to say. It was not *x*, but rather *y*." But no. We cannot add a single word after the ballot is cast, just as we cannot add any nuance when casting it. We cannot clarify anything – or even add a paltry footnote – once we have voted (oh, to be able to stipulate that my vote not be interpreted in a certain way). Our political life has lost its language. There is no language, only clumsy, crude signals that someone else will interpret on our behalf.

8.5 "Paper Stones"

The absence of words that permeates elections reflects how the central, discursive dimension of politics has been wounded. Voting, for its part, has been losing its most important communicative facet. The act of voting, in fact, has become very similar to throwing stones. The metaphor of "votes as stones" has its history partly set out in a beautiful book published by Adam Przeworski and John Sprague under the title of *Paper Stones*. As the authors describe in the book, the first socialists, enthusiastic that expanded suffrage would enable them to defeat the bourgeoisie through elections, made references to these "paper stones" that would allow them to leave behind their strategy based on barricades and clandestine action. The bourgeoisie, it was assumed, could be defeated, without violence, now that the political game was made fairer through the establishment of elections open to all.

In my view, the metaphor of "paper stones" holds promise, and it works well on many levels. First of all, the idea alludes to the potential power of universal suffrage. Voting is a tool that, in principle, allows us to assert, vehemently and with authority, certain points of view, for example, through the massive approval or rejection of a given electoral proposal. However, and at the same time, the idea of "votes as stones" also has a graphic quality that makes clear the dark, heavy, crude nature of the main political communication tool that we possess. This tool, as we saw, rather than helping us, blocks the possibility of conveying an accurate account of our beliefs. The crudeness and darkness of the vote prevents the electorate from expressing the multiple, fine-grained nuances that voters would often like to express through the ballot.

As I understand it, the metaphor is most suitable for how it represents what happens during and immediately after voting. In practice, we vote without saying a word; marking a box on the ballot is like a single, sudden bang. Like throwing a rock. Sometimes, when we throw a rock, we produce a loud noise. Immediately afterwards, however, people will sensibly ask what the people meant by the outburst. There will be no shortage of explanations: politicians who stand to benefit or risk losing power will rush in – running as fast as they can – to fill the void that follows the bang with words, giving their interpretation and final meaning to our actions. Yet, as we already know, anyone will be able to interpret what happened almost however they like. Supporters of the incumbent government, after an apparently overwhelming defeat at the polls, will be able to say: "I have understood the voters' message. They support us, but demand that we change our economic policy." (I write these notes a few days after the beating that Argentine President Mauricio Macri took in the August 2019 primary elections. His response was almost the same. He said: "I have listened to you and you are right, that is why I am taking these economic measures" – assuming that the citizens' complaint was limited to the "economic adjustment" his administration had implemented in his first term.) The opposition, on the other hand, might read the result of the elections (as occurred in the election being used as an example) as: "this overwhelming vote indicates that the people reject everything that this government has done." A more audacious opponent may even maintain: "this overwhelming vote means that the people have finally opened their eyes and vindicated everything done by the government that preceded the current one." We could easily continue collecting diverse (and mutually contradictory) interpretations to lopsided electoral victories. Once again, none of the interpretations can be objectively refuted: the opacity of what we "said" through our votes is so thick that no one can "decipher" it in any authoritative or definitive way. We threw our "paper stones," and they made a lot of noise, but nothing has become clear because of it.

8.6 Irrational Voters or Dysfunctional System?

A crucial problem that derives from the dilemmas just described is that the "irrationality" of the electorate is often blamed for election results.

We hear it all the time, as soon as the results are revealed: "How is it that the people have voted once again for those who oppress them?" "How is it possible that the people do not realize that this government is working against them?" "The people must have grown accustomed to being abused." "The people are masochists." "What did you expect from an ignorant society?"

Of course, part of that rhetoric is just that, folkloric rhetoric, and part of it stems from the desire to give quick answers to results that we dislike, consider adverse, or do not know how to explain otherwise. Yet there is generally much more to such comments. In Brazil, for example, after the election of President Jair Bolsonaro (a situation not very different, by the way, from the election of Donald Trump in the United States), many people blamed the "ignorance," "foolishness," "racism," or some "anti-democratic" character of the people who voted for Bolsonaro (or Trump) as a way of accounting for the result.[2]

However, on the heels of our previous observations, it should be clear that the truth we face might very well be quite different from what those immediate assessments of the elections suggested. Without the least complacency, we could not only argue that many other factors explain the results of those elections – or of any election whose result displeases us – beyond the "irrationality" of the electorate, but also, and above all, we might question the very identification of some collective "irrationality" as the cause. There are many reasons to doubt those assessments, the most obvious of which being, since the electorate is essentially blocked from making its position clear through the vote, it makes absolutely no sense to complain of the interpretation that we ourselves – those who criticize the results – attribute to them. It makes no sense to deprive the citizenry of their capacity to express their opinion by forbidding any qualification of their vote, and then point accusingly at the result as if it carried a specific, forceful message. The problem is not, in general, that citizens do not know how to make good decisions, but rather that they are not really given the opportunity to decide on anything. Someone might reply: "If the people already make so many mistakes with the little decision-making power they have, the last thing we should do is delegate more authority for them make decisions on other issues." Here again, however, the retort misses its mark: the issue is not that the public makes bad decisions, but rather that they do not have the necessary opportunity

[2] See, for example: https://brazilian.report/power/2018/08/28/esther-solano-jair-bolsonaro/.

to talk and clarify through dialogue what they want to say and the contours of their position.

The size and severity of the problems I am thinking of is more clearly seen when we focus on what we called the issue of "electoral extortion": elections through which we seek to express *x*, but through which our vote for *x* can also be understood (naturally, especially because we have no the opportunity to clarify what we meant by *x*, or emphatically reject misinterpretations) as affirming *y*, where *y* is a claim that we directly reject. Allow me to return to the example of Bolsonaro. The first Bolsonaro voter I spoke to in Brazil after he won the presidential election was a black female activist who was fully aware of her racial and gender rights and the racist and homophobic discourse expressed by the President-elect. Her surprising choice, as she made clear to me, had nothing to do with any desire to quash the rights of the groups with which she identified, but rather with her desire to remove from power the previous government, which she considered highly corrupt. The only instrument at her disposal for this was voting for Bolsonaro, and she had made use of it. There would be time later – she mused, sensibly or not – to reset the country back on the right path. In Argentina, months later, many people who identified themselves as opposed to the previous Kirchner administrations (the "*anti-kirchneristas*") went on to vote for a ticket that brought the Kirchner clan closer to power, as it represented the only means to expel President Mauricio Macri from office. Many of these voters could never have imagined – even a very short time before – voting to bring those they had fought back to power. However, they saw no other path within their reach, given the primal urgency they felt in the face of the prospect of giving Macri another term. In any case, I am not especially interested in the relevance of one election or another, or even those I am using as examples: who won and why is not the point. I do not want to delve into the justification for the voting behavior just described, but focus instead on the limitations of our electoral tools and the "extortion" to which they subject us. It is very common for voters to want to express, with their vote, a plurality of issues, and for the electoral system to situate that person in the midst of tragic dilemmas such as the one we have attempted to capture through the idea of "democratic extortion." It is far too common, for example, that when faced with the difficulty of expressing or articulating all our preferences, we are forced to sacrifice some strong preferences, ones we hold dearly, to stake a position on another or other values that, at the particular moment, take priority. That is, faced with the direct impossibility of honoring the two or three preferences that rank most highly, we must often choose, exclusively, one of them, and sacrifice the rest for its sake. We are forced to attempt to affirm, through our single vote, our first preference, which leads us to "quash" in the same gesture all the other preferences that, if possible, we would have expressed. Worse yet (as perhaps is the case of the examples cited), the voters in question may feel forced to vote for options that they repudiate (referring to the examples, they might say: "the only instrument I had at hand was voting for Bolsonaro/Kirchner") because voters must assign priority to the most pressing of the many objectives that they would like to support (that objective in both cases being the removal of the incumbent or former president, whether Macri in Argentina or Lula in Brazil). It is difficult to assert, in either case, the irrationality of the voters in question: they deployed the only means offered by the institutional system to ensure their first preference was expressed but, as is often the case, putting their support behind it forces them to sacrifice or jeopardize other very significant preferences (perhaps at the expense of their second highest preference, which could very well be that someone like Bolsonaro would never attain power or that the *kirchneristas* would never regain it). There is no irrational voting behavior here, only a system that habitually forces voters to choose one among their many demands and that then allows their vote to be read as affirming something that they would actually reject. The crucial problem here is not that of irrational voters, but rather the dysfunctional system. That is why we need to do more than wag a moralizing finger at the voters. We need to radically change the representative system that extorts, distorts, and abuses the voters. Above all, we need to give the floor back to the voters, create the institutional channels for listening to them, and, ultimately, make genuine dialogue possible.

9

Checks and Balances

Combining "Institutional Means and Personal Motives"

9.1 The Key to Modern Constitutionalism: "Checks and Balances"

The system of checks and balances is, without doubt, the greatest contribution of North American constitutionalism to the long history of constitutional government. It is also one of the most important – if not the most important – features of constitutionalism that the United States exported to the rest of the Americas, from where it spread to countries across the oceans. Many other central and still characteristic aspects of world constitutionalism (typically, the separation of powers and the division of government into executive, legislative, and judicial branches) had already taken shape in the "common heritage" of humanity through the contributions of thinkers like John Locke and Montesquieu.

The mechanism of checks and balances must be understood as different, complementary, and corrective to the famous notion of the division of powers. The notion of the "division of powers" requires that power not be concentrated, and that different government functions be allocated to different bodies (the executive branch serves the "managerial" function; the legislature is tasked with establishing the laws; and the judiciary interprets them to resolve conflicts and determine how they apply in specific cases). The notion of "checks and balances," meanwhile, refers to the articulation between these different branches of power. For a long time, the proposal of "strict" separation between the different branches of power prevailed in the United States (as it would beyond its borders). The idea of "strict separation," on the one hand, signified the principle that no branch of power should undermine, meddle, or interfere with the power of any other and, on the other, ensured the predominance of the "most powerful" branch, that is, the legislative branch (as Maurice Vile explains in an essential book on the subject). The idea of "strict separation" was developed during the French Revolution and came to the United States through the "radical" writings of politicians such as Thomas Paine (who, recall, was the primary intellect behind the "radical" 1776 Pennsylvania Constitution in which "strict separation" was the guiding principle). However, for several reasons (which included the fear of the "dangers," "hardships," and "excesses" of the legislature), a different constitutional dynamic took root between the branches of government in the United States. This dynamic was not one of "strict separation," but rather one of checks and balances. In accordance with this approach, each branch of power was given limited room to intervene in the actions of the others to control and counterbalance potential errors or excesses (the President was given veto power; the judiciary the authority to declare laws invalid; the legislature the power to impose initiatives on the executive and conduct political trials, among others).

There are two quotes that I find enormously revealing about the ends, merits, and serious flaws that still distinguish the "checks and balances" mechanism. The quotes come from two of the masterminds behind the 1787 Constitution, James Madison and Alexander Hamilton.

The first quote comes from one of the most cited paragraphs of The Federalist Papers, No. 51. The phrase, from Madison, reads:

> The great security against a gradual concentration of the several powers in the same department, consists in giving to those who administer each department the necessary constitutional means and personal motives to resist encroachments of the others. The provision for defense must in this, as in all other cases, be made commensurate to the danger of attack. Ambition must be made to counteract ambition. The interest of the man must be connected with the constitutional rights of the place. It may be a reflection on human nature, that such devices should be necessary to control the abuses of government. But what is government itself, but the greatest of all reflections on human nature? If men were angels, no government would be necessary. If angels were to govern men, neither external nor internal controls on government would be necessary.[1]

The second quote comes from one of the most notable speeches that Hamilton made during the Constitutional Convention on June 18, 1787, and is enormously significant for its grasp of the serious problems that still affect the system of "checks and balances" today (despite the fact that, with notable exceptions such as Robert Dahl, this quote has not nearly received the attention it deserves).[2] Hamilton breaks it down in this way:

> In every community where industry is encouraged, there will be a division of it into the few & the many. Hence separate interests will arise. There will

1 https://avalon.law.yale.edu/18th_century/fed51.asp.

2 https://avalon.law.yale.edu/18th_century/debates_618.asp. Dahl's quote can be found in his short but great book, *A Preface to Democratic Theory*, ch. 1, I, Hypothesis 4.

> be debtors & creditors &c. Give all power to the many, they will oppress the few. Give all power to the few, they will oppress the many. Both therefore ought to have power, that each may defend itself against the other.[3]

The Hamilton quote brings out, in my opinion, the principle and logic upon which the notion of "checks and balances" are founded: the principle involves avoiding mutual oppression, and the logical strategy to implement the principle is giving equal power to majorities and minorities so neither can overpower the other. Madison's quote, meanwhile, makes clear the content and *modus operandi* of the system. The key idea – which deserves repeated emphasis – is that those who administer the various branches of government should be provided the *constitutional means* and have *personal motives* to resist encroachment from the other branches. Then, and given the assumption that individuals – and especially men in power – are primarily motivated by self-interest, egoism, or personal ambition – "personal motives" – the system of "checks and balances" proposed levering these (unattractive, we might say) motivations for the common good. This was made possible by the "constitutional means" that were to be attributed to the different branches of government: veto power for the President; powers to invalidate laws for judges; powers of overrule for legislators; and so on. Hence, for example, the expectation that the President would curb any irrational, excessive, or precipitous measures of the legislature (to cite a common reproach of the local legislatures by the federalist elite, decisions to issue paper money) through the powers or competences allocated to the executive (say, by vetoing), not out of virtue or altruism but, rather, merely out of their own self-interest or ambition. Ambition – as Madison stated in the quote – was to "be made to counteract ambition" (in this case, the ambition of legislators, the representatives of the indebted majorities who were willing to impose their interest, destroying the rights of the others would be counteracted by the ambition of the creditors in the minority). This was a system that, as Bruce Ackerman has argued, "economized" on public virtue.

The logic at work, as can be seen, was essentially similar to Adam Smith's economic vision. In fact, Madison proposed the same framework

[3] In the same vein, Madison argued that the owners should have a "share" in the government, to ensure the "invaluable interests" of the owners, and thus "balance and stop the other group." In the original sentence: "landholders ought to have a share in the government, to support the ... invaluable interests (of property) and to balance and check the other (group)" (Farrand 1937, vol. 1, 431).

for behavior as Smith had suggested for the economy (using institutions to channel even the worst motivations towards the collective good). Madison, however, focused on constitutional institutions: designing the institutions correctly, so that they played to the "natural" self-interest of each individual, would suffice to achieve better conditions for the collective (the conditions envisioned being willingness to negotiate and power to block oppressive policies from either faction). The aggregate ambition on both sides could benefit the collective welfare if the constitution was able to harness it.

With the help of the two quotes, allow me to examine and evaluate in more detail this centuries-old tool that developed in United States constitutionalism.

9.2 Institutionally Channeling "Civil War"

The "checks and balances" system is attractive in many aspects. Without doubt, its "realism" must be praised. The underlying conception of human behavior was anything but naïve (on the contrary, it was solidly pessimistic). Madison clearly understood the importance of limiting power. Born with an appetite for history, he knew very well the tendency, inherent in politics, to abuse and oppress through power. The system he devised reacted to the tendencies (particularly that of the "factional spirit") that, as we will see, the "strict separation" system simply lived with (and perhaps even fed). All these factors count in favor of his system for "mutual control."

Of all the virtues that could be considered characteristic of the new checks and balances model, surely the most important was the one that provided its raison d'être in the United States; that is, its ability to encourage opposing factions to come to agreement, thus preventing "mutual oppression." The merit of the system, in this respect, lay in its capacity to channel through institutions a conflict that threatened to descend into civil war. In this sense, the model was a true success. Allow me to give a brief account of this deep conflict that broke out during the "founding moments" of North American constitutionalism. The conflict allows us to understand better the reasons why the response of checks and balances was conceived in those circumstances, and, concretely, the kind of conflicts to which it provides a remedy.

Civil war was on the verge of exploding in the United States very soon after the colonies' break from England. The country had been left economically impoverished by the war, and politically extremely divided.

The most impoverished sectors (the "debtors") were eager for an end to the hardship and injustice they suffered. In his most important text (Federalist No. 10), Madison had already referred to the inevitable and insurmountable divisions between "property owners and propertyless"; the "creditors and debtors"; the "wealthy groups" and those with "minor interests." In the years following the Revolution of 1776 that brought independence from England, the lower classes, many of whom had put their lives and everything they owned on the line to support the cause, found that what followed independence was not – as had been promised – prosperity. Rather, they found waiting the opposite: imminent risk of losing what little they had left to pay off debts incurred during the war. Then, in a way never seen before, the number of lawsuits filed to collect on debts shot up (in Massachusetts, 3,000 such suits were filed in Hampshire County between 1784 and 1786, and in Worcester County, more than 4,000 in 1785 alone). This led to sudden, widespread social unrest, which initially found expression in armed uprisings: Luke Day led a mobilization of 1,500 people in Northampton, while Daniel Shays went down in history for the revolt he led (now known as "Shays' rebellion") aimed at preventing the courts in Worcester from convening.

Following this initial period of armed uprisings came a development just as concerning. The unrest was similar, but its expression could be described as "institutional uprisings." Indeed, in many states where a majority of voters were in debt, the local legislatures were dominated by their representatives and laws were passed to provide immediate aid and alleviate suffering (typically, by cancelling debts or, especially, issuing local paper currency). Those practices caused a direct shock to the ruling class of the time, because – as historian Gordon Wood has pointed out in his study of the period – what had previously only ever been achieved in situations of anarchy or the absence of law was now implemented through legal institutions (Wood 1966, 405–406). There were the "factions" against which the entire national constitutional project that sprung up at that time was oriented, for the "weak" institutional structure prevailing at the state level (which lacked any system of "checks and balances") appeared unable to contain or counteract them. In "Vices of the Political System," Madison had laid out the "vices" of those state legislatures – defects that a new national constitution ought to expunge. Specifically, Madison spoke of the "multiplicity," "mutability," and "injustice" that he felt characterized the laws being passed at the state level.[4]

[4] https://founders.archives.gov/documents/Madison/01-09-02-0187.

In historical details such as these we can often find nodal points that help explain the emergence, the justification, and finally the central success of the system of "checks and balances": it was a system that provided institutional channel to divert armed rebellions such as those of Shays and remedied, at the same time, the institutional ills that the institutional design in place until then had proven incapable of solving. Thanks to the new scheme of "checks and balances," the institutional system would be in a position to contain the "excesses," "hardships," and "injustices" of the previous one.

9.3 Erroneous Antidemocratic Logic

The problems presented by the system of "checks and balances" are numerous and very serious, to the point that it is difficult to understand the inertia which has enabled it to remain intact. In other words, it is not clear how the system is still considered a proper or "natural" "fact" within modern constitutional systems rather than the object of urgent attention and radical modifications.

Here I am only going to deal with three problems that affect the checks and balances model, although I consider it relevant to at least mention several others. On one side are all the problems that the defenders of the "strict separation" system (including, saliently, Thomas Paine) recognized very early on: the system was confusing (it did not clearly define the powers that each branch of government should exercise); it was complex; and it weakened, above all, the most democratic organ of government. On another side, the system did not appear equipped to work as well when the same faction retained control over most or all of the branches of government (I will return to this point later). In addition, the indifference of this model to "civic virtue" and its reliance on individual "egoism," which thus becomes the main "fuel" of the institutional system, which it tends to regenerate and reproduce, is problematic. In any case, I would like to underscore three problems that suggest that "checks and balances" not only represent a very inefficient tool, but also one that is normatively unattractive and in serious tension with our most elementary democratic intuitions.

A Thin Conception of Democracy, or Undermining Majority Rule. Above all, I would highlight the very surprising way (especially in terms of the lack of debate over them) in which the mechanisms of checks and balances arose in direct rejection of the democratic ideal. The quote from Hamilton frankly and directly affirms this. Hamilton maintains that if a majority has the (institutional) capacity to oppress the minority, they will do exactly that, just as the minority would oppress the majority if it had the ability and opportunity. From this affirmation, the federalists derived the need to give both groups equivalent (veto) power to avoid "mutual oppression." This phrase, as I understand it, perfectly sums up the objective that defines the system, as well as its main virtue and defect. The intention is – as I have already said because it is very important – avoiding "mutual oppression" between majorities and minorities – but the cost in democratic terms is enormous because the solution is giving the minorities equivalent institutional power to prevent potential abuses by the majorities. That is exactly what the "checks and balances" system purported to do.

Indeed, the Federalists opted for a scheme (of "checks and balances") through which each sector of society would have veto power against the opposing group on the basis of the assumptions (i) that society was fundamentally divided into two groups (minorities and majorities/debtors and creditors/large landowners and small holdings); (ii) that the members of each of these groups were fundamentally motivated by self-interest; and (iii) that members of each of these groups could be incorporated into the institutional scheme (through a system combining direct elections – which favored the election of representatives of ordinary citizens – and indirect elections – which favored the election of members of the elite). The original idea was to concentrate the power of the most numerous groups (the "debtors," "small landowners," and "poor") in the potentially most "powerful" (and "dangerous" or "threatening") organ of the institutional system, that is, in the lower house of Congress, while minority groups would dominate all the other indirectly chosen government organs – the Senate, the executive, and the judiciary. This way – it was hoped – no "faction" could impose its "sinister" volition on the others. It is worth adding that this way of understanding the organization of power, which linked branches of government to different sectors of society – to ensure, simultaneously, political and socioeconomic balance – was the same understanding that was operative in the distinct "mixed government" projects developed in England. The British model was (for this very reason) admired by many North American elites, although they tended to express their praise in hushed voices.

The proposed "checks and balances" scheme denies, implicitly but clearly, a basic tenet of democracy by directly undermining the elementary bases of the democratic ideal, which require majority rule to occupy a central role in the institutional structure. Naturally the power of the majority must be subject to controls in constitutional democracies and minorities warrant special institutional protection, but it is possible to devise other mechanisms to force majorities to "think twice" or review their initiatives. Such initiatives are viable and warrant consideration as they take seriously both the rights of the majority (the right to pronounce its preference or demonstrate its weight in political decisions), and the rights of minorities (the right to respect for its fundamental interests). What is surprising and unacceptable is seeking to ensure protection of minorities by endowing them with power equal to that of majorities, that is, by putting an end to the principle that majority rule prevails. The resulting scheme of "checks and balances" thus intended to avoid mutual oppression by giving the majority and minorities the same level of institutional power, an affront that any constitutional democracy should reject. It is and should be possible to give special protection to minorities without replacing majority rule or hollowing out the basic democratic essence of the constitution.

A Fundamentally Inefficient System, or Two Faults That, Together, Yield a Compounded Problem. When Madison proposed countering ambition with more ambition as the driving principle of the new system, he opted for combining institutions and motivations in a way that was as attractive as it was dangerous. What drew interest was how, without demanding noble heroism from anyone and promising to derive sustenance from everyone's worst intentions, the new system of checks and balances promised to redirect institutionally selfish impulses such to make them contribute to the common good. But was the promise sensible? Can we really expect some good to emerge from the sum of two evils? Or should we rather expect the result to be some "bad compound"? (As Karl Marx once said to Joseph Proudhon: "It claims to be synthesis but is nothing more than a compounded error.")

To begin with, Madison himself warned, shortly after the system of checks and balances was implemented, that it did not operate effectively when different powers of the government are controlled by the same party (Luo & Przeworski 2019, 5). It seems clear (and it should have been clear from the beginning) that (to the extent that it is not possible to limit each branch of government to the representation, direct or indirect, of a given social sector) that the risk of a majority taking control of more than one branch of government was obvious, thus putting the entire system of "checks and balances" into crisis.

The possibility just mentioned (of a system that loses its equilibrium when the "factional majorities" take control of more than one branch of power) should have been foreseen in advance. However, it is possible that, at the time, such a scenario was far-fetched (it was not foreseeable, it seems, that the majorities would ever gain control of the executive or judicial branches, or even both houses of the legislative branch). In any case, the "founding fathers" should have at least realized the genuine possibility of other anomalies that were far less removed from practical reality. Some analysts during those founding moments actually anticipated that opposing factions that controlled different branches of power, when confronted and acting out of pure self-interest, would not sit down to negotiate among themselves. Rather than negotiate to avoid "mutual oppression," they would likely take aggressive stances, unleashing an "institutional war," using their institutional competences (the "checks" they held over the other branches) to block the other faction from obtaining what it wanted.

This is what, for example, Nathaniel Chipman argued. Chipman rather casually predicted that institutional "war" or "stalemate" would result from the ("normal" and predictable) situation where different groups controlled different branches of government. Chipman thought foreseeable a "perpetual war of each against the other, or at best, an armed truce, attended with constant negotiations, and shifting combinations, as if to prevent mutual destruction: each party in its turn uniting with its enemy against a more powerful enemy" (Chipman 1833, 171).

The situations that Chipman predicted and others like them have indeed become "normal" in the political lives of our countries. We can find examples everywhere of opposing political parties that have roughly equivalent the same amount of power who, instead of collaborating, seek to gain a comparative advantage by blocking the initiatives of their rival, leading to direct conflict or institutional paralysis. (Recall, to take a well-known case, the confrontation and mutual blockade unleashed between the Republican and the Democrat Parties in the United States related to the health program promoted by President Barack Obama, "Obamacare.")

Taking into account the institutional design of the "checks and balances" imagined by Madison, and the type of motivational assumptions that he and the Federalists in general adopted, at least one other institutional scenario can be imagined, one as scary and unattractive as the previous scenarios (and one that also occurs frequently in our countries). I mean the situation (which, in my opinion, should have been the most obvious and expected of all) in which (i) self-interested representatives (ii) who detain control over broad powers (including the "power of the purse" or the budget and that of "the sword" or military power) are

(iii) only held accountable by weak "popular" or "external" controls (as determined by the constitution) and (iv) come to agreement on a set of mutually beneficial conditions for themselves at the cost of harm suffered by the majority of the citizenry that lives outside the government structures.[5] In fact, one would reasonably find the extremely negative social result (where the political elite works collectively for their own benefit) much more probable than its opposite, which is the one promised by Madison and many Federalists. Madison and his colleagues argued that the comparable power of each group would allow them to coerce each other to negotiate laws favorable to the common good (preferring "action" to "paralysis"). Many of the situations that we suffer in our countries, and that lead us to speak of a "crisis of democracy," elicit pessimistic scenarios similar to those just described. We collectively recognize that the "political class" (or "the caste," as the political class has been labelled in Spain) protects itself through measures and laws that favor it at our expense.

A System That Discourages Dialogue, or Civil War by Other Means. The last of the serious problems that I would like to highlight in relation to the system of "checks and balances" is related to the disincentives it creates for democratic dialogue. I am referring to dialogue within and between the different branches of power, and between them and the citizenry. Forms of conversation come to mind like public hearings, civic assemblies, mechanisms for public consultation like referenda and special votes, panel discussions, and so on. For those of us who understand democracy as a system structured around the principle of conversation among equals, the objective of public discussion must be an absolute priority: the value of any democratic system directly relates to its proximity to or distance from the effective practice of that ideal.

In this sense, what I maintain is that the system of "checks and balances" that, as I said, was devised to institutionally channel a "civil war" fulfilled (not fully, but to a large extent) its original purpose in the country for which it had been intended (the United States). However,

[5] Jon Elster came to the conclusion that this situation is more typical when he refined his study of constitutional creation (through the use of the metaphor of "Ulysses and the sirens"): we cannot expect the creators of the constitution "to tie their own hands" when writing the constitution. The most reasonable expectation is that they "tie everyone else's hands," leaving their own hands "untied" (an example of this might be found in the 1787 US Constitutional Convention, where the delegates established protections for the rights of several minorities, but left the "problem" of slavery, in which many had direct interests, "out of the Constitution" (Elster 2000).

and as is obvious, that partial success (redirecting, with the help of the Constitution, the worst oppressive impulses), did not imply similar success in the area of public deliberation: the Constitution did not aspire to, nor was it intended to promote public deliberation. On the contrary: the Constitution reflected genuine preoccupation with the prospect of high levels of citizen involvement in the discussion of government affairs (hence its interest in "separating" rather than "linking" citizens and public officials). In short, encountering constitutions poorly equipped for the promotion of public debate should come as no surprise, since their object (and, in particular, the objective of the system of checks and balances) was to stop a war, not to promote dialogue (an objective, I insist, that has not changed since the biases of the first constitutional movements against citizen participation were incorporated).

Public dialogue (between branches of government, or between citizens and public officials) was thus discouraged, in different manners and forms depending on the country. In fact, it could be argued that all the instruments for "checks and balances" are in tension with the regulative ideal of dialogue. Its purpose, I repeat, was to "arm" – in Madison's language – each branch of government with "defensive tools" against the "certain attacks" by the others. "Vetoing" a law is described as "dealing a mortal blow" to the law (a "blow" that cannot be seen as a call for dialogue); initiating a political trial is akin to "firing at" the official under prosecution in order to remove them from the political game; judicially invalidating a law essentially implies banning it (in an even stronger sense, the great jurist Robert Cover spoke of "jurispathic" decisions; Cover 1985). In other words, the tools of checks and balances bear little resemblance, even in principle, to tools designed to encourage dialogue. Rather, they resemble instruments meant to close it down. They provide the means for political leaders to wage a different kind of war, one fought through institutions.

In short, our model of constitutional organization can be considered valuable in several diverse and important respects (preventing "mutual oppression"; channeling "civil war" through nonviolence; etc.), but it does not promote collective dialogue. It does not forbid it, nor is it incompatible with it, but it does not favor it. In fact, it often helps discourage or block it. This should not be surprising in light of the very poor and very restricted vision of democracy that underpins the system. Moreover, as we will see, the system can be considered responsible for many of the institutional problems that have come to characterize modern constitutional democracies: institutional paralysis or constitutional "hardball," hostile confrontations, elitism, and inefficiency. These difficulties, as is obvious, are caused by many factors (the high levels of poverty and inequality typical of our democracies is certainly one), yet – as I have attempted to make clear in this chapter – these factors doubtlessly include the particular institutional design of our constitutional systems.

10

Presidentialism

Busting the Checks and Balances

The "Liberator" of the Americas, Simón Bolívar, has been revered in Latin America since the days of his heroic deeds (at the beginning of the nineteenth century) up to the present day. However, many of his colleagues and fellow citizens watched his moves with extreme suspicion. In particular, many saw him as an ambitious, larger-than-life figure who sought to become the equivalent of a king in the nascent republics, albeit without a crown. Bolívar was never shy about expressing his own thoughts on the subject. In one of his many references to the role that he envisioned for himself, as the President of the Republic that was taking form in Bolivia, he declared:

> The President of the Republic, in our Constitution, becomes the sun which, fixed in its orbit, imparts life to the universe. This supreme authority must be perpetual, for in non-hierarchical systems, more than in others, a fixed point is needed about which leaders and citizens, men and affairs can revolve. "Give me a point where I may stand," said an ancient sage, "and I will move the earth." For Bolivia this point is the life-term President.
>
> (Bolívar 1951, vol. 1, 190)

Bolívar had been in charge of drafting the Constitution for the country, and he reserved the supreme post for himself. That is what led many of those around him to their distrust. In particular, both his more liberal and extremely liberal colleagues – the radicals of his day and age – found cause for suspicion and alarm in his enthusiasm for concentrated power. In the end, they – as convinced republicans – recognized in Bolívar's discourse the same type of authoritarian aspirations against which they had risked their lives during the very long struggle for independence. They found it completely unacceptable that the person who had led their epic fight for emancipation now sought to replicate the forms of the old order.

A not insignificant number of the most renowned liberals of the time thus set about forming plans to get rid of Bolívar. The Colombian liberal-radical, Florentino González, was one of them. Historian Gerardo Molina described González as a "fiery young man . . . who did not hesitate to contemplate an assassination attempt" to finish Bolívar (Molina 1987, 97). We find the same extremism in another notable Colombian liberal, Ezequiel Rojas. With Bolívar in mind – and reflecting on the conspiracy to assassinate the Liberator on September 25, 1828 – Rojas wondered:

> Can the constitutional head of a society that destroys the Constitution and its legitimate government be guilty of high treason? Yes: it is not possible that he is not guilty. If he commits the crime after usurping the sovereign power and investing himself with absolute power, so that there is no law other than his will? Yes: it is not possible that he is not guilty. Should anyone who commits such a crime go unpunished? No: a thousand times no. Is there a moral and legal obligation to obey the leader who usurps public power and who governs without title or right? No: a thousand times no. Are his associates obliged to uphold the Constitution and the legitimately established Government? Yes: they are obliged: all of law imposes it. Are they obliged to suffer the absolute power and tyranny of the usurper? No: no right imposes that obligation. Have they the perfect right to rebel against such a government, destroy it, punish the usurper and reestablish the violated institutions? Yes: a thousand times yes: doing otherwise is not possible. Is it a crime in the eyes of the law or morality, when such an act is executed? No: acting otherwise is not possible.
>
> (Restrepo Piedrahita 1997, vol. 1, 298)

The intense dispute that took place in Colombia, in any case, followed the pattern of conflicts that were already familiar in the region after similar experiences in Venezuela. That is where the tension first intensified between the more radical revolutionaries and the conservative spirit embodied by Bolívar who, in the name of consolidating independence from Spain, sought to join political and military power in a single figure – him.

In fact, the Venezuelan Constitution of 1811 – the first national constitution promulgated in Latin America – was inspired by French revolutionary constitutionalism and included, among its multiple clauses, key articles aimed at avoiding abuses by the executive, articles that seemed addressed to someone whose first name was Simon and last name was Bolívar. Such was the Constitution's repudiation of concentrated power that it ordered the creation of a tripartite executive (three heads of government instead of one), contrary to the trend that began in the United States, where the presidential system established a unipersonal executive and continues to this day. According to Article 72 of the 1811 Venezuelan constitution: "The constitutional Executive Power of the Confederation will reside in the federal city invested in three democratically elected individuals." The Constitution also required, in Article 73, that the heads of government be natives (born in) and current residents (for the past ten years) of Venezuela. These clauses not only demonstrated the constitution's strong anti-presidential attitude but also its pronounced anti-Bolivarian bias (Article 73 was expressly written to make it impossible for Bolívar to take control of the executive).

Such initiatives by his Venezuelan counterparts outraged Bolívar who immediately intensified his attacks on the "Frenchified" radical groups to whom he attributed the language of the first Venezuelan Constitution. Taking advantage of its quick demise (difficulties in consolidating the country's independence as a single nation basically prevented the Constitution from being implemented), Bolívar railed against the 1811 charter, blaming it (I repeat, a Constitution that was never implemented) for the political crisis of the moment. In his famous "Cartagena Manifesto" of 1812, Bolívar wrote: "among the causes that led to the fall of Venezuela, the nature of its constitution must be placed first; I repeat, it was as contrary to its interests as it was favorable to those of its opponents."

Such examples – important public figures looking for alternatives to tyranny; constitutions apparently written to curb Bolívar's presumably despotic ambitions – express, in extreme manner, what many liberals and radicals thought in the early days of Latin America's independent political life. Indeed, after centuries of authoritarian oppression, after years of struggle and sacrifice to put an end, once and for all, to the rule of the Spanish Crown, these figures found unacceptable any political initiative with defects in its republican pedigree. Numerous examples in the decades that followed independence illustrate this sentiment. For example, the Peruvian Constitution of 1823 also adopted – in exceptional circumstances – the tripartite executive. One of the delegates in the constitutional convention, Sánchez Carrión – who would later take a sharp ideological turn and become a minister under Bolívar's dictatorship – justified the tripartite governing board (*junta*) with the quip that three people do not come together in order to oppress. He also declared that "the presence of a single person in command evokes for me the image of the king, that is, a word that implies inherited tyranny" (Basadre 1949, vol. 1, 12). The establishment of weak executives would go on to become a distinctive mark in Peruvian constitutionalism.

Another extraordinary example of the anti-presidential bias of the Latin American liberals and radicals is found in the Colombian Constitution of 1863. Drawn up at the Convention of Ríonegro by the representatives who would later be called the "radical Olympus," the Constitution of 1863 included somewhat unusual clauses, at least compared with current standards, that were unanimously and unequivocally aimed at preventing the concentration of power in the executive. Three of these clauses deserve particular mention. The most extraordinary, Article 65, stated: "The term of those Designated to exercise the Executive Power will be one year, beginning from April 1 following their election." Executives who only spent one year in power! Furthermore, Article 15, dedicated to the fundamental rights of the people, includes notable references in the light of Latin-American history. For example, it enshrined a completely unlimited right to express one's thoughts: defamation did not constitute a crime, nor did personal criticism constitute a "violation of honor." All speech was authorized. Just as notably, it established a robust right to bear arms and ammunition, and to freely trade them. The idea was that an armed society would minimize the risk of concentrated power – authoritarianism could then be resisted, if it materialized – "from below."

These short anecdotes contain several lessons to which we will return. For now, let me just say this: since the inception of independence in Latin America, politicians have learned to brandish democratic discourse that masked authoritarian projects. Moreover, we must remember how, for many long decades, liberals and radicals confronted leaders who – despite their discourse to the contrary – revealed their autocratic inclinations after reaching power. It is also worth remembering, at this juncture, that the conservatives systematically favored initiatives that centralized territorial power and concentrated political power. I point out these facts, which may be of some interest to those interested in the region's history, because they will help us understand worrying institutional developments, ones particularly linked to the presidential system – developments visible in Latin America since its first experiments with constitutional democracy, and ones that today seem evident across much of the world.

10.1 Creating the Leviathan

The thread that runs through this chapter involves the imbalance generated within the system of "checks and balances" by the presence of super-powerful executives (what some have called "hyper-presidentialism" (Nino 1997)). In many of our countries – clearly those in Latin America – the evolution over time of hyper-presidentialism has led to crisis for the entire system of balances conceived by the original liberal constitutional thinkers. Today we find ourselves with institutional systems plagued by limits and controls that have been gradually "dismantled from within," generating a phenomenon that is at once identified as if it were new and also described as "democratic erosion" (a phenomenon which we will explore at the end of this book). Tom Ginsburg and Aziz Huq have rightly recognized that "the most formidable motor of erosion [of the entire institutional system] would be the presidency" (Ginsburg and Huq 2018, 141). This situation, one currently presented as the rule rather than the exception with respect to many modern democracies, should largely (though not exclusively) be seen as an endogenous product of the institutional system, much more than the result of personal pathologies (authoritarian leaders or unenlightened representatives). Moreover, the situation should be seen much less as an unfortunate novelty of our time than as the unfolding expression of, to large extent, a poorly designed institutional system. We are witnessing the slow, unfortunate, coming of age of the Leviathan our constitutional heroes created.

10.2 A Poorly Designed Institutional System

In the constitutional construction of the Leviathan, the example of Latin America is interesting. Not, of course, because that is where "the origin of it all" can be found, but because the case very visibly makes manifest the decision to build a constitutional system centered on the executive, which expressly, from the outset, fought to "break down" the main proposals meant to ensure a "balance" of power. In Latin America, as I will argue, the unfortunate decision was due to what I would call, without hesitation, a major design error.

From the time of independence, enlightened, even brilliant, discussions of constitutional matters have taken place in the region, and a number of interesting institutional mechanisms were conceived. This does not mean, however, that very relevant mistakes were not made, such as the one we are going to review next that relates to a peculiar variation of the "checks and balances" model (an "impure" model, as we shall see). In the United States, meanwhile, the original (or "pure," as I shall call it) design of the "checks and balances" system turned out much more promising, but nevertheless also, and from the outset, open to serious flaws. Basically, and from the "foundational" obsession with the overreach of legislative assemblies at the local level, the systems of checks and balances created were highly skewed against Congress, which was taken as the most threatening institution of all the existing ones. Hence the faith put, somewhat naively, in balancing the power of Congress with a strong executive (in charge of the armed forces and the administration and, thus, a significant portion of the budget). Unfortunately, the executive little by little expanded its authority (as would, by other means, the judiciary), until it attained a threatening degree of control over the entire system. The fact that this model was vulnerable from the beginning to such developments (the self-expansion of the executive and judicial branches) speaks to the limits of the much-revered American model of "checks and balances" that were evident since its formulation. In any case, at least for now, I will stop my sermon here in order to focus momentarily on the description of the imperfect or "impure" model of the Latin-American "checks and balances." As a model of controls it has clearly failed, and has also made abundantly clear, perhaps to the point of exaggeration and from the start, the internal defects embedded in the nucleus of the checks and balance system.

10.3 The Problem with the Pact

Argentine jurist Juan Bautista Alberdi was one of the most important and influential constitutional theorists in Latin America during the "founding" period of his country (1850–1880). He was one of the thinkers who best understood the relevance of constitutional design for the newly independent republics, and he was also one of those who best understood the modes of its operation. However, for different reasons, Alberdi also bears much of the responsibility for the construction of a deeply flawed institutional system – one largely predestined to failure.

After decades of fratricidal warfare, when (in the case of Argentina) the liberal factions seemed to have dealt a definitive blow to the conservative dominance of politics, Alberdi was interested in ensuring the inclusion of conservative leaders in the creation of the "new order." Contrary to many of his compatriots who were more intent on exacting revenge, Alberdi tried to ensure that the emerging "new order" represented some "convergence" between the groups that had clashed for so long.

Almost from the moment of Argentine independence (1810), liberals and conservatives had waged war to the death, exterminating each other in the most brutal fashion. Now, however, after almost half a century, the possibility of finding some common ground between the opposing factions was opening up. This is the moment when, throughout the region, the "liberal-conservative pact" began to take shape, a pact that would leave an indelible mark on the institutional life of all Latin America and one that had been simply unimaginable up to that point.[1]

In some cases (e.g., Argentina in 1853, Mexico in 1857) the pact made it possible to gather the two factions who had been at each other's throats until then (unitary versus federal in Argentina and liberal versus conservative leaders in Mexico) around a table to negotiate a new constitution. In other cases, such as Colombia, reconciliation between liberals and conservatives took place more gradually, only concluding near the end of the century (1886), as the government's liberal policies (which had reached an apex during the mid-nineteenth century presidency of José Hilario López) slowly grew more conservative. In Chile, meanwhile, the "fusion" of liberals and conservatives also occurred towards the end of the nineteenth century, but in this case the process went in the other direction: the country's conservative, authoritarian, and antidemocratic leadership (emblematically represented by the figure of Diego Portales) gradually became more "liberal." Towards the end of the century, this order (which had become the only reliable model for "political stability" in Latin America) entered crisis as it could no longer resist the pressure to give into long-delayed liberal reforms. Regardless of the particular path followed, the profound changes that Latin American societies underwent starting in the middle of the nineteenth century forced changes in the prevailing model of constitutional organization. The pendulum had swung from an original conservative constitutional order, to a liberal one, and then stabilized around a new order that grew out of the pact between liberals and conservatives.[2] I focus now, then, on the case of Argentina, because it is extremely illustrative of the institutional design problem.

[1] The reasons that explain this pact are difficult to unravel, and clarifying them, for the moment, is unnecessary. (Perhaps it was the fear of the arrival of a democratizing wave – a "red wave" – like the one that had occurred in Europe in 1848? Battle fatigue in the face of so many senseless deaths? The maturity – earned at the expense of brutal violence – of a new ruling class? Or that, with time, the conservatives had grown more "liberal" and the liberals more "conservative"?)

[2] The new structure for the "organization of power" that was designed then is basically identical to the one that still exists today in most Latin-American countries. To put it another way: all the constitutions of the region continue to reflect the constitutional form devised at the time: they are all divided into two major sections, one devoted to establishing enumerated rights and the other establishing the rules for the organization of power.

10.4 An "Unbalanced" System of "Checks and Balances": The "Alberdian Error"

The Argentine Constitution of 1853 offers one of the most interesting examples of the new constitutional model that gained momentum in mid-nineteenth century Latin America. It is an apt embodiment of what "liberal-conservative" constitutionalism became in the region. A distinctive product of the pact, the Argentine Constitution attempted to combine the aspirations of both factions in every clause. As we will see, adequately combining claims of rival groups in the same text is not a simple task.

In Argentina, as in so many Latin-American countries, instead of coming to agreement on one set of norms, the claims of the groups previously in conflict were bundled/accumulated, granting part of the demands of one group and part of the other's (we will return to the problem of "bundling" with greater detail). The result was, in this case as in many others, ill-fated. This is because what one group wanted was habitually contradicted, directly or to a large degree, by the constitutional vision inserted into the text by the other group. As a result, constitutions with deep internal tensions were created.

The most visible manifestation of this tension can be found in the scheme for organizing power. There, the exemplary Argentine Constitution ended up crudely, if not brutally, combining the United States' scheme of checks and balances with the model of authoritarian presidentialism that was developed in Chile; this was the model that, as we noted, had gained recognition across the region as the only "successful" standard of political stability in the nineteenth century.

The main representative of Alberdi's ideas in the Argentine Constituent Convention was Benjamin Gorostiaga. During the debates, Gorostiaga described the Argentine constitutional model as "cast in the mold of the Constitution of the United States, the only model of a true federation that exists in the world." At the same time, however, the constituents followed Alberdi's advice regarding the organization of the executive. In this regard, Alberdi's directives were clear. As Alberdi explained in his most important book, *Bases*, concerning the part of the Constitution related to presidential powers, "our Spanish-Argentine Constitution must be separated from the example of the federal Constitution of the United States," to emulate instead the Chilean model, which endowed the "executive power [with] the means of enforce respect [for the Constitution] with the efficiency of a dictatorship." He added, as to leave no doubt: "Time has shown that

Chile's solution is the only rational one for republics that were monarchies shortly before" (Alberdi 1981, ch. 25).

The presence of a strong president was essential in the phase that was beginning, Alberdi believed, to avoid repeating the errors which Latin American liberalism had traditionally made. Alberdi was very familiar with these mistakes. Time and again, when the Liberals replaced the Conservatives in power, they opted for a system of robust freedoms while weakening and restricting the power of the authorities in order to avoid authoritarian relapses. The result, time and again, was that each time liberalism succeeded conservatism in power, it quickly succumbed to the wear and tear of its exercise. Lacking the tools to endure the attrition or repair the damage, the liberal regimes promptly lost power.

With these antecedents in mind, Alberdi wrote, thinking about the new Constitution and the difficult history that preceded it:

> Regarding its energy and vigor, the executive power must have all the powers made necessary by past events, for the conditions of the country, and the greatness of the purpose for which it was instituted. Otherwise, government will exist in name, but not in reality; and if there is no government, the constitution cannot exist, that is, there can be neither order, nor freedom, nor the Argentine Confederation.

This is where the Chilean model comes up as an alternative. In Alberdi's opinion, "Chile has shown that between the absolute lack of government and dictatorial government, regular government is possible; that of a constitutional president who can assume the powers of a king whenever anarchy disobeys his republican authority as president." Let me underscore that last part: what Argentina needed was "*a constitutional president who can assume the powers of a king whenever anarchy disobeys his republican authority as president.*"

The combination proposed by Alberdi, then, was based on the model of "checks and balances" adopted in the United States and the authoritarian model proposed first by Juan Egaña (in Chile's 1823 Constitution) and then by his son Mariano (a decisive figure in the debates over the 1833 Chilean Constitution). That is how Argentina – as eventually almost all the other Latin-American countries – ended up granting the executive much broader "additional powers" than those of the expressly presidential US Constitution itself.

Emulating the Chilean model, the Constitution of Argentina grants the President, among other powers, the power to declare a state of siege, during which "constitutional guarantees" are suspended in that "province or territory where there is a disturbance of order" (Article 23), the power to deploy federal troops to restore order by virtue of the government's republican nature (Article 6), and the power to appoint and remove government ministers at his or her discretion (Article 86). These special powers (through the state of siege, federal intervention, etc.) reserved to the President have allowed different authors (i.e., Carlos Nino) to refer to this specific political regime as *hyper*-presidentialism.

At least judging by current standards, it seems clear that the system that took form then, in terms of its organization of power, was "mortally wounded" from the beginning. How could the proposal of a disproportionately strong executive be squared with a system that seeks to organize itself around checks and balances? I believe that the problem should be clear in the eyes of people living in the present day (although I am not sure the question itself is "obviously" clear), but I would like to say something even more forceful. What I mean is that the problem should have been obvious even in the mid-nineteenth century: even back then it should have been clearly recognized that the attempt to organize power combining those two models was misguided.

Sometimes I imagine what two of the great constitutional thinkers of the era, James Madison and Juan Bautista Alberdi, would have talked about had they met. In my daydream, each is familiar with the other's work and there was ample opportunity for each to clarify their points and correct the other. In particular, with regard to the place of the executive within the "checks and balances" framework, I think Madison would have urged Alberdi to introduce drastic modifications to his model. He would have asked Alberdi:

> How can you begin to combine these two antagonistic proposals? The logic of checks and balances requires powers of mutual control. Each branch must have comparable strength to put in check the others. The legislature must fear the executive's veto power; the executive and legislature must fear judicial review; the executive and judiciary must fear Congress, which has the ability to impeach the president and amend laws that sideline the judiciary, and so on. Above all, the power of each branch of government over the others must be roughly proportional if not equivalent. Otherwise ambition, as I said, cannot be counted on to counteract ambition. It is therefore unacceptable that the firepower of one of the branches of government be vastly superior to that of the others. In that case, the equilibrium of the entire structure is lost and the system of checks and balances breaks down. The entire logic of the system falls apart.

In other words, Alberdi's model tried, on the one hand, to put in place a system of "checks and balances" like the one used in the United States while, on the other hand, he devised an all-powerful executive following the Chilean constitutional tradition. This composite model of "impure" mutual controls on one side is contradicted by the exaggerated power of the executive. Can anyone be surprised, then, when the system of "checks and balances" immediately breaks down? Can anyone be surprised in the face of this inevitable breakdown? Would anyone argue that they do not understand why the different parts of the control system begin to erode or are destroyed by improper encroachments by the executive, one by one, as soon as the system begins to operate?

10.5 The Political Left and Presidentialism

I would like to conclude this chapter as I began it; that is, thinking about certain details in the history of Latin-American political-constitutional thought in a new light. If we paid attention to what was said at the beginning of this chapter, and then observe the consolidation and spread of the strong presidentialist or hyper-presidentialist models across Latin America, we would see at least one unexpected anomaly. At the beginning of the chapter, we briefly pointed out an attitude that seemed common among Latin American liberals and radicals: they all identified conservatism as the "enemy" and believed the concentration of power was a necessary component of conservative mindset. That is why they designed so many, often extreme responses, to combat the stubborn return of conservative priorities – from one-year presidential terms, tripartite executives, powerful legislatures, to – surprisingly – expressly justifying the constitutional grounds of tyrannicide!

As the pages went by, we saw how, after a while, the political situation changed in this regard. For reasons that are not obvious liberals and conservatives came to an agreement in the middle of the nineteenth century (perhaps, we suggested, fearing the advance of the nascent European strand of radicalism in the Americas). At that point, liberals and conservatives began to come around and reinforce the many elements they had in common (concern for order over anarchy, particular protections for certain rights, such as property). In the process, they pushed aside or left in abeyance the differences that had kept them at each other's throats for decades (especially their differences over the concentration of power and the role of the Catholic Church in government).

Latin-American radicals habitually remained opposed to conservatism because of their extreme disagreement over political matters: the radicals took as a fundamental assumption the sovereignty of the people, while the conservatives apparently distrusted democratic principles just as fundamentally. This disagreement was effectively translated into the preference of the former for more horizontal and inclusive forms of government (expanded political rights, stricter controls on representatives, popular assemblies), while the latter insisted on the more vertical and exclusive forms of government (strong restrictions on the rights to vote or run for office, concentrated government powers, hyper-presidentialism). The differences were obvious: one side preferred horizontal and inclusive organization of power; the other a vertical and exclusive one.

Occasionally, because of the resistance that certain versions of liberalism provoked in both groups (radicals and conservatives), bridges between them were established (the close collaboration between the republican Pedro de Ángelis and Juan Manuel de Rosas in Argentina is a good example). Radicals and conservatives alike were suspicious of the liberal obsession with individual rights (in particular, the rights of freedom of religion and expression), and in some cases the two factions came together to "tear down" the "wall of separation" that the liberals erected between the State and individuals through a list of rights.[3] In any case, however, the bridges between republicans and conservatives were scarce, clearly more of an exception to the general rule of the antagonistic relationship between them.

In this framework – resistance, mutual distrust, hostility, suspicion of bad faith, violence – the evolution of Latin-American radical thought is surprising, particularly since the early- to mid-twentieth century. This was the political group that had fought hardest against hyper-presidentialism, to the point of endorsing assassination, the faction that had stood up to the model of concentrated power demanding the return of power "to the people," the force that had opposed liberalism, scorning their obsession with declarations of rights. It is surprising, then, that the radicals ended up turning their backs on their previous identity, throwing out their most established convictions, and beginning the twentieth century by embracing a program almost indistinguishable from the one their enemies had advanced.

[3] It should be noted, however, that conservatives were primarily opposed to liberalism because of its perfectionist, moralizing, and authoritarian project. The radicals, meanwhile, opposed liberals because of their indifference to material conditions. The radicals believed adequately addressing the "social question" urgently required redistributive reforms, rather than any new list of rights.

The most notable aspect of this stark turnaround involved their progressive, uncritical adherence to the ideals of concentrated power (for an interesting analysis in this regard, see Dyzenhaus 2004). Fed up, perhaps, by so many failed democratic initiatives, or seduced by the apparent opening for urgent reforms that they had long sought, many radicals switched, from one moment to the next, in one movement on a command from above, aligning themselves unconditionally and without question with authoritarian leaders in exchange for the leaders' promise to carry out their primary demands (i.e., from Juan Domingo Perón, to Getulio Vargas, Fidel Castro, Hugo Chávez). They justified their decision with, for example, the argument that the "control of power" discourse, concern for balance among the government branches, or protections against abuses of power amounted to formalistic excuses, bourgeois concerns, and empty legalisms. Unfortunately, as history would show time and again, those who tasted absolute power often became unwilling to democratize it, especially after realizing the benefits afforded by the position they had attained. The radicals frequently ended up defending what they previously condemned, while they waited indefinitely for the changes they had been promised.[4]

I will stop here, having noted the importance and abruptness of the ideological or strategical shifts in Latin-American radical thinking – the political left – and having posed the question, still open, of what exactly it is that explains or justifies them.

[4] In other common cases, as we shall see, the radicals opted for another path, one that was also incongruent with their traditional position: seeking social change through the consecration of new rights. These radicals became experts in the struggle for new social, economic, cultural, multicultural, and human rights. They specialized in enumerating, advocating, demanding, judicializing, litigating, and adjudicating them, in order to render them operational. In this sense, their aspiration for equality, social justice, and the welfare of the most disadvantaged was channeled into the formal, legalistic path that they had habitually repudiated for so many years. Later we will return to this shift, its implications and its limits.

11

Rights

Citizenship As Repository of Rights

"The mass of the citizens is the safest depository of their own rights."

Letter from Thomas Jefferson to John Taylor, 1816.

I want to devote this chapter to the idea of "rights" that occupies such a central, perhaps even the most important role within modern constitutionalism. In particular I want to reflect on the tensions that arise between the conception of rights and that of democracy itself. To begin the reflection, I am going to start with one of the foundational texts on the subject by the English philosopher John Locke in which he refers to the meaning and importance of the idea of "rights" – the rights that belong to each and every one of us equally – in association with the notion as controversial as it has become influential – of natural rights.

In his *Second Treatise on Civil Government*, written in 1689, Locke discussed, among other subjects, the principles that should organize civil government. In particular, he emphasized that all people were born "equal" in at least one important sense. He argued that everyone was born with certain "natural," inalienable rights: rights that no one had the power to grant or to deny anyone else. These are rights given by God to each person. Locke then spoke of three fundamental rights: the right to life, liberty, and property (estate). Ultimately, these rights made it possible to understand the mission of every civil government – the government's main task being the protection of those rights – and also facilitated recognition of the principles that should structure political life.

Locke elaborated and expressed his thoughts with the specific purpose of refuting another influential thinker of his time, Robert Filmer. In his well-known work *Patriarcha*, Filmer had defended a vision contrary to the one that Locke would defend. Indeed, Filmer held a "patriarchal" view of power according to which the king was authorized to exercise his power without any regard for the will of the governed, like a father's dominion over his children. Alarmed by this view, Locke set out to refute it. The four central claims presented by Locke in his attack against Filmer were:

(i) There exist certain inalienable rights (life, liberty, property);
(ii) The first duty of the government is to protect the inalienable rights of the people;
(iii) Authority is legitimate to the extent that it rests on the consensus of the governed;
(iv) The people have the right to resist and overthrow any government that does not properly respect their basic rights.

The principles set forth by Locke on that occasion left an imprint on the political thought of the Western world that can still be seen. Within them are ideas that many have repeated in an original or modified fashion, ideas that others have bitterly rejected, and ideas that have been taken up more or less explicitly in many contexts – in any case, the ideas have proven difficult to ignore from the moment they were first formulated.

Surely, the most extraordinary "journey" of Locke's ideas to other lands and other contexts is the passage it made to "the other side of the Atlantic," since Locke's writings had a direct and explosive impact in the thirteen colonies during the revolutionary movement. As is well-known, the American Declaration of Independence, originally written by Thomas Jefferson, reproduced almost verbatim the ideology advanced by Locke. That is to say, one of the most influential documents ever written, one of the most cited manifestos in the history of the Western world, explicitly and openly reiterated principles from Locke's *Second Treatise*. The American "Declaration of Independence" begins by affirming:

> *We hold such truths self-evident: that all men are created equal; that they are endowed by their Creator with certain inalienable rights; that among these are Life, Freedom and the pursuit of Happiness. That to guarantee these rights, governments are instituted among men, deriving their legitimate powers from the consent of the governed; that whenever a form of government becomes destructive of these principles, the people have the right to reform it, or abolish it, and to institute a new government that is based on said principles*, and organizing its powers in such form, as to them shall seem most likely to effect their Safety and Happiness. Prudence, indeed, will dictate that Governments long established should not be changed for light and transient causes; and accordingly all experience hath shewn, that mankind are more disposed to suffer, while evils are sufferable, than to right themselves by abolishing the forms to which they are accustomed. But when a long train of abuses and usurpations, pursuing invariably the same Object evinces a design to reduce them under

> absolute Despotism, it is their right, it is their duty, to throw off such Government, and to provide new Guards for their future security.
>
> (italics added)

If we compare the four fundamental ideas presented by Locke to the heart of Jefferson's "Declaration of Independence" (italicized in the above quote), we immediately recognize the amazing similarity of the two texts. The essential core of this set of ideas, which occupies such an important role in modern thought, is not only the premise that all people have certain rights, but also that these rights are *natural* and *self-evident*. The relevance and impact of this notion warrants pause for reflection.

11.1 Natural and Self-Evident Rights: Rights As "Planets"

The conception of rights expressed in the United States "Declaration of Independence" taken from Locke resonated in many other contexts (including, especially, the Latin American context). For this reason, it makes sense to explore in some detail how the texts themselves relate to the ensuing discussion that continues to this day. I will focus, in particular, on two interrelated questions I consider fundamental that derived from what has already been said.

From Where Do Rights Derive Their Strength? The first fact I would like to remark is that the idea of rights, which has represented one of the articulating axes of every constitution and which is manifested in the basic claims made on every government – the idea of inviolable, inalienable, unconditional, undeniable rights – rests on dark and elusive foundations. These rights are – Locke argued – what God gives everyone. But what does that mean? What precisely is it that God gives us, and how do we recognize it? "Don't worry" – the American "Declaration" seems to answer – "these are self-evident truths, which we all recognize." Self-evident truths, we may ask ourselves? What exactly might those be? How do we recognize them? Rights seem to rest on, unfortunately, an elusive foundation that we are told is ours but that slip through our fingers when we try to grasp them. They are rights that should be recognizable just by thinking about them, but that are fleeting: they disappear in front of our gaze. That is how serious they are.

A curious notion of rights took root then that continues to the present. Rights are conceived somewhat the same way as planets in space. They are out there, out of reach, regulating our lives, waiting for us to "discover" them. Rights like planets that are removed from any process of human creation. Rights are like planets that we are able to visualize with the proper tools (lenses, telescopes, or other technical equipment). We think of rights as if they are in no way a product of our democratic life – they are neither the product of our imagination, of our contemplation, of our legislative volition (rights – in Locke's words – cannot be granted or denied by governments). Notwithstanding, rights are called upon to wholly regulate our democratic lives, establishing inviolable limits.

Here are some initial indications that reveal the nature of the problem we are facing. In an earlier draft of the "Declaration," in referring to "natural rights" Jefferson did not appeal to the idea of "self-evident truths" (which was what was added to the final version), but instead to the idea of "sacred and undeniable" rights, which also happens to resonate in perfect harmony with Locke. In edits Benjamin Franklin made to that initial draft of the "Declaration," Franklin introduced the idea of "self-evident truths," which he felt gave even more force to the idea of "natural rights." (Franklin also intended to reinforce the reference to Locke by the change, but Locke actually spoke of "self-evident truths" in a narrower sense that was not directly linked to "natural rights.") So our first problem is that the drafters sought to give added strength to an idea (that of "natural rights") that will indeed require extraordinary force to stand up (enough to support the affirmation that the government must devote all of its energy to protecting them?), but at the same time they were looking for support in theoretical appeals that are difficult to grasp and recognize.

Let us look at a significant manifestation of this problem, which comes to us through an anecdote that is as entertaining as it is disturbing. Jefferson is at work writing the first draft of the "Declaration." He decides to follow, neatly and carefully, Locke's example. He puts down: "that all men are created equal; that they are endowed by their Creator with certain inalienable rights; that among these are Life, Liberty and Property." Jefferson takes a break to rest. On reflection, a doubt comes to him. He asks himself: "Property?" He cannot shake it: "Property, really? Is property really one of the three most important rights?" He keeps thinking. After a while Jefferson shakes his head: "It cannot be." He erases that "property," and comes up with another, the idea that would be forever recorded in the final version of the "Declaration of Independence." Jefferson thus pens what would become the final version of that line of the "Declaration": "that all men are created equal; that they are endowed by their Creator with certain inalienable rights; that among these are Life, Liberty and *the pursuit of Happiness*" (emphasis added).

The idea of "property," which played such a crucial role in Locke's theory (you could say that everything he wrote was meant to justify nearly absolute protection to property rights), vanishes. The notion of "property" has been replaced by that of "pursuit of Happiness." Possessing a right to "happiness," a fundamental right to it that would be protected by the government, seems excellent. Yet something else is at stake, something altogether different. What matters is this: Jefferson, one of the most influential thinkers in the history of mankind, and one of the most influential developers of the notion of "natural rights" that we still carry with us, is working on his list of *self-evident* natural rights (or, which boils down to the same thing, "sacred and inalienable" natural rights). He jots down the first two of those rights in absolute serenity (we can picture him: "Life . . . without a doubt! . . . Freedom . . . of course!"), but when he gets to the third one, doubt sinks in, a doubt so deep that he changes his mind, erasing "property" and replacing it with the tantalizing but elusive idea of "the pursuit of happiness." "Wait a minute" – we might ask ourselves – "weren't these rights supposed to be natural and self-evident?" Yes, they were supposed to be "self-evident," but as soon as we began to think about them, the right vanishes, and we start to think maybe it isn't self-evident. Although we parade them as "self-evident" rights, one of the most important figures in the history of their theorization does not even finish writing them down before he is overcome with doubt. The anecdote, which you may find trivial, clearly reveals fascinating and radical facets of the problems associated with the idea of "natural and self-evident rights," the idea around which, ever since, we have tried to structure our coexistence – the idea that is still called upon to define the main mission of government. Natural rights may well be "self-evident," but perhaps not as much as we would like.

"Self-Evident" Rights, But to Whom? There is another question, intimately connected with the previous one, that might help us comprehend the type of problem in which we find ourselves. I recently pointed out that "natural rights" claim for themselves extraordinary strength that is justified – as those who first invoked them claimed – by the fact that "we all easily recognize them." I just suggested, however, that this certainty – which seems obvious today – is far from true: we tend to disagree strongly over which rights are the most fundamental (we saw what happened when Jefferson tried to pen "his" list).

I want to move to a related topic now, one that has to do with the question of the person who actually sees, perceives, recognizes, or comes up with the "self-evident" rights. Locke referred to a notion of "self-evident truths" as those truths that did not require complex reasoning to understand: they were so clear that they were presented as maxims or even axioms, like principles irrefutably proven long ago by science. Jefferson, for his part, seems to have taken an even more "popular" approach to the notion of "self-evident" principles. Apparently, his notion of "self-evident truths" was influenced by the work of a philosopher from Geneva, Jean Jacques Burlamaqui (who was the first to articulate the idea of "pursuit of happiness" that Jefferson would incorporate into the "Declaration"). Burlamaqui radicalized the sense of "self-evident" that appeared in Locke: for Burlamaqui "self-evident" meant rights that were directly evident, evident to anyone.

However, this disagreement over the definition of "self-evident" represents the core of a very serious problem: is it really about "self-evident" rights for all? Note, in this sense, an extreme escalation of the difficulty that was subtly incorporated into the "The Federalist Papers" by the conservative Alexander Hamilton, specifically in No. 31, an apparently abstract, philosophical, speculative text. In it, Hamilton referred to "self-evident truths" proposing a new approach:

> There are certain primary truths, or first principles, upon which all subsequent reasonings must depend. These contain an internal evidence which, antecedent to all reflection or combination, commands the assent of the mind. Where it produces not this effect, it must proceed either from some defect or disorder in the organs of perception, or from the influence of some strong interest, or passion, or prejudice.

Hamilton seems to take here a crucial, decisive step out of the world of "self-evident to anyone" that Burlamaqui or Jefferson evoked. In Hamilton, rather, we read an approach much more in line with the elitist theoretical ideology typical of many Federalists. According to this theoretical approach, widely shared among the participants of the US Constitutional Convention, the political capacities of the great majority could not really be trusted because the ordinary citizens' reason was clouded: crude interest blinded the discerning eye of reason, in much the same way the passions were believed to prevent them from making reasonable political decisions. According to Hamilton, then, many ordinary citizens would presumably be unable to recognize these "self-evident truths" because they suffered from "some disorder or defect in the perceptual organs" or were blinded by their selfish interests. Ultimately, this is the same argument that Madison himself clearly advanced in many of his writings (we saw, for example, what Madison wrote in The

Federalist No. 55: "in all very numerous assemblies, of whatever character composed, passion never fails to wrest the sceptre from reason"). It is worth emphasizing and remembering this idea, which Madison presented – as he so often did – with the conviction of a mathematical deduction and the rigor of a law of nature: in *every* large assembly (the ones where ordinary citizens make up the majority), passion (irrational behavior) will prevail.

The discussion up to this point should make clear the significance of Hamilton's precision in the Federalist No. 31, why his understanding to "self-evident" truths was so common among the leadership of the time, and why it is so worrying. From one moment to the next, without much clarification, he adopts the idea of the "primary truths" upon which all the rest of the theoretical construction of the constitution would depend, introducing a major, decisive adjustment. All of a sudden, those principles "on which all the reasoning that must follow" are not nearly as "self-evident." In his account, there is room to believe that a good portion of the population will not be able to perceive them. Hamilton tells us this is because "there is some disorder or defect in the perceptual organs." In the end, the apparent explanation – he adds – has to do with "some great interest, passion or prejudice" which affects most people, but not all.

This vision of rights, based on the demanding and controversial conception of "natural rights," would exert its influence up to the present day. Many of the most important jurists of our time, in fact, seem to subscribe, more or less explicitly, to the "natural rights" approach. The extraordinarily influential reading that the philosopher Ronald Dworkin proposed of rights – comparing rights to "trump cards" – represents a current and sophisticated version of the natural rights tradition. Later, we will return to this tradition and related approaches in order to examine its influence and implications.

11.2 Bentham and the Idea of "Natural Rights" As "Nonsense upon Stilts"

As I understand it, the idea of "natural rights," or at least the conception of them that has its roots in that idea, became and has remained dominant ever since. This approach, which was clearly the one subscribed to during the "founding moment" of United States constitutionalism, found its place in US Constitution. That vision, I would add, was also adopted in Latin American constitutionalism, and we continue to find it, as we will see, in doctrinal studies and juridical arguments in contemporary legal literature. In fact, recourse to it tends to prevail in the disputes that endow law with meaning.

However, I would like to acknowledge, before moving on, very different approaches to the same question, ones that appeared at around the same time Locke's theories were gaining popularity. As we will see, an alternative vision began to develop at almost the same moment in which the vision of "natural rights" was erected, a contrary vision which sought to reject Locke's argument outright. In this view, whose main proponent was Jeremy Bentham, the very notion of "natural rights" was complete rubbish, or "nonsense upon stilts," as Bentham famously wrote.

Bentham elaborated his critical position in "Anarchical Fallacies," an essay written between 1791 and 1795, but not published until 1816. In it he harshly attacked the "Declaration of the Rights of Man and the Citizen" adopted by the French National Assembly shortly after the French Revolution. Bentham argued that the idea of "natural rights" employed by the French manifesto was elusive, evasive, and susceptible to impermissible abuse and excess, such as those that occurred during "The Terror" after the French Revolution (a revolution that, in other ways, Bentham supported). That is why he described the notion of rights in such harsh terms as a "perversion of language," an "ambiguous," "sentimental" idea that promised "anarchic consequences."

For Bentham, what it was important to recognize was that rights are created by law, and law is the product of the sovereign will. That is why it could not be said, as Locke did, that rights could not be granted or denied, or that they derived from God, and that is why it was impossible to speak, as the French manifesto did, of a "natural" origin of rights. Rights were *created* – they were the product of laws – and thus did not pre-exist government. As Bentham remarkably declared in reference to property rights (in his work "Theory of Legislation"): "Property and law are born together, and die together. Before laws were made there was no property; take away laws, and property ceases."

Bentham's approach to rights runs directly counter to the idea of "natural rights" expressed by Locke and the most influential theorists of the French and American Revolutions. Fortunately, this alternative tradition also has influenced constitutional thinking – although I assume much less forcefully – up to the present day. Take as an interesting example – one of particular relevance to the discussion of Latin American constitutionalism – a book written by Carlos Nino on the subject, *Ethics and Human Rights* (Nino 1991). The book literally opens, in the first line, by staking out an approach contrary to that of "natural rights," one that also understands rights as merely products of human creation: "Undoubtedly, human rights are among the great inventions of our civilization" (Nino 1991, 1). In other words, Nino was saying, when we speak of rights, we are talking above all else about something "invented," that is, a collective creation.

I chose the example of Nino because he had a fairly significant impact in Latin America, but I could have chosen many others. I could have referred, for example, to the constitutionalist Cass Sunstein's statement – in an interesting book on social rights – that "rights must be understood as instruments designed to protect the most important human interests" (Sunstein 2006, 203). Sunstein's vision (aligned with what is known as the "interest theory" of rights) reflects something similar to what Nino said: rights should not be understood as "natural," "pre-political," or "pre-governmental." On the contrary, when we speak of rights we must speak of them as human creations – in the end, as mere instruments that we have devised because they help us better protect the things that matter most to us.[1]

Lastly, we could describe rights, according to this alternative tradition, as human creations destined to address the most serious tragedies faced in times past. After a period of autocratic government, people resolved to create the first "Declaration of Rights," establishing liberal rights intended to protect our lives and our most basic freedoms, erecting a protective barrier against the risk of repeated abuses. The memory and fear of abuse of power move us to do what we can to prevent future abuse. They move us to affirm, constitutionally, certain human interests (life, freedom of opinion, freedom of thought, physical integrity, etc.) that are of utmost importance to us. Formulating a list of rights (liberal rights, in this case), represents a way of declaring publicly (typically through a constitution) that we have learned from history and past experience that we have a propensity to commit certain unacceptable abuses of power, and that we want to make it clear that we want to protect certain fundamental interests, abused in the past, in the most meaningful way that we can.

Similarly, the social rights that constitutions began to incorporate into their texts after the Mexican Revolution of 1910 can also be read as

[1] Another contemporary philosopher, Thomas Scanlon, takes a similar but more refined approach. For him, rights should not be seen as "natural" for that implies they are alien to human designs. On the contrary, in Scanlon's opinion, the claim that someone has a right (Scanlon is discussing moral rights, rather than legal ones) means engaging in reasoning completely dependent on empirical and historical considerations of the type: "What would happen if there were no such barrier (meaning the right in question)?" "How would individuals and institutions tend to act if they weren't faced with such limitations?" (Scanlon 1984).

a direct response to impermissible abuses. Including social rights in the constitution conveyed the message that the extreme social injustice that had been the norm for decades were now recognized as unacceptable. At the same time, the revised lists of rights also publicly recognized previously neglected interests (ones left off the "old" lists of rights or "first generation rights") that were now to be highly protected. The same occurred with the newest (or "third generation") rights, such as environmental and multicultural rights.

Finally, the human rights that many countries have more recently incorporated into their constitution (or endowed with "supra-legal" status) represent a response to the tragedy of massive human rights violations, genocide, and mass extermination. Once again, giving legal recognition to these rights offered a way of expressing loudly and clearly – in a public declaration of commitment – our recognition of the extraordinary gravity of such violations and our intent to defend as basic qualities of humanity rights that protect against torture, forced disappearance, and other atrocities.

11.3 Rights versus Democracy

At this point, we might ask why this dispute, which was so important and which started so long ago in the seventeenth century, is still unresolved. Is the dispute relevant to what we are going through, to the way we organize ourselves today? I have no doubt that it is, and that it holds extremely pertinent insights. First of all, as I will argue, the dispute in question is crucial to an issue of extraordinary importance: I am referring to the relationship between the idea of rights and that of democracy.

I want to begin the analysis with reference to fundamental conflicts faced every day that reveal, from their surface to their deepest level, the relevance of our understanding of the relationship between democracy and rights, which in turn brings us back to our understanding of the idea of the rights themselves. If, for example, we take for granted the idea of rights as "natural rights," then we will tend to say, along with Locke, that any question over rights must be outside the control of any government. The response to the conflict in question would "precede" government and be "pre-political" – independent of anyone's will. If, on the other hand, we start from a vision like Bentham's, we will tend to respond the way he talked, for example, about property rights: the "right" is born and dies with the law, so if the law changes, the right changes too. Clearly, then, the seemingly abstract and distant theoretical discussion is absolutely relevant to current, concrete social conflicts and tensions. Allow me to illustrate my affirmation with some examples.

For the purpose of illustrating what is at stake, imagine, for example, South Africa after the end of apartheid. The government, to respond to the aberrant crimes committed by the outgoing regime, decides to exchange "truth for justice" and consequently "reward" with an amnesty those accused of crimes who are willing to confess what they did and where the bodies of those they killed are buried. The government could justify its decision to pardon cruel murderers, for example, by arguing that what the relatives of the victims want above all is to know where the bodies of their relatives are buried, and they know the more traditional response to such crimes – criminal prosecution – will motivate the perpetrators to remain silent; to avoid conviction, no one will confess. The government's "deal" could be considered impermissible by some people depending on their idea of "rights." For example, people who subscribe to the idea of "natural rights" might protest that national and international law requires that crimes be tried and convicted. They would argue that these basic questions about criminal guarantees are independent of anyone's political will – be it the will of a majority of voters or of the government in office. These people would believe the truth and reconciliation policy was simply unavailable for the government to pursue, since the question exclusively concerned the rights of the victims to justice.

Let us take but another important example of capital gravity, also involving actual developments in the recent past. In Colombia, after many decades of armed conflict and laborious negotiations, a peace agreement was signed between the government and some of the insurrectionary organizations – groups responsible for atrocious crimes that had been in hiding. The terms of the agreement generate enormous controversy, so in order to bestow it with democratic legitimacy, the government decides to submit it for approval by the people through a vote. Again, depending on one's conception of rights, one might consider the government's proposal (organize a process of collective consultation to determine whether or not the majority of citizens supports the agreement) as reasonable or, on the contrary, find the government's behavior completely impermissible. In this sense, for example, the renowned Italian jurist Luigi Ferrajoli – famous for his firm position on legal guarantees and defense of a legal position in the "natural rights" tradition – expressed strong opposition to the Colombian government's initiative. He emphatically proclaimed that the right to peace cannot be put to a vote. The decision was, in his opinion, unavailable to any government and therefore absolutely outside the discretion of the majority.

Through examples such as these, we see how an apparently abstract theoretical controversy has concrete and dramatic repercussions for fundamental questions of daily politics. From a position anchored in the tradition of "natural rights," certain legal questions of immediate importance can be considered outside the realm of politics – beyond, as we shall see, the "sphere of democracy." Meanwhile, from a position anchored in the opposite conception – rights as purely legal creations – the controversies in question (granting amnesty, entering into a peace agreement) appear as eminently democratic issues.

11.4 Rights As "Trump Cards" against Majorities

I have already acknowledged my judgment that the conception of rights currently dominant – at least in the American context – is rooted in the "natural rights" tradition. Now I would like to demonstrate the weight and implications of this tradition on the present through the work of contemporary jurists who have also been directly involved in the discussion of public issues of primary importance (which will help us to recognize the significance, relevance, and implications of their arguments).

I begin with brief references to the arguments of Ronald Dworkin, one of the most important legal philosophers of the last fifty years. Dworkin's theory, as I understand it, has not attained majority support among scholars despite its incontrovertibly enormous influence, but I have chosen it anyway because it provides one of the most sophisticated, current visions of the democracy-rights relationship from the tradition rooted in the notion of "natural rights."

Among the many lessons from Dworkin's "legacy" of decades of reflection on a wide range of issues in the theory of law, perhaps the best-known is his likening of rights to "trump cards." According to Dworkin's analogy, a right is like the ace of spades that trumps all the other cards in the deck. Dworkin used this metaphor to reflect on the relationship between fundamental rights and democratic politics, or, more precisely, between individual rights and collective objectives. Dworkin's position was clearly anti-utilitarian (Bentham, for example, was a utilitarian, that is, someone who believed that rights should serve the achievement of general objectives, collective benefits). Dworkin's anti-utilitarian vision was based on the affirmation of a fundamental principle that ran through all of Dworkin's academic work: the principle of equality (or, more precisely, as he immediately elaborated, a fundamental "right to equal concern and respect" (Dworkin 1977, 180, 182, 227).

A real-life example of Dworkin's analogy can be found during the Vietnam War. At this point in the mid-twentieth century, the US government made many general, global decisions (including censorship, compulsory military service, deploying troops, and so on) that challenged or disregarded certain individual rights. From his first writings, Dworkin defended the rights of those who protested against the war, the rights of conscientious objectors, and the right to civil disobedience. In all these cases, Dworkin's position could be synthesized through the trump card analogy: the persecuted individuals, in each case, held "trump cards" (their rights to expression, freedom of conscience, etc.) that beat the government's cards – the "general objectives" or "policies" that justified the draft, censorship, etc. If people in society did not recognize the greater value of protestors' cards (the individual rights at stake), it was because they reasoned from a degraded, unacceptable (ultimately utilitarian) vision of law and rights. In the view of rights as "trump cards," then, having a right means saying that one holds a "winning card" that cannot be overcome by generalities such as collective benefits, public policy, the general interest, and common good.

I wanted to offer examples like these because I think they help make Dworkin's position more sympathetic and bring out the more attractive side of the "natural rights" tradition. In any case, and before taking up another prominent jurist's work within that tradition, I would like to anticipate a serious problem that I see in positions such as Dworkin's – a problem that we have actually already encountered in this book. Many and maybe even most of my readers might very well agree with Dworkin's position in relation to the Vietnam War and the value of free speech, even or especially in a time of war, and the right of the citizens to protest against the war. The problem is that the "legal solution" offered to the conflicts mentioned, while it may even seem clear, falls well short of being self-evident. We have to remember and acknowledge the problem inherent to the notion of "self-evident" rights, meaning we have to ask what those "self-evident" rights are, and who has the authority to determine them (maybe the judges?). To put it another way: if there is any distinguishing feature of public life in societies like ours, it is not consensus, but rather disagreement; this is, in Jeremy Waldron's apt expression, the "fact of disagreement" (Waldron 1999). In circumstances where there are deep and reasonable disagreements over values, insisting on the idea of rights as "trump cards" presents a serious problem. As Waldron (a long-time colleague of Dworkin's with whom he repeatedly clashed) might say: it would be fantastic if people agreed broadly and extensively about the most difficult and important issues, and thus were able to mediate and solve all conflicts encountered through the consecration of forcefully definitive and unchallengeable solutions. Unfortunately, however, we disagree. We do not agree on what is important. We do not agree on the proper way to frame the major social conflicts that we encounter. We do not agree on the values that our society should prioritize. In this context of deep disagreement, the criterion of rights as "trump cards" becomes part of the problem, not the solution.

11.5 Rights and the "Sphere of the Undecidable"

A less sophisticated and interesting version (in my opinion) of the "natural rights" tradition, but one just as influential as Dworkin's theory of rights, is that of the Italian jurist Ferrajoli, whom we have already mentioned. Where Dworkin's arguments exerted enormous influence in Anglo-Saxon circles, Ferrajoli's position continues to have great influence in the Latinate and Spanish-American ones.

Even more radically than Dworkin, Ferrajoli distinguishes two different domains or "spheres" within the legal discipline. The first – the *sphere of the undecidable* – is where fundamental rights and guarantees operate, while the second – the *sphere of the decidable* – is the sphere of democratic decision-making. The two spheres – Ferrajoli maintains – are distinct and separate without overlap between them. The "sphere of the undecidable" is portrayed in Ferrajoli's work as particularly removed from any majority control. The Italian professor associates the idea of the "undecidable" with the contractual tradition in liberal thought – which builds from, according to his description, authors ranging from von Humboldt to Constant and Tocqueville – and the proposals of renowned contemporary political philosophers, among whom he cites the Italian Norberto Bobbio (known for his idea of "inviolable territory") and the Argentine Ernesto Garzón Valdés (who spoke of the "forbidden preserve").

In recent writings, Ferrajoli has clarified the notion of the "sphere of the undecidable" through statements such as these:

> This sphere of the undecidable . . . is not lawfully decided (or not decided) – is nothing other than what in democratic constitutions an agreement has been made to remove from the will of the majority. And what is it that the constitutions establish as limits and bounds on the majority, as preconditions of civil life and at the same time reasons for the pact of coexistence? Essentially . . . the protection of fundamental rights – the first among which are the right to life and personal liberty – and there is no majority will, nor general interest, nor common or public good, to which they can be sacrificed.
>
> (Ferrajoli 2008, 212–213)

Many of the ideas related to the tradition of "natural rights" that we have reviewed in previous pages resonate clearly here: the idea that the issues that matter most to us, ones related to fundamental rights, fall outside the democratic terrain; and the idea of rights as claims that prevail (like Dworkin's "trump cards") over invocations of the "general interest" or "common good." Ferrajoli's position is thus categorically counter-majoritarian: he believes in safeguards that cannot be set aside by even a unanimous decision by the citizens. The position expressed by Ferrajoli in this regard leaves no doubt about its extremity. In his words:

> In a different way from the questions belonging to what I have called the "sphere of the decidable," fundamental rights are removed from the sphere of political decision-making and belong to what I have called the "sphere of the undecidable" (either yes or no). Their specific characteristic is thus that such rights are established in the constitutions as limits and bounds on the majority precisely because they are always – from the rights of freedom to social rights – against contingent majorities. What's more, this is the logical way to ensure your guarantee. Whenever you want to protect a right as fundamental, it is removed from politics, that is, from the powers of the majority, and from the market, as an inviolable, unavailable and inalienable right. No majority, not even unanimously, can decide to abolish or reduce it.
>
> (Ferrajoli 2008, 55)

Paragraphs like the previous one underline, in effect, the meaning and radicalism of Ferrajoli's position and those like it. This robust, influential, contemporary version of the "natural rights" tradition has proven decisive in many major court cases. In fact, on many occasions, at the highest levels of national and international justice, courts have justified decisions of crucial public importance by citing the most strident expressions of the conception. In doing so, they have made clear the devastating implications for democracy that positions such as the ones examined hold.

A significant illustration (with apologies to readers already very familiar with it) is the *Gelman* case that went before the Inter-American Court of Human Rights. It involved an amnesty law passed in Uruguay to address the massive crimes committed by the Uruguayan dictatorship during the 1970s and 1980s. The problem implied by these amnesty laws was discussed in the South African and Colombian examples, but the difficulties in this case take on particular relevance in this case for unexpected reasons. Unlike almost all the amnesty laws passed in the Americas over the last fifty years, the Uruguayan amnesty laws were not decided hastily and arbitrarily by dictatorships or authoritarian governments, but rather through a fully democratic process. Furthermore, the amnesty law, or "Expiry Law," passed by the Uruguayan Congress received harsh public criticism (I am referring to Law 15.848, on the Expiry of the State's Punitive Claims, promulgated on December 22, 1986). Due to the controversy, the law was sent back to the people not once but twice for direct vote. These "popular consultation processes," moreover, involved significant collective debate before the votes were cast (in 1989 and 2009).[2] These details are important because they are absolutely exceptional within contemporary democratic politics: a public decision of utmost importance – absolving people of horrible crimes – was adopted in Uruguay after an extensive (and still unfinished) process. The process began with a vote in Congress and was later twice confirmed by the society through popular consultations held under irreproachable conditions in terms of public discussion.

The extremely democratic justification of the norm pushed the dispute between the two rival conceptions over rights to the limit. On the one hand, the tradition anchored in the idea of "natural rights" unconditionally considered the amnesty law invalid: no government or majority ever had the authority to take a decision of similar magnitude (which pertained to the "sphere of undecidable"). On the other hand, in the Benthamite tradition that understands rights as fundamentally human creations, the Uruguayan amnesty is acceptable because of its democratic credentials.

As it predictably should have, the conflict over the validity of the Uruguayan amnesty law eventually reached the nation's highest court (in the *Nibia Sabalsagaray Curutchet* case, decided on October 19, 2009). Uruguay's high court decided the case fully in line with the tradition of "natural rights." Following very closely the theory of the Italian legal philosopher Ferrajoli, it affirmed that basic questions about rights fell within the "sphere of the undecidable." The Court reasoned:

> As Luigi Ferrajoli argues, the constitutional rules which establish the principles and fundamental rights guarantee the material dimensions of

[2] The first consultation was organized through a referendum organized by the National Pro Referendum Commission created in 1987. The vote was held in April 1989 to decide whether to annul the first four articles of the law, but instead the law was upheld (by 58 percent of the votes). Years later, and with the *Frente Amplio* in power (a coalition whose electoral platform had not included any proposal to repeal or annul the law in question), 340,000 signatures were collected by public interest groups (more than the 260,000 necessary) to call a plebiscite. The plebiscite concluded on October 25, 2009. It also proposed annulling and declaring void the first four articles of Law 15.848. The law, however, was once more upheld, this time by a slimmer majority (approximately 48 percent of the votes were in favor of the initiative to annul).

> the "substantive democracy" which refers to that which can not be decided or is to be decided by the majority ... under penalty of invalidity ...

Directly reproducing the same author's words, the Court went on:

> the issues pertaining to what I have called "sphere of the decidable," fundamental rights are subtracted from the sphere of political decision-making and belong to what I have called "sphere of the undecidable" ... Whenever you want to protect a right as fundamental, it is removed from politics, that is, from the powers of the majority ... as an inviolable, unavailable and inalienable right. No majority, not even unanimously, can decide its abolition or reduction. (*Nibia Sabalsagaray Curutchet* case, p. 32)

Notably and – in my opinion – more seriously, the Inter-American Court of Human Rights (Inter-American Court) also ruled on the *Gelman* case, adopting an even more extreme position than the Uruguayan Court regarding the relationship between democracy and rights. After invoking Ferrajoli's work on the subject ("the protection of human rights constitutes an impassable limit to majorities, that is, to the forum of the 'possible to be decided' by the majorities in the democratic instance"), the Inter-American Court resoundingly disqualified the Uruguayan attempts to validate the amnesty laws because of their strongly (I would add) democratic nature.[3]

I believe this case illustrates, in a dramatic and highly visible way, the remarkable practical and political implications of taking as a starting point one or the other position (Lockean or Benthamite) with respect to rights and their relation to democratic values.

[3] On the one hand, the Inter-American Court denied importance to the most significant legal aspect of the case; that is, that an exceptionally democratic decision to affirm the validity of the challenged norm was not merely a "formal" property of origin (i.e., the Court considered the deep democratic debate of the case, later consolidated with two direct consultations with the public, as a merely formal question – and not as a fact of exceptional substantive value). On the other hand, and even more seriously, the Inter-American Court also affirmed that the fact that "the Expiry Law was approved in a democratic regime and was further ratified or endorsed by the citizens on two occasions does not automatically or by itself grant it legitimacy before International Law." In this way, again, the Inter-American Court minimized (considered as minor, basically irrelevant) the extraordinary turn of events that had taken place in democratic terms: the fact that the society of Uruguay had been entirely engaged and responsibly carried out an open and continuous process of democratic debate to resolve one of their deepest disagreements.

12

Social Rights and the "Engine Room"

12.1 The "Exorbitant" Mexican Constitution of 1917

The 1917 Constitution of Mexico was an extraordinary legal milestone: it divides what came before from what came after, and was itself something of a miracle. The direct and legitimate child of the radical Mexican Revolution of 1910, that constitution was the first national constitution, in the history of humanity, to include a long list of social rights. (The famous Weimar Constitution, another pioneering charter – though it was much more modest in social matters than the Mexican Constitution – would only be approved two years later, in 1919.) The Mexican Constitution brought social constitutionalism to the world. Its significance derives not simply from being comparatively decades ahead of its time (most constitutions that added social rights would only appear in the middle of the century or later). It is also significant because it incorporated social rights in a very detailed, precise, complete, and exhaustive way – to the point of exaggeration. The 1917 Constitution leapt suddenly, almost without warning, into the legal world.

There is no room to doubt either the *grandeur* or the excess of the revolutionary Constitution of 1917 – revolutionary not only in origin but also in terms of its social content. The two main articles on social issues attempted – each in its area – to cover absolutely everything. Article 27, referring to "property," contains no fewer than eighteen subsections (!). Article 123, in reference to "labor," has fourteen of its own. Article 123 alone could have been presented, in another legal system, as an entire Labor Code (a Labor Code incorporated into the constitution!). It covers everything from the maximum duration of the workday, conditions for after-hours work, the legal working age, mandatory days of rest, labor regulations for pregnant women, the minimum wage, equal conditions for labor negotiations, the workers' share of company profits, overtime pay, mandatory health and hygiene standards, the obligation to provide workers with education and training, regulations in the case of accidents at the workplace, the right to strike, the right to organize, dismissal without just cause, abusive employment contracts, social security, paid holidays, conditions for the suspension or termination of workers, and so on.

For a possibly minor but curious fact, one that gives an idea of the charter's "excess," consider the following. If we excerpted that tremendous text so that it only consisted of Articles 27 and 123, we would still be left with 5435 words. Article 27 has 3665 and Article 123 has 2770. The entire US Constitution is around 4500 words long. The comparison might offer a decent indication of the kind of strange "animal" we are dealing with.

Because of its pioneering character, because of its ambition, because of its excessiveness, the Constitution of 1917 represents a curious case, an exception to the rule, even an object of worship. It is revered for its content (it remains in force, whether by virtue or in spite of the many reforms it has undergone), but perhaps even more so for what it represented historically. Not long ago (in 2017), its centenary was celebrated in political and academic circles across the globe with respectful tributes and proud festivities.

In any case, and without wanting to spoil the celebratory mood in what follows, I would like to look at the 1917 Mexican Constitution both in terms of what it meant and the principles undergirding it. I want to reflect not only on what has been the main focus – its transformative character – but in particular on the implicit limits that it incorporated. I will argue that the Mexican Constitution of 1917, for all its greatness, also launched a model for thinking and writing about constitutionalism that has brought serious problems. I will argue that the venerated, revolutionary Constitution was not truly the direct or legitimate child of the 1910 Mexican Revolution, but rather that, in some sense, it represents the "conservative" expression of that revolutionary moment. I want to present this argument not out of any desire to be a nuisance, but because I believe that the argument might help us understand the role played by the Mexican constitution in introducing a constitutional model that we must now confront as an urgent problem.

12.2 The Mexican Constitution of 1917: A "Conservative Moment" in the Revolutionary Movement

As indicated, I will now argue that the 1917 Constitution that came out of the Querétaro Convention deserves to be seen, more than as the first revolutionary constitution that enshrined social rights, as a late expression of a conservative moment, which came at the end of a very long constitutional process that began with the Mexican Revolution of 1910. Again, I am not making this argument out of any desire to stir controversy for the sake of attention, but rather out of the desire to understand the change in the "constitutional game" for which it is responsible. Representing the "last stop" that the constitutional train of the Mexican revolutionaries made, their 1917 Constitution was the first of a whole series of constitutions, especially in Latin America, to be written in the same way, and to conceive of constitutionalism as it did; that is, in equally deficient manner. I will argue that it inaugurated, more than the era of "social constitutionalism," the era of "social authoritarianism" propped up by constitutionalism.

For anyone familiar with Mexico's history, this affirmation should not be complicated to understand. Let us look at some of the details from that country's long revolutionary period, starting with the origin of the revolution itself: radical, supported by the common people, with indigenous blood running through its veins. As had almost become a tradition in Mexico's political life, the break with the "old conservative order" – in this case the "order and progress" project led by the dictator Porfirio Díaz – was led by radical revolutionary groups with large indigenous support (this pattern goes at least as far back as 1810, when indigenous groups and a group of revolutionary priests headed by Hidalgo and Morelos led the struggle for independence from Spain). The period of Porfirio Díaz's authoritarian reign, often referred to as the "Porfiriato," had already gone on for more than a quarter of century.

To confront and overthrow General Díaz's military apparatus, mobilizing an equivalent force was necessary, representing an extraordinary feat. Two sources of support for the radical uprising stood out more than any others: peasants and indigenous groups. From the north came troops led by Pancho Villa and, from the south, they came led by Emiliano Zapata. The "Porfiriato" had not only consolidated a military regime; it had also articulated, to strengthen its foundation, efficient legal mechanisms, for which Díaz had assembled some of the most notable Mexican jurists of all time, among whom Justo Sierra and Emiliano Rabassa played a special role. That might explain why, together with the urge to dismantle the "Porfiriato" completely, the revolutionaries coupled their military campaigns with several attempts to legally reconstruct the Mexican state. These initiatives to lay the organizational foundations of a new revolutionary order were varied. Of all the conventions that they established and the documents they issued, I will only point out the following for now.

The Plan de la Villa de Ayala, or Plan de Ayala. This was signed by a group of military officers in Zapata's army (the Zapatistas), the vast majority of whom had been peasants before the revolution, on November 28, 1911. The agreement signed in Ayala denounced, above all, the dangers facing the revolution (and in particular, the revolution's leader at the time, Francisco Madero). The "Plan" also included a detailed program for vast reforms, starting with land reform. It laid out, for example, a scheme for the recovery of lands "despoiled" during the Porfiriato. It called for expropriating large landowners – with compensation – because "the vast majority of Mexican peoples and citizens no longer even own the land they walk, while they suffer the horrors of misery" and nationalizing the assets of opponents to the "Plan" (Gilly 1994, 97–98).

The Manifesto "To the Mexican People." This manifesto was issued by the Zapatistas in August 1914. In the letter, the Zapatistas rejected military government and any electoral reform that did not include profound social reforms. The manifesto called for convening an assembly of "the heads of the fighting groups, the representatives of the people up in arms" as well. Also of note, it expressed support for the basic principles of the Plan de Ayala: expropriation, confiscation, and restitution (Gilly 1994, 156).

The "Programmatic Letter" Written by General Manuel Palafox* in *September 1914. In this letter, Palafox voiced support for the agrarian revolution demanded by the Zapatistas and the principles of the Plan de Ayala. Similarly, the military leader requested a "convention formed by the revolutionaries of the republic," destined to elevate "to the rank of constitutional precepts" the three great "agrarian principles" of the Ayala Plan: "restitution of lands to the peoples or individuals who were dispossessed in the shadow of bad governments; confiscation of the assets from the enemies of the Ayala Plan; and expropriation for public use" (Gilly 1994, 157–158).

The Aguascalientes Convention. The assembly that took place in Aguascalientes represents the great precursor to the Querétaro Convention. It was attended by representatives of the Northern Division led by Villa and, importantly, of the "constitutionalist" army under Venustiano Carranza's command. However, the majority of the representatives were career soldiers rather than peasants. Only well after the convention was underway would some Zapatista representatives join, although they would end up dominating the debates. Originally indigenous and peasant, the movement against the "Porfiriato" had begun to take on a different character, one less linked to its revolutionary beginnings. The purpose of the meeting, in any case, was to put an end to the bitter disputes that had ignited between the different rebel factions. One of the most notable jurists of the time, Luis Cabrera, declared his aspiration that the convention would be "larger than that of 1857" and "the first in the history of . . . Mexico" to legislate according to real needs of Mexicans (Gilly 1994, 165). After a difficult start marked by mutual suspicion, the Convention adopted some important decisions, including, as in previous instances, the vindication and approval of some of the Ayala Plan's basic proposals. Yet the Aguascalientes assembly also left the haunting impression that something had been irreparably broken. It was in this new context of mistrust and disputes among opposing factions that General Venustiano Carranza, head of the Constitutionalist Army, proposed a constituent assembly to meet in Querétaro.

In light of these antecedents, it becomes easier to understand the meaning and limits of the Querétaro Convention. If the Ayala Plan had been dominated by the most radical political wing – the Zapatistas – along with the predominantly agrarian and peasant interests, Aguascalientes was the product of a mixture of diverse political factions (led by Villa, Carranza, and, at the last moment, Zapata), along with significant participation of more homogeneous social groups from the military sector. Put simply: the political and legal process was becoming more and more conservative. Then came Querétaro, at which the will of the most dominant political faction (and most conservative, that of Carranza) found the greatest (although not exclusive) expression along with the interests of (again, not exclusively) the most affluent social sectors. The Congress of Querétaro began on November 21, 1916, and quickly divided into two camps: the more conservative faction associated with, for example, Luis Rojas and Félix Palavicini; and a radical or "Jacobin" faction led by Francisco Múgica.

12.2.1 Constitutions with "Two Souls": Social Conservatism

The previous section tells the story of the potential of and challenges faced by the Querétaro Convention. In one aspect, the Convention is indisputably the culmination, the heir, of the revolutionary movement. In another, the Convention also represents, as I claimed, the conservative moment of that long process. Unsurprisingly then, the constitutional model that saw the light at that assembly sought to express some convergence between these two influences.

One episode that occurred at the Convention can, in my opinion, be understood as a key metaphor that characterizes the moment. This was a speech delivered by the man who had gone from leading the Constitutionalist Army to heading the executive of the new Mexican government, Venustiano Carranza. Indeed, the now President and "First Chief" of the Constitutionalist Army, Carranza gave the inaugural speech of the Constituent Assembly on December 1, 1916. In it, Carranza laid out all his optimistic expectations for the Convention. He also made very clear the boundaries that he was not going to allow the Convention to cross. To be more precise, aware of the deep desire for profound reform that moved a significant part of the delegates, Carranza stressed that he was not willing to accept constitutional changes that undermined the long established political tradition of concentrated power. To make his case, Carranza appealed to the familiar American conservative discourse. He argued, for example:

> The people . . . have needed and still need strong governments, capable of containing undisciplined populations within order, populations disposed to excesses at every moment and with the most futile pretext . . . Order is a condition of freedom, and without order freedom is impossible . . . The Legislative Power, which by nature of its functions always tends to intervene in the functions of others, was endowed in the Constitution of 1857 with powers that allowed it to obstruct or make the task of the Executive Power more cumbersome and difficult, or to subject it to the capricious will of a majority easy to mold in times of turmoil, when bad passions and bastard interests regularly predominate.

Carranza covered all the typical tropes of conservative and authoritarian thought in the region: anarchy, lack of order, social indiscipline, whimsical majorities prone to excess, the irrationality and passions of common citizens, the importance of strong government, and the value of reinforced authority. Brutally put: Carranza suggested that the delegates were free to institute, through the Constitution, diverse initiatives and crucial reforms. In fact, he seemed to tell them: "If you want to incorporate social clauses unlike any other in any country in the world, go ahead, do it." However, in the same breath, Carranza let it be known that he was not going to allow any questioning of his own authority, the power of the executive. The threat of anarchy, in his opinion, was still alive – perhaps more than ever – and he was unwilling to cede a shred of his military powers or coercive instruments of control.

That is how this strange animal was born, "split" constitutionalism with "two souls," one legal body that had two heads. A new constitutional model saw the light that, regarding the organization of power, maintained the principles of the typical nineteenth-century conservative model (the elitist political model that became the standard in the region between 1850 and 1890). Regarding its declaration of rights, meanwhile, the 1917 Mexican Constitution opened the doors for social reforms never seen before. Mexico had ushered in, with the most spectacular fanfare and excitement, a new phase of constitutionalism: social and reformist in spirit, conservative and authoritarian in practice. This new constitutional form would be consecrated in many countries – certainly in Latin America: on one side they kept an organization of constitutional powers in the eighteenth- to nineteenth-century style (concentrated powers, a lopsided system of checks and balances, counter-majoritarian mechanisms and other manifestations of democratic distrust); and on the other, they added declarations of rights that were updated, robust, wide-ranging, and boasted a strong social profile, just like the Mexican Constitution did, as if emblems of the twentieth century.

12.3 The Animal Stirs: From the Fourteenth Amendment to "Social Authoritarianism" in Latin America

As we know, the Mexican Constitution came shortly before the promulgation of the 1919 Constitution of the Weimar Republic, the creation of the International Labor Organization (also in 1919), and the emergence of the welfare state and embrace of Keynesian economics.

Half a century earlier, a few years after its Civil War, fought over the issue of slavery, ended in 1865, the United States ratified the Fourteenth Amendment to its constitution in 1868. The first section of the amendment established the "Clause of Equal Protection."[1] This modification meant to combat discrimination in the name of equality significantly changed United States law but, again, the effect of the changes tended to stagnate in the area of rights without affecting the organization of power in the country. More precisely, the very serious inequalities of power

[1] The first clause of Section 1 reads: "All persons born or naturalized in the United States, and subject to the jurisdiction thereof, are citizens of the United States and of the State wherein they reside. No State shall make or enforce any law which shall abridge the privileges or immunities of citizens of the United States; nor shall any State deprive any person of life, liberty, or property, without due process of law; nor deny to any person within its jurisdiction the equal protection of the laws."

between races, developed over scores of years, backed by law and reinforced by the Constitution, remained effectively untouched. After a promising but short-lived start (the "Reconstruction" period that ended in 1877 and whose achievements were quickly reversed), political participation of Black Americans was discouraged and no restorative measures were implemented to repair the accumulated disadvantage and afford the group what the law had explicitly denied them (Fiss 1976). The constitutional power structure, in this sense, maintained its resistance to the social change that the spirit of the time demanded.

Generations later, as in the rest of the region, the United States would be shaken by social crisis – a product of that rife inequality that had been neglected for so long and was unleashed by widespread, planetary economic crisis. In 1944, President Franklin Roosevelt sought to address some of these social inequalities through a variety of measures, including a proposal for constitutional amendment, in the name of a "Second Bill of Rights" (Sunstein 2006). These kinds of political initiatives were picked up by the judiciary, particularly by the Supreme Court when Earl Warren presided over it, whose jurisprudence approximated a recognition of constitutional social rights (welfare rights). In fact, in a series of important rulings (*Griffin*, *Gideon*, *Douglas*, *Boddie*, *Harper*, *Shapiro*, *Goldberg*), well analyzed by Sunstein, the Court began to advance an interesting position, one recognizing the benefits of social welfare not as merely institutionalized "charity," but as necessary conditions for the "blessings of liberty" (Sunstein 2006). Soon after the election of President Nixon (1968), however, the Court began walking back this position (Nixon was able to appoint four new judges, changing the ideological profile of the majority). Although the backtrack was not expressed in all areas, it did take place in the area of social and economic rights, which were promptly denied constitutional status. In short, and as argued by the constitutionalist Frank Michelman (one of the very few North American constitutionalists who took the problem of inequality and social exclusion seriously) in an article about "protecting the poor through the Fourteenth Amendment": "the Court has directly shielded poor from the most elemental consequence of poverty: lack of funds to exchange for needed goods, services, or privileged of access" (Michelman 1969, 9).

In Latin America, meanwhile, the Mexican social model of constitutionalism inspired reforms which reproduced the same dichotomy created in Mexico: yes to the long lists of social rights; no to the introduction of commensurate changes in the organization of power. In this sense, most of the new constitutions that appeared (or were modified) during this period incorporated lists of social rights, in some cases as complex and rich as Mexico's: Bolivia, in 1938; Cuba, in 1940; Uruguay, in 1942; Ecuador and Guatemala, in 1945; Argentina and Costa Rica, in 1949. However, as we will see, they maintained extremely vertical power hierarchies.

The two greatest expressions of this new constitutional template that emerged in Latin America were surely the constitutions adopted in Argentina under President Juan Domingo Perón and in Brazil under President Getulio Vargas. I want to highlight these cases because of the extraordinary political and historical importance that each regime would acquire and, also, because of the salience with which each confirmed the central features of the new model.

Indeed, the cases of Brazil under Getulio Vargas and Argentina under Juan Domingo Perón offer the clearest and also most extreme examples of the new regional constitutional model – social conservatism. It is worth remembering that both Vargas and Perón came to power in the mid-twentieth century with the help of the armed forces (Vargas as a result of the 1930 Revolution led by military offers; Perón in the elections held after the 1943 military coup in which Perón himself played a leading role). Both leaders found support not only in the lower social sectors – among the incipient working class – but also among part of the upper classes who feared the presence of leftist and revolutionary forces in their respective countries (the Communist Party in Brazil and anarchist and socialist groups in Argentina). Both promoted substantial social reforms with the intention of permanently changing the socioeconomic structure of their countries, integrating traditionally marginalized and disadvantaged sectors into the formal economy – and these were extraordinary achievements. Both leaders also implemented "corporate" regimes that increased representation by organizing new interest groups but also favored the concentration of powers and were accompanied by restrictions of freedoms. (Vargas ruled as a dictator during his first years in power and launched a period of "xenophobic nationalism," Villa 2011, 53; Perón developed a hyper-personalist presidency, imprisoning and torturing political enemies.)

Most importantly for our purposes, both Vargas and Perón promoted social constitutions that, for the first time in the history of each country, included long lists of social, economic, and cultural rights. In fact, Vargas promulgated two constitutions during his time in power, one in 1934 and the other in 1937, while Perón promulgated Argentina's 1949 Constitution, which lasted until the military coup of 1955. Analysts characterize the

Brazilian Constitution of 1934 in terms of its two main features; namely, its strong corporate character and its serious engagement with the social question (Lima Lopes 2008, 36). The new Constitution included entirely new sections that addressed social and economic order (Title IV), and, regarding the second feature, the family, culture, and education (Title V, Chapter I). Articles 120, 121, and 122 were particularly decisive in shaping a new social policy. Among other novelties, the new social clauses prohibited paying different compensation for the same work, established regulations on the minimum wage, the eight-hour workday, rights to paid vacations, and healthcare for workers. Meanwhile, the 1937 Constitution was characterized by its "centralizing and anti-federalist character" (Lima Lopes 2008, 362). It maintained most of the social clauses of the previous Constitution, although it did not recognize the right to strike, which it considered "antisocial" (Article 139). The new Constitution's outlook could be characterized as illiberal, anti-idealistic, and undemocratic (da Silva 2011).

In Argentina, the Peronist Constitution of 1949 included, among other novelties, Chapter 3, which consisted of a single article divided into four sections: labor rights; the rights of the family; the rights of the elderly; and the rights to education and culture. The first section became known as the "Decalogue" of workers' rights and established fair and dignified working conditions, health protections, the right to social welfare, and social security, among others. In addition, the Constitution added Article 40, which held that the exploitation of wealth must be directed to the welfare of the people in accordance with the principles of social justice. The Constitution also deepened state intervention in the economy, in the name of general interests, and it established that the state would also run the public services that – under no circumstances – could be "sold or transferred for exploitation." Like the Brazilian Constitution, the Argentine did not recognize the right to strike, and also eliminated the jury system, which had previously been part of the country's constitutional tradition.

The constitutions implemented by Vargas in Brazil and Perón in Argentina reflect in an emphatic, perhaps exaggerated way, the dimensions of the constitutional problem created by the Mexican model: these were constitutions elaborated by authorities holding disproportionately concentrated political power. On the one hand they opened the doors wide for the inclusion of new social rights while at the same time they locked down the political system by maintaining broad powers for the executive.

In my opinion, the prospects for social rights were compromised from the start within this dangerously ambiguous constitutional framework.

The new constitutional model was effectively "split" into two parts (one referring to the organization of power, the other referring to citizens' rights), each of which was written by, and was under the control of, a different authority. In fact, as we shall see, the new social constitutions made the rights they incorporated dependent almost exclusively on the good will of the executive. The legislatures in these contexts were, in most cases, well under the President's control, so the entire constitutional order largely fell within the broad authority of the President.

12.4 The "New Latin American Constitutionalism": Constitutionalism That Was Already Old at Birth

This section takes up where the previous one stopped to point out a significant development. In recent years, Latin American constitutionalism has undergone major reforms, leading some to speak of the emergence of a new constitutional movement: "New Latin American Constitutionalism." For example, Brazil reformed its Constitution in 1988; Colombia in 1991; Argentina in 1994; Venezuela in 1999; Ecuador in 2008; and Bolivia in 2009. The origin and modes of creation of some of these constitutions caused astonishment and drew particular attention because they were much more open and inclusive than in the past. Racial, sexual, and indigenous minorities, for example, took an interest in the constituent processes and mobilized to make their demands heard. The inclusive quality of the "new constitutional moment" may also explain the additional content they incorporated. Citing a few merely to provide some illustration: references to gender equality were incorporated into the constitutions of Argentina, Bolivia, and Colombia; (curious but interesting) references to the "rights of nature" were added to those of Bolivia and Ecuador; new protections for the environment found constitutional expression in Brazil, Chile, Colombia, and Costa Rica; references to cultural pluralism or the multicultural character of the new constitutional order in Bolivia, Colombia, Ecuador, and Mexico; mechanisms of popular initiative in Argentina, Brazil, Colombia, and Costa Rica; referendums or popular consultations in Bolivia, Brazil, Guatemala, and Honduras; openness to linguistic pluralism in Bolivia, Ecuador, and Venezuela; affirmative action programs in Ecuador, Mexico, Nicaragua, and Paraguay; revocation of mandates in Bolivia, Ecuador, and Venezuela; new forms of popular control over public policies in Bolivia, Brazil, Mexico, and Nicaragua; and references to the right to housing in Argentina, Brazil, and Colombia.

Reforms like these (remembering that I only mentioned a limited, non-exhaustive sample for the purpose of illustrating the phenomenon) are interesting in that they sought to protect the unprotected sectors within the most traditionally unprotected ones. I mean: these were constitutional reforms that, among other things, placed a very special focus on the rights of the many groups that had been neglected, even after the social reforms promoted since the Mexican 1917 Constitution. For the first time, National Constitutions seemed to take (what Hannah Arendt called) "the social question" seriously. This is, indisputably, an important achievement.

However, if we look at the results of these reforms – their legacy – we must also recognize another characteristic. In a remarkable way, the reforms of the so-called "new constitutionalism" were born too "old." What I mean is that the reforms reproduced the same old Latin American constitutional model – that of the constitutions "split in two." All the new or newly reformed constitutions, in effect, neatly reproduced the old constitutional model keeping its two traditional components fundamentally intact. On the one hand, then, the new constitutions maintained the same type of concentrated (and, ultimately, elitist) organization of power as was typical of the second half of the nineteenth century in Latin America (in some cases, reinforcing presidential powers even more). On the other hand, these new constitutions reinforced their declarations of rights, following the same logic as in the previous wave of reforms at the beginning of the twentieth century: new, longer lists of rights (adding human, social, economic, cultural, multicultural rights) aimed at "recognizing" groups that had not been properly recognized in previous waves. That is why we can speak of a "new" constitutionalism that is too "old." The model imagined by Carranza for Mexico remained, for all intents and purposes, intact: rights for everyone in the style of the twentieth century (and now the twenty-first century); power for the few, in the style of the eighteenth and nineteenth centuries.

12.5 Rights versus "Engine Room"

In my previous work, I have often alluded to the problem with constitutions' "engine room" (Gargarella 2014). The metaphor was simple in that I meant that the (Latin American) model of constitutionalism had failed because, in obstinately seeking real change by incorporating more and more constitutional rights, it left virtually untouched or unchanged the most important part of the constitution – the organization of power that

I called the "engine room." I was suggesting that there was a problem in treating the constitutional text as if its various parts were autonomous – as if significant changes could be made by altering one section or article while leaving the rest as it was. I was particularly interested in the difficulty that arose when – a practice that has become the rule in Latin America – supposedly profound reforms were introduced in the declarations of rights, giving them a new, social, democratic, and avant-garde character while the existent elitist, retrograde organization of power that was hostile to democracy remained intact. This is why I argued that the constitutions created had "two souls" and compared them to Janus: one face looking back to preserve their conservative past; another pointing forward, towards a bright, egalitarian future. What I suggested was that an effective reform would not only introduce significant change to one section of the constitution, but also should adjust the other section(s), accordingly.

This argument is not only based on the important consideration that the constitution be consistent (as important as consistency is), but also on the risk that, within the framework of an internally contradictory constitution, part of the constitution will directly undermine the other. The risk is particularly salient and serious when, as in Latin America, the reform is intended to substantively modify the constitutional section referring to rights, while the part relating to the organization of power is basically left untouched. This is so because the latter – and this is why I call it the "engine room" – contain the levers that control the implementation of the rest of the constitution. If Congress does not (or is unable to) pass laws to implement the incorporated reforms, those rights will effectively "remain in the books." If citizens cannot access justice in any simple, straightforward way, an ambitious structure of rights will likely remain "dormant." Without adequate means of mobilizing the executive, that branch may or may not "execute" the reforms created according to its own needs and political ambitions (this last problem proved to be the most decisive on in Latin America where, since the nineteenth century, hyper-presidential regimes continue to predominate).

All the very serious (and predictable) problems cited above as examples have flared up repeatedly in recent years. In almost all of Latin America, for example – the heralded "promised land" in terms of social rights – extraordinarily robust declarations of social rights were transformed immediately, and for decades, into "dormant clauses." Time and time again, systematically, judges have qualified such rights as "nonoperative," and legal scholars have largely gone along with them, arguing that the reforms introduced were "aspirational" (for an insightful analysis and criticism of these court decisions and scholarly contributions, reread Abramovich and Courtis 2002 or Courtis 2006). Similarly, new rights aimed at strengthening the decision-making power and oversight of the people, including referendums and plebiscites, died an early death in some cases – as in Argentina – because Congress, in charge of regulating those mechanisms, initially postponed them endlessly, long enough to introduce regulations that eventually made them nearly impossible to implement. Laura Eberhardt has similarly demonstrated in her doctoral thesis how the powers of revocation incorporated into Colombia's constitution ended up, fundamentally, and in all cases, reinforcing the powers of the President who was their target (Eberhardt 2017). In Ecuador, for another example, the new Constitution incorporated radical modifications in favor of citizen participation. Citizen groups, however, have systematically encountered nearly insurmountable obstacles to put them into practice (Ávila Santamaría 2009; Echeverría 2008).

The point is this: social, participatory, or democratizing reforms do not work well when the organization of powers remains concentrated, traditional, and conservative. Ultimately, I question whether it was ever even conceivable to believe that simply by changing the content of the bill of rights the constitution could ever be truly modified in terms of its effect. Was it reasonable in any way to believe that the traditional power centers – left fully intact – would voluntarily ply themselves to the service of the reforms advanced? Even more directly and crudely: Who thought that conservative judges would take their place at the forefront of implementing these new social rights to carry out their egalitarian transformation (instead of positioning themselves, as they quickly did, as the first line of defense for the established powers)? Who did it occur to that the executive branch, with all the power and privilege it enjoyed, was going to go along initiatives of popular participation that implied ceding much of its own decision-making power? Really, did anyone think that the executive would freely give up even a smidgen of power for the sake of social transformation and the empowerment of the people? Unlike the Baron of Munchausen, normal people are not able to pull themselves out of a swamp by their own hair.

12.6 Rights As Bribes? Another Take on Rights versus Democracy

At this point, I would like to add a few closing comments to tie the discussion of this chapter back in with our previous discussion of rights. The problem facing us (the problem of the "engine room") has to do with the amount, in some cases an extraordinary amount, of social rights that have been written or read into constitutions, while the whole institutional system the same constitutions establish seem to work against effective enjoyment of them.

This unfortunate situation should compel us to think about many things but here I would like to limit myself to only a few. First of all, many people intimately and genuinely committed to constitutionalism, to social change, to social justice, to equality, and to democracy seem to have been working their way down a dead end for almost a century. They have put extraordinary energy into improving the constitution, but they have put their effort in the wrong place. Concerned about equality and democracy, they have dedicated themselves, for decades, to obtaining constitutional recognition of social rights; to identifying and pursuing strategies for constitutional litigation; developing theory and doctrine to justify the application (and enforcement) of these social rights; untiringly criticizing judges who disparage them as (not directly operative) rights; conceiving remedies for their implementation; and on and on. In this way, unfortunately, however well-meaning and indefatigably, they have diverted (or squandered) forces they could have devoted to another much more meaningful struggle: the endeavor to democratize power and restore authority to citizens. Worse than that, by devoting all their efforts to the first task (that of strengthening the domain of rights), they seem to have failed to realize that without questioning the organization of political power and leaving it as concentrated as ever, they undermined the very cause that purportedly moved them (the cause of rights).

Indeed, these lawyers, activists, and scholars might respond to my assessment by recognizing their focus on social rights but denying indifference with regards the organization of power. They might also respond that the time is not right, that the conditions are lacking, but as soon they are, they will turn to the democratization of power. Until then, they might say, they will continue to concentrate on the fundamental reform of rights. Even if they did say as much, unfortunately, they would be wrong. This is because – and here is the tragedy – the two tasks are not separate or independent. Safeguarding rights cannot be attained by postponing, for a second time, modification in the structure of power. On the contrary. The lack of reforms in the organization of power, as we have seen, directly undermines or even makes impossible everything that they want to accomplish through rights. To put it a different way, working for a more just system of rights requires changing the power structure; that is, fighting for democratic political organization.

This "error," which has persisted for so many years, is curious, particularly because many of our predecessors did not fall into it at all. Think about Madison and his generation: they understood clearly from the start that the path to constitutional rights lay through the organization of organizations of powers in the constitution. The most obvious example involves their particular interest in protecting property rights. Unlike our contemporaries, instead of dedicating themselves to elaborating the first national constitution full of rights related to property, free trade, and contracts, they immediately focused their energies on the design of the structure of the constitution (to the point that the original US Constitution did not even include a list of rights). Of course, their elitist convictions drove them to take measures with which many of us today would disagree for ideological reasons. To a large extent, what they did was "tie the hands" of legislatures, which posed the main threats to property rights (that was, at least, the lesson they seem to have drawn from history). However, and beyond ideological disagreements, the truth is that the logic of Madison's constitutional reasoning was impeccable: since he and his supporters were especially interested in certain rights (property, contracts), they realized that the best means of protecting them (rather than having to include more rights in the constitutional text than they actually wanted) was making sure the structure of power tilted to their favor.

Note that the same observation about Madison and his contemporaries applies in Latin America, where the Argentine Juan Bautista Alberdi, the Venezuelan-Chilean Andrés Bello, or the Colombian José María Samper employed a similar logic. All of them seemed to take the same strategy as their North American counterparts; that of ensuring their special interests (property, contracts) not by incorporating them into the constitutions that they were formulating (which could mean having to compromise or include rights they did not want in the text), but rather by modifying the power structure in a way that made ensuring them much easier.

Our contemporaries, on the other hand, never seemed to understand this rationality. They seemed to say – as opposed to what their predecessors had perfectly understood – "because we are especially interested in *x* [in this case, let us say *x* is social rights], what we will do to get *x* is . . . agree to put many more rights, even ones that do not interest us, in the constitution. That way we do not have to worry, for now at least, about the organization of power."

All of which leads us to a big question: Why is it that such skilled people – many of the finest jurists and activists of recent decades – concentrated their work so exclusively in the area of rights? Why did they give up on modifying the power structure in such a way as to help advance their egalitarian ideals? Was it naivety? Bad faith? A misunderstanding? Short-sightedness? Was it, rather, that they themselves benefitted from the service they provided in the existing power scheme? Could it be that, in fact, those who held power allowed them to "entertain themselves" with rights advocacy, while they themselves took advantage of the system to preserve and shore up their privileges?

We do not know. However, it is an important topic, one that has generated much reflection in our time. Personally, and without addressing the "moral" conclusions of so many colleagues, my objective opinion is that it was caused by an erroneous approach to constitutional logic – a misunderstanding of how constitutionalism works. Other contemporary authors, such as Samuel Moyn, have insisted that the over-obsession of many academics and legal activists with human rights in recent years has been very harmful to objectives such as equality and social justice. The cause of human rights, in particular, seemed to represent the "last utopia" to which they devoted all their effort, thus failing to see that, while internationally making ground in favor of those rights, the welfare state was hollowed out, the free market strategy was enshrined, and inequality rose just as fast as ever. Academics and legal activists who had lost faith in the promises of communism, socialism, and social reform, continued, however, undaunted, litigating for human rights (Moyn 2010, 2018).

Australian professor Rosalind Dixon has made similar observations, but reached an even harsher conclusion. She has compared the new social, economic, and cultural rights recently incorporated by constitutions as "bribes." Dixon has accordingly maintained strong "skepticism in relation to the processes of expansion of constitutional rights," suspecting that they were "granted" by the minority groups in power to co-opt or "bribe" groups capable of challenging them (sexual minorities, indigenous groups, ethnic minorities; Dixon 2018).

In any case, I would like to end this chapter by reiterating a key point for those of us who hold a robustly democratic view of constitutionalism: when we recognize that rights are the result of democratic politics – that is where they emerge, take form, and have effect – we must immediately realize that the best service we can give them – if those rights truly interest us – is to fight for a radically more democratic organization of our society.

13

Judicial Review

"It Seems Something of an Insult"

> When citizens or their representatives disagree on which rights we have or what those rights entail, it seems something of an insult to say that this is not something they are permitted to sort out by majoritarian processes, but that the issue is to be assigned instead for final determination to a small group of judges.
>
> Jeremy Waldron 1999, 15

13.1 The "Democratic Objection" and Hamilton's Defense of the Judiciary

Federalist No. 78, written by Alexander Hamilton, is one of the most notable essays of the entire collection. One may disagree with him (in my case, I disagree with almost everything he says) but still admire his accomplishments greatly. In a mere three or four pages (the same length as all the other Federalist Papers), Hamilton examines the judiciary in a historically unique manner. Its uniqueness is not only due to the remarkable clarity, synthesis, and careful reasoning of the essay's treatment of public matters of the highest import. The essay is especially unique because of the lucidity with which Hamilton discusses, specifies, and responds to all the major issues surrounding the judiciary: How should judges be chosen? What qualities and qualifications should they have? Why is long tenure and job security so important? How should judges interpret the Constitution? What virtues can we expect of and what risks should we fear from this branch of power? All in just four pages! However, none of these qualities explains why Federalist No. 78 caused such a stir or why we are still talking about it today. It is because Hamilton addresses the most controversial aspect of judicial authority in all of history, judicial review of constitutionality and its democratic justification. Of all the great responses to the question, Hamilton's was the first, and he expressed it with admirable sharpness, simplicity, and forcefulness.

In order to make sure everyone has a grasp on what I am talking about: the justification for judicial review has been debated for more than two hundred years. The controversy arose because, even before the Constitution of the United States came into force, many people questioned the extent of judges' authority. More specifically: from the beginning, many wondered how it was possible for judges to override the laws passed by the legislature. They suggested that doing so (invalidating a law) should be considered an affront to democracy: How could courts be allowed to invalidate a law, if the laws represented the will of the people? If this were allowed – they added – it would mean the judges had greater power than the legislature itself – that is, power superior to that of the people! Judicial review of constitutionality (or, more precisely, allowing judges to declare laws unconstitutional) should thus be considered antidemocratic.

This is the criticism of the judicial function that occupied the center of serious studies of the judiciary for more than two hundred years ago and up to the present day. The underlying question is how the courts, which are made up of the authorities with the (comparatively) weakest democratic credentials (judges, especially in superior courts, are not usually directly elected by the people, nor can they be removed by popular initiatives), are able to impose their decisions over the will of the majority (as expressed through the laws of Congress). This is, in its most specific form, the objection to judicial review that remains with us – the point famously made by Alexander Bickel when he wrote about the "counter-majoritarian difficulty."

This is where the wonder of Hamilton's short text becomes apparent: in less than four pages, indeed, in a couple paragraphs, Hamilton does two equally remarkable things: first, he recognizes the problem (which many of his contemporaries did not even perceive), and then he offers a devastating response (a knockout blow, in fact, one that would leave his rivals practically speechless for almost a century).

First things first: at the dawn of this particular "founding moment" of constitutionalism, the "democratic" criticism of the scope of judicial power was already surfacing. Some of the critics were "antifederalists" who opposed the "federalist" project for a new Constitution. Together, they launched multiple attacks against the proposed Federal Constitution targeting each of its aspects. Perhaps because the proposed Constitution was under attack from so many angles, the criticism of judicial review (the "counter-majoritarian" or "democratic" objection) went relatively unnoticed. Therein lies Hamilton's first coup. While many of his colleagues still failed to recognize or understand, or simply disregarded, the "counter-majoritarian objection," Hamilton decided to take it on the volley. Immediately, without hesitation, Hamilton realized that the objection crucially strikes at the very heart of the Federalists' intentions. He knew he could not let it go unanswered, and that an immediate, forceful response was critical. And that is what he set out to provide.

One of the antifederalists who opposed the national constitution – one whose identity we still do not know – signed his many articles against the project as "Brutus." Brutus attacked several of its aspects: the immense powers that the new central government was going to have; the heightened risk of tyranny; and possible loss of freedom. But his most accurate blows were directed against the judiciary. He was among the first to bring the counter-majoritarian objection to center-stage. He wondered how could it be – as we would say today, in a democracy – that the will of the people, expressed through the decisions of Congress, is overcome by the decisions of judges? Does not this mean that the will of the judges will prevail over the will of the people in the new government? Where does this centralized power, held by the Supreme Court, leave the states? [1]Hamilton immediately recognized something important and powerful in that criticism, and the need to clear it up immediately. His colleagues, however, seemed impervious. Hamilton thus alludes to Brutus, without directly naming him, when he is halfway through Federalist No. 78. He goes on the attack. He comes out to meet his pugnacious rival, writing: "the rights of the courts to pronounce legislative acts void, because contrary to the Constitution, has arisen from an imagination that the doctrine would imply a superiority of the judiciary to the legislative power . . ." Hamilton's recognition of Brutus's objection appears in these three lines: the right attributed to the courts – Hamilton observes – "has raised certain doubts," because it is alleged that the competence of judges to challenge the authority of the laws "would imply the superiority of the judiciary over the legislative power" (the "democratic objection").

Next comes Hamilton's powerful response, in one short paragraph – the response that would define the course of the discussion to this day (and partially remove the question from all debate for generations). Hamilton replies, with surgical synthesis and precision, that the objection misses its mark because it is based on a misunderstanding. With the agility of an expert swordsman, he responds by avoiding the blow. To put it another way, he takes out all the sting of the objection by granting its

[1] See, for instance, Brutus: "The Problem of Judicial Review," https://teachingamericanhistory.org/library/document/the-problem-of-judicial-review/.

crucial, impelling, most powerful essence. Hamilton recognizes and highlights, in effect, the power of what we now call the "democratic objection," and responds that the concern is justified (indeed, he admits that it is absolutely relevant), but counters that the error lies in the criticism's presupposition.

Hamilton turns the table on his opponent by turning the argument upside-down. He says the objection is well taken, but ill-founded. He criticizes it using his opponents' own terms, and in particular their most important argument – the democratic argument: "You are forgetting what is most important" – Hamilton seems to be saying to his critics – "in your haste to criticize us, you have forgotten the most crucial point."

Hamilton points out that those who criticize judicial review and thus defend the "superiority" of the legislature (as an organ that expresses the "will of the people") have forgotten the most relevant factor of all: the Constitution. And what happens when the Constitution enters the debate? It reveals the error of the criticism because (this is the central idea of Hamilton's response) it is in the Constitution, and not in the legislature, where the alleged "will of the people" truly resides! So, the proper reasoning should go as follows: when a judge invalidates a law passed by Congress in the name of the Constitution, the judge is not imposing his own will on that of Congress and, thus, negating the will of the people. On the contrary, the judge is *restoring the will of the people* (!) as *expressed in the Constitution*, and preventing it from being negated by Congress. That is, according to Hamilton, the justified, and fully democratic function of the judiciary: it is simply the custodian of the will of the people as expressed in the Constitution, and its mission is to act as its guardian, preventing other government organs – the legislature in particular – from violating it. Confronted by any attempt to undermine the people's will, the judiciary's duty is unequivocally clear: the judiciary must ensure that the people's will as expressed in the Constitution prevails over the will of the legislature, which is expressed through the laws of Congress. Here are the exact words Hamilton used in that short and historic paragraph that forever changed the discussion about constitutional review:

> It is not otherwise to be supposed, that the Constitution could intend to enable the representatives of the people to substitute their WILL to that of their constituents. It is far more rational to suppose, that the courts were designed to be an intermediate body between the people and the legislature, in order, among other things, to keep the latter within the limits assigned to their authority ... If there should happen to be an

irreconcilable variance between the two [the Constitution and the law] . . . the Constitution ought to be preferred to the statute, the intention of the people to the intention of their agents. Nor does this conclusion by any means suppose a superiority of the judicial to the legislative power. It only supposes that the power of the people is superior to both; and that where the will of the legislature, declared in its statutes, stands in opposition to that of the people, declared in the Constitution, the judges ought to be governed by the latter rather than the former.

13.2 The Most Famous Court Case in History: *Marbury* v. *Madison*

In the previous section, I stated that Hamilton's brief argument in The Federalist No. 78 forever shaped the debate over judicial review in the face of the "democratic objection." However, the truth is that, in practice, the argument that actually settled the discussion was formulated by Supreme Court Chief Justice John Marshall in 1803 (who did not initially realize that its core element had already been presented by Hamilton) in the most-cited court case in history – *Marbury* v. *Madison*. I must insist that what Chief Justice Marshall did in that case, knowingly or not, was nothing more than reformulating what Hamilton had already said more than a decade earlier, merely applying its implications to a specific case. It is in this sense that the Hamilton-Marshall line of argument was can be said to have changed the history of the debate over judicial review and the "democratic objection."

It is also worth taking note of the special juridical and political nature of *Marbury* v. *Madison*. The case was juridically special because it enshrined in judicial practice something that the Constitution of the United States itself does not mention (and neither would most of the constitutions molded after it): the right of the judges to invalidate legislative acts. It is for this reason (because it provided the instance from which constitutional review was "invented") that it is so frequently cited (it is surely the most cited court ruling in the history of constitutionalism). Its extraordinary political importance relates, meanwhile, to more mundane reasons: after the democratic President Thomas Jefferson was elected to replace the outgoing conservative President John Adams, Adams tried to "pack the bench" by appointing judges who were political allies. This would enable Adams, in a sense, to continue governing after leaving office. The massive and urgent appointment of judges prompted a scandal over "midnight judges" – judges who had been appointed the night before Jefferson took office. The rush to secure these appointments was such that the appointments were not finalized before Adams' term ended. Once he entered office, Jefferson took advantage of the incomplete process to block the appointments, refusing to sign the last forms necessary for the judges to assume their functions. These were the circumstances when William Marbury, one of the newly appointed judges, filed suit demanding his appointment be completed, bringing the case to court.

In order to keep sight of the subject that matters to us at the moment, remember that this was a case of the utmost political importance, which courts were called on to resolve, and which would surely set off all sorts the controversies, theoretical and political, regarding the role of the judges: Did it really come down to judges to decide, in the last instance (to have "the last word"), what the Constitution required in these situations (in short, were the judges ultimately in charge of defining the meaning of the Constitution)? Jefferson, upon learning of the decision (which, as we shall see, worked to his favor at the moment, but would prove to be a handicap in the long run), clearly saw what was happening and immediately "yelled blue murder." He immediately realized Marshall was conceding him "the battle" (Marbury would not win his lawsuit or receive his appointment), but signing his defeat in "the war." Through his decision, Marshall consecrated and gave legal force to a remarkable competence (basically, giving judges the power of "the last word" to decide constitutionality), which was not clearly expressed or recognized in the Constitution. From then on, judges would have the authority to impose the "ultimate interpretation" of the Constitution, *invalidating the norms that – according to their interpretation – contradicted it.* Hence Jefferson clamored angrily against the decision, claiming that all branches of power had the same right, stating that all of them had the same authority to "say" what the Constitution meant (Jefferson went on to advance what we now call a "*departmentalist*" approach to constitutional control, according to which all "government departments" have the same right to participate in the interpretation of the Constitution). Still, what triumphed was not Jefferson's theoretical objection over who interpreted the Constitution, but Marshall's argument, which, as Jefferson anticipated, was essentially the same as Hamilton's. Following Hamilton, as we shall see, Marshall argued that judges were the simple guardians of the Constitution and *that they therefore had no other choice but to invalidate the laws* that they found in contradiction with what the Constitution required. Let us look at the very heart of Justice Marshall's decision:

> It is a proposition too plain to be contested, that the constitution controls any legislative act repugnant to it; or, that the legislature may alter the

> constitution by an ordinary act. Between these alternatives there is no middle ground. The constitution is either a superior, paramount law, unchangeable by ordinary means, or it is on a level with ordinary legislative acts, and like other acts, is alterable when the legislature shall please to alter it. If the former part of the alternative be true, then a legislative act contrary to the constitution is not law: if the latter part be true, then written constitutions are absurd attempts, on the part of the people, to limit a power in its own nature illimitable.

In other words, taking up Hamilton's position, Judge Marshall's main argument was that the justice system had for its mission safeguarding the Constitution where the will of the people resided. In a system (like all of our systems) where there is the "constitutional supremacy" (i.e., the Constitution represents "supreme law" because it occupies the highest point in the "legal pyramid") the judges, simply, "have no other choice." If they believe that any law contradicts the Constitution, they must invalidate and take it out of the game.

More precisely, Marshall argued, the judges have only two options to choose from when they notice a conflict between some law and the Constitution – a situation many described as the unescapable "iron dilemma" observed by Marshall. According to Marshall, *the first of these two alternatives was conceivable, but absurd*. It boiled down to the argument that, in the event of conflict between a law and the Constitution, the primacy of the law should be upheld. This alternative was completely unacceptable – ridiculous – because it implied that the Constitution was basically useless (if the law won out in cases of conflict between it and the Constitution, then the Constitution did not establish any real limits and did not serve any purpose). If the law was in the end superior to the Constitution, then why bother having one? (Constitutions would then be nothing more, in Marshall's words, than "absurd attempts by the people to limit a power that is unlimited in nature.") Given the absurdity of this first alternative, Marshall pointed out that only the second could be taken seriously. Marshall thus only considers valid the alternative possibility: if the Constitution represents the "supreme law" of the land (the "law of laws"), and a legislative norm is passed that contradicts it, the norm should be struck down as unconstitutional. *In a conflict between the two, it is the law that must "lose" against the Constitution and be declared invalid*. In Marshall's terms, what was enshrined in this way was a truth as powerful as it was obvious, that is, that all "law contrary to the Constitution is not law."

We thus arrive at the consolidation of the Hamilton-Marshall argument that, for almost a century, would represent the unquestionable "truth" on the matter. Such was the force of this simple reasoning that a different line of reasoning, one that had gotten off to an ambitious start at the time, was shoved out of the public sphere for decades, as if it had never existed. Indeed, Marshall handed down his ruling in 1803, and the discussion over judicial review and the "democratic objection" was only meaningfully reengaged at the end of that century: a theoretical knockout that lasted close to a century. However, the "winning" argument was far from watertight; in fact it was full of holes. It took some effort to find them and, for many people, it is still as if the discussion stopped there, frozen in time, settled by Marshall's decision, once and for all. In the next section, in any case, I will start to show where the holes in this "victorious" reasoning lie.

13.3 Judicial Review and Democracy: Failed Arguments

The line of argumentation presented by Hamilton-Marshall in defense of judicial review and against the "democratic objection" was, as we saw, indisputably successful. For many activists, jurists, and academics, the discussion over it simply ended then and there, as if there was nothing left to dispute in the face of such arguments. However, as we will see below, the "Hamilton-Marshall" line of reasoning actually does contain notable flaws – I would even say insurmountable ones. I would like to focus, above all, on one of the strongest arguments against the "Hamilton-Marshall" line: an argument involving "interpretative gap." Still, I want to emphasize beforehand that this very successful argumentative position is vulnerable to several other lines of criticism in addition to that of the "interpretative gap."

Indeed, with the passage of time, the problems posed by the Hamilton-Marshall proposal have become clearer and clearer, problems which for decades had remained unquestioned. To begin where we ended the presentation of Marshall's decision in *Marbury* v. *Madison*, the Chief Justice's "iron dilemma" was actually very problematic, dubious, and in the end not nearly as hard as "iron." The judge appealed, as we recall, to an almost irrefutable "logic": only two alternatives were available to the Court faced with a law that violated the Constitution. The first alternative was – Marshall declared – simply absurd (validating any law contrary to the Constitution), so only the second alternative was available (requiring the court to invalidate any law contrary to the Constitution). The truth is, however, that what the judge held as incontrovertible holds room for enormous doubt.

I mean that Marshall presented as a matter of "logical" reasoning, as an irrefutable syllogism, a conclusion that was actually highly debatable. It so happens that many alternatives are in reality available to judges called to make a decision on the constitutionality of a law. The availability of more than two alternatives therefore cracks the "dilemma" presented as "iron"-hard. To take a highly relevant example, we might look to the situation unfolding in France around the same time as the "constitutional moment" in the United States. The context in that country following the French Revolution was very distinct in that a strong anti-judicial climate was apparent. The French judiciary was perceived as closely associated with the absolute monarchist "*ancien regime*," which generated enormous suspicion of the judges' motives. For example, authors such as Montesquieu expressed the opinion that judges should be seen as simple "mouthpieces of the law": they did not possess the slightest competence to question the validity of a law passed by Congress. Congress, from this perspective, embodied the "sovereign will of the people." One consequence of this interpretation of the sovereign will in France, within the context of deep suspicious of the judges' role, was taking action to prevent judges from challenging the legislature. Hence, within the framework of the first Revolutionary Constitution – the French Constitution of 1791 – a study was commissioned to examine the role of judges with regard to laws that appeared to be in tension with the Constitution. The conclusion of the study was unequivocal: even when a law appeared to conflict with the Constitution, judges could not invalidate it. The judges were to *send the rule back to Congress.* A practice of referral to the legislature was thus conceived. Pausing for a moment, we may agree or disagree with this mechanism. We might consider it justified or illegitimate, efficient or ineffective, attractive or repugnant. Notwithstanding, and this is what is important to us, we cannot deny that the alternative exists, and its mere existence shows the fallacy of the "iron dilemma." Remember, the Hamilton-Marshall argument held that judges could only choose between two paths of action. In fact, if a judge fails to realize that there are other viable, reasonable alternatives beyond invalidating the law passed by Congress, that judge is in error. (To anyone who might argue that the legal referral mechanism did not exist in the United States, I would point out that neither did judicial review – it was a power that the judges gave themselves as if it existed!)

The problems of the line of reasoning offered first by Hamilton and later by Marshall do not end there; indeed, that is only where they begin. In truth, each of the logical steps of the argument, when examined closely, is vulnerable to serious objections. I will take an especially visible example on which I do not want to dwell long. The fundamental assumption behind Hamilton and Marshall's reasoning was that the Constitution – not Congress – embodied the "true will of the people." That assumption, however, as should be obvious, is also questionable. It may be valid as a working hypothesis, as a provisional and momentary assumption, but if we expect the proposition to bear the full load of its implications, then we run into problems. I point this out now, at this point in history, but in truth the assumption in question was much more vulnerable back when the argument was made. Indeed, considering the number and magnitude of the groups (racial minorities, women, slaves, and on and on) that had no part in the drafting of the US Constitution (and the original constitutions of Argentina, Chile, Ecuador, and so on, are probably even worse in this regard), the affirmation that the Constitution expresses the "will of the people" is, more than an exaggeration, "nonsense upon stilts." In any case, I do not want to press this line of argumentation since, I am inclined to concede, many of the constitutions in force today have "remedied" those original deficits of popular legitimacy, either because they have "earned" democratic legitimacy over time (which some might dispute), or because they have undergone reforms instituted through more plural and inclusive constituent assemblies.

Another important criticism of the Hamilton-Marshall argument that I will only touch on is the "intertemporal objection." This is an argument that has been advanced, for example, by the constitutionalist Bruce Ackerman, towards the end of the twentieth century. Ackerman, like so many of his contemporaries, tends to be sympathetic to the "Hamilton-Marshall" justification, but not without significant reserve. Ackerman accepts the principle of constitutional supremacy – the argument that the Constitution, not the Congress, embodies the "true will of the people." He also accepts the idea that judges "have no reasonable alternative" other than invalidating laws that violate the Constitution. What Ackerman criticizes, however, is the idea that the only point of reference from which judges can ascertain the "will of the people" is the text of the Constitution as it was written a hundred or two hundred years ago. Ackerman argues the "true will of the people" is, in effect, found in the "original"

Constitution, but that it has also found expression in subsequent moments where the people steadfastly "stood up" with a similar level of insistence, amplitude, and depth to the original "founding moment" of the Constitution.

Let me illustrate this through an example that especially interests Ackerman. The civil rights movement of the 1960s – fighting for racial equality and justice – involved extraordinary levels of mobilization and activism that were translated into political disputes, legislative twists and turns, and dozens of court decisions for and against initiatives meant to promote racial equality. The primary, ultimate result of the long social and political process and legal and moral disputes were a series of public decisions (e.g., the Supreme Court's decision overruling the discriminatory legal principle of "separate but equal"). This result, in Ackerman's opinion, deserves recognition as a constitutional reform: it represents, in fact, a new "constitutional moment" as important and as equally relevant as the original constitutional moment. This is because the process contains all the virtues and distinctive characteristics that justified assigning relevance to the original moment of "constitutional creation" (political mobilization, public debate, disputes in Congress, judicial interventions, etc.). What matters about Ackerman's argument for the moment is its response to Hamilton and Marshall that judges cannot affirm the prevalence of the Constitution over a law in question by limiting (as Hamilton and Marshall requested) their "comparison" of the law to the text of the Constitution. If the norm in question (let us say, one that establishes nondiscrimination on racial grounds) is the product of a "constitutional moment," then that norm – and not the "old" text of the Constitution – should prevail. Although I am not in a position to present and defend Ackerman's position in more detail here (beyond its more or less obvious strengths and weaknesses), the truth is that it represents another worthy challenge to the Hamilton-Marshall argument.

After this quick overview of a couple of the many arguments that challenge the dominant position on constitutionality control, we find ourselves in a better position to delve into what I believe is the decisive objection against the Hamilton-Marshall line of reasoning.

13.4 The "Interpretative Gap" Argument

As indicated, I believe that the "decisive argument" against the dominant, standard position on the justification of judicial review and its resistance to the "democratic objection" is what I have called the "interpretative gap" argument. Now I would like to explain this argument and its importance in greater detail.

The basic idea of this argument goes as follows: if the Constitution were a document whose interpretation was simple or more or less straightforward, or if we all shared a common interpretative formula (consensus on how the Constitution should be understood), then the arguments of Hamilton and Marshall would be fundamentally sound and defensible. Despite the problems already mentioned (some of which might have solutions, while others might persist), we could agree with Hamilton and Marshall that, in the areas where the Constitution represents the "supreme law," judges are obliged to "safeguard" it, and in this context there is a very strong argument in favor of allowing judges to invalidate laws that violate the Constitution. As Marshall himself wondered: "What else are we supposed to do?"

However, in situations where we strongly disagree over what the Constitution (or the laws) establish, the authority and legitimacy of allowing judges to decide constitutionality comes into question. I will try to illustrate this crucial question with an example that might help understand it.

For the first part of the example, imagine that the Constitution says that Senators shall serve terms lasting four years, but the Senators want to extend it, and so pass a law saying that their terms, from now on, last five years. In this situation, since the Constitution represents the "supreme law" and the judiciary performs the role of "guardian" of the Constitution, a judge is called upon to decide on the law's constitutionality. The judge reads where the Constitution says "four years" and then reads the law that says "five years." The judge concludes that, in fulfilling her mission to ensure the Constitution's supremacy, the law goes against the constitutional text. Confirming a law that authorizes Senators to serve for five years, would mean assuming that the Constitution (which in this case explicitly establishes four-year terms) does not speak to the matter. Since the judge's task is to preserve the prevalence of the Constitution, and the law clearly goes against the Constitution, the judge invalidates the law: "Law contrary to the Constitution is not law."

If all cases were as straightforward as this one; if all our norms were (as in this case) as transparent in meaning; if there was no room for interpretative doubt; if the norms in question (as in this case) boiled down to "numbers" (or similarly pristine symbols of undisputable meaning); then, basically, we would not have any problem with constitutional interpretation and there would be no significant doubt regarding the authority of the judge to decide the case. The judge could tell us, with good reason:

> I have decided as any of you would have done. Anyone can read the same words that I read, can compare the law and the Constitution, and see that the law that says five years and the Constitution says four years. I have no choice, just as any of you would have none in my place: declare the law unconstitutional and thus invalid.

Despite the considerable objections to the judges' authority that we have already seen, the reasoning in this case would be close to irreproachable. However, let us look at a slightly different scenario.

Now say the Constitution, like so many constitutions around the world, speaks of the rights to "life" and "liberty." The law in question, meanwhile, does not mention either term, but does speak of "abortion." How should the judge make the comparison now? In the previous case, we read "four years" in the Constitution and "five years" in the law. We compared the two – a judge, a lawyer, a carpenter, a child, anyone would come to the same conclusion: the second text is inconsistent with the first. But what now? Does the idea of "abortion" contradict the idea of "life"? Does it contradict the idea of "freedom"? Here we are faced with a major problem! It would not be surprising if almost none of us agreed on how the two texts should be compared. For many people, the idea of "abortion" contradicts the constitutional requirement of respect for "life." For others, the idea of "abortion" expresses what the Constitution says when it speaks of "freedom" (e.g., the freedom of women to decide what they do with their bodies). No matter what position we may hold, the truth is that we are faced with enormous doubt and complication! Unfortunately, dilemmas like these are not the exception, but are rather the most typical ones in our legal systems. This is because, among other reasons, the texts are not transparently clear; they are often imprecise; sometimes they were lazily written; other times they are purposefully ambiguous; they do not only involve numbers; and, furthermore, because we do not share an interpretative theory or algorithm to resolve disagreements. Much more seriously, constitutions – every constitution – is plagued (necessarily, I would say) with principles, abstract clauses, open concepts: every constitution seeks to express commitment to certain fundamental values (equality, freedom, dignity, justice). The problems of interpretation that we encounter in any text, be it a book, a poem, or a legal treatise, are even more extreme when we are dealing with the Constitution. We face an abyss that I describe as germane to (or generated by) the "interpretative gap."

The crux of the matter is that, when the interpretative difficulty is this serious, the judge can no longer say, as she did when invalidating the law to extend the length of the Senators' mandate: "My decision is the same as yours, it is the same decision that anyone would reach if they were presented with the same texts that I have read." In the face of clear, transparent, indisputable texts (perhaps possible if the Constitution only contained numbers), the legitimacy concerns surrounding the judges' authority would be practically nil. The judge could reasonably argue that it makes no difference that she took the decision, because anyone else would have come to the same decision, had they been in her position.

The question is completely different, however, when we are dealing with issues like abortion, or thousands of others. To take some recent examples, does the passing of a law to regulate media outlets honor or violate the freedom of expression? Does the prohibition of a racist demonstration violate the constitutional right to free assembly, or does it uphold the rights of other groups to assemble? Does banning a Nazi political party go against respect for ideological freedom? All these issues activate different interpretations that overcome the justification of judicial authority and democratic legitimacy that was evident in the first scenario. When everyone agrees on how to interpret community norms, problems of democratic legitimacy vanish. The more disagreement there is over the interpretation of our community's legal texts, the greater the problem of judges' democratic legitimacy. These instances lead us to ask ourselves why the judges, and not us, are in charge of determining how the Constitution should be read. Why, if they have as many doubts as we do (e.g., when comparing the ideas of "life" and "freedom" to "abortion"), are they the ones to decide, and not us, the correct interpretation? Why, in a democratic society where the will of the people is taken as sovereign, should the judges' interpretations prevail in disagreements over ours? The point is: if judges are ultimately left in charge of deciding all the tough cases (is abortion unconstitutional? Is the media law constitutional?), it is as if they are in fact governing society. Allowing them to make these interpretative decisions places them, in effect, above the politicians and, ultimately, the rest of us. In other words: the "fire" that Hamilton and Marshall sought to "put out" – the "democratic objection" – has come forcefully and irremediably roaring back.

13.5 Law Goes Global: International Courts

As an appendix to this chapter, I would like to dedicate a few final lines to a larger problem that deserves more extensive treatment: the globalization of law and the emergence of international tribunals. I am interested in examining, among other things, whether the emergence of "global law" forces us to rethink or set aside the type of objections to judicial review explored so far.

Over the years, starting from the recognition of "universally" shared problems – problems that extend beyond one country's borders (including, for example, genocide, Nazism, or fascism) and the consequent need for and urgency of legal answers to these shared difficulties, the international expansion of law began – very particularly at the end of the Second World War. The European Court of Human Rights, for example, was established in 1959. We can also point to the signing of the Inter-American Convention on Human Rights, in 1969, as a result of which two other international bodies were assigned competence to intervene – once again – in the face of the most serious human rights violations: the Inter-American Commission on Human Rights and the Inter-American Court of Human Rights. These are early examples of that growing call to internationalize the law – a call that has spread across much of the West since the mid-twentieth century. Taking examples such as those mentioned as a basis, I would like to pose a few questions about their relevance to judicial organization and the concern raised in this chapter about the democratic legitimacy of courts.

International tribunals that were created to respond to very serious human rights violations that the States themselves appear unable to confront or resolve raise questions such as the following: *Does the democratic objection still make sense when it is no longer clear where sovereignty lies (because "those affected" is often the whole of humanity and often no pertinent universal political body exists)?* Is the democratic objection relevant when we are no longer talking about democratic communities (e.g., when the issue is rights violations committed by dictatorial regimes), or when the communities in question are incapable of or recalcitrant to prosecuting the massive violations?

Consider, for example, the very important case *Velásquez Rodríguez* v. *Honduras*. This was both the first decision in the history of the Inter-American Court and the ruling that defined the Court's profile during its initial stage (as Jorge Contesse has described it, the case set "the ethos that would govern the Inter-American Court" for many years, Contesse

2015). Starting with *Velásquez Rodríguez*, the Inter-American Court clearly demonstrated an "interventionist" stance: the Court showed it was willing to confront local political authorities and "impose" non-negotiable, unassailable judgments for failures to respect rights.

In that case (which I chose because it helps understand the nature of the problem at stake), the Court found that the state security forces of Honduras had violated numerous clauses of the American Convention for their involvement in the forced disappearance of Ángel Velásquez Rodríguez, a student at the National Autonomous University of Honduras. They had violated Velásquez Rodríguez's right to life, right to humane treatment, and right to personal liberty. In response to the serious failure of the local authorities to prosecute the crimes, the Court ordered Honduras to pay monetary compensation and carry out an investigation of the student's disappearance. Honduras objected to the Court's decision with the interesting argument that the victims had not exhausted the available domestic remedies (a necessary requirement for cases to be referred to the international system). The Inter-American Court, however, rejected this argument in a way that made clear its "interventionist," even "aggressive" stance. It stated that "the international protection of human rights" was based on the need to protect victims from "arbitrary excesses of governmental authority." Because the petitioner alleged the lack of adequate domestic remedies – the Court concluded – international protection was not only justified, but also "necessary and urgent."

Now let us return to our initial question: In the context of international law, violations of rights that are an affront to humanity, and states that unabashedly resist efforts to try those accused of the them, is it not absurd – and directly insulting – to consider the validity of the democratic objection? The internationalized stage of law could allow us to recognize and address problems that the difficulty of localized parochialism prevented us from in the past.

It is my sense that these considerations do not change the substance of the discussion – they situate the matter at a "higher level" – but at the root the objection remains relevant unless the nature of the problem we are analyzing is modified. As I understand the framework of the international application of law, the essence of the dilemma remains relevant, and therefore there is no reason to vary the position that we laid out in the previous pages. The exception – I insist – lies in cases where the problem is of a different nature, as in the case of *Velásquez Rodríguez* v. *Honduras*. In this case, as in the other early cases decided by the Inter-American Court, that defined "the ethos" that would govern the Court in its initial stage, the Court was dealing with authoritarian states and dictatorships. In this respect, but only in this respect, the problem is different in nature from the problem of the democratic objection. But in our recent history (at least, since the creation of international tribunals), this situation represents more the exception than the rule, within the framework of international relations. In the face of dictatorships, in effect, the entire discussion on democratic objection dissolves: we are dealing with a problem of a different nature that may justify exceptional measures and decisions on the part of the international community. Faced with these types of extreme situations, we might accept initiatives that we would not in principle justify in normal circumstances: international boycotts; pressure campaigns; even armed intervention. This does not mean that any of these extreme measures are justified without regard for their content or the procedures that led to them, or that they would be justified in other cases. However, in principle, the intervention and decision of an international tribunal, such as the Inter-American Court or the European Court of Human Rights, does not seem controversial (again, depending on the decision taken, the remedies adopted, etc.) in relation to the actions of dictatorial or authoritarian governments. These international tribunals were created as a result of somewhat, however weakly "democratic" agreements between states, and enjoy – because of the way in which they were formed – a degree of democratic legitimacy. The degree of legitimacy is lower than the legitimacy of, for example, that of a democratically elected legislature or even, I would say, than that of local courts, but in any case, without a doubt, they do possess a degree of legitimacy that is greater than any dictatorial government. This "relative advantage" in terms of legitimacy, typically in relation to a dictatorship, makes comprehensible (and partially justifies) the "initial ethos" that moved the Inter-American Court in its early days when it handed down many important decisions against dictatorial governments that earned it international respectability.

However, in many other cases the international court does not enjoy more democratic legitimacy than the defendant and the substance of the democratic objection problem remains. Consider, for example, the aforementioned *Gelman* case, where the Inter-American Court took up an amnesty law passed by the Uruguayan Congress in irreproachably democratic conditions. As we have already seen, the discussion on the matter in Uruguay was so deep, so widespread, and so long-lasting that we could reasonably say that the amnesty law finally consecrated in Uruguay had acquired extraordinary democratic credentials seldom seen in modern times. Recall that the amnesty law was ratified by not one, but two (!) popular votes, both of which were preceded by extensive processes of collective discussion.

In *Gelman* v. *Uruguay*, the Inter-American Court was no longer dealing with an authoritarian or dictatorial regime (the Court's concern for its democratic legitimacy waned after the initial phase of cases against authoritarian regimes). In *Gelman*, the defendant-state under investigation was not only fully democratic, but had also carried out extended public discussions over the proposed measure, which is almost unheard of in our time. For those of us who think about the law in terms of a commitment to democratic dialogue, what happened in Uruguay was remarkable and deserved recognition – whether we like the Uruguayans' decision or not.

However, the decision of the Inter-American Court could not have been worse. Completely disregarding the democratic process that involved prolonged and inclusive discussion, the Court held in this regard, removing all relevance to the extraordinary democratic legitimacy of the measure at stake:

> The fact that the Expiry Law of the State has been approved in a democratic regime and yet ratified or supported by the public, on two occasions, namely, through the exercise of direct democracy, does not automatically or by itself grant legitimacy under International Law.

In other words, the Court first swept away ten years of democratic discussion, denying the value of the two popular votes (consultations that, I emphasize, had been preceded by a broad and inclusive process of collective deliberation). Then, and even worse, the Court, completely ignoring the pertinence of interpretative disagreements and the special value of public discussion on the matter, simply declared that the incompatibility of amnesty laws with the American Convention "does not derive from a formal question, such as its origin," but from its material aspect. To put it another way, the exceptional value of the democratic procedure (particularly in a case like *Gelman*) was dashed with a single blow. It (the public debate, the first open consultation, the popular mobilizations, the second consultation) was reduced to mere "formal" facts, nothing with legal weight.

Let us now return to the "interpretative gap." In the previous section, I reasoned that, unfortunately, the difficulty posed by the "democratic objection" is aggravated when (i) we disagree over the interpretation of basic elements of the law and (ii) we do not support a single formula on how to resolve the disagreement. Since there are no epistemic authorities who can correctly or even adequately solve such problems on our behalf, we must take up the issue ourselves, and discuss it democratically. The decisions on which policies should be adopted to address the darkest episodes of our past and our worst collective traumas must be taken through collective discussion.[2]

[2] This is particularly the case when the requirements of international law on crimes against humanity and amnesty laws are not clear. Simply, and in order to finish illustrating the point, the Inter-American Court held in *Gelman* that the incompatibility of the amnesty laws with the American Convention "does not derive from a formal question, such as its origin," but rather from its material aspect: why it was committed, and the action in question ran afoul of international law, which requires the prosecution and punishment of the crimes that were pardoned by the law. To substantiate its position, the Court contented itself with citing, "the obligation to respect rights enshrined in Article 1(1) of the American Convention" (paragraph 189 of Gelman). That article – the court added – obliges the States to "prevent, investigate, and punish all violations of the rights recognized in the Convention, and seek, in addition, the reestablishment, if possible, of the violated right and, where necessary, repair the damage caused by the violation of human rights" (ibid., paragraph 190). The text, however, of Article 1.1 of the American Convention, does not actually include at all the detailed series of strict obligations enunciated by the Inter-American Court. Article 1.1 of the Convention reads as follows: "The States Parties to this Convention undertake to respect the rights and freedoms recognized herein and to ensure to all persons subject to their jurisdiction the free and full exercise of those rights and freedoms, without any discrimination for reasons of race, color, sex, language, religion, political or other opinion, national or social origin, economic status, birth, or any other social condition." In other words, one of the main reasons alleged by the Inter-American Court to condemn Uruguay for its failure to comply with current International Human Rights Law had to do with an Article of the Convention that does not make explicit reference to the duties of "preventing," "investigating," "punishing," "restoring," or "repairing" the "damage caused by the violation of human rights" – the duties with which the Inter-American Court alleged Uruguay had failed to comply. Ultimately, this example helps us understand why we should prefer democratic discussion to judicial decisions when dealing with basic moral problems and the most abstract commitments of our right. Often, we simply disagree, and no person or international body is qualified or has the required legitimacy to decide with authority for all the others.

14

Constitutional Interpretation

When the "Interpretative Gap" Widens

To make the type (and severity) of problems we face when we speak of constitutional interpretation easier to understand, it may make sense to start with an example like the following. Let us imagine that we are before a higher court that functions respectably well. Let us say we are talking about a court in the style of the (revered and much discussed) nine-member Supreme Court of the United States. The court represents the highest interpretative instance in the country: we may assume that there are very few people within this community who are as well-trained in legal knowledge as the members of the Court. Most of the judges are studious, well-prepared and, importantly, each has a fantastic team of clerks and assistants culled from the best law graduates across the country. They are a fabulous pool of experts in terms of skill and knowledge.

Let us now see the results as reflected in the court's recent decisions. For the sake of the example, let us say they are the court's last four decisions (that I will make up to illustrate my point better). In the first decision on gay marriage, the court's decision was unanimous with all nine judges supporting it. In the other three cases, as is more frequently the case, the decisions were divided. On a case involving the right to bear arms, the decision was made by a six to three majority; in the next case regarding taxes imposed on telecommunication companies, the court voted seven to two; and in the third case, involving abortion, the most divided decision of all, the decision was made by a five to four majority. Many people might read the varying majorities positively as a sign that the court thinks deeply about each case independently and without fixed ideologies.

Still, let us think a moment more about the meaning of these changing majorities mean and the message they tell us. The fact that a collegial court regularly reaches fragmented decisions (five to four; six to three; seven to two) does not only speak to the court's reflective and impartial nature. It implies and reveals, above all, that even in the highest interpretative instance of the country, even among the most technically prepared legal teams, even among those who have studied the meaning of the law the most, *disagreements on how the law should be interpreted are deep and happen almost every day!* The implication is even greater and much worse, for the examples "chosen" indicate the level of discord at the highest level of interpretation in the country on the most important public matters (abortion, gay marriage, taxes). These results mean that five of the judges (or six, or two, or four), have a similar enough opinion of the law's ultimate meaning to form a majority while the remaining four (or three, or seven, or five) believe that in fact the law means the opposite! This is the alarming situation we find ourselves in on a daily basis when it comes to legal interpretation.

To give an adequate sense of the dimensions of this panorama, we should remember that the first promise of the "rule of law" is equal treatment (Allan 2016, Dyzenhaus & Thorburn 2016). The law promises us, from day one (and this is what, in principle, gives law the legitimacy it claims): "It does not matter who you are, what your name is, what your race, sex, or ethnicity is. The law will treat everyone equally. The rules are the same for everyone. This is the difference between states that respect the rule of law and authoritarian states where your fate depends on the discretionary will of the person in power." The sample of high court decisions discussed above, however, examples that can be found on any given day in any moderately organized legal community, call into question that "first promise" of the rule of law to treat us as equals, understood as not treating us in any discretionary manner. Our examples suggest, on the other hand, that our fate decisively depends on *who* makes up the tribunal. This deserves careful attention. It means that, for example, if I am being tried for the consumption of some drug, my fate – in some cases my life, rights, and freedom (e.g., whether I am released or sentenced to ten years in prison) – will depend a lot not on what the law in force in my community *says* but on the reading of the particular judges chosen to interpret the law (for instance, whether they find that the constitutional right to "privacy" implies full protection for personal consumption as "private" and protected behavior, or find that I can be prosecuted for what I thought was allowed). Unfortunately, and after more than two hundred years of constant reflection on interpretative theories, we remain very far (as far as ever) from reaching any basic agreement on the matter.

14.1 What Interpretation Is Not

As we already know, the (self-assigned) capacity of judges to invalidate laws as unconstitutional confers extraordinary power to them. That capacity and the enormous power it brings would be basically irreproachable, if (i) the task (of interpreting the law and determining its compatibility with the Constitution) was simple and obvious, or (ii) if we agreed on ways of resolving interpretative disputes (if we had some consensus for an "interpretative formula"). We saw towards the end of the previous chapter that constitutional interpretation is not simple or obvious: the law is not clear; it is imprecise, ambiguous, full of "gaps"; and the Constitution is not transparent (it is not reducible to numbers and pure logic). These problems are typical of "natural language": they appear when we read a book, try to understand a novel, listen to a speech, or go to the movies. The language with which we speak and write is plagued with these ambiguities and inaccuracies, whether we read a legal text or Borges, or Cervantes. The problem is more serious in the case of constitutional law if the Constitution – as any constitution does, as it must do – expresses commitment to general values and principles ("life," "freedom," "equality," "dignity").

We must then ask the other question: Are there shared "formulas" for interpreting the Constitution or resolving interpretative differences? Are there, for example, specific legal theories that, after serious study, enable us to interpret the law and the Constitution well enough to rise above doubt? If the answer was yes, then we would have found the way out of our problem: the solution would only be a matter of studying and working more. Unfortunately, this is not the case, as the following examples make clear.

First of all, interpreting the Constitution is not comparable to solving mathematical problems. If it were, we could require our judges to obtain the required skills to reach the correct result the same way we ask mathematicians to learn and deduce complex proofs. If the two tasks were comparable, we would assume that problems only have one correct answer and that the answer is the same no matter who performs the analysis: they just need be very intelligent, have all the relevant information, and possess the requisite knowledge. However – as we saw – this is not the case: law is not an exact science. On the contrary, interpreting law involves a number of value judgments (balancing ideals such as justice, freedom, equality, dignity, etc.) over which we currently disagree and will continue to do so. Correctly interpreting the law is not achieved by study alone. (Curiously, or not, for as much as a giant that Ronald Dworkin was in legal theory, for a good part of his life he was committed to the idea that all difficult cases only have one "correct answer." He spoke of the "correct answer," however, only as a working hypothesis: in his writings, only a fabulous judge – "Hercules," Dworkin called him – could actually find the answers.)

Unfortunately, interpreting the law is not comparable to translating between languages either. In translating texts or speeches – say, a speech from Norwegian or Russian into Spanish – we could reasonably argue that the more we prepare and study (the better we know both languages), the better the chance of performing well. We know that, in translation, there are correct ways to accomplish the assigned task (say, translating a text from Russian to Spanish). Most of us will not get it right, but we will improve with better preparation. If we work hard enough, study variants, interact with native speakers and pick up their jargon, we will undoubtedly do better: our translation will then reflect, in an increasingly irreproachable way, the text that originally read in Russian. Eventually, someone might be able to say that the translation is more or less perfect. We could disagree on fine points, such as the best equivalent of this or that term, but regarding the truly important substance, we will agree wholeheartedly. Those of us who speak both languages well (Norwegian and Spanish; Spanish and Russian) will recognize a job well done, more or less perfect. If interpreting the law were similar to translating languages, then we could reassure ourselves: again, we would just need to appoint the most intelligent judges who have studied the most. When a difficult case came up, we would simply turn to the best judges who, like the best translators, have acquired the most knowledge. Because they know the most, they will know what the law requires so we can resolve the case.

Alas, more disappointment: interpreting the law is not like solving mathematical problems or even like translating between languages. Two legal experts can be very intelligent and have studied hard all their lives, yet still arrive, at the end of the day, at two different conclusions regarding the law in the specific case. Worse still, they may even come to (believe it or not) directly antithetical conclusions! Unfortunately, this is not uncommon. It happens every day, all the time, every moment (think of all the five to four and six to three decisions in US Supreme Court cases).

14.2 The Multiplicity of Interpretative Theories

These problems have to do, above all, with our deep disagreements over how to "read" the law and how to balance the implicit, fundamental value judgments that every legal system incorporates with regard to the specific facts of the case at hand. I have suggested that these serious problems would cease to be if we shared interpretative theories (which we apparently do not) that would enable us to resolve our disagreements. Again, however, we have no such broadly accepted interpretative theory. On the contrary, we have at our disposal (and so, therefore, do judges) interpretative theories of all stripes and for every taste, even – or especially – theories that tend to lead opposite directions. Therefore, it should not be surprising for some judges to read the law one way while the judge sitting in the next chair arrives at the opposite solution (again, this is why we have, even in the highest courts, so many five to four and six to three majority decisions: even at the highest level, we frequently find opposite interpretations). Allow me to go into a few more details.

In the first place, after more than two hundred years of studying constitutional interpretation, we have not even come close to solving the problem. Secondly, interpretative theories have become very sophisticated in recent times, but this has not widened the margin of agreement (reinforcing the first point): today we have more diverse, well-founded interpretative theories than ever and, many times, they are totally incompatible with one other. Scholars seem to agree on the starting point: we all tend to recognize that in order to understand and interpret a text, we must read it. We must first read the norms in question to see if they contain the information needed for resolving the case (alike when, in our imagined example case, the Constitution said that the Senators' mandate lasts four years but a law is passed determining that it will last five, what we did is read both texts and spot the contradiction). In most everyday cases, however, the commonalities between interpretative theories tend to end right after the initial reading of the norms: legitimate doubts and reasonable disagreements immediately surface. The important question that arises, then, is how these interpretative disagreements over the law should be resolved.

We are thus confronted by an enormous variety of responses (which tends to deepen disagreement further still): we have theories that suggest one answer, and others that advise the opposite. I will list a few of the available theories below for illustrative purposes only. Let us imagine, to take a real case, that what is at stake is the meaning of the respect that the Constitution extends to "private life" in the context of a government that wants to criminalize sex between people of the same sex. Below are some contemporary interpretative theories that will guide us to different responses.

Original Intent (Originalism). Some theories recommend paying attention to the "intentions" of those who wrote the applicable norms (e.g., a judge might cite a letter from Alberdi – the "ideologue" of the Argentine Constitution – to his rival Sarmiento that makes it clear that Alberdi considered homosexuality a purely private act). In a similar (but by no means identical) way, there are interpretative visions that ask us to resolve interpretative disagreements by considering the other writings of the authors of constitutions, or by trying to reconstruct – counterfactually – what they would have affirmed, had they faced the current situation (e.g.: What did the convention delegates who wrote the text under analysis say during the debates? Or, in the case of the counterfactual: What conclusion would they have reached in this case, if it had been presented to them, in light of what we know they said in analogous cases? Some conclusion may be drawn from their opinions on religious dissent or people who engaged in "vicious" behavior).

Original Meaning. Another interpretative approach suggests we interpret the meaning of the term in question ("privacy," for example, and in this case), according to the meaning of the term at the time it was written and incorporated into the Constitution (e.g., how the idea of "private morality" was understood in 1853, the year the Argentine Constitution was adopted). The famous United States Supreme Court Justice Antonin Scalia subscribed to this type of interpretative vision, which he called the theory of "original public meaning" (a vision to which he referred saying: "I take the words as they were promulgated to the people of the United States, and what is the fairly understood meaning of those words").[1]

"Living Text" (or "Living Constitutionalism"). Some consider that the Constitution cannot be "anchored in the past" and that its meaning must therefore be updated in accordance with the community's current values (e.g.: "Would we now say that the right to private morality protects sexual acts between consenting adults?"). The Constitution – this school maintains – must remain in force as a "living text."

Traditions. For some jurists, the way to resolve existing interpretative disagreements in a community requires paying attention to the dominant

[1] Scalia presented this view in a speech given at the Catholic University of America on October 18, 1996 (Scalia 1996).

legal traditions and practices within the society in question. Carlos Rosenkrantz, President of the Argentine Court between 2019 and 2021, has proposed this interpretative path on more than one occasion, in the first instance, when disagreements in difficult cases arise (just after assuming the Presidency of the Court, Rosenkrantz maintained that). In any case, the text of the law should play – in his opinion – a primary role in the law's interpretation, and that the text could only be "expanded or contracted according to the way in which the community understood the rules throughout its history and through the canons it created over time").

"Majority Thinking." Similarly to the approach above that examines a community's legal tradition, others attempt to resolve the deep doubts that certain legal texts generate by taking into account the current, majority, democratic opinion (e.g.: "What position on LGBTQ rights did the party in power today put on its electoral platform?" Or, similarly: "What do most people in the country currently think about LGBTQ rights?").

Systematic Interpretation. For still others, doubts over a term in the Constitution should be resolved, firstly, by trying to understand how the particular clause is integrated within the whole constitutional text – comparing, for example, the text of the clause in question with related articles or rights (asking, for example, what the implicit value of "privacy" is in a Constitution that provides very strong protections for the freedom of expression, freedom of association, freedom of thought, etc.). The different sections and clauses of the Constitution must be interpreted – this approach holds – harmoniously, comprehensively, and systematically.

Teleological Interpretation. An alternative suggestion for correct constitutional interpretation invites to look not at the past or present to determine what others thought or think, but to focus instead on the ultimate "ends" of the norm, on the objectives that the norm is meant to serve (asking, for example, what the purposes outlined in the Preamble to the Constitution tell us about "privacy" and other relevant norms, or what the "invitations to progress" mentioned in the Preamble imply).

Comparative Law/Prevailing Doctrine. One last example of alternative interpretative theories suggests that we resolve our interpretative disagreements by taking into account the jurisprudence of other jurisdictions in similar cases, or what their dominant doctrine is now (e.g.: "According to the European Court of Human Rights, homosexuals have the right to be respected as equals in terms of their most personal preferences").

These examples are a sample of the many interpretative theories currently available to facilitate the resolution of disagreements over the meaning of law. For the moment, I only want to highlight two crucial issues.

The interpreters of the law (we can call them the judges) have available to them all the theories mentioned (and many others), which they may choose among according to their own knowledge and criteria. In the end, all adopt some theory, whether consciously or not, without having to justify their choice. The point should be now obvious. As Hans Kelsen put it in his noted *Pure Theory of Law*, "There simply is no method ... by which only one of several meanings of a norm may gain the distinction of being the only 'correct' one ... All methods of interpretation developed so far lead only to a possible, not a necessary, result, never to one which is alone correct" (Kelsen 1967, 352).[2] This is why – he concluded – "the question which of the possibilities within the frame of the law to be applied is the 'right' one is not a question of cognition directed toward positive law – we are not faced here by a problem of legal theory but of legal politics" (Kelsen 1967, 353).

Worse still, judges are free to choose the interpretative approach "to their liking" today, and a contradictory theory tomorrow (and choose yet another the day after tomorrow, and so on, as many times as they want). Judges can also bring in various contradictory theories to support their interpretation, or use a certain interpretative theory to reach the desired decision in one case, and an opposing theory in another case. Such strategical choices obviously (and also remarkably) carry no personal consequences. Whether judges choose one approach or its opposite, the institutional and personal cost is almost null, for nobody is going to punish them, institutionally, for it.

However, it should also be emphasized that the results obtained by following one interpretative theory over another are – understandably – often radically different. Typically, judges can reach one decision or its exact opposite by choosing one or the other interpretative theory. Returning to our example, it is not difficult to imagine that a judge who makes reference to the rights extended to homosexuals in an eighteenth

[2] He added: "The interpretation of a statute, therefore, need not necessarily lead to a single decision as the only correct one, but possibly to several, which are of equal value, though only one of them in the action of the law-applying organ (especially the court) becomes positive law. The fact that a judicial decision is based on a statute actually means only that it keeps inside the frame represented by the statute; it does not mean that it is *the* individual norm, but only that it is *one* of those individual norms which may be created within the frame of the general norm" (Kelsen 1967, 351). For a similar, contemporary approach, see Guastini (2017). I thank Paula Gaido for the references.

or nineteenth-century constitution would tend, although not necessarily, to reach a restrictive or negative decision on the right to gay marriage. Similarly, we could expect judges who rely on interpretative theories that, contrariwise, emphasize the importance of interpreting norms according to their "current meaning," to reach an opposite conclusion of acceptance and tolerance with respect to the rights of homosexuals.

The truth is that, given everything that is at stake, the power that this decision-making capacity confers, and the low cost of strategically choosing one interpretative path or another, judges are left in a very privileged situation and operate within the framework of very dangerous incentives. Their situation makes it easier for them to act in the least desirable way of all. In the face of difficult cases that they must resolve, the attitude we least expect and want from them would be deciding first the type of conclusion they would like to reach based on their preferences and biases, and then choosing the interpretative instrument that best serves them to get to that conclusion. That is to say, it would not be surprising – given the incentives – for judges to start by asking themselves what they are inclined to decide and then to search for the technical or legal "excuse" that allows them to support or justify (to cover with the "color of law") what they have already decided in advance. As Jeremy Bentham once put it (referring to "Judge and Co." and the "sinister interests" that they pursued), common citizens have enormous difficulties "to unravel the mysteries in which Judge and Co. have involved all legal proceedings, under cover of which they have with so much success pursued their own peculiar and sinister interests" (Bentham 1843, 253).

All of the above, as should seem clear, raise very serious questions about the quality of our rule of law, the scope and limits of our rights, and, therefore, the effective limits of our freedoms.

14.3 Look to the Past or Think in the Present?

To better understand the implications of the difficult interpretative situation in which we find ourselves, I would like to simplify the problem and frame it in a more limited, simpler perspective. I propose that, instead of managing the enormous diversity of interpretative theories that exist and those available to judges, we concentrate exclusively on two main sets. In the Anglo-Saxon world at least, for decades the discussion has revolved around two main groups of theories, those related to what we call originalist theories on the one hand and, on the other, theories linked to living constitutionalism (theories that interpret the Constitution in terms of values that are currently "alive"). In some way, it could be said, these two large groups of theories bring together a good part of the interpretative proposals reviewed above. Simply put, those related to "originalism" ask us to resolve our interpretative disagreements by looking back (i.e., pay attention to the traditions of the country, the original meaning of the text, the intentions or will of the constituents; the way the term in question was defined when it was used, etc.); while the other group of theories (those related to the "living text" approach) ask us to focus on the present in order to find the appropriate legal response (i.e., by taking into account the majority or democratic assessments; relying on the current meaning of the terms and values in dispute; etc.).

Let us imagine, then, a situation in which we only have available these two theoretical approaches (and refer to them as): "originalism" and "living text." Let us keep in mind that both types of theories appear supported by understandable, reasonable foundations ... but yet also contrary! Let us look at what one or the other "interpretative path" can tell us:

Why "Originalism"? What the "originalists" tell us boils down to the affirmation that the meaning of the Constitution cannot be subject to anyone's discretionary will. Originalists reject interpretative choices made by speculating what the judge believes or would "like" the Constitution to say, or what, according to his personal convictions, the Constitution should say. As citizens who live under the rule of law, we believe the scope and limits of our rights must not be subject to the discretionary will of judges: we want interpretations to be "tied" to what the rules say, and not to anyone else's inclination. It makes sense to remember that "originalism" regained popularity in the 1960s during the tenure of socially "activist" and progressive Courts, especially the famous "Warren Court" (the US Supreme Court under the Chief Justiceship of Earl Warren, 1953–1969). The Warren Court stood out particularly for its "activism" in cases related to civil rights and the discrimination historically suffered by Black Americans. These courts issued vibrant judicial decisions recognizing the rights of Blacks Americans in areas ranging from employment discrimination, housing and school desegregation, access to public spaces and services, voting rights, due process, and so on. In this context, many legal professionals (mostly conservatives, but we can set this question aside for now), began to formulate their complaints against what they perceived as inappropriate judicial activism. Their complaint was basically that the Court was handing down very bold decisions – very attractive to many, too progressive for others – but ultimately decisions based on what the Justices wanted the Constitution to say, not on what it actually expressed (e.g., nowhere does the Constitution say that Black Americans have the right to go to the same schools as whites). These judges were thus failing, in the Originalists' view, to fulfill their mission of ensuring respect for the Constitution. In order to reduce the exaggerated use of discretion for which they denounced the "activist" judges, they proposed judges "tie their hands" by adhering to the "fixed" meaning of the Constitution that – they suggested – was found in the past, in the law's origins. *Against the discretion that they associated with their legal adversaries, the Originalists then offered, as a distinctive characteristic of their own response, a great virtue: certainty!* The Originalists argued that if judges have doubts about the meaning of a constitutional term, they should not look for it out in the world wherever they want: they ought to tie their hands, to put aside desire and preferences, and to study constitutional history. There, at the origins of the text, they will be able to find what the law says, in its original, first, fixed, and permanent meaning.

An immediate retort to the Originalists might be: "Conservatives! Why fix the meaning of the Constitution in what was said by its authors, 50, 100 or 200 years ago?" This critique of "originalism," however common, is not very good. What the Originalists demand is not keeping the Constitution unchanged; they are not saying that what was written a century or two ago should prevail until the end of time. No. What they are saying is compatible with an ever-changing Constitution. What they demand is constant respect for the original meaning of the Constitution (which may require, if the Constitution is two hundred years old, going back to what the "founding fathers" of the Constitution said two hundred years ago, or, if the Constitution has only been effect for a day, because we just reformed it, then going back to what the delegates said yesterday).

Why the "Living Text"? Contrary to the position of "originalism," the defenders of the opposite position – interpreting the Constitution as if it were a "living text" – also have valid points. Basically, they defend the idea that the basic norms of the community cannot be frozen in their original terms. This must be so, the defenders of the "living text" tell us, for constitutions that aspire to remain in place for tens or hundreds of years. To remain relevant, the law must adapt to new needs, goals, and knowledge. We cannot expect that, in the twenty-first century, basic moral issues – such as those related to the rights of sexual minorities – will be decided on the criteria of the few white, wealthy, and conservative men who wrote the Constitution two hundred years ago. It is also completely unreasonable to undertake a difficult and costly process (politically and economically expensive) of constitutional reform each time there is relevant change in normative criteria. Judges must therefore, when deciding difficult cases that stir uncertainty over the correct interpretation of the Constitution, take into account the new agreements, shared assumptions, and aspirations of community that have developed since the text was written.

Ultimately, both the Originalists and those who interpret the Constitution as a "living text" have important points in favor of their positions. However, before moving on, we should acknowledge the uneasiness that this short presentation provokes. At stake are the scope and limits of our fundamental rights, and we see – from the start – that very influential suggestions on how those rights should be understood are often contradictory.

14.4 Looking to Past or Present for Often Opposite Results

Depending on which of the theories reviewed we subscribe to the "originalist" approach (leading us to think about the past) or the "living text" theories that invite us, on the contrary, to read the law thinking about the present, it seems clear we will often obtain – although not necessarily – opposite results. This situation should be alarming in itself, because it implies that the same written law is compatible with one result and its opposite, depending exclusively on the identity of the judge in charge of interpreting it. This situation seems completely inconsistent with the most elementary promises that the rule of law tries to make in terms of legal certainty and "equal treatment."

To understand the dramatic, real, effective implications of the situation, consider the following. first: interpretative differences tend to appear more intensely – naturally, I would say – in the most difficult public cases where our disagreements surface with greater salience. For example, at the beginning of the twentieth century, one of the deepest economic crises of the modern era broke out (what we call today the Great Depression in the US and, in Argentina, the "Crisis of '30"): the old societies of "order and progress" were crumbling, and they faced profound social demands sometimes expressed in violent confrontations against the government. In this context, many countries began to explore forms of "economic intervention" aimed at repairing the worst consequences of the economic and social crisis. The "Welfare State" – the New Deal, in the United States – would end up gaining support as a possible solution to the disaster of those years. Today, we recognize the importance of the emergence of the "regulatory state," which at the time imposed controls and limits on the use of private property and sought to provide a social "safety net" for the people most in need. However, in its initial moment, the "regulatory state" encountered harsh resistance, particularly from judges who, "interpreting the law," affirmed that the state's proposed economic regulations were not valid because they were "contrary to the Constitution." The truth is that, in a majority of countries, the constitutions said nothing against economic regulation or limits on property rights. However, time and again, the judges rejected the initiatives of executives and legislators. They thus delayed for many years, in the face of an extraordinary social emergency, the emergence and consolidation of the Welfare State.

In the United States, for example, and in the context of deep economic crisis, the judges blocked economic regulations for more than thirty years! The first time the United States Supreme Court rejected a regulation of this type came with *Lochner* v. *New York* in 1905. On that occasion, the Court considered the limits the executive sought to place on working hours in bakeries unconstitutional, and did so based on an "originalist" type of argument. The judges showed that the Constitution said nothing about bakeries, work hours, or economic regulations. Moreover, according to the Court majority at the time, an anti-statist or preference for free market values and private property was evident in the drafters' original intentions. With its decision, the Court dealt the government a devastating blow, which it would repeat in around two hundred other cases! Only in 1937, with the decision in *West Coast Hotel Co.* v. *Parrish*, after a long process of social mobilization, political insistence, social conflict and unrest, and – above all – extreme pressure from the executive and legislature would the Court modify its position – thirty-two years later! In the meantime, what we now remember as a successful economic program (the New Deal, one of the most remarkable reform programs implemented in human history), had been mercilessly blocked by the courts, time and again.

(In those days, President Roosevelt communicated regularly with the citizens by radio – the famous Fireside Chats – giving listeners an account of his concerns, particularly about the changes needed and the poverty and suffering of so many citizens, but also how the courts prevented him from using legitimate political power to change the state of affairs. How was it possible – Roosevelt wondered – that his political initiatives, so obviously necessary, were resisted by the judiciary using those arguments?)

In Argentina, to illustrate the same problem with another example, the situation was basically the same as in the United States around the same time. From the beginning of the twentieth century and for about thirty years (a period also marked by serious social crisis and the fearful rise of the "regulatory State") the courts confronted or sided with the "regulatory" government through untempered argumentative shifts. Appealing to the "original will" of the "creators of the Constitution" (in particular, to the will of Alberdi), typically anti-statist judges contrary to all regulation led by Antonio Bermejo, the conservative President of Argentina's Supreme Court from 1905 to 1929, struck down as unconstitutional the economic regulations pursued by the State (e.g., the rent controls sought by the radical President Hipólito Yrigoyen to alleviate the plight of the poorest). As the Court said in *Hilleret* (1903), the Constitution could not be interpreted from "theories and precedents that are not in harmony with the immediate sources of the fundamental law"; they could not disregard "the needs and desires of the time in which [the Constitution] was dictated [nor neglect the meaning that was given to it through] historical documents and numerous rulings." However, on other occasions, and with opposing arguments in the style of "living constitutionalism," the majority of the Court sided with the government's policy and the "regulatory state." As the Court held in *Avico* (1934), it was necessary to "adapt the text, liberally and humanely, to the realities and demands of modern life, without lagging behind in obstinately seeking what had been, a hundred years ago, the thinking of the authors of the code when writing this or that article."

To summarize a decades-long, oscillating judicial history, I would say the Argentine Court assumed a strongly anti-statist position contrary to all state regulation in the economy in cases such as *Hilleret* (1903), but became an advocate of state economic intervention in *Ercolano* (1922), returning to the opposite stance again in *Mango* (1925), and finally buried its anti-statist bias in *Avico* (1934). That is, a jurisprudential back-and-forth that lasted thirty years (one of the most stable periods in the Argentine Supreme Court's history) that drew from both opposing argumentative theories. Meanwhile, people were unable to pay their rent; others fell into poverty; and many died in misery. Shifting their interpretative approach, the judges moved from one position to the other, without difficulty or much concern for the dramatic consequences of their actions.

Examples like these show the divergent results generated in specific cases from the use of an interpretative line or the other; the ease with which judges maneuver between interpretative changes; and the tremendous practical, political, economic, and social consequences that they have.

14.5 Radicalizing the Critique of Constitutional Interpretation

I would like to conclude this critical analysis of constitutional interpretation by intensifying it. Intensifying the criticism simply requires looking at it in some greater detail to better describe the urgency of the situation. The point, someone might say, is that we have two strong, powerful, but competing approaches, so we should simply decide on one. The question is which of the two is most promising and most persuasive. They might suggest we see which one works best, and stick with that one. The problem is, however, that the premise of such reasoning is false: we do indeed have two opposing approaches, but both are completely implausible and untenable in any of their most common versions. I will explain why below, examining each of the two approaches briefly and successively.

The Radical Problems of "Originalism." I will start with "originalism," which as we saw promises a great virtue – "certainty" – to counter the wide margin of discretion enjoyed by the adepts of living constitutionalism. While the latter theories would allow judges, ultimately, to say what they want the law to say (replacing the intention of the constitution's drafter and, through them, the people, with the discretionary will of the magistrate), the Originalists would assign a "fixed" meaning to the Constitution. Whenever doubts over its meaning arise – the Originalists told us – we must interpret the Constitution according to the original will of its authors based on the meaning of its terms at the time. The great problem with "originalism," unfortunately, is that if there is one thing this theory cannot offer, it is precisely certainty. The whole theory depends, although its adherents deny it, on extraordinary levels of uncertainty that reach pure discretion.

To see why, imagine that we take originalism seriously, in its best form. The theory instructs us that, for example: "the Constitution must be interpreted according to the original will of its creators." "Very well" – we amiably respond – "but please clarify for me which of the different drafters' will we should take into account." After all, we find many different intentions expressed in constitutions, many in conflict. Must we take into account, then, only the will of those who wrote the Constitution (all? some? the main ones?). Or should we rather consider the intentions of those who wrote the relevant section, clause or article? Should we lean towards the decisive figure in the conception of that particular article? Or prefer, instead, the will of those who participated in the debates over it, even if they did not write it or did not conceive it theoretically? Note, moreover, this early problem: by definition, the Constituent Conventions of complex societies are also, and insofar as they are fairly representative, plural. This means that, within any Constituent Convention, we are naturally going to find people who hold opposing, conflicting, and contradictory views. Thus, our interpretation will depend on which perspectives that we choose to take into account, whether we find a "constitutional" testimony of one "author" or a rival one. For example, take the case of the United States Constitutional Convention, where very different positions on all the important issues were discussed – such as the system of "checks and balances." In the face of doubts generated in the matter (i.e., can the President decide, by himself, to intervene in an armed manner in an allied country, if that ally is the object of a "sudden attack"?), we find no clear answer when we read the debates looking for an answer, because we can easily find opposing positions among its main members: Hamilton, for example, always favored deference to the authority of the President in case of doubts. Madison, meanwhile – as a great defender of "balance" – thought otherwise. What do we do when an article was written by people holding antithetical views (a common case, I insist, in (nearly all) constitutional conventions made up of representatives with opposing views) who were eager to leave their mark on the final wording? Article 19 of the Argentine Constitution, for instance, refers to "private morality": the first line of the text, demanded by liberals, endorses respect for the "private actions" of people while the second line of the article, written by conservatives, conditions respect for private actions on not affecting – in the final wording – "order and public morals." How is a legal construction of this type – exaggerated perhaps, but ultimately not anomalous – to be applied to a specific dispute (say, the State's attempt to criminalize homosexuality)?

And what about the "founding fathers" who influenced the constitutional text but who did not directly participate in its writing? This is the case, for example, of Thomas Jefferson in the United States. Jefferson – undoubtedly one of the main theoretical leaders of the moment – was in France during the debates. How do we "evaluate" his intention and will, taking into account that he was not an effective party to the Constitutional Convention? Then there is the perhaps more extreme case of Juan Bautista Alberdi in Argentina. Although he spent most of his life abroad in exile, Alberdi is considered the ideological author, directly and fully, of many of the clauses of Argentina's Constitution, which were decisively influenced by a manuscript he wrote prior to the

Convention. If we are to take into account only the intentions of those who wrote the constitutional text, Alberdi's position should not be taken into account, but rather only the intentions of his "scribes."

Another important question is whether we should take into account only the expressed will of these people (although, in truth, we have not yet been able to determine the will of whom), or should we also take into account their private intentions? Must we also evaluate *counterfactually* what they did not say but think they would have said, according to what we know about them? As Mark Greenberg put it, "contemporary" originalism, in its different forms (from "textualism" to "intentionalism") appear to be "confused to the core" (Greenberg 2020, 143), in its incapacity to tell us "what a reasonable (interpreter) is supposed to be seeking" (Greenberg 2020, 114).[3]

This leads to the question of where we are to look to deduce the will of these people. Should we limit our study to what they expressed at the Constituent Convention? What about the letters they wrote to (or the communications they had with) people "outside" the Convention? What about their writings or correspondence after the Convention ended? Note, for example, that the famous Federalist Papers were written to persuade the population to vote in favor of the Constitution. They were originally articles published in local newspapers in order to garner popular support for the charter that they had already written. To assume The Federalist Papers are a "natural" or obvious source of relevant interpretative material to determine the will of some of the members of the Constitutional Convention, after the Constitution has already been written, would imply, for example, that – in the present day – we should take as relevant interpretative material the comments of conventional delegates made in a late-night television talk show, or tweeted on the constitution's anniversary. Are we supposed to deduce the will of an author by reviewing the thousands of communications made, to anyone, at any time, that include any opinion on the Constitution? That would be ridiculous. So why is taking seriously as relevant interpretative sources – and The Federalist Papers are taken seriously – a series of essays published in "rags" that were more about marketing a finished product than part of the public debate, not also ridiculous?

3 Greenberg considers that the same Antonin Scalia "played an outsized role in propagating these confusions," which he himself once denounced – thus, when he referred to "the great degree of confusion that prevails" in the field of statutory interpretation" (see Greenberg 2020, 143, 109).

We should also ask ourselves about the proper degree of abstraction of the principles expressed or written by those "founding fathers" so long ago. As an example, the principle of equality established by the Fourteenth Amendment to the US Constitution, read at a very "low" level of abstraction, refers exclusively to equality between "whites" and "blacks" following the Civil War. However, if we read these references at a "higher" level of abstraction, we find egalitarian allusions that seem to apply to and may help us understand matters of gender equality. At what level of abstraction, then, is it appropriate to read that clause, recognizing that the "level of abstraction" chosen may have enormous consequences?

In short, the interpretative world proposed by "originalism" promised above all certainty to counter the subjective discretion of its rival approach. However, we hardly pay any attention to what "originalism" entails to attain that certainty, and when we do, we encounter countless problems whose solutions are unclear if not inexistent: we do not know whose "original intent" to take into account; where or when to cull the "intent" from; what level of abstraction the principles warrant; and so on and so on, ad infinitum. Sadly, we must draw the conclusion that "originalism" cannot assure us interpretative certainty.

The Radical Problems of "Living Constitutionalism." Once we understand the nature and (in my opinion, insurmountable) severity of the problems inherent in the "originalist" interpretative approach, we are in a better position to recognize similar problems on the side of "living constitutionalism." This is because, again, it is not clear what living constitutionalism really means when taken seriously. More specifically, it is not clear how we are to apply the approach in specific cases. Should we transpose the terms and principles of the Constitution to their current or present meanings, or to the meaning shared by the community? How? To honor the dictates of "living constitutionalism," we should take into account, then, the will or the claims of whom? From whom how? From whom when? From whom, as expressed through what means?

Let me illustrate the problems with a recent example from Argentina where, since early 2018, notable public discussion has taken place around the issue of abortion (an example that we will return to later in more detail). Depending on where we look to unravel the "current thinking" of the community on the subject, we find very different results. The President at the time – who made clear his personal convictions against abortion – supported holding hearings in Congress to take the issue up. Argentine civil society, very much influenced by Catholic tradition, was actively involved in the discussions and tended to take, according to various polls, a much more liberal position than was traditionally the case. In party politics, and more specifically in the Congress where discussion of the issue had been silenced for years, the issue suddenly gained so much prominence. After centuries of being silenced, the subject now seemed omnipresent. Finally, a liberal reform initiative was undertaken. The measure obtained a narrow but very important victory in the lower house, but was ultimately defeated (closing the matter for discussion) by a slim minority in the Senate. The project to liberalize abortion ended there. Let us imagine that, in this context, the Supreme Court was forced to reconsider its somewhat ambiguous position on the subject and opted to follow the criteria of "living constitutionalism" interpretative approach. The question is what a court willing to give special weight to the new community understandings about the law should take into account. Should special weight be attributed to the will of the President, who, on the one hand was personally against the practice but on the other hand "liberally" allowed democratic deliberation for the reform to proceed? Or should weight be given to the majority opinion that, according to polls, seemed to favor liberalization? Or the sentiments of the majority political parties that, until 2018, had blocked discussion of the issue? Or the will of Congress, which buried the debate after their votes (the Chamber of Deputies in favor, the Senate against)?

Note the implications of seeking to recognize and honor the "current will" regarding abortion. Depending on the institution, public figure, or group that we take into account, we will encounter contradicting results. Furthermore, as several of those possible sources demonstrate, the result also depends on the moment or time we consult them (e.g.: political parties, public figures, civil society organizations, and the citizens themselves had all sometime in the past shared an apparently hostile or indifferent position towards abortion that seems to have started to change significantly in recent years). What should count as "current" – yesterday, last month, last year . . . or last century?

These examples, moreover, open important questions about the appropriate methods for determining the "current will." For instance: Do surveys "reveal" what citizens really think or feel about controversial issues? Or are political expressions, by congressional votes, for example, a better indication? Furthermore, we have yet to determine who has the authority to decide what the "current opinion" on any topic is. The jurist John Ely put it poignantly by asking how a "living constitutionalism"-type theory could justifiably be employed by judges, for the task would effectively require the judiciary to become extremely familiar with the "current thinking" of the community. This seems highly paradoxical after having gone to so much effort, in institutional terms, to "separate" judges from the citizenry for the sake of their "independence" (e.g., by shielding them from political influence through ample compensation, life tenure, etc.). There seems something irrational, then, in expecting the judges to do a certain kind of work after having institutionally trained them to do exactly the opposite (at least in the sense of disregarding majority preferences).

In conclusion, the two main interpretative theories suffer from very serious shortcomings that show their structural fragility. That fragility noted, it is time to return to our initial concern: finding a reliable interpretative "formula" that would allow anyone at all ascertain the standard "correct" result of a legal dispute, at least anyone with the requisite amount of study and intelligence, and thus eliminate the "democratic objection" against conferring ultimate authority on judges to determine the meaning of the Constitution. When we realize that there are no indisputable interpretative formulas or shared methods for resolving interpretative differences, the "interpretative gap" broadens even more, leaving us staring down into a dark, bottomless abyss: today, through constitutional interpretation, judges can literally decide anything they want. The problem of the democratic legitimacy of those charged with constitutional interpretation has returned with potent force, as the reasonable doubts expressed by "Brutus" over judges' authority to decide, for the people, what matters most to them, have been established, for all intents and purposes, as "certainty."

Before closing this chapter, I would add a small additional point, of particular public-political relevance in many Latin American countries (and beyond). In the fragile institutional contexts typical of Latin American countries, the political and/or economic power centers have extraordinary incentives to gain control over the judiciary. These powers (political, economic) know that control over the "judicial key" of interpretation gives them control over almost everything that matters. Through the help of "friendly" judges – or the active collaboration of politically engaged or committed ones – they know they can obtain legal enforcement for their abusive practices. If, for example, the Supreme Court puts its "seal of approval" on such excesses of power (e.g., by legitimizing censorship, legalizing the persecution of opponent, and so on), those currently in power will be shielded from internal and external criticism, in that even authoritarian leaders will be able to defend the legality of their actions, and it will also strengthen their own claims to legitimacy. This is very bad news for the (already) fragile democracies we inhabit.

14.5.1 *Some Notes of Caution*

In the previous paragraphs, I presented a very skeptical position regarding constitutional interpretation. Allow me, then, to add a few notes of caution (and perhaps optimism), before continuing my analysis. To begin with, I do not deny the existence of "clear" and "easy" cases, where we all tend to agree about the meaning of the law. Second, I am mainly focusing my attention on a specific (hopefully small) set of cases, namely those legal dilemmas that Ronald Dworkin described as "hard cases" (Dworkin 1975, 1977). More specifically, I am thinking about situations of profound legal disagreement, which refer to ideologically contested cases, related to fundamental constitutional issues.[4] In addition – if I may – I want to admit that my views on the judicial system may be unduly biased, given the place where I was born and the context in which I grew up.[5]

In sum, there are different factors and circumstances (personal, contextual, theoretical) that explain, to a large extent, my disenchantment and lack of hope towards constitutionalism, the role of judges, and legal interpretation. Surely, then, the realities of other countries – I mean more solid and stable democratic countries – may allow other readers greater margins of optimism than those I find in my region. I also understand that in many of these countries (i.e., the United States, Germany, England), the use of judicial precedents (and the use of some interpretive techniques, such as analogical reasoning) allows the legal community to approach to issues like constitutional interpretation with less anxiety and fewer worries.[6] Likewise, the existence of more stable legal practices and

[4] Remarkably, Dworkin did not provide a clear definition of "hard cases": He mainly referred to those cases that arise when "both in politics and law . . . reasonable layers . . . disagree about rights"; "no established rule can be found"; etc. (Dworkin 1975).

[5] In fact, it is difficult, in a country like mine (Argentina), to believe in the virtues of judges and in the possibilities of constitutional interpretation. Our entire constitutional history has been marked by political instability and the presence of "politically dependent" judges. Let me illustrate what I am saying: the previous century (the twentieth century) was characterized by recurrent coups d'état (six coups d'état in total: in 1930, 1943, 1955, 1962, 1966, and 1976), which usually implied changes in the composition of the main courts, and consequent changes in the content of the main judicial decisions and in the existing line of judicial precedents.

[6] I would always remember, however, what some empirical studies on judicial behavior and constitutional interpretation have revealed us, on these matters. Think, for instance, about the studies carried out by Cass Sunstein, David Schkade et al., in the context of US Federal

the presence of more solid interpretative conventions favor the strengthening of the rule of law. All these factors can result in higher levels of trust towards the judicial system, in general, and the task of constitutional interpretation, in particular.

14.6 Constitutional Interpretation in a Community of Equals (or "from How to Who?")

The difficulty of constitutional interpretation represents a very serious problem for the law – one that we have not been able to solve, nor come close to, after more than two hundred years. Everything of essence boils down to what the Constitution means in specific cases – how to resolve difficult cases on any important public issue (abortion, social rights, privacy, free expression, etc.) – and yet we seem bogged down in clumsy answers. We have already become familiar with the theoretical swamp in which we are bogged down: "Do we need some kind of dictionary to solve the interpretative problem? Must we carry out scientific socio-historical-anthropological research to unravel our ancestors' intentions? Would carbon-dating the original constitutional manuscript reveal anything? Or, on the other hand, should we conduct a survey?" The difficulty of this important and complex problem is clear, yet it still seems unusual that, after centuries, we remain in complete uncertainty. Much worse is that we continue to maintain simultaneously two primary responses that contradict each another: one to look backwards to unravel the past with some secret formula; and one to look around us in the present to deduce a similar mystery. Unfortunately, this situation favors the emergence of discretionary readings about the law and its content.

How to think, then, about the constitutional interpretation, in these circumstances? How to do it in the face of difficulties such as those discussed above? Of course, I do not intend here, in this brief space, to

Courts (i.e., Sunstein, Schkade, Ellman, & Sawicki, A. 2006; or Sunstein, Schkade, & Ellman 2004). Examining the work of federal judges, they have demonstrated that, in "ideologically contested cases, a judge's ideological tendency can be predicted by the party of the appointing president; Republican appointees vote very differently from Democratic appointees. Ideologically contested cases involve [. . . issues such as] affirmative action, campaign finance, the rights of criminal defendants, sex discrimination, piercing the corporate veil, racial discrimination, property rights, capital punishment, disability discrimination, sexual harassment, and abortion" (Sunstein et al. 2004, 304). It seems that in such fundamental and controversial cases, what is written in the law is less relevant than the ideology of the interpreter.

solve a problem that the legal community has not been able to solve for more than two hundred years. I will simply suggest some ideas and observations in this regard.

In the first place, the analysis presented in the previous pages draws our attention to the fragility of most of the interpretive theories that we have. As we have seen, even the most widely accepted theories show themselves, upon closer examination, to be weak, inconsistent, and imprecise. To make matters worse, after more than two centuries of reflection on the matter, we still lack clear criteria to prefer any of these theories (i.e., originalism) over the others. This is where the fragility of interpretive theories intersects with what Jeremy Waldron has called "the fact of disagreement": there are not, nor are we expected to find, solid and indisputable methods of resolving our main disagreements on constitutional interpretation.

What can we do then, at this point? I return here to Waldron, to say with him: what we need is to pose ourselves a question about "authority" in politics. The question is: "Who is to have the power to make social decisions, or by what processes are social decisions to be made, on the practical issues that competing theories of rights purport to address?" (Waldron 1999, 244). In other words, in the face of our disagreements, we need to accompany the question about "how to interpret" with another question about the "authority" to intervene and decide, in such situations of uncertainty. For Waldron, the main answer to this question is: "The people whose rights are in question have the right to participate on equal terms in that decision" (Waldron 1999, 244).

In the framework of this work, my answer to the question about "authority" is somewhat different from that offered by Waldron. I would respond by saying "the community of equals" has to have the final authority to decide in such circumstances (the difference with Waldron's position is greater than it seems, since Waldron declares to be speaking, finally, of "the representatives of the people, in the Congress").

We now have some modest but important answers to some of the crucial questions posed by constitutional interpretation. In fact, we do not have a clear answer to the question of "what" ("what interpretive theory to use"), but we have some possible answers to the question of "who" should decide – "the community of equals" – and "how" it should decide – "through a conversation among equals."

Let me then illustrate how the "conversation" could develop in the "community of equals," in the face of the serious interpretive problems we have. In order to do so, let me return to our initial example, this is to say, the example of the "immigrant community" recently settled in the "promised land." Recall that they too faced serious interpretative problems from the beginning. The "original charter" they made on the ship represented their "Constitution" with minimal regulations to organize their collective work in the new land ("we will all work, every day, except on Sundays"). Then, once at their destination, conflicts begin to arise, forcing them to ask questions like: "Why don't we work on Sundays?" "Is it forbidden?" "What about people of other religions who rest from work on Saturdays?" Take, for example, the case of Francesco: he found that he could no longer work the land on cold winter mornings because the climate had aggravated his already serious respiratory problems. He wanted to know, then, if the "regulation" that required "work" from all members of the community "allowed" him to stay home and cook for the rest. "Does that qualify as work?" – he wondered. This problem, for the purposes of our work, undoubtedly represents an interpretative problem. How could we solve the problem, in a community of equals? We suggested the answer at the time, considering the case "easy." Community members would come together. Knowing Francesco, they would converse with each other, and arrive (imaginably, not necessarily) at a shared solution. They responded, looking at the regulation (but also taking into account everything they knew about him, including, in a nondefinitive but still relevant way, their affection for Francesco): "But of course you can stay home, of course cooking is work." Someone else might have added, with a grin (or not): "Housework is very hard work, we already know! Look at María and Carlos, who spend all day cooking!" I am not interested, of course, in idealizing or romanticizing the response that I imagine to be typical in a community of equals. What I am interested in is drawing attention to the decision-making process, to contrast it to the alternatives that we know.

The response of the community of equals seems light-years removed from the alternatives that are currently available and predominate. Of course, none of the immigrant community breaks out a dictionary to see check the current definition of the word "work." That is not how they resolve their conflicts! Let us imagine, to take another example, that one of our "founding fathers" – the patriarch Don Vincenzo – has, after providing so much guidance during the "original" moment of writing those rules in the little notebook, passed away. His colleagues would remember what he had said, and incorporate it where relevant in discussions. Yet would someone go find an old letter he once wrote, looking for some indication, some clue in the dedication perhaps ("Look at what he said in this letter to his wife: 'I always remember you fondly, working alone in the kitchen . . . '") to determine whether kitchen work is work? The suggestion is preposterous. They might read the letter out of curiosity, if they wanted, but they would all understand – in the community of equals – that the problem faced was theirs to solve, not Don Vincenzo's. The words of the departed often move or enlighten us, but they cannot "determine" our responses to conflicts in the here-and-now.

The same applies to the "living constitutionalism" alternatives. It would be unusual, in the face of our dilemma, to decide through some "secret vote" or a show of hands a final decision without any discussion. Our imagined community must "own" the problem, it is theirs, even if it affects Francesco in a special way. They need to give reasons, listen to others – people they trust, with whom they spend their days – rather than imposing an impersonal decision. In extreme circumstances, yes, they could resolve the matter through a vote, but it would not be ideal and it would probably be offensive, since they have both the opportunity and the need to exchange views about what happens to the community, about the difficulties encounter (in this case, interpreting a foundational text).

Someone might ask what would happen if the community grew so large that it became unreasonable to hold group discussions about every issue. In that case they could, for example, create a committee or "representative commission," entrusting it with finding the problems that we can no longer solve on a daily basis through collective discussion. Yet, surely, if that committee claimed it was deciding something on their behalf, according to their will, when it was actually imposing its own will; or if the committee did not consult the collective, when it could have, before deciding divisive issues, the group would take such behavior as an abuse of power. They did not choose the committee to "rules over them" or impose its will, but rather out of efficiency, division of labor – to save time for everyone, so everyone was not needed to do "everything." For the same reason that, once the society has grown, they will not all till the land or cook the meals: the labor and the benefits belong to everyone, but they cannot all take care of everything all the time. They help each other, then, by delegating.

In short, as I understand and hope, our "community of equals" example might be fertile. It might provide a basis on which we may begin to think of ways to solve our most serious, bicentennial, stagnant legal problem, one with no apparent solution: the problem of constitutional interpretation.

***

Appendix: Judicial Review and the "Conversation among Equals"

In his article "The Arduous Virtue of Fidelity," Professor Ronald Dworkin tried to answer the following question: What is the correct answer to the question of what our Constitution means, no matter what or who is given final interpretive responsibility? (Dworkin 1997, 1251). Here, I have been partly following his invitation, to then depart a little from it. In my opinion, once we clarify certain basic questions about the first problem – the problem of interpretation – we are in a better position to think and decide about the second question – the problem related to the "interpretative authority."

According to the analysis so far presented (on democracy, constitutional interpretation, and the judicial function), we can define at least two things. First, we have reasonable and persistent disagreements concerning matters of common and public interest (disagreements that also affect the fragile interpretative theories that we have). Second, we think that those disagreements should be dealt through a process of collective conversation. This starting point – I submit – helps us articulate a better approach to the role of judges in a constitutional (dialogic) democracy. In what follows, I would like to advance a few brief considerations on the role of constitutional justice (a subject to which we will return, in different ways, in the following chapters).

Let me begin with two claims. First (and contrary to what judges usually do, in the name of the Constitution), judges should allow the community itself to decide about its own fundamental issues, through collective dialogue. Second, and contrary to what some legal doctrines suggest (i.e., the doctrine of "political questions") they should concentrate on safeguarding the (procedural) conditions of the collective dialogue.

These brief initial "directives" already allow us to formulate some interesting clarifications. On the one hand, we can affirm that the usual doctrinal discussion about whether we should have "activist" or "self-restrained" judges is wrong. We should consider, instead, that in some specific cases judges should allow politics to decide (i.e., on "substantive" issues), while in other types of cases judges should be very active (i.e., safeguarding the procedural conditions of democratic dialogue). In the same way, the previous proposal helps us better confront the traditional "counter-majoritarian" objection. When we establish that judges should focus on safeguarding the procedures of democratic conversation, the "democratic critique" tends to dissolve (and this would be so because now judges would dedicate themselves to work "at the service" of the democratic debate).[7]

From my previous analysis, someone could conclude that I defend a "procedural" model of judicial review, like the one famously proposed by John Ely in his important book *Democracy and Distrust* (1980). On that occasion, in fact, Ely proposed judges to focus on guarding against systemic biases in the legislative process.[8]

Although there is an obvious connection between Ely's procedural theory, and the one I am here proposing, the differences between the two approaches – I claim – are equally relevant (for reasons that should be now evident). These differences have two main sources. On the one hand, my view is based on a "dialogical" conception of democracy, which is very different from the "pluralist" conception of democracy that lies behind Ely's scheme.[9] On the other hand, Ely's theory was conceived for a particular social and political context, and here I will be interested in rethinking that background and consider instead other problems or "dramas," more pressing in our era.

Let me begin with the first difference, related to the diverse conceptions of democracies that we consider. In my view, and guided by a deliberative conception of democracy, judges should set aside cases that they deal with today, and at the same time, begin paying attention to other cases, which today they tend to set aside. Thus, and for example, they should start examining with *strict scrutiny* (I mean, with a high presumption of invalidity) those laws passed in Congress with the necessary majorities, but without public debate, or unsupported by public

[7] I am well aware of the difficulties confronted by this view (i.e., "what should be considered a 'procedural matter'?"; "what could count as an improvement of public debate?" etc.). I do not think, however, that these difficulties are insurmountable, given the capacities that judges have demonstrated for engaging in fine distinctions; the priority we are giving to the public debate; and the instruments that are now available for developing an institutional dialogue, between the branches, and between the branches of power and the people.

[8] In *Democracy and Distrust* and following what the US Supreme Court had established the famous "footnote 4" of the "*Carolene Products*" case (*United States* v. *Carolene Products Co.*, 304 US 144, 152, 1938), Ely proposed judges focus on two main tasks, namely to "keep open the channels of political change" and to provide special protection to "discrete and insular minorities."

[9] In this respect, I share Cass Sunstein's critique of Ely's pluralist approach. Sunstein claimed, "against Ely," that "the American system should not be considered one of interest-group pluralism, with the courts assuming what Ely describes as an 'antitrust' role of assuring the conditions for political competition. The deliberative aspirations of the system require the courts to do something other than provide a fair system of horse-trading" (Sunstein 1993, 144, 104).

reasons, or just expressing the demands of interest groups. As Cass Sunstein once put it:

> the Court requires some independent 'public interest' to justify regulation. A reference to political power is, by itself, insufficient. In no modern case has the Court recognized the legitimacy of pluralist compromise as the exclusive basis for legislation ... Representatives must deliberate rather than respond mechanically to constituent pressures; but decisions to redistribute resources or opportunities, or to adapt the preexisting structure of entitlements and preferences, may well be based on an effort to promote the public good.
>
> (Sunstein 1985, 49–51)

Similarly, this renewed starting point could lead judges to strictly examine legal and institutional reforms that could negatively affect the public debate (e.g., – and these are my own opinions on the matter – they could follow what the US Court said in a case like *Red Lion* – related to public debate and the *fairness doctrine* – while at the same time resist the possibility of making public speech dependent on money – *Citizens United*?).[10] As John Rawls put it, in his examination of some of the US Court's decisions in the area: "what is fundamental is a political procedure which secures for all citizens a full and equally effective voice in a fair scheme of representation" (Rawls 1991, 361). Unfortunately – he claimed – "the Court fails to recognize the essential point that the fair value of the political liberties is required for a just political procedure, and that to insure their fair value it is necessary to prevent those with greater property and wealth, and the greater skills of organization which accompany them, from controlling the electoral process to their advantage" (Rawls 1991, 360).

[10] Let me add another important difference with Ely's approach, which I will not develop here. According to Ely's view, as far as procedures work well, political majorities are free to take the decisions they wish, even concerning issues of private morality. By contrast, for the view that I want to advance here, in what concerns issues fundamentally related to our private lives – and following Millean premises – each person should be allowed to live as she wishes: each individual is taken as "sovereign" upon her own life, and thus responsible for the way she wants to live. For this view, there should be no laws imposing a particular religion or enforcing a particular morality or discouraging certain sexual choices, etc. Also, for this view there should be no judicial decisions enforcing a particular comprehensive conception of private morality – in this respect, judges could only prevent legislators to impose others the dominant or prevailing morality. As Carlos Nino put it: "The validity of personal ideals does not depend on the satisfaction of the requirement of impartiality. Accordingly, collective discussion and decision are not substantially more reliable than individual reflection and decision for arriving at morally correct solutions in this regard" (Nino 1997, 203).

Let us now focus on the second difference that distinguishes Ely's proposal from the one that I am suggesting here – a difference related to the "contextual background" of each of these views. Let me begin by characterizing Ely's approach, following Stephen Gardbaum's excellent review of it. According to Gardbaum, Ely's theory was "consciously parochial," since it was destined to deal "exclusively with the case of the United States Constitution, and almost entirely with the Warren Court" (Gardbaum 2020, 1). Like Gardbaum, I also think that Ely's theory "must be broadened, refined, and updated in order to fulfill its potential for relevance and application" (Gardbaum 2020, 1).

Now, although this discussion would require a separate and more detailed development, in what follows I would simply content myself with pointing out some imaginable "re-updates" of Ely's proposed scheme. Let me just list some possibilities. First, while Ely's theory is (in his own words) a "*representation-reinforcing approach*," my own approach would rather be oriented to the *democratic reconstruction* of an already seriously undermined scheme of controls. This would require judges, for instance, to work with a *presumption contrary to the concentration of powers.*[11] Second, while Ely's scheme aims to "*keep open the channels of political change*," the one I suggest would be oriented (for said reasons) to promote the *democratic debate.* Third, while Ely's scheme requires judges to provide special protection to *discrete and insular minorities*, my proposal would (also) urge a similar concern for the fate of *impoverished majorities*. In this sense, and in order to honor the values of public debate, judges could make a special contribution to public debate by providing special protection to the voices of socially marginalized groups (i.e., in cases related to social protest).

I conclude this brief introduction on a skeptical note. I recognize that judges not only lack the necessary incentives to engage in a dialogic exercise (such as the one I propose), but also find more limits than opportunities to act "dialogically," in the context of our prevailing institutional system. In other words, nothing prevents judges to decide in

[11] In similar terms, and thinking about the US during the Trump years, Professor David Strauss wrote that "If there [is] a significant risk that the administration's actions reflected a systematic undermining of liberal democratic values, then the courts [should] rule in a way that limited the president's powers. The courts may have [] reasons to think there was the kind of threat to democratic institutions that justified them in choosing, among the legally plausible conclusions, the one that limited executive power, irrespective of whether that would otherwise have been the better view of the law " (Strauss 2018, 373; Stone 2018).

accordance with the requirements of a dialogic theory, but – in addition – nothing in the institutional system helps them or induces them to decide in such a way – rather the contrary. Under present conditions, I would conclude, a "dialogic" exercise of the judicial function seems desirable, possible, but also unlikely. We, advocates of the dialogic view, should therefore recover James Madison's teachings (in Federalist Papers n. 51) and focus our attention on the judges' "constitutional means" and "personal motives." Our question should then be: What kind of institutional changes would a dialogic approach demand us to promote (so as to provide judges with the required "means" and "motives")? The good news that we have is that, presently, judges have, at their disposal, different "tools" and "remedies" that are perfectly consistent with the requirements of dialogic constitutionalism (instruments that, years ago, were simply ignored or considered to be utopian, i.e., public hearings; "round tables"; "meaningful engagement"; etc.). The bad news, however, is that the inertia of the "old system" seems still too powerful.

15

Constitution Making

Speaking with One Voice in Multicultural Societies

15.1 Ulysses and the Constitution

15.1.1 Ulysses 1: Ulysses Tied to the Mast

In 1988, Jon Elster published a memorable book, *Ulysses and the Sirens*. In the text, Elster used as a metaphor the myth of Ulysses (who tied himself to the mast of his boat so as not to succumb to the charm of the sirens' song, and to ensure the safe arrival at destination), to reflect on the tensions between constitutionalism and democracy. He meant the tensions that we have already encountered, that derive from questions like: How can a document written long ago (the constitution) resolve in advance the main questions that come up in a democracy centrally organized around majority rule (questions related to political organization, fundamental rights, etc.)? What really governs in such a community: the will of the citizens – the living people walking around – or "the will of the dead"? What justifies placing so many fundamental decisions, in a democratic country, far from the immediate reach of the citizens themselves?

Elster used the myth of Ulysses to help frame the problem and offer solutions to several of the questions preoccupying him. The main idea is that when Ulysses decides to tie himself to the mast, in order to pass safely by the sirens' island and reach his destination, he is not "enslaving himself." He does not "irrationally" tie himself to the mast to deprive himself of freedom because he has lost his mind. On the contrary: Ulysses asks to be bound, not to be deprived of freedom, but to gain it! And his decision is no irrational impulse, but completely lucid reflection! He knows where he wants to go, and he does not want to stray from his course. The act of tying oneself to the mast can thus be seen as a fully rational attempt to attain greater freedom, not less.

The metaphor of binding oneself (to a mast or to a constitution) allows us to understand the purpose of establishing a constitution. Through the dictation of a constitution, a society effectively ties its hands, not irrationally to deprive its freedom, but as a purely rational act to ensure future freedom: to avoid getting lost on the way; to avoid deviating from the set course; to avoid succumbing to temptation. What temptation? The temptation to crush adversaries whenever the opportunity presents itself; to persecute opponents when we hold power; to censor the press when it criticizes us. The constitution is the means we use to keep our freedoms intact by preventing the abuses that tempt anyone – ourselves included – with power. By committing to a constitution, then, as a society, we "tie our hands," but we do it as a (purely rational) means of "freeing ourselves" (Stephen Holmes has published some excellent reflections on the subject, inspired by the work of Elster, Holmes 1988).

15.1.2 Ulysses 2: Ulysses Unbound

In the year 2000, Jon Elster published another fantastic book, *Ulysses Unbound*. In this new book, Elster refuted part of what he himself had written in his previous work in an admirable (and without a doubt, uncommon) exercise of honesty and intellectual curiosity. Comments of some colleagues from his country of Norway led Elster to conclude that he had been wrong in his previous diagnosis (not to mention very important dissimilarities between the myth of Ulysses and constitutionalism that strained the analogy).[1] The main error in his analysis had to do with the risk that, in numerous, unequal societies like ours, a minority ends up in charge of writing the constitution that "ties the hands" of the rest, leaving their own "unleashed." To reverse the metaphor, Ulysses would tie the hands of his crew and take advantage of the temptations and the short-term benefits at the others' expense. Put this way, the metaphor could be crudely applied to the story behind the United States Constitution itself: the authors of the Constitution, mostly slaveholders, defined the basic principles of the new country's political organization. They also provided protections for fundamental rights and freedoms, but nevertheless swept the issue of slavery under the rug as if the problem did not exist. They benefited from this abuse, which they ended up covering with legal protection, thanks to their power of influence.[2]

1 Elster tells of receiving the advice from a Norwegian historian (Jens Arup Seip), who told him: "In politics, people never try to tie themselves, they only try to tie others" (Elster 2000, ix).

2 It is interesting note, in this regard, what can happen when a serious problem is left out or concealed in the constitution: eventually it explodes violently, as in this case, into civil war.

The correction that Elster proposes to *Ulysses and the Sirens* is also indicative of the nature and difficulties inherent to the issues we are analyzing. What should the text of a constitution include, if we intend it to regulate the democratic life of our society? How can we incorporate the claims, hopefully diverse, contradictory, of the many sectors of the community into a single, common text? How can we guarantee mutual respect towards the conflicting demands of all? Who should have the definitive authority for the content of that common constitution?[3]

15.2 Constitutions That Speak with One Voice in Multicultural Societies

It is, without a doubt, difficult to write a single constitution for societies that are plural, multicultural, and diverse: Whose voice should prevail? Or how do we separate and order all the voices talking at once? In the history of constitutionalism, many paths to deal with the growing social, legal, and ideological complexity of our societies have been explored, and this is a good time to look at a few of them.

Imposition: One's Own Voice, As If It Were Everyone's. The worst option of all is, without a doubt, exclusive "imposition" of one faction's will over the others: it is the last possibility that we would like to see today. This happens when one group gains dominance – through number, wealth, power, might, influence, whatever – over the rest and imposes its own criteria: "we get what we want, and the rest will have to work it out for themselves." In Latin American history, which began with close to a century of fratricidal struggles between opposing factions after independence, this was the most common option. Liberals against

[3] The problem that forced Elster to abandon Ulysses' example is, I believe, parallel to the one affecting even the best studies on (the difficult to grasp) issue of the "constituent power" (this is an issue that I shall not examine here with more detail, although I discussed some of the problems associated with the concept in Gargarella 2020). I am thinking, particularly, about Joel Colon Ríos' important book *Constituent Power and the Law*. In his book, Colon Ríos insistently (and reasonably) refers to abstract entities such as "constituent power," "sovereign," "popular will," "the people." The problem emerges when Colon Ríos needs to go from theory to practice – this is to say, from an abstract notion such as "constituent power," to practical instances where that specific power is exercised. In those situations, Elster's problem reappears (recall: "in politics, people never try to tie themselves, they only try to tie others"). More precisely, a collective power that can be properly justified, in the abstract (i.e., constituent power), becomes much more difficult to defend, in actual practice when a particular person or entity, say, the Executive Power simply claims to be acting on behalf of "We the People" or the "sovereign will," and decides consequently.

Conservatives; Unitarianists against Federalists; the capitol against the periphery. The winners imposed rules that they hoped would subdue their opponents or simply established their own values as if they were shared by everyone. These disputes were unsurprisingly reflected in the treatment of religious freedom in the constitutions, for the factions held diverse, often opposing beliefs. For example, all the conservative constitutions adopted in Latin America between 1810 and 1850 established, to greater or lesser degree depending on the case, Catholicism alone as the state religion. On some occasions, the establishment of Catholicism as official religion was accompanied by the prohibition and persecution of those who practiced any other religion; in other cases, the establishment brought with it the privilege of state financing; in still other cases it was only public worship of other religions that was barred. Article 5 of the 1833 Chilean Constitution, for example, stated: "The Religion of the Republic of Chile is the Roman Apostolic Catholic Church, excluding the public exercise of any other." Article 38 of the 1886 Colombia Constitution, meanwhile, affirmed that the Catholic religion was that of "the Nation," and that the public authorities were in charge of protecting it and making sure it was respected "as an essential element of the social order." Of course, in all these cases, what determined the official status of the Catholic Church reflected the identity of the forces that had established the constitution, and that identity was also evident in many other aspects of the shared constitutional order. To continue with the example of Colombia (I insist, towards the end of the nineteenth century), the 1886 Constitution required that public education be "organized and directed in accordance with the Catholic Religion" (Article 41) and that the press, although free, would also be held responsible for attacks on a number of values ambiguously defined by the State: the "honor of the people," the "social order" or "public tranquility" (Article 42). The constitutional practice, in these cases, directly reflected the authoritarian government that the constitutional text was meant to legitimate. And this was perfectly common.

Silence: Leaving Things Undecided. A second possible option, also very common since the origins of constitutionalism, was to pass over in "silence" subjects where there were diverse "conceptions," particularly when in conflict. Silence tended to be the solution when the parties were not able to find a path or "formula" to resolve their disagreements. In such situations, the parties sometimes decide to leave the central issues dividing them "unresolved." As the constitutionalist Cass Sunstein argued, sometimes the most sensible and rational thing to do is simply "leave the question undecided" (Sunstein 1996, 3). A very interesting example of this response occurred in the Mexican constitutional debates of 1857. The place of the Catholic Church and religious tolerance in the new ordering was the subject of one of the longest and most intense disputes. Unable to resolve it, the delegates opted for indecision. It should be remembered that the religious issue was a particularly pressing issue in Mexico at the time because of the enormous privileges that the Church enjoyed. Many liberals opposed ratifying the unfair advantages that the Church had acquired over the years. Ultimately, the liberal delegates decided – revealing the transactional nature of constitutional deal-making – to support leaving the religious question out of the constitution. In this way, at least, the constitution could not be used for religious persecution or intolerance.

The value and consequences of this option, however, are difficult to evaluate. Divided communities understandably seek basic agreements on the most important issues, and for their sake might give up on resolving all differences in one fell swoop. In this sense, "silence" may be advisable. However, as we shall see, putting aside or concealing basic problems often proves to be unfair, ill-advised in the circumstances, or outright mistaken. When the drafters of a constitution make the decision not to deal with the most conflictual or divisive issues (or some of them), they also deprive themselves of an important opportunity to incorporate resources or mechanisms relevant to the conflict in case. Should the differences between the groups come to a head in the future, the groups might find in the constitution the means or motivation for resolving the conflict. It is also true that sometimes the necessary resources may be indirect (an impartial judiciary, for example). However, in addition to the problems specifically associated with these types of alternatives, experience shows that passing over the most serious problems in silence often turns out to be "very bad advice."[4]

Bundling/Accumulation: From John Stuart Mill's "Dream" to His "Nightmare." A third possible response to mitigating conflicting or directly opposed constitutional demands is to "bundle" the interests in tension of the different parties. In cases of opposition and tension in the

[4] In a different case than the one I examine here, that of the United States, the Federal Convention was silent on the country's conflict over slavery (although the complexities of this case make a straightforward assessment impossible). The result was the outbreak of the Civil War between the South and the North – a war that, of course, cannot be attributed to the Constitution, but the Constitution cannot be considered completely alien. For example, many people in the South, to this day, continue to maintain the war was fought over states' rights vis-à-vis the federal government.

claims, when the relevant forces chose "not to let the problem pass" in silence, the strategy of "bundling" was generally preferred in countries from the Middle East to Latin America (see Lerner 2013). In these cases, the members of the convention tried to simply to insert into the constitution ("one on top of the other") as many of their different claims as they could, leaving the tension between them unresolved or totally intact. We shall see, beyond the obvious and foreseeable difficulties, that this strategy is also problematic.

The Argentine Constitution (in its original 1853 version, which remains largely intact and relevant to our discussion) offers several examples of the potential and risk of this strategy. During the "founding" moment of Argentina, as in several other Latin American countries, liberal and conservative groups clashed, often violently, on various issues, and particularly on the religious question. Specifically, the liberals favored religious tolerance while the conservatives wanted to make the Catholic Church the state religion. Faced with these conflicts, the delegates to the Constituent Convention of 1853 – a Convention that included representatives of the liberal and conservative groups – decided first, in response the demands of the conservatives, to grant special status to the Catholic Church in Article 2 of the Constitution ("The federal government supports the Roman Catholic Apostolic Church"). At the same time, but now in response to the demands of the liberals, they adopted a scheme of religious tolerance through Article 14 ("All the inhabitants of the Confederation enjoy the following rights . . . to freely profess their religion"). In other words, they included both contradictory commitments in the Constitution.

The same cumulative strategy (although expressed in an even more worrying way) is found in one of the most interesting articles of the 1853 Argentine Constitution – Article 19 – on private morality. In its initial formulation, which appeared in the first constitutional documents and in the first draft of the 1853 document, Argentina adhered to a typically liberal formula in this regard.

According to Article 19, the State would ensure the protection of private morality, "the private actions of people," to the extent that such conduct did not harm third parties. The initial formulation of this commitment (advocated by liberals such as the convention delegate Gorostiaga) was embodied in the first line of Article 19, which I will characterize as *John Stuart Mill's dream*: a constitutional clause enshrining the philosopher's "harm principle." However, during the constitutional debates, the representatives of the conservative groups – led by the delegate Ferré, from Corrientes – expressed his opposition to that and other liberal clauses and his refusal to sign the agreement as long as the text remained written in such liberal terms. This threat enabled the conservatives to introduce changes, including the reformulation of Article 19. The revision in this regard deeply altered the initial text, converting the clause inspired by John Stuart Mill's ideals into something closer to what we could call *Mill's nightmare*. Basically, conservatives would only endorse the liberal commitment to respect "private conduct" to the point that private actions "in no way offend public order and morals." This condition seriously compromised the entire original purpose of the article and left great uncertainty regarding the borders between "private" and "public" morality.

Note that these kinds of "inconsistencies" in constitutions still in force, such as Argentina's, are not uncommon in the history of constitutionalism, and are in all cases very serious. Again, a community may decide not to make a definitive pronouncement addressing all its serious conflicts, choosing instead to leave matters in varying degrees of ambiguity or trying to generate commitment to the charter by "granting something to everyone." In the case of the most divisive social conflicts, however, we must give much more serious thought before seeking recourse to these constitutional responses. I will only point out one very worrying consequence in this regard. The strategies mentioned do not resolve in any way the substantive conflicts, to begin with, and the resulting constitutional text will either not disallow or will allow, in the future, government action that is either biased (which I discuss next) or confusing and contradictory. Such constitutions contribute greatly to the confusion and biases by bundling opposing claims – all of which receive official state endorsement.

The example of Argentina illustrates this clearly. After the country's Constitution entered into force, the conflicts between liberals and conservatives in religious matters continued, making their way into the courts on numerous occasions. An initial worrying observation is that, as sociological studies of the legal system in Argentina show, most of the country's judges are practicing Catholics. Leaving the resolution of conflicts over the bounds of religious values in public life to judges belonging to the dominant religion offers an insufficiently impartial framework for resolving the conflicts. A second concerning observation involves the frequency with which local courts (even at the highest level, if not as frequently) have had difficulty resolving in good faith and in accordance with the law the disputes that come to them over the constitutional protection of each individual's religious convictions. This is because the Constitution includes clauses that judges can explicitly and directly cite to support one decision or its opposite. When deciding cases on the most sensitive privacy issues (drug use, homosexuality, abortion, gay marriage, etc.) the judges systematically oscillated between liberal and conservative decisions, for both of which they could always refer to the explicit wording of the Constitution.

Synthesis: Overlapping Consensus. The last response to the problem of mediating contrasting demands in the same constitution that I am going to explore is what I am referring to as *synthesis* – a ploy similar to the idea of "overlapping consensus" formulated by the great twentieth-century political philosopher John Rawls (Rawls 1991). In this approach, the dissenting groups make an effort to reach a common solution, which they approach from very different perspectives without repudiating their principles. Rather, they find the points that they have in common so they can establish a lowest common denominator between all the pertinent groups' claims (as Rawls would say, however, this is a more morally justified arrangement than a mere *modus vivendi*). In order to reach a synthetic agreement, each party is expected to set aside or suspend certain relevant aspects of its own proposals.

An interesting example of a "synthetic" response in practice is found in the debates that took place in the United States regarding the religious question. The situation of religious tolerance in the United States was very complex, for many of the first settlers were members of religious groups that had suffered persecution for their beliefs in England. Organizing the norms for public life in the newly independent country were thus particularly important to many people worried that the same scheme of persecution and intolerance might be reproduced. In the end, the majority of the groups who participated in the US Constitutional Convention accepted the non-establishment clause that was made part of the First Amendment. All the groups made a commitment, if and when they came to power, not to impose their own beliefs on others. This interesting result, at least in light of the strategies discussed above, may have been made possible by several reasons, including self-protection, reciprocity, a culture of tolerance, secularism, and so on. (Not surprisingly, the First Amendment represents one of Rawls' main examples to illustrate his reflections on public reason, state coercion, and "overlapping consensus.")

As I hinted, the strategy of the "synthesis" is more interesting and promising than the previous responses to conflicts over what to include in constitutions, insofar as it reflects genuine agreement between the parties reached after each looked for shared convictions that might bring them together. It might represent a "path to explore" for those interested in respecting both the other parties' position and government by all, but the importance of the end result means it should not be undertaken lightly. As with any difficult journey – like that of Ulysses – making it to the intended destination depends on commitments made at the beginning. If only some of the disagreeing groups make a genuine commitment to find common ground, the chances of reaching a final conclusion that is satisfactory to all of them – the most impartial one possible – diminishes exponentially. This important lesson explains the modification in Elster's analysis from Ulysses and the Sirens to Ulysses Unbound.[5]

15.3 A Plebiscite for Everything Aggravates the Problem: The "Hourglass"

Another attractive proposal to address the risk of a minority gaining control of the Constituent Convention and pushing through solutions to the majority according its own criteria is designing the constituent process so everyone potentially affected by the constitution has a voice in it. There are different ways of going about it. Jon Elster himself has explored some of the possible forms this might take in a series of works using another metaphor. Comparing the process to an hourglass, he suggests a procedure that would have ample public participation at the start and end of the process, the way an hourglass is wide at the top and bottom, and restricted participation in the middle (Elster, Gargarella et al. 2018). More precisely, this would involve popular elections for the

[5] Again, the Constitution of the United States provides good examples. As we already saw, the approach I called "synthetic" and Rawls called "overlapping consensus," describes the process behind the country's non-establishment clause, but was clearly not employed for all social conflicts. On the contrary, the US Constitution offers good examples of the more usual approaches. If in some cases, "overlapping consensus" is found; in others, only the vision of one group prevails; and in still others the conflict is silenced in a way that ends up being detrimental. With regards the issue of slavery, for example, the Constitution's silence now seems, paradoxically, deafening. How could the same constituents who had demonstrate so much lucidity in finding common ground in their differences over religious matters opt for such an unfair path regarding human equality? I will not dwell on it here, but I am interested in pointing out that the way the problem was treated, as well as the course of action chosen undoubtedly depended on many factors, but fundamental among those factors was the identify of those who came to the agreement. Undoubtedly, the absolute absence of any representatives from the most disadvantaged group of all – the slaves – could go a long way to explain the final decision of those who were there (mostly slave owners): Ulysses unleashed again.

Constituent Convention delegates, which would then meet privately, after which the results would be subjected to the citizens' consideration through some type of direct consultation.

This proposition does indeed possess interesting inclusive features. Unlike some of the conventions previously discussed that were directly controlled by the ruling elites, this option effectively involves "all those potentially affected." However, we should resist our instinctive attraction to such proposals, at least not if the "popular consultations" are held in the usual way. We must always ask ourselves if the procedure truly favors more open, transparent, and inclusive dialogue. My first reaction is that it would not. A lot of people weigh in at the beginning and end of the process, but play almost no part in the discussions or solution-searching. This is a problem. On reflection, however, the procedure is even more problematic than my first impression suggested. To give an idea of the problems I have in mind (problems entirely related to those we examined with regards the shortcomings of periodic elections, to which I will refer), allow me to offer the example of the 2004 Bolivian Constitution.

After the draft of a new Constitution had been completed, the country's president, Evo Morales, submitted it to a popular ratification process (interesting note: the Constitution had also begun in promising fashion by calling for the participation of a vast range of social groups. However, and for different reasons, that initial opening was quickly sealed, and the Convention ended up taking place within the guarded confines of a military garrison). Still, the invitation to hear the people's voice seemed extremely significant. Following the unfortunate irregularities in the early phases, the people would directly give its opinion on the country's new Constitution! "Everyone potentially affected" were called to vote.

The first problem that immediately became clear was the length of the Constitution: 411 articles, and hundreds and hundreds of sections and subsections. The sheer length made offering any meaningful feedback extremely complex, even for citizens who took the invitation very seriously. Skeptics might point out that, if the citizens truly took the invitation to have their voice heard seriously, they would read it anyways. Even if we did grant the skeptics' point, problems remain. It would not be strange for someone to like some parts and reject others. The Bolivian example is very illustrative in this sense. To take a single, widespread example of the mixed feelings among voters, many were attracted to the clauses related to social and economic rights for indigenous communities (a traditionally neglected social sector in Bolivia, despite their large numbers and presence). At the same time, those same voters were repulsed by the powers that it granted the President and the terms for re-election. Without going into more detail than necessary, and considering only those two elements of the constitution's ocean of articles and clauses, the dimension of the problem is still obvious. The odds on finding parts of a constitution 411 articles long that we like along with parts we detest are pretty high. Popular consultations in this context actually exaggerate the "electoral extortion" disorder that we already dissected. Not only are people prevented from asking for some revision or additional nuance, they are forced to vote for the "complete package." Presumably, *they will have to pronounce themselves in favor of proposals they absolutely reject in order to obtain the promises that they value even more.*

In this sense, popular consultations worsen the citizens' connection to the constitution. Now, not only will they have to put up with constitutional regulations that they emphatically repudiate, but their vote for the constitution will be interpreted as approval of those abhorrent element. The voter will have no way of clarifying the error, no way of marking their reservations regarding specific parts of the text. Although they may be keenly affected by the unwanted facets, they will no longer have grounds to complain. If they did, the authorities would be able to argue that they are doing what the people asked them to do, by approving the constitution, that they accepted the task on their behalf, not out of any self-interest.

15.4 Inclusive Constituent Assemblies

It was not long ago that most constituent assemblies were restricted to elites with varying degrees of citizen representation. In the case of the United States, the Constitutional Convention was held behind closed doors with its back to the citizens. They were even unaware that the convention was held for the purpose of writing a constitution, which is why it was necessary to hold "open" votes in each state to crown the supreme charter produced by the "hidden" debates.[6] In France, meanwhile, the Constituent Assembly of 1791 was also written by a reduced elite composed of representatives of the "three states": the clergy, the aristocracy, and the "commons" (mostly lawyers). The next French constitution, the revolutionary Jacobin Constitution of 1793, was also produced by an

[6] The popular ratification process, however important, does not negate that the Constitutional Convention and the subsequent vote to ratify it were always in the hands of small minorities (which, it goes without saying, did not include women, the poor, Blacks, slaves, indigenous peoples, and so on).

"enlightened" minority, but it was – unlike the previous one – approved by more than 90 percent of the 1,800,000 (male) voters. In Latin America, at least throughout the nineteenth century, constitutions were purely pacts among elites unconcerned in all cases with majority support (only after the Querétaro Convention of 1917 in Mexico would constituent assemblies with more significant social participation become common, which was also reflected in their results, i.e., through the adoption of social rights, indigenous rights, etc.). Latin America became a fertile region for new constitutions during the twentieth century when the very serious legitimacy deficits of the nineteenth-century constitutions were largely repaired by the institution of democratic elections. Then, at the end of the twentieth century, much more inclusive constituent assemblies, with greater minority and, especially, indigenous minority, representation than ever before, were organized in the region, processes that concluded with popular ratification. Often mentioned examples in this sense are Venezuela (1999), Ecuador (2008), and Bolivia (2009).

My personal assessment of those processes is, as you might guess, unenthusiastic. The good news is that they reveal the seriousness of the problems we must resolve: the generalized democratic deficit; social exclusion; inequality, which is also political; and the alienation of important sectors of the community in relation to public life. It seems clear that awareness of these problems is increasing and renewed attempts to repair them through new modes of constitutional creation have been made. The bad news is that, in none of the cases cited, do we find a genuine, open, participatory process – capable of escaping the "trap" or eluding "capture" by the dominant (political, economic) elites of the moment.[7] We have already made reference, moreover, to the limitations inherent to the "popular endorsements" that followed each of these constituent processes. We can reasonably ask ourselves if ratifying the referendums by popular vote ended up giving democratic legitimacy to the new constitutions, or whether they actually only strengthened presidential authority

[7] Very problematic signs of government "capture" can be seen in even the most apparently participatory constituent processes (Bolivia, Ecuador, Venezuela) of the day, if we look at them in any detail at all. To give the briefest inkling, I would just note that the Bolivian process, which began auspiciously with promise for social openness, ended its debates, as we saw, sealed within the confines of a military installation; in Ecuador, the president of the Convention, Alberto Acosta – the leader of the promising environmentalist-indigenous movement that propelled the process – was forced to resign hastily from his post after he recognizing the severe limitations that the government imposed on his position and competences; in Venezuela as well, beyond its participatory promises, the constituent process was tightly monitored by President Chavez's loyalists.

by asking the people to endorse packages that were already wrapped and sealed.

A relevant change occurred in the early twenty-first century, however, with the emergence of a new type of constituent assemblies, which, in my opinion, can genuinely be considered inclusive deliberative processes. As we will see later, in cases such as the extraordinary Icelandic crowd-sourced process (2009–2013), or in the developments in Ireland that started with its 2012 Convention, citizens were allowed to intervene actively and directly in discussions at the constitutional level. In the case of Iceland, the constitutional process (which included multiple stages that were organized in various different ways) concluded with an Assembly composed exclusively of citizen volunteers (representatives of political parties were not allowed). The ensuing debates were fed by questions sent from the citizenry at large through electronic platforms. It is thus possible to speak of the first "crowdsourced" constitution drafted directly by citizens, an unprecedented experiment in the history of constitutionalism. In the case of Ireland in 2012, meanwhile, the constitutional discussion was left to an assembly comprised of a mixture of ordinary citizens (two-thirds of its members) and elected politicians (the remaining third). The citizens were selected through a sort of lottery.

As we will see, there is much to reflect on, discuss, and learn from the experiences of deliberative assemblies such as the one just mentioned.[8]

[8] At this point, I cannot properly analyze other interesting and influential proposals regarding how a constitution-making process should look like. Let me just say that the model of the "conversation among equals" that I advance greatly differs to other alternative views, such as those proposed by Andrew Arato or Joel Colon Ríos, as I have tried to demonstrate on other occasions (see, for example, Gargarella 2020, Gargarella 2022). As we know, Arato's "post-sovereign" model is based on the exclusion of "any single agency, institution or individual that claims to embody the sovereign power and authority of the constituent people" (Arato 2017, ix). However, I do not think that such a model reproduces or resembles, in an attractive way, the model of "conversation among equals." Let me just mention one possible criticism to Arato's suggestion, by reproducing the words of Melissa Williams. As she put it, "[from] a democratic point of view" the legitimacy of the conventions and round tables – basically, the post-sovereign paradigm advanced by Arato – is 'clearly lacking' . . . [w]hy is the round table a legitimate representation of the people at all even if we accept the Lefort inspired idea that the people must be represented in a multiplicity of institutional forms in order to resist the temptation of reading its identity as settled or unitary?" (Williams 2019). I would say something similar regarding Colon Ríos' attractive view (which I do not think differs from mine in what concerns the value he assigns to the new citizens assemblies). Colon Ríos advocates for a constitution-making process that closely follows the "instructions" given by the sovereign ("We the People") through plebiscitary mechanisms (i.e., constituent referendums). For reasons

These processes hold great promise, although they must still overcome important limitations (limitations that, in the case of Iceland in particular, ended up "stifling" the results). These experiences rebut the eighteenth- and nineteenth-century prejudice that effective participatory constitutional processes, open to all, were utopian dreams impossible in large societies. Against the more democratic constitutional reforms typical of the twentieth century, these experiences show that social participation does not need to be limited to the moment before and moment after the constituent debates, but can also occur during the debates themselves. Finally, with regard to the most recent participatory initiatives at the end of the twentieth century, these experiences show that the role of citizens not need be limited to flatly approving or rejecting a text entirely formulated by others (even when proposals were submitted electronically, they were rarely taken up). The processes in Iceland and Ireland demonstrate that it is possible to implement a radically different model of constitutional creation that is, at the same time, fully inclusive and fully deliberative. The problem remains, still, whether the entrenched powers will allow such experiences to assert themselves and consolidate.

that should now be clear (reasons that refer to the differences I established between a "conversation among equals" and a plebiscitary process) I do not find particularly attractive the particular plebiscitarian alternative that he defends (see my objections to his view in Gargarella 2020).

16

The Birth of Dialogical Constitutionalism

In this chapter, I would like to examine the most interesting recent development in constitutionalism, a "dialogical" approach that seeks to bring the practice in line with the regulatory ideal defended here as a "conversation between equals." Although a careful approach and more precise definitions are required, which I will attempt to provide, the starting point is the idea is that the currently dominant institutional system (which we might characterize as the "checks and balances" system) pits the branches of government against each other. For example, if the executive and legislative branches are controlled by different parties, they tend toward open confrontation or "armed truce." If, on the other hand, one of the branches has a clear advantage over the other – whether due to popularity, support in votes, etc. – then that branch tends to impose its dominance over the other power. The system of incentives for the different branches of power seems to facilitate and favor conflictual relations (e.g., presidential veto powers, impeachment, judicial review). The different powers are not institutionally encouraged to engage in "conversation," dialogue, or cooperation.

In recent years, however, and in different ways, the landscape has begun to change. Decisions and reforms have occurred that, in one way or another, "lubricate" the gears linking the different branches of government and favoring a more cooperative attitude between them. In what follows, I will exemplify these changes from two cases, one "judicial" and the other "political." As an example of the first, I will refer to a well-known decision by the new Constitutional Court of South Africa: *Grootboom*. As an example of the second, I will refer to the now famous "notwithstanding clause," a political reform adopted in Canada. These cases will allow us to describe in greater specificity what a "dialogical" approach to constitutionalism may imply.

16.1 The *Grootboom* Case in South Africa

South Africa is still, even after the end of apartheid, marked by strong social injustice and inequality. At the same time, along with a few other countries in the "Global South," like India and Colombia, certain traits of South Africa's institutional structure, particularly its Constitutional Court, have proved forcefully resilient (Bonilla 1993). It is therefore unsurprising that the highest court has intervened to mediate serious social conflicts, or that it has often done so in a creative, original, innovative way. Some of the most influential decisions made by the highest South African court specifically involved critical social issues: poverty, the rights to housing and health, and state violence, among others. The case to which I will refer can, in some way, be considered the one where "it all started." I am referring to the *Grootboom* case decided in 2000, involving a complaint filed by of more than 900 plaintiffs (which included more than 500 children). The case concerned families who were expelled from an informal settlement on private land that had been designated for the construction of low-income housing. The plaintiffs, invoking the progressive Constitution of South Africa, demanded protection for their most basic rights after their possessions and homes were destroyed. The South African state had behaved as was its custom against squatters up to that point, by razing the settlements with bulldozers and expelling the inhabitants with police force. The government's attitude only started to change with the *Grootboom* decision, forcing a reconsideration of the relationship between law, judges, and disadvantaged groups.

The case can be grouped within a set of notable decisions handed down by the "new courts of the Global South," but even among them it represents a watershed. For many, *Grootboom* represented "the first time" that a national case provoked similar reflection in the international arena over the role of courts in critical social situations. To understand the unusual amount of interest aroused, it makes sense to look at the background that framed the case and explains its fame.

As we know, around the beginning of the twentieth century, constitutionalism began to open up to the "social question" that it had until then blatantly ignored. The constitutions that emerged or modified from that point began to explicitly recognize social, economic, and cultural rights. Those constitutions opened another question, however, about who was in charge of implementing and enforcing the new rights. In particular, does the adoption of these constitutional commitments mean that the courts entrusted as "guardians" of the constitution can now intervene and order the political branches to fulfill their duty? For example, the 1996 South African Constitution speaks of the right to housing and health. That being so, may the members of a marginalized group go and request from the courts that, in compliance with the Constitution, they be assigned a home or given access to health services?

Questions like these revive concerns that we have already examined, ones related to the links between constitutionalism and democracy, between politics and justice, between legislators and courts. More specifically, can courts justifiably, in a democracy, order the construction of housing or define the contours of a health plan? The answer to these questions has always been negative, and for several good reasons. Among them are:

- In a democracy, the courts do not and should not have control of the budget: community spending must be decided democratically, and resources allocated according to collectively defined options.
- Furthermore, the courts do not have the necessary technical support or expertise – that the Congress does – to manage and provide oversight for these expenses.
- Moreover, it is one thing for the courts to ensure respect for classical liberal rights (e.g., by lifting some form of censorship, which does not "cost anything"), and another for them to ensure respect for social rights, which imply enormous economic costs.
- And again, if judges order the political branches to carry out actions that incur expenses, they violate the division of powers, since doing so encroaches on an area (budget management) that is the legislature's constitutionally established responsibility.
- Finally, courts are to decide individual cases. Programs that follow general regulations (e.g., the health budget) must not be distorted (or directly depleted) because court orders require excessive spending. For example, a judge could order that the public health ministry provide a person suffering from a strange illness with the healthcare needed for that person to survive. The measure may seem fair, but if the necessary healthcare is extremely expensive, it might drain the ministry's budget. As a result, an apparently fair decision may actually result in depriving thousands of people basic medical care – care that is more affordable but just as vital to those people. The funds that could keep them alive will have been spent in order to respect the judge's decision.

These are some of the reasons why the social rights incorporated in Western constitutionalism since the beginning of the twentieth century have been largely blocked. Sometimes conservative political administrations have refused to implement such rights; sometimes Presidents who employ progressive discourse have preferred keeping the funds available for social expenses in their discretion (rather than as a universal and inalienable requirement); and, most frequently, the courts, for different reasons (sometimes for conservative beliefs, often times alleging deference to the democratic process), have stayed out of the question, shunning the political role of the legislator by deciding – on the basis of an individual case – political questions that society had to answer collectively (e.g., how to organize the health budget or the housing policy).

It was in this political and theoretical context that *Grootboom* was decided. In the squatters' lawsuit, they appealed to Article 26 of the South African Constitution, which establishes the right of every person to "adequate housing." They also cited Article 28, which establishes that every child has the right to "basic nutrition, shelter, health services and social services." The plaintiffs – and rightly so – did not take these constitutional declarations as merely poetic or rhetorical aspirations.

The decision of the South African Court, was remarkable for, among other things, the way in which it safely and prudently navigated these troubled waters. The ruling would thus transcend the obstacles despite its relative modesty (and also because of it). What the Court did was, above all, order the political branches to design a "coherent and coordinated" plan that made clear how they were going to comply with their constitutional obligations. The plan, the Court also argued, should be organized by the State and define the "reasonable measures" that it would take to provide relief to people who "do not have access to land, nor a roof over their heads, and are living in intolerable conditions."

On the basis of that scant information, let us examine what the Court achieved with its decision. The Court (i) made it clear that the social clauses of the Constitution established rights that deserved as much respect as classical liberal rights and that the squatters were absolutely right to invoke them. The Court (ii) also demonstrated the capacity to recognize and order the implementation of these social rights without replacing or taking the place of the legislator: it was the legislator who was in charge of determining the proper policies, setting priorities based on general criteria, and determining how the budget would be allocated. The Court simply – but also radically – told the legislators that they must comply with the constitutional obligations that they had neglected up to that point. Similarly, (iii) the Court showed absolute respect for the reasonable demands that can be placed on the institutional system, even from very robust and demanding visions of democracy. Indeed, the Court basically "initiated a dialogue" with the political powers without imposing any concrete solution on them (it did not tell them "to implement a housing plan, which I have now set for you"; but rather, "you have these constitutional obligations and how you comply with them is your decision to make through the political process"). In this way, the Court began a deliberative process that simultaneously drew on and recognized the democratic prerogatives of the other branches, as well as the basic independence and security of the citizens that democracy requires (Sunstein 2001).

The *Grootboom* decision gained some of its fame for its precision, technique, and theoretical basis, and also some because it came out "at the right time and in the right place": it was a culminating moment in the *era of rights*, when the doctrine was eager to reflect on what courts should do with the social clauses of the Constitution and their proper role. It was also a time when most scholars were still extremely timid, offering conservative or simply inappropriate answers. A single but illustrative example in this regard is the article against social rights (in fact, it was titled: "Against Positive Rights") published in 1993 by the brilliant and very prolific constitutionalist Cass Sunstein after closely studying the nascent constitutionalism in the new Eastern European democracies. Just weeks after *Grootboom*, at the beginning of 2001, Sunstein published another article going in the opposite direction, expressing his fascination with the South African Court's decision ("Lessons from South Africa" was the article's subtitle). What had *Grootboom* taught him? Something simple and fundamental: it was possible to give legal force (to enforce) social rights, in a way that was completely sensitive to the demands of the Constitution in line with a robust conception of democracy. (see, in general, Gloppen et al 2010).

16.2 The "Notwithstanding Clause" in Canada

In the years of *Grootboom* at the end of the twentieth and beginning of the twenty-first century, law seemed actively moving in the direction of more democratic constitutionalism. In this sense, the political correlate of *Grootboom* could be seen in the 1982 political reform carried out in Canada through the adoption of a "Charter of Rights and Freedoms" that replaced the existent "Bill of Rights." In particular, this reform consecrated the so-called "notwithstanding" or "override clause." The Charter of

Rights and Freedoms in Canada also represented a political turn in relation to the traditional constitutional state that was in force until then. Just as the South African Court's had been "modest" in judicial terms, Canada's reform was modest in political terms. However, it opened the door for initiatives and reflections that had previously seemed utopian or distant. As we will see, the adoption of the "notwithstanding clause" helped outline a course that was perfectly navigable. Nothing more and nothing less.

The Canadian reform was very profound for a Commonwealth country unaccustomed to its southern neighbor's approach to the law (i.e., with courts actively defending established bills of rights, reviewing legislation for constitutionality, and so on). This said, the "notwithstanding clause" was included as an apparently minor "addition" to the now famous "Section 33" of the Charter, at least compared to the significance of replacing the country's existing Bill of Rights. The Charter was meant to remedy some of the defects ascribed to the previous declaration of rights, and entailed, in practical terms, a transfer of power from the country's federal governments to the federal judiciary.

In a country where the question of federalism was particularly prominent due to the diversity of ethnic minorities and linguistic differences (which continue to cause controversy today), the announced change generated enormous reservation. The "notwithstanding clause" (initially resisted and then grudgingly accepted by Prime Minister Pierre Trudeau, at the request of the provinces) was devised to moderate those fears. The clause returned the "last word" to the political organs, after (and against) adverse decisions by the courts on matters of rights. More specifically, "Section 33" established that the national or provincial legislature would have the power to insist on the application of its legislation for a period of five years "notwithstanding" a ruling by the Supreme Court that the legislation was inconsistent with the rights enshrined by the Charter.

The Canadian reform – particularly the "notwithstanding clause" of Section 33 – sparked fabulous academic controversy for the way in which it "restored" authority to legislatures, thus opening a hitherto unthinkable, nonexistent channel of "dialogue" between the government branches (Bateup 2007; Hogg & Bushell 1997; Manfredi & Kelly 1990; Roach 2001, 2004). Constitutionalist Mark Tushnet wrote, for example, that it was this seemingly minuscule reform that gave rise to what we now call "dialogical constitutionalism" (Tushnet 2009).[1]

[1] We may find interesting approaches to "dialogic constitutionalism" also in Bachtinger et al. (2018); Levy et al. (2018); Sigalet et al. (2019); Young (2017), among many others.

Let me specify the importance of the notwithstanding clause in terms of "constitutional dialogue": (i) it implied recognition of the "democratic objection"; (ii) it proved that, in the framework of a democratic society, the courts' self-assigned power to pronounce the "last word" on constitutionality was a serious problem; (iii) it made clear that the prevailing institutional systems, as they were organized (i.e., the familiar structure of "checks and balances") did not facilitate democratic "dialogue"; (iv) it showed that certain institutional changes can (and deserve to) be undertaken to restore the "last word" to the democratic organs of government; and finally (v) the adoption of the "notwithstanding clause" demonstrated that the path of institutional reform is both possible and necessary, if the overall goal is promoting democratic dialogue.

16.3 The Spaces for Dialogue Expand: "Public Hearings," "Prior Consultation," and "Meaningful Engagement"

Normative (the Canadian "Charter") and jurisprudential reforms (*Grootboom*) were neither the first nor the only indications of the emergence of a new dialogical paradigm in constitutional matters (Gardbaum 2013). Yet they were catalysts for a succession of new events that were already in the air, and have become symbols of that new phase that was beginning. The reputation of the South African Court and the confidence in the Canadian institutional system legitimized and encouraged many innovations that deserve to be inscribed as defining this new stage. For the moment, we can speak of a "dialogic" stage in modest terms: we speak of changes in the ways in which institutional power is organized, and in particular changes that operate on the traditional forms of the relationship between the branches of government. In traditional forms, the link between the "branches" was more rigid (marked by the "aggressive" veto and powers) and allowed the judiciary to effectively have the "last word" (any judicial decision adverse to the democratic one was virtually final). With the arrival of this innovation, on the other hand, the institutional system seemed to open up, little by little, step by step, to new, less "violent" forms of interaction, and politics once again gained some prevalence, for example by asserting its right to speak the "last word." This occurred, in *Grootboom*, through *a Court that was active, but at the same time deferential to politics; while in Canada, it took place because of a "clause" that attempted to place legislatures at the center of decision-making power.*

The changes at different levels produced during this (ongoing) stage have been extremely important. I want to mention (only) three of these institutional innovations that have helped to make this new "dialogical" paradigm more visible: public hearings, prior consultation, and meaningful engagement.

Public Hearings. In many countries (especially in Global South countries such as Argentina, Colombia, Brazil, and Mexico), both the Congress and judiciary have begun calling public hearings to gather information and different points of view that do not otherwise enter in political deliberation. Let me briefly illustrate this through an exemplary case (at least during the early stages): the *Mendoza* case in Argentina (the first decision was in 2008). On that occasion, the Argentine Supreme Court, whose democratic legitimacy was still fragile, decided to intervene in a complex "structural" case through a series of measures to gain access crucial information; fulfill its role as "custodian" of constitutional rights; and show deference to the political branches, and thus respectful of the legislature's "democratic dignity." The case involved a highly polluted river (the *Riachuelo*) whose contaminated tributaries seriously affected more than a million people, generating a conflict that crossed various jurisdictions and authorities (national, provincial, municipal). Faced with a "structural dispute" that had remained unresolved for decades (neither governments nor courts had dared to deal with it), the Argentine Court convened, starting in 2006, a series of public hearings in which brought together delegates from political authorities (including, especially, the Ministry of the Environment), representatives of industries responsible for the pollution, and, above all, the communities most affected. In the hearings, the situation was discussed collectively and the political authorities were commissioned to present a plan for cleaning up the pollution that would be subsequently evaluated by those summoned. Disregarding the challenges that faced the court at every stage, it revealed the potential of judicial "openness" to civil society as well as the richness of public dialogue that could be promoted and monitored by the courts (Benedetti & Sáenz 2016).

Prior Consultation. Another type of initiative that has helped both to renew the traditional forms of the decision-making process and, above all, include "voices" usually absent from such processes were derived from the approval of the International Labor Organization Convention 169. The Convention was meant to favor the consideration of demands and interests of the indigenous communities in public decisions that could directly affect them. It included a variety of clauses designed to guarantee respect for the culture, ways of life, and institutions of indigenous peoples. In particular, the agreement included the right to *prior consultation* of these communities in the event of legislation that put their main interests at risk. The first section of Article 6.1 of the Convention referred to the obligation of member states to "consult the peoples concerned, through appropriate procedures and in particular through their representative institutions, whenever consideration is being given to legislative or administrative measures which may affect them directly." Meanwhile, the second part required the parties to the agreement "to establish means by which these peoples can freely participate, to at least the same extent as other sectors of the population, at all levels of decision-making in elective institutions and administrative and other bodies responsible for policies and programs which concern them." Internal incorporation of the Convention by the majority of countries that signed on was slow, and application was even slower, but it gradually gained acceptance and recognition at the national and international levels. At present, clauses of "prior consultation" are invoked and implemented in a variety of cases of primary public importance – particularly when governments grant mining concessions in areas inhabited by communities. Given the sensitive nature of the environmental risk and interests involved, disputes related to the exploitation of resources and "prior consultation" have been the subject of constant litigation, both locally and internationally.

"Meaningful Engagement." The South African Supreme Court also demonstrated its creativity and commitment to democratic debate in cases involving socially marginalized groups. Once again, in cases involving the illegal occupation of land and eviction by the State, the Court intervened, forcing the parties to "dialogue in a committed way" until an agreement an agreement was reached. The first time the Court formulated this response was in *Olivia Road* (2008), a lawsuit filed against the Municipality of Johannesburg for the expulsion of some 67,000 people living in more than 300 rundown buildings (Liebenberg 2012). The Court ordered the parties to begin a process of meaningful engagement, which implied that they immediately make "an effort to resolve the differences and difficulties ... in the light of the values of the Constitution ... and the rights and duties of the citizens concerned." The Court monitored the agreement and its implementation to ensure its compatibility with the requirements of the Constitution. Here again, the South African Supreme Court produced an institutional innovation aimed at ensuring respect for fundamental rights (in particular, those of the most vulnerable groups in society) in a manner consistent with the obligations imposed by the constitutional framework.[2]

16.4 The Potential of the Incipient Dialogical Constitutionalism

The above examples illustrate the increasingly widespread "constitutional dialogue" that is, however, still a long way from becoming prevalent. Here and there, institutional innovations appear, ones seeking to make the seemingly impossible probable: more open, more impartial, more inclusive decision-making processes. These experiments have usually come to be through practical problem-solving than theoretical creativity. Theory, for that matter, has generally shown little institutional imagination and much inertia. It always seems to be "following from behind" (trying to understand, and in the best of cases, to justify) the advances that appear in practice.

I speak of "advances" because these practices have, in one way or another, strengthened the democratic foundations of constitutionalism. We have spoken, in effect, of practices included under the general umbrella of dialogical constitutionalism insofar as they have helped to take the "last word" away from the courts (the "notwithstanding clause"); to affirm greater judicial deference to politics (meaningful engagement, public hearings); to include in the decision-making process the "voices" of groups habitually marginalized from the decision-making process (meaningful engagement, public hearings, prior consultation); and to facilitate more collaboration between the branches of government (the "notwithstanding clause"; public hearings, meaningful engagement).

Allow me, in any case, to list seven important virtues of the particular this type of practice related, although not exclusively, to the functions of the judiciary, which is perhaps the most discussed and criticized of the

[2] Initiatives such as "meaningful engagement" or public hearings were just some of the measures promoted by the judiciary that have promoted public deliberation and improve dialogue with and among the political branches. These and many other similar initiatives were unthinkable not so long ago. In recent years, for example, exceptional decisions such as the so-called unconstitutional state of affairs created by the notable Colombian Constitutional Court were formulated to intervene on a structural problem (Cepeda 2004; Rodríguez Garavaito 2011). There have also been judicial initiatives aimed at ensuring that voices are not unfairly excluded (as, for example, in *Doctors for Life*, also from the South African Supreme Court) and cases in which the courts exhorted the political powers to act on issues they had neglected or where the courts established some limits for political action, i.e., including the deadline by when the political branches must act (as in *Badaro*, of the Argentine Supreme Court).

government branches, both because of its unjustified omissions the dimension and forms of its interventions. The innovative "dialogical" judicial practices such as those mentioned allow us to:

(i) *Reconcile the ideals of constitutionalism and democracy.* In the first place, the emergence of this type of initiative reveals possible links between constitutionalism and democracy, dissolving the tensions and contradictions that we usually find between the two commitments (Elster & Slagstad 1988). In other words, the different branches of government are able to exercise their constitutional competencies in perfectly consistent ways – even in the demanding terms of a robust conception of democracy.

(ii) *Come closer to meeting the demands of a deliberative model of democracy.* Measures such as those examined help to vindicate a very robust "deliberative conception" of democracy – a conception that usually encounters resistance because of its abstract or remote nature, or because people feel its demands are unreasonable. All the examples examined help to see that it is perfectly possible – to the extent that it is genuinely desired – to bring constitutional practice closer to the ideal of deliberative democracy (i.e., more debate, more inclusiveness in decisions, and more citizen participation).

(iii) *Avoid the traditional "counter-majoritarian objection."* The mentioned exercises of the judicial function seem impervious to the counter-majoritarian objection, insofar as they prove that judges can fulfill their mission as "guardians" of the Constitution, safeguarding rights and the democratic process, without offending the "democratic dignity" of legislation, or overruling political decisions (a quality that has even been recognized by the scholars critical of judicial control and supportive of the "democratic objection," who are showing openness to what they have called "weak" forms of judicial control or "weak constitutionalism" (Tushnet 2008; Waldron 2009, 2016).

(iv) *Moving beyond the "final word" debate.* For years (and this point directly relates to the previous one), the debates over judicial review have remained anchored in discussion of the judicial "last word." The theorists ask if judges should have the "last word" in institutional matters, or if legislators should. The developments discussed show that forms of institutional collaboration and reforms that favor fluid "dialogue" between powers are possible (Kramer 2005).

(v) *Transcend the "binary" views of judicial functions.* The judicial function has habitually been studied on the assumption that the task of judges is binary: either validate or invalidate the law. The function of justice seemed reduced to it, as if this were natural. Practices such as those examined help us to see the limits of this attitude: we now know that judges, if they wish, can transcend that binary, unattractive, theoretically poor, and descriptively incomplete approach to their function.

(vi) *Transcend the dichotomy between "judicial activism" and "self-restraint."* One of the most common and unproductive debates around judicial control, for decades, has focused on the distinction between "activist" and "passive" courts (or courts and judges that exercise "self-restraint"). The truth is that the classification is unattractive for several reasons. Mainly, the categorization fails to represent what it is called on to justify. For example, it generally identifies "activist" judges as ones who hand down progressive decisions and the "self-restrained" ones as the most conservative, when in truth the argument that the most activist judges are conservative and vice versa is just as viable. The dichotomy has also failed in normative or evaluative terms. For example, many defend one or the other attitude (i.e., "yes to judicial activism!" or "down with activist judges"), as if judges tend to act one way or the other all the time. Again, the truth is that (as might have already been made clear) there are times when judges should assume a more active role (e.g., to ensure affected groups have a voice in decision-making processes) and times when a "passive" or deferential role is justified (i.e., those related to the content of democratically established policies).

(vii) *Enrich the discussion on judicial "remedies."* Also in relation to the previous point, the practices examined have helped to enrich our reflection on the available "remedies" that justice might order. In this sense (and returning to the previous point), "active" intervention by the judges (in defiance of the political powers) may be reasonable if the chosen "remedy" generates dialogue along the lines of the South African Supreme Court's imposition of "meaningful engagement"). Resistance to intervention or "activism" by judges may also be reasonable when the courts choose a more intrusive "remedy" ("imposing" their substantive criteria upon legislators).

17

Why We Care About Dialogue

17.1 The Debate Over Abortion in Argentina

The discussions that took place in Argentina over abortion in 2018 were exceptional for several notable reasons. (see Bergallo, Jaramillo and Vaggione, comps. 2018). Firstly, there was the abrupt emergence of this debate into the public sphere and the depth and extension that it immediately took on. Legalizing abortion was an issue that had been promoted by feminist groups for decades, but it went from periphery to center-stage in the public sphere almost from one moment to the next.[1] It is worth remembering the October 2017 elections in Argentina. None of the political parties on the ballot, except for a small Trotskyist group, included abortion reform on their electoral platform. The other parties had understood, perhaps rightly, that simply raising the issue could lose them votes, which was unacceptable for any party that wanted to improve its electoral chances. Between the end of 2017 and the beginning of 2018, however, topics that are usually silenced began to emerge with unprecedented force, both inside and outside the country.

The *Me Too* movement against sexual harassment, above all, took off at that time. Similarly, in my country, Argentina, activists, artists, journalists, and academics against gender violence joined a campaign that had emerged in 2015, *Ni una menos*, breathing new life into it. By January 2018, the collective began to demand reform of Argentina's abortion law: the demonstrations reached unprecedented numbers and lasted for months. This occurred right after an intense electoral period (in late 2017) in which the issue of abortion was still "taboo" or contrary to the electoral interests of any party. Abortion became the dominant, overwhelming issue on the agenda public, the issue that seemed to mobilize everyone.

[1] In particular, the National Campaign for the Right to Legal, Safe and Free Abortion Project had promoted a bill for the Voluntary Interruption of Pregnancy Law in 2006. It was presented for the first time, for treatment by the Congress in 2007. They would have to present it seven more times, until it was admitted for discussion in 2018 for the first time.

Shortly thereafter, after more than a decade of steadfast advocacy, discussion of the Voluntary Termination of Pregnancy project began in the Chamber of Deputies in April 2018. The lower house of Congress organized extensive debates that lasted for more than two months. In the notable *public hearings* organized by the legislature more than a thousand speakers, from the most diverse places, experiences were heard: from academics and legal professionals, to doctors and high school students, to women who had undergone illegal abortions, sex workers, and more. The quality and intensity of these public debates was, in my opinion, extraordinary.

Moreover, the collective debate began, first and foremost, in the streets, which were flooded for months by protesters for and against the initiative. Once again, the people who came to the demonstrations were from a wide range of backgrounds and profiles. The youngest students stood out, in a very special way, demonstrating unprecedented activism, as well as, it must be said, fixed views (on a difficult and complex subject).

The debate moved, in equally unparalleled fashion, into a political context marked by extreme division and polarization (what was then called, in Argentina, the "political rift"). People from opposing political camps who disputed every other issue came together behind a common cause. More importantly, they came together precisely, around the most divisive subject of all, the example that many teachers use, in the classrooms, to explain social discord and controversy.

The debates, in which young people and professionals, people with advanced degrees and people who had not finished high school participated, turned out to be very rich (although they also included many dogmatic testimonies and slavishly ideological sermons), so much so that many people adjusted their initial positions. As a result, some participants (and many legislators), directly changed their positions on the matter, while many others – among whom I count myself – added nuance and sophistication to their previous position. We all learned from those debates (I emphasize this: the debates do not necessarily, nor usually, convince the person who thought A, after hearing arguments to the contrary, to hold the non-A position. The result of debates is normally that, after a process of exchange of arguments, said person goes on to support a more nuanced version of A, and becomes more sensitive to the opinions of their opponent).

Finally, the Congress voted down the reform initiative. In the Chamber of Deputies, the law was partly approved with 129 votes in favor, 125 against, and 1 abstention. It was rejected by the Senate after a vote of 31 in favor, 38 against, 2 abstentions, and 1 absent. The political weight of the most conservative provinces in the north of the country ended up decisive, but even so, by only a handful of votes.[2]

In any case, nothing of what has been said tarnishes, nor is it capable of hiding the extraordinary nature of what happened: *the very strong and surprising outbreak of the issue; the demonstrations in the streets; activism; the richness of the debates; the enthusiasm; the involvement and massive participation of young people, the public commitment demonstrated; etc.*

In what interests us, the lessons are varied: against what was expected, and against what the theory could have predicted or supposed, in a massively Catholic country where the Church permeates public life, and despite large conservative bastions, the abortion debate emerged overnight in remarkable scope and intensity. Against the assumption that public debate does not lead to anything, the discussions were remarkable, changing many minds and refining the opinions of many more. Against the idea that public debate is meaningless when large power centers (the Church, the media) take strong positions, the citizens knew how to enter and navigate the discussions with enormous freedom. Against the notion according to which people do not change their opinion when their self-identity, religion, or deepest values are called into question, many of those who changed or qualified their initial position did just that. In short, the experience proves that almost everyone who thought they understood the Argentine people, from the theorists to the politicians, systematically had it absolutely wrong.

17.2 Why We Are Interested in Dialogue

I hope the previous example helps to better understand, from a practical perspective, the central themes of this work with which we have been struggling laboriously from the start. What is the value of dialogue, why does it matter to us, and what can it bring us? I use the example of abortion to point out why, in the face of disagreements of this kind, the defenders of the dialogic approach argue that (i) it is important to *take a decision*; (ii) it is important that the decision be *deliberative*; and (iii) it is important that the deliberative decision be

[2] The pro-abortion initiative would be discussed again two years later, and would finally be approved December 30, 2020.

inclusive. It is for the sake of reaching an inclusive deliberative decision that we care about dialogue.

Let me start by recalling what I said at the very beginning of this book. In a *diverse society, marked by the fact of disagreement and composed of individuals of "equal dignity," decisions on matters of common concern should be debated and resolved by all*. As Michael Sandel put it, we can only arrive at the common good "by deliberating with our fellow citizens about the purposes and ends worthy of our political community" (Sandel 2020, 227). The first point that I would highlight, in light of this discussion and the example of the abortion debates in Argentina, is that debate helps us to recognize the importance of committing ourselves collectively to resolve our disagreements. This is because (as Jeremy Waldron argued), we live together and we are going to continue living together, predictably – because we need it, because we want it, because we have no alternative.

In this framework, we disagree, and we are motivated to make decisions on the issues on which we do not agree: we need to continue living together. Furthermore, the example of abortion helps us to see that (despite the illusion of many, who might have thought that nondecision implies, in a certain sense, neutrality or respect for everyone's view) not deciding implies taking sides in a certain way that ends up benefiting some, and harming others – while explicitly saying that "we choose not to act." Thus, for example, when the government does not take active measures in the matter of abortion, it tends to allow, in fact, many people to die as a result of the poor conditions in which illegal abortions are performed; many people to go without the medical assistance they deserve; many people to lack the protection and recognition they need. Similarly, when the government does not intervene in matters of climate change, it implicitly condones the big businesses that go on polluting the planet. When the government does not take measures to ensure public security, it may promote an "every man for himself" attitude where the most powerful end up protecting their lives, their interests, their properties, while the most disadvantaged are all the time at serious risk. In short, always, but particularly in diverse and unequal societies such as ours, the fact that we do not make decisions on certain relevant public issues normally implies – concretely – taking sides, usually with those who are the best situated, and who then benefit even more. Faced with serious matters on which we disagree (such as abortion), not shirking the responsibility of making a decision is very important.

What has been said can serve, in any case, more to justify decision-making on those issues on which we disagree, than to justify inclusive decision-making. However, we have already examined the why of the value of collective, socially *inclusive* decisions. When the issue at stake has the potential to affect all of us, or many of us, in a serious way, it becomes especially relevant to listen to the point of view of all "those affected." *In a society of equals, where we all appear united, at least and above all, by our "equal moral dignity" – where we all deserve the same respect – the voice of each one matters, and must be counted in the same way.* (Recall the example of abortion, and what it suggests about the importance of collecting the testimony of all those involved, before deciding on the matter.) We need to recognize, when making a public decision on the subject, everything from the immense pain that women who have abortions go through, to the sufferings of those who went through an abortion in illegal conditions, to the anguish of those who – added to the pain of the loss – were prosecuted and later punished (criminally and morally) for interrupting their pregnancy, to the doubts and fear of the doctors and the inexperience or inability of the police personnel to deal with such cases, to the testimonies of the social workers involved in the case, to the despair of girls facing similar predicaments, to the infinite trauma of women raped (and forced to have a family). The inclusion of diverse, opposing points of view, particularly those most affected, in these cases, can be crucial, simply to decide with the most complete information, especially in light of what has been said: even assuming that we are honest people, of good faith, it is nearly impossible for us to put ourselves in the shoes of those most affected, especially if we do not hear from them directly.

What has just been said can help to understand why, in plural societies, marked by disagreement, it is important to make decisions after recognizing and considering everyone's point of view. But what has been said does not sufficiently, not yet, explain the value of *collective debate*. The debate matters, because it is not simply a matter of throwing testimonies into an empty box, as in bad group therapy, nor of simply providing data to those who intend to decide on everyone's behalf, so that the decision is at least better informed. Collective debate is also about helping each other, to think better, to correct each other, to learn from what the other affirms and how they say it (their bodily attitude, their gestures, their pain or enthusiasm, their joy or suffering). It is about removing the prejudices that we have about what the other does or says, after knowing them. It is about others being able to point out those issues on which we reason badly, or show us the inconsistencies that exist between what we say today and what we thought yesterday. It is about educating each other in civility, in the practice of giving and rejecting arguments, of listening to the other, one at a time, of learning that in a plural, democratic society, no one has the right to decide in their own way, and in the name of all the others. To return to the example of the abortion debate.

In it, many were able to change their initial positions, after the debate; many were able to partially change, or qualify, their starting positions, even – also – positions that seemed fixed from the beginning. And this is so, at a time (like that one) of deep "political rift," social division, crossed anger, and around one of the most complex and divisive issues of all.

17.3 What Kind of Dialogue Are We Talking About, When We Talk About Dialogue?

In recent years, the discussion on the relationship between judges, the Constitution, and the "people" (in a broad sense) changed significantly, in line with what has already been examined: the presence of the "democratic objection," institutional crisis, the lack of legitimacy of justice, citizen protests, etc. In this framework, the emergence of "dialogic" theories and practices (again, in the broad sense), generated enormous appeal among members of the legal community. This is so, not only because "jumping on the bandwagon" early is an easy path to recognition in reputational terms (positioning oneself at the theoretical vanguards of the moment) but, above all, because "dialogical constitutionalism" offers an excellent "umbrella" from the usual rain of criticism of the dominant modes of exercising the judicial profession (referring again to judges' lack of democratic legitimacy, etc.). Hence, the appeal of the dialogical paradigm has become very widespread and many have gone to pains to become leading or active members of that theoretical camp. The great problem was that many judges have asserted their "membership" without making any fundamental changes to the way they always practiced the law (only now they seek protection for their decisions under the "umbrella" of dialogue). The result is that the dialogical paradigm, shortly after its birth, has been emptied of any real meaning.

For this reason, it is highly important to specify why it is that we are interested in dialogue, lay out from the start what types of dialogue are appropriate for which purposes, and evaluate the genuine, existing institutional forms of dialogue on the basis of those parameters.

Here I will attempt to describe "dialogue" in terms of the criteria established and defended in the previous pages: deliberation, inclusion, equality, public interest. And I will do it, essentially, focused within the framework of the Constitution; that is, I will be thinking in terms of *constitutional dialogue* or *conversation.* I will argue, in line with the analysis that we have been working our way through, that the discussion about the Constitution and the principles that underlie it in a democracy should be the product of egalitarian and inclusive conversation among all the "potentially affected" (and not, for example, imposed from above). To clarify this brief definition in terms of what it rejects and in what it denotes:

- We are referring, first of all, to an exercise of argumentation that revolves around the content of the Constitution and how to interpret that content.
- This exercise includes public discussions that have an obvious legal, constitutional component but, just as importantly, address public issues of primary significance (I am not thinking of an argumentative exercise that deals with "mere legalisms" or legal formalities, but in public discussions on immediate, substantive policy choices to address, for example, environmental protection, public safety and security, health services, even abortion and social rights).
- This exercise in collective argumentation cannot be reduced to the platitude that "life is a classroom" and thus every interaction we have in our daily lives represents "dialogue" and "learning." The dialogue I am referring to is specifically related to the disputes over the Constitution that play out above all in classrooms, in newspapers, in seminars, and, in the context of sharp social conflict, at street demonstrations and protests. (See J.Parkinson & J.Mansbridge, eds., 2012).
- For the rest, it is assumed here that the dispute over the meaning of the Constitution does not only involve "words" and "public reasoning," but also gestures, acts, emotions ("banging on the table"). Protesting outside the home of a judge (or a doctor who performs or refuses to perform abortions), for example, may be condemnable for different reasons and also justified to greater or lesser degree, but it still must be considered part of our deliberative exercise inasmuch as it is form of criticizing those who exercise public power or of decisively intervening in matters of prime public interest. As Owen Fiss argued (in an article that specifically refers to the phenomenon of picketing at the homes of doctors who perform abortions), political life does not begin or end in

elections. It is linked, in a very special way, to what happens in between elections (Fiss 2005).

- I must emphasize, in a special way, that the notion of dialogue I am referring to must be inclusive, and not simply in a rhetorical or decorative sense: an inclusive dialogue is one in which the people most affected themselves – each one of them, wherever possible – should have a central role in the discussion, and should not keep quiet even if and when others speak on their behalf. Of course, someone might say that, in societies like ours, made up of millions of people, the possibilities for truly inclusive dialogue are zero. However, the example of the discussions over abortion in Argentina directly contradict that affirmation. Those discussions were incredibly complex, difficult, intricate, controversial, divisive (in an already polarized society), and yet, in different ways, and in a concrete sense, "everyone" took part in them. I mean the discussion was largely forced into people's living rooms by the fact of the massive street demonstrations that were well organized institutionally and successful in inclusive terms. The example (I repeat, of a challenging topic in a difficult social context) proves that it is not true that inclusive discussion can only function either as an unreal, unattainable, regulative ideal or in simple cases and small communities. We can work to develop the institutional foundations for open and public discussion or we can decide not to, but whatever we choose to do, this modality of dialogue – it must be acknowledged – is far from impossible or utopian.
- I must also emphasize that this notion of dialogue is not rhetorical. Dialogue does not occur in a setting where others make speeches and decisions which we applaud. Dialogue is not the same as accepting or rejecting what others have decided. Dialogue requires forums that make conversation possible, and procedures that organize it and reserve space for the exchange of arguments, mutual correction, and transparent and complete information to all.

I hope these points have helped map out the contours of the idea of dialogue to which I have been referring throughout this work so that it is easier to understand how it applies to the institutional setting as well as what it implies in constitutional terms (how the idea of dialogue is linked to the narrower sense of constitutional dialogue or conversation). At the same time, the above points may also help us to keep clear in our minds the conception of dialogue on which this work *does not rely*, or *directly rejects*: primarily, conversations that are fundamentally unequal, whether because of status or wealth or any other stark asymmetry; conversations where genuine, effective dialogue does not take place; or exchanges that are not genuinely inclusive. A common and particularly illustrative example of what is rejected here would be the following. Imagine that a traditional authoritarian father summons his family members to the dinner table to discuss some important issue (e.g., about how to deal with economic difficulties they are experiencing). Imagine that, in an unusual exercise of tolerance, the father listens to what his wife and children have to say. Then, tired of listening to their arguments, he bangs on the table and says: "That is enough, you have worn me out." This common situation makes clear the obstacle that inequality (of power) poses for genuine dialogue. In contexts of strong inequality, the dialogue, despite its outward appearance, eventually reveals its true nature: a nonhorizontal exchange, one therefore of little value, for an essential component is missing, this being the condition that all participants be on an equal footing.

17.4 "Real-Life" Constitutional Dialogue

Once we have defined and clarified the parameters for what we could call constitutional and democratic dialogue, what can we say about concrete, known, "real-life" practices of institutional dialogue as it has been described in the previous pages? As I understand it, the clarifications made in the previous pages put us in a better position to understand and evaluate the practices that we called "dialogic" or "dialogical" in the previous chapter.

In my opinion, we are now in a position to argue that the institutional dialogical practices discussed are ultimately and generally unsatisfactory, even though I may have referred to them (at least partly) as well-directed. They might qualify, in principle, as dialogic practices in that they concern issues of public interest; they broaden the narrow framework set by traditional institutional channels; and they put emphasis, in some cases, on practices that move past the courts' power to have the "final word." In general terms, however, the "innovations" are still too distant from the basic guidelines defined above for genuine deliberative democracy. This assertion does not necessarily or completely detract from the value of the dialogical examples as deliberative practices, but it should remain clear that these practices are still far from what could reasonably and realistically be expected from practices characteristic of a deliberative community.

Allow me to review the practices that we highlighted in the previous chapter to make this clear and that indicate we have only begun on a slow path towards deliberative constitutionalism.

On the Notwithstanding Clause. Let us begin with Canada's "notwithstanding clause," which in fact, at least in the way that it has been consolidated in practice, can hardly qualify as a genuinely deliberative exercise. What has been achieved by it is indeed extraordinary, in terms of the value of the institutional reforms that it has made possible and the limitation it put on the "last word" of judges, enabling legislatures to recuperate some leadership, among others. However, in practice, not only has the "notwithstanding clause" been rarely employed, but it has been used in less attractive ways than expected. In what matters most to us, Section 33 – even in the purest and most refined form of the exercise – has not been able to establish any effective practice of "dialogue" (as confirmed by some of the scholarly literature, Petter 2003). As we said before: constitutional dialogue is more than returning authority to the legislature. Legislative authority is important, but on its own we do not call it dialogue. In reality, what the "clause" has been used for (I insist, despite the interesting contribution it has made to institutional innovation, that goes beyond its symbolic value) was giving the legislator one more "shot," another "card to play," a chance to let the legislature "bang on the table" last. What we call dialogue implies equality, social inclusion, and the exchange of reasons, and the "notwithstanding clause" is something else.

On Public Hearings. What about the heralded public hearings, particularly those convened by courts? We have already attested to an attraction to public hearings for various reasons, particularly because of their potential to enrich decision-making processes by including alternative points of view and voices that are usually absent. Such initiatives, however, have been routinely undermined in their implementation. One particularly important reason for this is that: *in the absence of clear and equitable rules to regulate hearings, their value ends up dependent on the discretionary powers of those who organize the hearings.* As a result, the fairness and value of public hearings come to depend, decisively, on the goodwill (i.e., the discretion) of public officials (whether political or judicial). Therefore, if the officials have a vocation for impartiality, or are animated by altruism, we can expect impartial and fair hearings. If they are not, however, or if they seek to use such audiences for other purposes (e.g., simply to recuperate some of their legitimacy), then we have no reason to expect hearings to be effective in any relevant way, and even less reason to expect this promising practice to fulfill its potential. A curious aside is that, *in the scheme set up to leverage the ambitions of individualistic "demons," constitutional dialogue ended up depending on the goodwill of altruistic, self-restraining "angels."* For this reason, judicial hearings such as those mentioned, tend to be held when the judges want, and not to be held when the judges are disinclined. They begin and end when the judges say so. In the same way, what the speakers say in the hearings is generally taken into account when the judges considered it appropriate, and exclusively in the way the judges considered relevant: none of the participants ever knows why their testimony mattered or not, why it was taken into account, in what way, or why it was simply ignored.[3]

On Meaningful Engagement. Similarly: What can we say about the practice of *meaningful engagement* promoted by the South African Court? These types of judicial initiatives interested us particularly because of their inclusive nature – their potential to involve "all those potentially affected" in the discussion of relevant public issues. This potential, so attractive, is dependent, again, on the discretionary will of those in control of the judicial process. If – as seems to be the rule – public institutions such as the Supreme Courts enjoy complete freedom to say when and how "meaningful commitments" are to be expressed, then the potential of the practice is severely diminished (as ended up happening in South Africa).[4]

On Prior Consultation. Finally, how to evaluate the practice of the aforementioned prior consultation? So far, I would say such initiatives have shown extreme promise in terms of the unique opportunity they offer for directly enriching the decision-making process by including the point of view of some of the groups most affected by the proposed project. Perhaps because of this power and the threat that this practice holds, prior consultation has been strongly resisted by the authorities in power, politically attacked, and subjected to extreme litigation. In any case, the battle continues, and it remains to be seen to what extent, in the coming years, the egalitarian and emancipatory potential of this tool may or may not be genuinely consolidated.

[3] In this regard, the aforementioned work by Benedetti and Sáenz is very illustrative (Benedetti & Sáenz 2016); and also, for Brazil, that of Miguel Godoy (Godoy 2017).

[4] It is worth recalling, in this regard, what happened in the *Joe Slovo* case, which was the first relevant case in which the South African Court again referred to "Meaningful Engagement" after introducing it in *Olivia Road*. In *Joe Slovo*, the Court adopted "a much weaker and unjustified version" of the institution that it had set in motion in *Olivia Road*, as if it had not defined sufficiently clear principles framed in the values of equality and social justice of the Constitution in the first instance.

The jurisprudence over prior consultation that has been developing, both at national and international levels, is still ambiguous and it remains to be seen how the disputes will evolve. It can be affirmed, however, that in the framework of our tremendously deficient institutional systems, the promise of prior consultation – even in its most modest versions – is extraordinary: citizens directly called upon to give their opinion on projects that will have crucial impact on their destiny. This, I insist, is extremely important, especially in the institutional framework in which we operate.

In any case, despite the practice's promise, it should also be emphasized that *a public consultation is not the same as a public conversation: it is not dialogue*. It is, in any case, I affirm, a fundamental element of dialogue and a means to enrich dialogue a great deal. Yet we are seeking something else: debate, mutual correction and assistance, an exchange of information, precisions and clarifications elaborated collectively through *an open, continuous, unfinished conversation*. Those qualities are what we mean when we talk about dialogue.

18

"Democratic Erosion"

18.1 An Autobiographical Note

I write this book in an academic context dominated by a problem known as "democratic erosion," and indeed it is in that context that I have largely been motivated to write it. In order to give an account of the dimensions of the problem as I personally see them, and the specific meaning of "democratic erosion" (and particularly the "erosion" part), I will grant myself permission to introduce this chapter with a short autobiographical tale about this book's genesis. I hope this little story will help to clarify the precisions on which I have repeatedly insisted.

I decided to relocate to the United States in early October 2019 to write this book. My intention was to distance myself from the sometimes overwhelming commitments in my home country and to devote myself to writing with only the company of good libraries and friendly teachers. The situation in the United States also seemed conducive to writing about the general theme that was my focus: the widespread sensation of (what has been correctly called) "democratic fatigue" that I have sometimes tried to describe in my legal scholarship as a settled state of "legal alienation": a shared sense that the norms that our leaders institute, in our names, are completely alien to us.

I noted that the American political context seemed very pertinent to my concerns, and thought it would incite to advance quickly in my project. I arrived in New York at a very special moment, when an unfit, heedless, unthinking man sat in the Oval Office while American society appeared politically more intensely divided than ever in my own memory. Many of the professors whom I would like to consider colleagues are currently writing about the ways that a presidential impeachment could be pursued.

The moment before I board the plane on October 9, another colleague and friend contacts me from Barcelona. He wants to know if I want to collaborate with him in a court case. He asks if I want to help him prepare a brief against a decision about to be handed down, one that is sure to generate social unrest: the conviction for sedition of nine pro-independence leaders after the failed (for various reasons) attempt to declare Catalonia politically independent from Spain. I must decline the invitation to take part because it could very well consume the little time I have to lay the foundations of this book, but I do so with a heavy heart, as I read the news of the massive protest demonstrations erupting in Barcelona on a scale never seen before.

This very morning – I am writing these words on October 26, 2019 – I wake ready to make some contextual notes intended to support the arguments in this chapter on democratic "erosion" and "fatigue." I am about to do a little research to help me frame and convey my sense of the problems I want address, but first, like every morning, I make some coffee and read the newspapers. As soon as I open the first one, I am overcome by the news I read. I am too numb to assimilate everything I see. Just when I was about to explain what I understand by "democratic erosion," I see that one of the columnists I read every Saturday like today, has devoted his column of the day about the peremptory need to "avoid a tragedy in Argentina." The column is relating the situation in my country to what is going on in neighboring countries, speaking of "popular uprisings, the repudiation of constituted power, deaths, repression, destruction, threat to governability." The columnist, Eduardo Fidanza, talks of "desperate voters who could say of the ruling elites the same thing that Jacobo Burckardt said of the great personalities: 'they are everything that we are not.'" It is from today's newspaper.[1]

I put off reading about the mobilizations in Barcelona and the demonstrations in France (where the increasingly violent "yellow vests" protests continue), to spend a little more time on the "wave of fury" taking over Latin America. The urgency and timeliness of the subject is such that I barely notice an analysis of the situation in Venezuela, where a UN report, prepared under the direction of former Chilean President Michelle Bachelet, speaks forcefully of 6,700 deaths in one year and a half and five million people who have gone into exile. No, I do not have the bandwidth to assimilate that tragedy. I am focusing on what happened yesterday and what will happen tomorrow in the rest of the region.

I say yesterday and tomorrow and in the literal sense. I say yesterday, because on October 25, the largest demonstration in the history of the

[1] La Nación, last consulted on October 25, 2019: www.lanacion.com.ar/opinion/columnistas/votar-y-acordar-la-utopia-del-dia-despues-nid2300691.

Chile took place: *more than a million people* took to the streets of Chile to pressure the government of Sebastián Piñera to undertake structural changes. The newspaper says that similar demonstrations had not been seen for at least thirty years, when Chileans took to the streets after the 1988 plebiscite called for the national election that ended General Pinochet's dictatorship. The protesters' slogan is: "Chile, wake up, we are not at war" (the President of the country, with astonishing clumsiness and a striking lack of sensitivity and awareness of the situation, had referred to the growing social problem and unrest by saying "we are at war"). In the few days since the protests broke out on October 18, there have been nineteen deaths in Chile and serious damage in most of the country's cities. It is also worth noting the event that unleashed the conflict: a slight increase in the price of the subway ticket, that a few days later, intimidated by the reaction, President Piñera reversed and replaced with increased social benefits. Yet the demonstrations demanding his resignation did not cease, but rather grew. Yesterday one million people took to the streets of Santiago.

These massive demonstrations in response to an increase in the price of services and demands for the President to resign, and the consequential cancellation of the increase by the President are all in reference to Chile, but I was reading the same account earlier this week about Ecuador. Just a few days ago (on October 14), President Lenin Moreno was forced to repeal Decree 883, which had eliminated the government fuel subsidy and unleashed a wave of protests, radicalized indigenous demonstrations, arson, and looting throughout the country.

I said tomorrow, too, because tomorrow is the day elections will be held, in my country, Argentina, but this year the political and social atmosphere is anything but enthusiastic (in Argentina, election day is traditionally a festive occasion). Instead, there is an air of sadness, anger, and disenchantment. The country appears not only economically, but also politically bankrupt. People are talking about a "political rift" (a term that has been used in many countries, from Spain to Venezuela) to describe the unprecedented hostility between the two main political factions of the country (another situation that Argentina has in common with many other countries). The person predicted to become the new Vice-President was already President of Argentina on two other occasions, and will assume her new position with six court orders for preventive detention and twelve confirmed convictions on her record.

I have made reference in just a few lines to similar events that occurred in just a handful of days in countries from Spain or France, to Argentina,

Chile, Ecuador, and Venezuela, but I could have spoken of almost any other Western nation, especially those in the Americas. I could have mentioned, for example, Bolivia – not what has happened in its recent history but rather what has happened since Sunday last, where there has been a succession of destruction, arson, and confrontations between security forces and demonstrators since allegations of fraud surfaced right after voting official began in their presidential election.[2]

Or, I could have looked at the divisions in South America's largest country, Brazil, and the catastrophic government of Jair Bolsonaro. Then there is the social tragedy unfolding in Nicaragua since the eruption of protests in 2018 against the government's reforms of the social security system, protests that have grown to denounce brutal police repression and demand the resignation of President Ortega. What about Mexico, currently in the midst of a "new national security crisis" that exploded after the ideologically left-leaning government lost another battle in its war against drug traffickers when it was forced to free the son of the Mexican drug boss, "el Chapo Guzmán," yielding control of the city of Culiacán to his criminal organization. If this was not enough, I could have mentioned Uruguay instead, where massive demonstrations have just taken place protesting the plebiscite "living without fear" public safety policy that includes conditions for deploying military troops in the country's cities.

There I was, enjoying a cup of coffee before setting off to find the sources that would help me explain in clear terms what I had in mind when I thought about the current crisis of democracy and "democratic erosion," but all I had to do was open the newspapers and I was crushed by distressing reports that all related to it. The situation is exploding in our faces, and is impossible not to see, even with our eyes closed.

18.2 "Democratic Erosion": A Previously Unidentified Species?

It was not that long ago that prominent social scientists were expressing renewed hope – even a certain optimism – for the prospects of improved democratic participation. Benjamin Barber published a book that found immediate success on "strong" democracies (Barber 1984); Jane Mansbridge had published another the year before that also praised participatory democracies (Mansbridge 1983). In recent years, however, the mood seems to be trending in the opposite direction: books upon

[2] For an overview see, for example, Maristella Svampa (2019).

books, article after article on the democratic crisis. The literature draws attention to the phenomenon of "democratic erosion": *democracies that no longer die in one fell swoop, but rather slowly, bit by bit.* Instead of succumbing from one day to the next after massive riots or a military coup, democracies nowadays are dismantled piece by piece from within. Through small, outwardly legal moves, democracies are emptied of their representational legitimacy and turn into their opposite. From the government "of the people, by the people, and for the people," we find ourselves with a government "of a few, managed by a minority, and for the privileged."

Indeed, in recent years, the entire front line of political scientists and many of the best constitutional scholars have begun writing about the same subject: democracy is going through its darkest hours; democracies are failing; democracies are not immortal. Here are a few illustrative examples:

- Noted political scientist Adam Przeworski had been writing on the subject for a number of years. He has just published a book on the issue entitled *The Crisis of Democracies* (Przeworski 2019) that speaks of "eroded" democracies dismantled gradually from within. He referred to the phenomenon as democratic backsliding.
- The constitutional law scholar Cass Sunstein published a book on the fall of democracy in 2018, wondering if the phenomenon – generally associated with exotic or far away countries – could also occur in the United States, the cradle of constitutional democracy: "Could it happen here too?" he asked (Sunstein 2018).
- Another renowned constitutional scholar, Mark Tushnet, along with other colleagues, edited a work on "constitutional democracies in crisis" (Graber, Levinson & Tushnet 2018).
- David Van Reybrouck advocated for more direct forms of democracy in addition to the traditional form of elections and famously spoke of "democratic fatigue" (Reybrouck 2017).
- The comparative legal scholar Tom Ginsburg, together with his colleague Aziz Huq, published a very influential book (one of the most notable and informed of the period), on *How to Save a Constitutional Democracy* (in fact, the book's original title was *How Constitutional Democracies Die*, but, on the advice of Supreme Court Justice Judge Ruth Bader Ginsburg, he gave it a more optimistic touch) (Ginsburg & Huq 2018).
- Another author working in comparative law, David Landau, wrote about rising "abusive constitutionalism" (Landau 2013).

- The political scientist Steven Levitsky published, together with Daniel Ziblatt, one of the most successful books written in the period, on the question: *How Democracies Die* (Levitsky & Ziblatt 2018).

What explains the sudden appearance of so many works on the democratic crisis – its erosion, its regression, its abuses, its dismantling, its fall, its death, its fatigue – in such a short period from so many of the best scholars of our time? I would like to reflect a little on the significance of the phenomenon, and how it connects with the concerns of this book.

18.3 Too Slow a Death: From the Crisis of Rights to the Crisis of Democracy

From the crisis of rights . . . A first comment on the growing thematization of the "slow death" of democracy relates to the shift in the literature's focus. Until a few years ago, the dominant paradigm was distinct in that it focused on what we could call the "crisis of rights." Think of the events that led to the Second World War, the unexpected rise of fascism and Nazism, and the ensuing genocide. Since then, much legal reflection has revolved on protecting rights as a means to prevent a tragedy similar to the one that had affected a large part of humanity: atrocious political regimes, war, massacres, death on a scale never seen before. As I stated above, a good deal of legal energy has understandably been devoted, for decades now, to the protection of rights: how to assign them legal protection; how to litigate for them; and how courts should respond to their violations. Many of the best authors of the time – such as Ronald Dworkin in the Anglo-Saxon sphere and Luigi Ferrajoli in the continental European and Latin American spheres – were expressions of that moment: their theories revolved around the perceived need for the protection of rights. Another way to characterize their reflections would be preventing genocide with the law's help. Law, as we know, has always played a part in with the worst dramas suffered by society. Humanity confronted the problem of genocide through conventions and international treaties establishing new rights and new local, national, regional, and international human rights courts to enforce them. The Universal Declaration of Human Rights was adopted by the UN in 1948; The American Declaration on the Rights and Duties of Man (which preceded the Universal Declaration and constitutes the first international agreement on human rights) was also approved in 1948 (the American Convention on Human Rights, or Pact of San José de Costa Rica, meanwhile, was signed in 1969); and the European Court of Human Rights was established in 1959.

In the 1970s, Latin America was gripped by the tragedy of violent dictatorships that regularly carried out "disappearances" and massive rights violations. This led to a powerful resurgence of the human rights movement – one that led many countries in the region to incorporate international law into their domestic order, usually assigning it a privileged status. In some countries, such as Argentina and Bolivia, human rights treaties were explicitly incorporated as constitutional norms. In other cases, such as Costa Rica and El Salvador, the treaties were conferred supra-legal hierarchy (Rossi & Filippini 2010). Some constitutions, such as those of Peru or Colombia, included interpretative clauses in their texts that made explicit reference to international law. Others, such as Brazil, made reference to the existence of rights not listed, among which are the treaties to which Brazil is a party. Chile established special duties in the area of human rights and required compliance to them by all state organs.

The rebirth of the movement for human rights was of such magnitude that activists and militants from the left – the ideological descendants of Marx who had historically repudiated the rights discourse for more than a century – ended up jumping on the human rights boat too. Allow me to say it again: it was a time marked by the drama of massive rights violations and subsequent constitutionalization of the human rights paradigm.

... ***To the Crisis of Democracy. "Termites" That Eat Away at Democracy.*** That we spent a couple generations immersed in the paradigm of rights is not bad in itself, but it is a historical fact. It is a fact that had a significant impact in preventing violations of basic human interests that, at the time, seemed the rule or normal state of affairs. We had become used to it but we are not any longer.

In the present day, however, a different paradigm seems to prevail, that of the democratic crisis. There is, as I understand it, widespread recognition that we are going through a new, very serious situation, about which we had not thought enough before. This does not mean that the rights crisis is over: rights continue to be seriously violated in a wide range of contexts. However, I would say that the rights crisis no longer seems to be the most pressing one. *The perceived urgency is related instead to widespread estrangement from our political systems; distrust in politicians; institutions that either do not deliver what they promise or provide just the opposite; and public organs whose function appears to be the creation and consolidation of new privileges*. These are the days of the "Arab Spring"; of the Argentine "May they all leave!" ("¡Que se vayan todos!"); of "Occupy Wall Street" in the United States; of Syriza in Greece and of Podemos in Spain (two anti-party political parties); the "yellow vests" (*gilets jaunes*) in France; the young pro-democracy activists in Hong Kong risking their lives; of bitter complaints against the political "caste" that has taken over our governments.

What I would like to add to the discussion of this "new" problem, the problem of democracy decomposing from within until it is too weak to stand, is also very much an "old" problem. Without going into detail, I will just recall the great political scientist Guillermo O'Donnell who spoke of the "slow death of democracy" for many years before studies of "democratic erosion" became fashionable (O'Donnell 2007) and who wrote extensively about the "brown areas" of democracy and related issues starting in the late 1980s and early 1990s (O'Donnell 2010).

Personally, I am tempted to go much further back than O'Donnell. The particular nature of problem about which we are thinking started much longer ago. To be clear, we are talking about the situation of democracies that do not crumble all at once, but fall apart piece by piece, while they are dismantled from within (or perhaps because they are dismantled from within) as if infested with termites (which brings to mind the Brazilian film "Aquarius" by Klever Mendonca Filho and starring Sonia Braga, where the walls of the old majestic family house are slowly eaten away by termites). What I am interested in showing is that the path that leads directly to our current "ills," starts, in truth, at the very "origin" of our constitutional tradition.

Remember, for example, what we saw when discussing the very imperfect system of "checks and balances" in Latin America. As we saw, these systems were implemented in the nineteenth century, borrowing the notion of institutional controls from North American liberalism but, nonetheless, very imperfectly, since they "mixed" the controls with the institutional demands of conservative groups that favored a "President-monarch." (Alberdi recommended, we will remember, the creation of an institutional system within which the President "can assume the powers of a king at the moment that anarchy disobeys him.") The institutional model designed then – I repeat, in the middle of the nineteenth century – was vulnerable from "day one" to constitutional dismantling from within, to democratic "erosion." We see the phenomenon of democratic backsliding already present two centuries ago. Of course, we know that Latin America was historically prone to coups d'état: that is how governments there tended to come to an end throughout the twentieth century. However, this is in no way inconsistent with the emphasis on erosion from within: "sudden death" always went hand in hand with "slow death." Both dynamics existed at the same time. The Latin American hyper-powerful president habitually sought to undermine the controls on his own office. Coups d'état (the "sudden death") tended to occur when the institutional attrition (the "slow death") reached a point where faith in the virtues of institutions to express and channel citizens' demands was completely lost. Just because this "slow death" phenomenon is especially visible in many countries today (or that the tendency for regime change through coup d'état in the Latin American region appears to have "stopped"), or that in the United States we seem to be witnessing the emergence, one that started decades ago, of "imperial presidencies" oriented towards throwing off the balance of the entire system of institutional control from within, does not mean that we are facing a new phenomenon. If anything, we are faced with a long-standing phenomenon that has taken on particular salience in the current circumstances, perhaps because the consequences are so serious and foreseeable.[3]

18.4 Repairing a Ship at Sea: Restoring Democratic Controls

Faced with the current crisis and the phenomenon (recent or not, but in any case now especially salient) of "democratic erosion," it is essential to carefully situate ourselves theoretically to properly recognize what is at stake and determine what adequate responses are available. My impression, however, is that much of the dominant literature on the subject has the enormous merit of having identified the problem of our time – a problem directly related to democracy – but I do not feel that it has been successful in terms of diagnosis and remedy. We have already noted one

[3] The extremely serious COVID-19 crisis, which broke out in early 2020, exposed the deterioration of our institutional system in the starkest way. The health crisis was then accompanied by an institutional crisis, which only aggravated the former. What we saw from then on was dramatic, but not surprising: Executive Powers that took the excuse of the pandemic to act (still more) discretionally; systems of "checks and balances" that could not respond to the demands of the time; decision-making processes that were shamelessly left in the hands of experts (so far removed from democratic debate); police abuses that were justified in the name of sanitary measures; social protests that were repressed by invoking the need to protect the people's health. A tremendous tragedy! I discussed some of these issues in Gargarella 2020a; 2020b; 2020c.

error in the diagnosis (the notion that the problem is new) so, in what follows, I would like to focus on possible remedies.

An important branch of the literature that deals with the subject seems to argue that the recent problem of democratic erosion originated in the gradual increase in the power of the executive branch, which led to the gradual dismantling of the system's internal control and was helped along by a general lack of political commitment and participation by citizens. This perspective suggests as a way of responding the recovery of *internal controls* (through a more active and vigilant citizenry) and, most of all, the strengthening of *external controls*, that is to say, the restoration of the democratic controls occasioned by the strong executive branches.

In this line of writing on the subject, I think in particular of the refined and empirically supported work of Ginsburg and Huq. As we saw earlier, Tom Ginsburg and Aziz Huq have argued that "the most formidable engine of erosion [of the entire institutional system] would be the presidency, which over time has acquired a plethora of more institutional, political and rhetorical powers beyond [those assigned by the Constitution]" (Ginsburg & Huq 2018, 141). They also emphasized that democracy demands from its members "a certain political morality" (Ginsburg & Huq 2018, 173). They explicitly maintained that "in the absence of that political morality, nothing in the toolkit of constitutional designers will save constitutional democracy. *Design, in short, can go only so far without decency*" (Ginsburg & Huq 2018, 173, italics added). I want to emphasize that notable point: *without a certain political morality, no tool will enable us to save these constitutional democracies.*

Even more radically, Ginsburg and Huq argue that the essential change needed in terms of political morality does not have to do with "incentives or stratagems," but rather "with beliefs and preferences," which are transmitted within "families, schools, churches, mosques, synagogues, workplaces, and social media networks" (Ginsburg & Huq 2018, 245). They conclude: "Without those beliefs, without a simple desire for democracy on the part of the many, the best institutional and constitutional design in the world will likely be for naught" (Ginsburg & Huq 2018, 245).

In my opinion, this kind of position has very serious problems, regardless the important contributions that Ginsburg and Huq may have brought to the discussion. I would like to quickly mention some of them. I have already referred to the error of considering as new a problem that, in truth, is not (and, similarly, there is also something problematic about thinking about the question in the light of political evolution in the

United States, despite the explicit efforts of Ginsburg and Huq to avoid all manner of parochialism). I would add that there is another significant problem with focusing on "political morality" and the terms with which they do it. The idea that the problem has more to do with "beliefs and preferences" than "incentives or stratagems" seems seriously wrong, especially since it ignores a factor that I have alluded to several times in this work, *the "endogenous formation" of character*. More specifically, the authors do not seem to appreciate the relationship between the alleged political apathy of the citizenry and a constitutional system with markedly elitist features, seeming to attribute the indifference instead to some choice or preference on the part of common people. Beyond the diagnostic error that this vision implies, at least in my opinion, I believe the approach ends up pointing us in the wrong direction by attributing to the citizens something for which the counter-majoritarian institutional system is originally responsible. Without intending to free anyone from their responsibilities (particularly citizens for greater or lesser degrees of "civic virtue," political participation, and respect for rights), I believe it is a serious mistake not to put the main focus of the analysis on the scheme built around principles of democratic mistrust, treating as "personal" a problem that is fundamentally "structural."

In this sense, it seems reasonable that citizens might rationally and sensibly choose to shun public affairs, tactically or temporarily withdrawing, in most cases, to a more private sphere, if what they encounter in the public sphere is neglect or aggression by those in government. If, as has happened so many times, active, constant public pressure (I recall in particular the 2001 demonstrations in Argentina that went on for months in the aftermath of the sovereign debt crisis demanding "may they all leave!") does not translate into meaningful change in the political system (again, in 2001, "everyone stayed"), citizens may well decide not to return to the streets except when the circumstances become truly unbearable, extreme. Why mobilize otherwise, if it commonly turns out institutionally useless despite the extraordinary effort? Similarly, if political activism is systematically and historically translated into severe violence, as in Colombia where for decades publicly assuming a leftist political position seemed to make you a target for assassination, it makes sense for citizens to be extremely cautious before entering the public sphere. Politics cannot just be for martyrs. Likewise, considering situations that are more similar to that of the United States, the institutional situation all seems markedly unfriendly to popular participation. There are very few incentives to vote (and a few disincentives to boot); the political influence of wealth is overwhelming; matters of collective interest are systematically decided by courts; civic activism is forcefully deterred (through, for example, "strong-arm" security policies that (boastfully) criminalize minor misdemeanors); and so on. In short, the view that Ginsburg and Huq present seems to take as a question of (bad) "attitude" or (poor) "character" – ultimately, of personal morality – the results of an institutional decision to penalize or render more difficult civic activism, rather than encouraging or facilitating it.

Returning to the diagnosis of Ginsburg and Huq once more, the political proposal for the restoration of "internal controls" ("checks and balances"), also rests on problematic assumptions in at least three different ways. First, my impression is that these authors tend to *conflate the problems of democracy with the problems of constitutionalism, as if they were identical.* To understand what I am saying, imagine that one day, miraculously, we managed to restore the old machinery of "checks and balances," putting an end to the widespread abusive practices of the executive, blocking it from future dismantling of control mechanisms, and so on. Even if we magically managed to achieve those ambitious goals, a central part of our problem of "democratic erosion" would remain fundamentally intact. On the one hand, people would continue to feel alienated from power and disconnected from democracy. This is because the problems posed by the crisis of constitutionalism differ significantly from those posed by the crisis of democracy. In other words, people do not feel politically alienated because, for example, judges have lost control of the executive or legislators are too deferential to it, or because there are too few limits on presidential power. *We the People* feel removed from politics because we have very few opportunities to participate meaningfully in the political life of our communities. Others take control over our affairs, telling us which direction the policies that matter most to us will take.

Secondly, I understand that these authors assume *a minimalist vision of democracy.* In this minimalist vision, the relevant decision-making power – control of the levers in the Constitution's "engine room" – ought to remain in the hands of a few, while the citizens ought to content themselves with the role of a distant and passive "monitor" of their rulers. As the authors explicitly state, citizen intervention in politics is basically limited to periodic voting (Ginsburg & Huq 2018, 244). Against this vision, as I understand it, a different vision with Jeffersonian roots deserves to be defended (as I have tried to do). In this vision, citizens must recover not only the power to limit what others do in their name, but, above all, recover decision-making power over their affairs ("a government is republican in proportion as every member composing it has his equal voice in the direction of its concerns").[4]

In any case, Ginsburg and Huq (as Robert Dahl or Adam Przeworski would, for different reasons), tend to subscribe to a thin Schumpeterian conception of democracy, according to which democracy is "an institutional arrangement for arriving at political decisions in which individuals acquire the power to decide by means of a competitive struggle for the people's vote" (Ginsburg & Huq 2018, 8). The authors perhaps subscribe to such a view, above all, for descriptive reasons (to enable comparison of as many political systems as possible). However, in this way too, they naturalize and end up taking as their parameter a model of institutional arrangement that, as I understand it, is a central part of the problem: a "minimalist" vision that contributes to political apathy and aggravates "democratic erosion" (given the "disengagement" that it promotes, or the "commitment" that it does not encourage, in terms of the relationship between citizens and their representatives).

The third criticism that I wanted to make of Ginsburg and Huq's approach is related to the fact that it seeks – to use Fernando Atria's phrase – *to revive dead ideas*, and in this case, "dead institutions" as well (Atria 2016). I mean that the institutional system as we know it presents irreparable structural deficiencies related to many issues but, in particular, to the system's incapacity or inability to represent and express the relevant points of view, demands, and needs of an extraordinary number of diverse groups. In this sense – as I have already argued – even were the institutional system entirely peopled by decent, competent, and "angelic" officials, it would be incapable of satisfying the basic functions expected of it. Look at, for proof, the enormous dissatisfaction and detachment from politics and sentiment of alienation and disenfranchisement in the most dissimilar of societies. Attempts like those of Ginsburg and Huq are laudable and well-intentioned. However, the attractive objectives they set seem to close our eyes to the fact that rebuilding a better system of checks and balances basically means "reviving dead ideas." The problem with their solution is not that it is impossible, but rather with its futility. We might perhaps, with effort and enormous difficulty, restore the machinery

[4] Proposals to Revise the Virginia Constitution: I. Thomas Jefferson to "Henry Tompkinson" (Samuel Kercheval), July 12, 1816. Available at https://founders.archives.gov/documents/Jefferson/03-10-02-0128-0002.

of mutual controls between government branches, but this would not repair the most important breakdown: citizen disaffection, fatigue, and widespread certainty that the institutional system will not help or represent us, that it does not respond to our demands, and that it will continue, primarily, to benefit a few. All this is also due – in a very central way – to deeper structural problems related, for instance, to the extraordinary difficulty of the existing representative structures to deliver on its original promise. The system was originally devised to represent us all, to serve as a "mirror" of society, to account for the enormous multicultural diversity of our societies. If the stated objective (restoring the old system of controls) is the main remedy offered in response to the problem of "erosion," then the "democratic objection" remains intact. To go back to the beginning of the book and "the shortest story ever written," we will wake up and the "democratic objection," like Monterroso's dinosaur, will still be there.

18.5 "The Final Stop": Congress As the Best Democracy Can Do?

In the previous section we looked at the difficulties inherent to one solution for "democratic erosion." The suggestion that the solution is "restoring the broken control system" is too narrow and, due to faulty diagnosis, does not address the essence of the problem which, as we saw, remains untouched. The discussion of Ginsburg and Huq's important work also helps us to discard a second and very fundamental line of response to the problem of hollowed-out democracy. I am referring to a line of argument that, in principle, is more promising than the previous one because, more than reviving checks and balances, it puts the accent on *a recovery of majority politics.*

I understand this approach as an improvement on the previous diagnosis. It clearly recognizes that *a solution to the difficulties faced that intends to use the existing counter-majoritarian system as a remedy is doomed from the start.* Hence the value of approaches that seek to recover the decision-making power of democratic politics. What such approaches focus on is reinvigorating the ailing representative system by "injecting" democratic politics into its sagging veins – particularly by strengthening the Congress.

There are many possible ways to present this response, but I would like to focus on one in particular because of its relevance to the framework of this book. The formulation I will use to represent this line of argumentation does not belong to the literature on "democratic erosion," however. It has been developing for dozens of years, largely through theoretical arguments over the judiciary's counter-majoritarian powers.

We are already aware of the centuries-long debate over judicial review and of the forceful resurgence in recent years of arguments that are particularly attentive to *the value of majority rule and democratic legislation* and concerned with moving those commitments back to the center of our democratic systems. I am particularly thinking of, as those familiar with these discussions may have anticipated, the work of Jeremy Waldron (author of a book with that very title: *The Dignity of Legislation*, Waldron 1999a). Waldron has advanced the most interesting and sophisticated critique of judicial review and defense of majority politics in the last thirty years.[5]

In recent years, Waldron has made some clarifications about his position. In his latest book on the subject, in particular, Waldron qualified his views on judicial review and the counter-majority problem. In *Political Political Theory*, in particular, Waldron has made it clear that his vindication of Congress is not a "second-best" choice, that is, one that is made out of the practical impossibility of obtaining a superior "first choice." No. His position is, in this sense, fundamentally identical to the one defended by James Madison in the famous Federalist No. 10. Waldron seems to make Madison's words his own when he maintains: "Under such a regulation, it may well happen that the public voice, pronounced by the representatives of the people, will be more consonant to the public good than if pronounced by the people themselves, convened for the purpose." Representation – for Madison, as for Waldron – appears as a "first option" and not by any means simply as a "necessary

[5] Waldron's position on the subject has evolved in that it has taken on greater nuance and has even changed slightly, compared to his starting point, but he has not abandoned its essence or critical content (which can also be said of other authors who have traveled similar paths, such as Mark Tushnet 2008). In his early writings (later compiled in his extraordinary book *Law and Disagreement*, Waldron 1999), Waldron presented the judicial review as an "insult," as "offensive" to our democratic dignity. He wondered: What do we say to those who have militated for a cause, put together their own movement, mobilized millions of people to the streets, and obtained a favorable legal change? What do we say to that person who has achieved a similar legislative success, if shortly after obtaining it, a majority of five judges invalidates the law, built patiently, for years and with a major political effort? In more recent years, as we know, he partially qualified his initial position (Waldron 2009, 2016), showing sensitivity to certain "variations of context" (how to respond to the problem in countries where Congress does not function properly, or is captured by elites, by criminal groups, etc.?), while accepting certain forms of judicial review consistent with the legislature's recovery of the "last word" (we will return to this topic later). In particular, his last book on the subject (*Political Political Theory*) explored possible ways in which the internal functioning of the legislature could be reconstructed (how to organize the decision-making process, how to rethink debates), in such a way as to make it back into a functioning democratic decision-making mechanism (Waldron 2016).

evil." I will quote Waldron in this regard, because his words on the matter are as careful as they are revealing. Waldron tells us: "*People have assumed from my own work on judicial review, based as it is on principles of democratic legitimacy and political equality, that I, too, must favor the people themselves voting directly as equals on the laws that are to govern them*" (Waldron 2016, 135, italics added). He goes on to affirm that any concession or limitation in this regard cannot be acceptable because it would imply (both at the legislative and judicial level) a delegation of authority that circumvents the political participation of the common citizen. Waldron concludes, however, such views are wrong, because representation constitutes, as regards the creation of laws, a better democratic alternative. And, as regards judicial review, the problem is not only insulation in relation to the people, but, and above all, their lack of adequate democratic credentials – which the legislator does possess.

That is to say, for Waldron, the challenge posed by systems of judicial review of democratic legislation (and the potential "offense" or "insult" of such review to our democratic spirit) does not require, as a response, direct citizen participation, as equals. A properly functioning representative system is simply enough – and much better. To support his argument, Waldron takes particular inspiration from the work of his colleague Nadia Urbinati. In line with Urbinati's thinking, Waldron argues that

> the abstraction that representation involves is particularly appropriate for lawmaking, which is a domain in which we are striving to produce abstract norms, abstract in the sense of *general*, rather than directives focused on some particular person or situation in the way that a bill of attainder is focused or in the way that a judicial decision might be focused, at least in the first instance. (Waldron 2016, 136)

Waldron's (in my view incorrect) defense of representative democracy over direct democracy ties in with his (in my view correct) defense of the "diversity" that is necessary in Congress. Indeed, Waldron's argument for diversity within Congress is extremely interesting, and includes important clarifications relative to the number of representatives the Congress should hold (Waldron emphasizes the need for large legislative bodies), as well as to the "presence" and the representation of "interests."[6]

[6] On "presence," in particular, Waldron says that Congress must reflect the full diversity of views that are embedded in society. "If there are ethnic differences, you want the legislature to include members of the different existing ethnicities": all the diverse conceptions of what is good, all the important interests, all the different experiences, must find a place in the Congress: the Congress must include diversity of opinions, but also diversity of experiences, and diversity of interests. This last point is no less significant – he clarifies – than the

Waldron concludes that, to the extent that Congress demonstrates the requisite degrees of representativeness, debating public questions in Congress is preferable to direct democracy. Why? Because representation helps to move the discussion to a more manageable level of abstraction: someone represents the northern district, another such-and-such state, another the Democratic Party: "We want our laws to consider people universally with regards certain aspects, and as we draft the laws, we also want our representatives to present the interests, concerns, ideals of the people, universally regarding certain aspects." The prioritization or presentation of interests is what, for Waldron, legislative debate is best for. Representation, as Urbinati says, helps to depersonalize demands and opinions in a way that makes deliberation more conducive. It represents what people of different classes have in common, and thus leads to "simplifying interests and assimilating issues." In addition, legislation requires time and careful deliberation, and in this sense, seems to have good practical effects: finding the time and space necessary for deliberation among thousands or hundreds of thousands or millions of people seems far-fetched.

18.6 Between Mill's "Best Judge" and Aristotle's "Wise Crowd"

Although I have followed closely, and with great attention, the evolution of this debate (and Waldron's work on it in particular), I should say that, for those of us who are concerned with the degradation of our democracies and aware that the corrosion has occurred from within the system (the problem of "erosion"), responses focused on restoring the "dignity of legislation" are – once again – completely insufficient. They are, granted, better oriented than those that do not give centrality to political debate and decision-making (in favor of repairing the system of checks and balances), but we still must ultimately consider them insufficient.

Congress, Self-Government, and the Dignity of Legislation. Above all, and as we have already seen, Congress is structurally incapable of representing and expressing the diversity of demands, voices, and points of view existing in society. Against what Waldron defends and seeks, we should insist on this: today it is structurally impossible to ensure that all lifestyles and the whole range of human experience will be represented in

importance that many theorists of democracy associate with representation allowing legislators to concentrate on the relevant "issues" rather than on individuals "interests." These theorists forget that "the impact of the measures on interest is usually the main issue."

Congress. In this sense, Congress is irretrievable. Its greatest promises have proven impossible to fulfill, perhaps because they were based on faulty or obsolete assumptions (e.g., societies comprised of a relatively few internally homogeneous groups and fundamentally self-interested individuals). Of course, in contexts as impaired as ours, where an elitist judiciary is the power that, in the last instance, makes the most crucial decisions (a judiciary that is more or less virtuous according to the hazards of its composition), vindicating the dignity of Congress is necessary, and very healthy. However, for those of us who recognize the insurmountable distance between legislative decisions and the self-government of the people, this claim that the "democratic train" does not go any further than Congress sounds at best very thin. As Karl Marx might put it, self-government requires much more than legislatures, and legislatures that work: it requires another type of constitutional organization, based on the sovereignty of the people.[7]

Congress As "First Choice." The previous point is reinforced with another that Waldron presents in an Aristotelian key. In several recent writings, Waldron has referred to Aristotle's notion of the "wisdom of the crowd." According to this idea, people acting as a "body" are more capable of making better decisions by adding or pooling together their knowledge, experiences, and intuitions, than any of its members can do separately. It is, finally, a criterion related to what I have defended in reference to John Stuart Mill's work, which I relate to a deliberative conception of democracy. This criterion is used by authors such as Carlos Nino in their epistemic defense of *deliberative democracy* (Nino 1991, 1997).[8] Nino's reasoning in support of his epistemic position, in summary form, goes as follows.

Nino explicitly starts from Mill's premise that each person is the best judge of their own interests. Putting ourselves in someone else's position is enormously difficult because it is nearly impossible to properly understand and weigh their interests and needs. Hence the crucial presence of each affected point of view in debates on issues of public or intersubjective morality. The idea is that the effective presence of all interested points of view increases the chances of making a well-informed decision and

[7] In Marx's terms: "In a democracy, the constitution, the law, the state itself, and insofar as it is a political constitution, it is only the self-determination of the people" (Marx [1843] 1978, 21).

[8] Waldron specifically criticized Nino's approach, in a tribute book to him, emphasizing the need for "decision" and not only – as he imputed to adherents of deliberative democracy like Nino – on "deliberation" (Waldron 1999b).

reduces the risks of partial decisions that are favorable only to some or biased against others, even if it is only biased against one single point of view! In other words, *the effective absence of the point of view of anyone significantly affected maximizes the risk of unduly impartial decisions.* And this occurs, as we saw, not necessarily due to bad faith or lack of empathy, but because of the difficulty indicated, which we all encounter, of understanding and properly processing what others perceive and value. Ultimately, the defense of a radically inclusive discussion is based on epistemic reasons: through such discussions we greatly reduce the risks of biased decisions, we increase our awareness of the various aspects and difficulties of what is at stake, and finally we create the necessary conditions for reaching the sought-after impartiality. Therefore, those of us who, like Nino, defend democracy from an argument that starts with John Stuart Mill's assumption, but also those who, like Waldron, defend democracy from the Aristotelian assumption regarding the "wisdom of the crowd," should all agree on the prime importance of citizen involvement in public decision-making: the importance of decisions made by the people themselves, as a "first option," not as a problem to be avoided. In other words: representation itself should be viewed as a "second best" option rather than the highest goal. These are the reasons that many of us believe – I would say rightly – that based on his work on judicial review and its reliance on principles of democratic legitimacy and political equality, Waldron should "support the idea that the people, by themselves, vote directly and as equals, for the laws that will govern them" – as Thomas Jefferson could have put it.

There Are Alternatives, and They Are Worth Trying. My third and last criticism of Waldron's understanding of the power of representative democracy and limits of direct democracy is based on practical experience. In recent years, we have seen evidence of the exceptional value and, above all, how well several concrete experiences of "deliberative assemblies" or "inclusive deliberation" have worked out. As we will see in the remainder of the book, the crisis unleashed by "democratic erosion" has led to the creation of problem-solving alternatives that involve much more inclusive public discussion in places like Australia, Canada, Iceland, and Ireland, among several others. I will specifically address and analyze these experiences in the next chapter, but, for what interests us here, I will only add that these experiences show in practice what we have already intuited from our theoretical discussion. If the procedure is organized properly, even in the context of extremely numerous, plural, complex, multicultural, diverse, and conflictive societies, inclusive debate is possible and, above all, worthwhile. Given the real existence of these alternatives, the emphasis on Congress, finally, is an unnecessarily limited, conservative emphasis.

19

The New Deliberative Assemblies

19.1 The "Pots and Pans Revolution"

Iceland has traditionally been recognized as a highly homogeneous, developed, and egalitarian country with a strong welfare state. In the mid-1990s, however, the local authorities became interested in the prevalent economic theories of those times favoring the "free market" over state intervention in the economy through "regulations." Reforms in the financial market were introduced to liberalize the flow of capital, which ended up making the country's banks and stock market attractive to investors, at least initially. For almost a decade, the country experienced an unexpected "boom" as foreign funds flooded in, which also left the country at the mercy of capital flux. As early as 2005, Iceland's economy began showing alarming signs of weakness, including high levels of inflation and a sudden change in the flow of capital: almost overnight, capital began to flow out of the market, and quickly. Now a prisoner to foreign capital and its fluctuations, the economic "shock" was immediately felt: the national currency depreciated by 70 percent; the stock market crashed; and interest rates skyrocketed. By mid-October 2008, the downward spiral seemed uncontainable. Faced with the crisis, the government decided to assert control over the country's three main private banks and declared the economy in a state of "bankruptcy."

For citizens, the situation was completely unimaginable in light of the tranquility, stability and well-being that had distinguished Iceland for decades. Approaching his seventieth birthday, the poet, lyricist, and gay rights activist Hordur Torfason – an early leader of the protests that broke out – would comment in an interview with *The Independent*: "I stood in front of the parliament building every lunch hour and asked people, 'Can you tell me what has happened in this country? Do you have any idea what we can do?'" The population began to take to the streets in great numbers in search of some answer and to protest against public authorities and private banks. Thus began the "pots and pans revolution."[1] The protests intensified the following January, and by the end of that month, citizens organized a protest demonstration against the National Parliament in Reykjavík, which would result in the largest protest in the history of the country.

The protests began to subside when the main government authorities (led by the right-wing Independence Party) resigned and a left-wing coalition took over. The new government, which appeared to side with the protesters, began a reform process that included the criminal prosecution of the former Prime Minister.

During the movement marked by social empowerment and collective mobilization, grassroots organizations began to fight for constitutional change "from below." The main drivers for the reform were a group known as the "National Assembly Anthill," which convened a first Assembly aimed at laying the foundations for the constitutional reform. It was a small step, but also a "revolutionary" step in constitutional terms: the Assembly – planned to define the basic principles for the future constituent assembly in a single day – was composed exclusively of (950) citizens chosen randomly on the basis of a questionnaire designed to yield a representative sample of the country (what in the academic literature is called a "mini-public"). This group would determine the guidelines for the subsequent Constituent Assembly. The Assembly would consist of twenty-five people elected from among hundreds of ordinary citizen volunteers. The selection would be balanced in terms of gender and incorporate a diverse range of professional backgrounds: from doctors and lawyers, to pastors, farmers, a museum director, a radio presenter, a trade unionist, a student, and a filmmaker (Landemore 2014a).

Radicalizing even further an already remarkable initiative, the Assembly would then open its doors wide for input from the rest of the population, who were invited to send suggestions and criticisms to the delegates through social networks. It would represent, according to one of those who put the final draft together, "the first Constitution in the world basically written from the internet." According to Professor Lawrence Lessig, a specialist in the use of new technologies, "for the first time in history, and using technologies typical of the 21st century, a Constitution was drawn up through a public, open and inclusive

1 www.independent.co.uk/news/world/europe/icelands-pots-and-pans-revolution-lessons-from-a-nation-that-people-power-helped-to-emerge-from-its-10351095.html.

process." The final constitutional project was presented to the Icelandic Parliament, on July 29, 2011.

19.2 The Spread of Deliberative Assemblies

It is as easy as it is common for people to dismiss the Iceland example because of the features we already noted – a small, distant, homogeneous, well-educated, peaceful country with a strong tradition of social programs and civic engagement – in short, an incomparable, almost exotic land. Interestingly, many valuable observations can be drawn from the Icelandic experience. Even more interesting, however, is that this phenomenon which, given the common dismissal of its relevance because of the Iceland's unique features, ought only to be possible in small, homogenous communities, was not. On the contrary, what happened in Iceland represented a more interesting and curious example of a new phenomenon that was spreading across the world. Indeed, the Icelandic experience was preceded by several similar ones in very dissimilar countries. At the same time, Iceland's "Anthill" example triggered other experiments that borrowed and improved on its model, most notably in Ireland. A new era of "deliberative assemblies" was born, one based on a new paradigm of inclusive discussion. The following overview of just a few examples (as I write, promising developments are underway in France as well) will support my affirmation while demonstrating their rich and extraordinary variety.[2]

The Australian Constitutional Convention (1998). A first important precedent about the emergence of these new assemblies occurred at the 1998 Constitutional Convention in Australia convened by the government of John Howard (1996–2007). Its mission was deciding whether Australia should become a republic, a decision that would then be put to a popular vote. The Assembly included, for the first time, and notably, "common citizens" as active delegates of the convention (which is why some referred to it as a "People's Convention").

The Convention was composed of 152 delegates from all the different states and territories of Australia. Half of the members were appointed by

[2] There has been a lot of academic reflection on deliberative assemblies and how to properly organize them, in recent years. Nobody has done so much for this purpose than James Fishkin, whose work on the matter definitely changed the subject and defined its content and contours. See, for example, Fishkin 1991, 1997, 2009, and also Fishkin et al. 2015. See, also, among many others, Setala 2017.

the federal government (thirty-six Commonwealth government appointed delegates and forty members from the Australian parliaments) and the other half were elected by voluntary mail-in votes (Winterton 1998). Here, unlike several of the cases that we will examine later, the designated citizens were chosen, not selected at random, and the proceedings were organized following the model of traditional parliamentary debates, rather than the model of deliberative mini-publics. The Convention ran from February 2 to 13, 1998, and was considered a great success in many ways because of, first of all, the significant public interest it generated, and also because of the involvement of ordinary citizens throughout the process. Numerous groups that had been completely excluded from the original 1890 constitutional discussions were thus able to participate in a crucial constitutional debate. In the end, a national referendum rejected the Convention's proposal that Australia convert to a republic.

British Columbia Citizens' Assembly on Election Reform (2005). The Citizens' Assembly of British Columbia had its origins, like many of the experiences that we are going to review here, in political crisis. It was spearheaded by a group of political leaders determined to change an imperfect electoral system but who found themselves unable to overcome the resistance of established political authorities. The solution they found for this tense political situation was creating a Congress of Citizens, whose members would be chosen at random from the voter rolls. One man and one woman were chosen from each electoral district and the proposals formulated by the Congress would be subsequently put to a popular vote. After an initial "training" phase, the Assembly held more than 50 public hearings and received more than 1,000 written submissions, after which its members deliberated on the proposals. In October 2004, the Assembly recommended that the existing "first past the post" electoral system be replaced by a "single transferable vote" system. The proposal received broad support, but not enough to meet the supermajority required to pass.[3]

Ontario Citizens' Assembly on Election Reform (2006). Shortly after the British Columbia remarkable example, the Canadian province of Ontario launched a similar proposal. In March 2006, a Citizens'

[3] The recommendation had to be approved by a 60 percent majority of voters and simple majorities in 60 percent of the existing seventy-nine districts. The latter requirement was met, but the general vote only obtained 57.7 percent of the required 60 percent.

Assembly on Electoral Reform was formed to review the existing electoral system used to choose the members of the Ontario Legislature. The Assembly met twice a month for six weekends in 2006. It also held numerous public meetings throughout the province and then took an additional six weekends to deliberate on the information gathered and elaborate its final proposal. In May 2007, the Assembly issued its recommendation that the province adopt a "mixed proportional" representation system (like the system in New Zealand). The recommendation was defeated by a higher margin than the British Columbia initiative (in Ontario, 63 percent of the voters were against changing electoral systems).

The Dutch Citizen Forum (2006). The Burgerforum Kiesstelsel offers another interesting example of a citizen assembly. The Dutch Forum was created by the Ministry of the Interior and Kingdom Relations and charged with examining options for electoral reform in the Netherlands. To choose the 143 citizens who eventually participated, an initial pool was randomly selected from the country's electoral rolls. Of this initial sample, 1732 citizens volunteered to serve on the Forum. The final 143 were randomly selected from this pool.[4]

The Forum was innovative both in its composition (only ordinary citizens were eligible) and in the lottery process used to select its members, but at the same time it differed significantly from the Canadian examples. Above all, the Forum had a national rather than a local dimension. Furthermore, in the Dutch example, the recommendations were presented to parliament, rather than to a popular referendum. It must also be said that the discussions organized by the Forum did not attract significant general attention.[5]

The "Crowdsourced" Constitutional Reform of Iceland (2009–2013). In the context of the crisis described at the beginning of this chapter, a process of constitutional reform was initiated in Iceland, driven "from below" by the citizen grassroots organizations. The process began with a

[4] However, to guarantee the representative character of the group, some additional characteristics were considered: the final composition had to reflect proportionally the inhabitants by province; there had to be an equal representation between men and women; and the group had to be representative of the country, also in terms of age (de Jongh 2013, 196).

[5] On December 14, 2006, the Burgerforum presented its final report to an outgoing People's Party (VVD) minister, recommending some minor changes to the electoral system. The Forum proposed a proportional representation system, in which voters would cast a vote, either for the party of their choice, or for the candidate of their choice. In April 2008, however, the proposal was rejected by the ruling coalition that controlled the parliament.

"National Assembly" formed to function as a representative "mini-public" composed of 950 citizens. Its purpose was to discuss the issues and values that should guide the reorganization of national institutions over the course of a single day.[6]

A Constituent Assembly later chose its members from a group of more than 500 citizen volunteers among whom professional politicians were ineligible. The final composition of the Assembly was made up of twenty-five directly elected delegates. The delegates were required to meet for three months (with an additional month if necessary) to discuss and then present a report on constitutional amendments. The 25 delegates elected to be representatives took, among their first measures, the decision to open the constituent discussion to the rest of the citizenry by accepting their input: anyone so interested could send their ideas or opinion to the representatives through social media and follow all the discussions from their home. The assembly's open sessions (they also held some closed ones) were filmed, recorded, and made available to the public (Landemore 2014a, 2020). The input gathered ended up totaling around 360 proposals and more than 3,600 comments on the different available platforms (Landemore 2014; Landemore 2020; Suteu 2015, Suteu & Tierney 2018).

The draft of the Constitution was finalized on July 29, 2011. On October 20, 2012, a nonbinding constitutional referendum was held. The proposals were approved by two-thirds of the voters (with around a 50 percent voter turnout). The proposals then moved to the Icelandic Parliament for ratification. The 2013 election, however, was won by opponents of the new Constitution, who ended up suspending the reform project.

The Irish Constitutional Convention (2012). Despite the rich comparative experience we have in popular and mini-public consultations, it is only in Ireland that we find an example involving two broad deliberative processes, one after the other. The first involves the Constitutional Convention held in 2012–2014, which became the main antecedent for the referendum on gay marriage (2015). This first process was soon followed by another Citizens Assembly (2016–2018), which became the main antecedent of the 2018 abortion referendum (Farrell et al. 2019).

As in other instances of deliberative assemblies, the Irish Constitutional Convention grew out of crisis – in this case, the Great Recession of 2010.

[6] They discussed issues such as democracy, human rights, transparency, public ownership of natural resources, and more rigorous control over the financial system.

The Irish government organized the Convention with the intent of reforming its rigid 1937 Constitution. Although the Convention was inspired by the previous experiences of British Columbia, Ontario, and the Netherlands, it differed from those in composition, as it combined ordinary citizens and elected politicians. As in those examples, however, the citizens were randomly selected. The ordinary citizens comprised two-thirds of the Convention, while the remaining third were elected members of parliament.

The Convention was meant to deliberate on several specific issues, including the overhaul of the electoral system and lowering the voting age; the limitation of the presidential term to five years; gay marriage; and two proposals aimed at increasing the participation of women in politics and public life. These topics were discussed over seven meetings during 2013. The Convention carried on for fourteen months, meeting on average once a month. The recommendations of the Convention were advisory rather than declarative. However, one of the recommendations of the Convention acquired special relevance: this was the recommendation, presented in the July 2013 report, to hold a popular referendum on gay marriage. That referendum was eventually carried out, resulting in the first popular consultation in the history of the country resulting from a process of public deliberation. The referendum to legalize same-sex marriage was approved in May 2015 with the support of 62 percent of the voters.

The Assembly of Ireland (2016). The 2016 Assembly was composed, as its direct antecedent had been, of ninety-nine randomly selected members along with ninety-nine substitutes. The selection process was coordinated by a market research company and one of the Supreme Court Justices and looked at four demographic variants: sex, age, social class, and region of residence.[7] The Assembly functioned as a deliberative mini-public. It generally met all day Saturday and Sunday morning once a month. The members were divided into seven- or eight-people groups who sat around a circular table with two other people. These were the facilitator who was in charge of ensuring the progression of the discussions as well as civil and inclusive conduct, and an assistant who took notes (Farrell et al. 2019, 116).[8] The assembly was, in general, very

[7] The Assembly was originally going to consider five topics, but it ultimately focused its energies on two of them, namely abortion and climate change, the issues where the national government was facing intense international pressure.

[8] A typical session consisted of, first, expert presentations (whose main ideas had been provided to the assembly members in advance); then presentations by civic organization;

successful, and in the end resulted in a referendum held in 2018 that legalized abortion in the country.

The Constituent Assembly in Chile (2015). In 2011, extended student protests in Chile exposed the weak democratic legitimacy of the political class: the social discontent revealed itself to be extremely deep, and unrelated to unfortunate circumstances. As a result of the social unrest, a "mark your vote" campaign was started in advance of the 2013 elections. It encouraged voters to mark their ballots if they were in favor of convening a Constituent Assembly to modify the Constitution, which after decades still carries deep imprints of the dictatorship that promulgated it in 1980. Surprisingly, more than 400,000 voters did just that. In response, shortly after being elected, President Michelle Bachelet announced in April 2015 that she was going to start a constituent process to replace the 1980 Constitution. The process began with an initial "pedagogical" phase to disseminate basic information to the public that lasted from November 2015 until May 2016. Then the most important "dialogue" phase began, involving discussions of reform proposals in citizen assemblies that were organized throughout the country. At the end of the process, more than 200,000 people had taken part in these very rich discussions. Following this stage, a group of experts charged with "translating" the results of the public discussions into a formal constitutional project. The interesting, although ever conflictive process, was bogged down when it made it to the Congress, whose responsibility was determining when it would be put on the congressional agenda for debates and how they would be structured. At this point, a lethal combination of deadlines established by the 1980 Constitution itself and waning political will on the eve of elections that the opposition was poised to win caused the reform project and everything that had led up to it to dissolve – including the citizen interest that the initiative had originally awakened.

19.3 The Era of Assemblies: A Short Initial Balance Sheet

This overview is only meant to illustrate an ongoing, evolving phenomenon that does not end with the experiences cited. However, it is true that it covers the cases that are most commonly cited as the most notable instances in this "early stage" of deliberative assemblies. Be that as it may,

then a question and answer period and small group discussions; and finally individual reflection time when each participant wrote down their thoughts.

and despite the limited scope, the sampled experiences can help us to better think about the phenomenon. In particular, the overview is useful because it provides a body of information that is not limited to the single case of Iceland. As I mentioned, the Iceland experience may appear too exotic to make any relevant inferences. With a broader panorama, the dimensions of the phenomenon can be better gauged, leaving us in a better position to evaluate it. From it, I propose the following initial assessment of deliberative assemblies:

(i) First of all, I would point out the cases mentioned help us to dispel a long series of prejudices usually associated with new assembly initiatives: The assemblies were not exclusively held in small, homogeneous countries like Iceland, but also in expansive, more populated and multicultural countries like Australia and Canada. Nor did the assemblies deal exclusively with abstract issues that were removed from most citizens' interests (think of the monarchy vs. republic question in Australia). They also addressed some of the most conflictive and socially divisive issues (leading to the referendums on abortion and gay marriage in Ireland). Furthermore, the debates were not limited to technicians, experts, and professionals. For the most part, they also included many participants who did not have advanced degrees or professional qualifications.

(ii) Relatedly, I would highlight the relevance of these inclusive discussion processes to certain assumptions common in the social sciences regarding the limits of participation and collective deliberation, many of which were challenged to varying degrees. I would like to draw attention to some of the established notions that these experiences invite us to revisit (many of which were also evident in our examination of the debate over abortion in Argentina):

Rationality and technical knowledge. One of the most extraordinary achievements of these processes involved public education. Ordinary people quickly became experts on issues of public relevance through the deliberative assemblies. After a simple process of information and collective discussion, the participants were often able to master complex technical content. The learning that occurs during these practices is very important, especially in an institutional context that often hinders or even actively resists the participation of the electorate in the discussion of public affairs, alleging (for example) their rational ignorance (with the support of the public choice school of political theory: Buchanan 2000; Pincione & Tesón 2006; Tullock et al. 2002). The proponents of this school build their theory by appealing to the lack of information and ("rational") knowledge of the citizens, which they argue is based on their ("rational") lack of interest in and motivation to tackle complex issues, which are defined as issues not of their immediate and direct interest (a subject to which I will return). The truth is that the deliberative experiences examined helped to demonstrate the obvious fallacy of the public-choice school's surprisingly resilient assumptions: even in the absence of crucial interest in the subject matter, people can be motivated to participate and learn about complex and divisive issues, and even become, without major difficulty and years of training, "experts." The example of the Canadian Deliberative Assemblies is quite extraordinary in this regard: they dealt with nothing more and nothing less than "electoral systems" – perhaps the most unattractive, technical, and complex field within political science. And yet, through the experience, ordinary people who did not have any strong interest at stake or technical training became experts. All that was necessary was organizing the process well in an open, deliberative and inclusive way.

Motivation. In addition, the Assemblies helped to disprove the widespread assumption in contemporary social science that most people are apathetic and poorly motivated to engage with complex political issues. On the contrary, I would argue, people distrust party politics and resist actively participating in politics when they realize that their voices or contributions will not be taken seriously, or that their contributions will be considered only when it can be used to support what has already been decided by others. However, *when citizens recognize that their input will or might seriously be taken into account, they become motivated to play an active part in the collective deliberation and make themselves heard in the interest of finding the best decision possible.* Now, some critics of the view I am here advancing may object to this point and claim that – sooner or later, and contrary to what I suggest – people are going to fall prey, once again, to political passivity, lured by the seductive chants of hyper-presidentialism and concentrated power. As one critic mentioned: "now, the world is populated by presidents under which they feel represented ... there are people that feel politically included (through an authoritarian, populist, messianic, anti-liberal President), not politically excluded."[9] I disagree, however, with this view, and I think that, in the end, it is based on a misunderstanding about the nature of my claims. In fact, I am not "predicting" that, after the coming of citizen assemblies, the world will change, the people will change, and nothing in politics will be anymore as it was before. My claim is much more modest than that: I am just saying that contrary to common and repeated criticisms, there are interesting and promising alternatives to our presently degraded democracies.[10] I am saying that it is not true that, under present conditions, a more inclusive and participatory democracy is impossible, or even unthinkable: we have good examples that strongly contradict these pessimistic claims. I perfectly understand, however, that the risks faced by these alternatives are enormous, precisely because of the way in which "the past always comes to limit the present" (I shall come back to this point immediately).

Deliberation and the transformation of preferences. The Assemblies also confirmed the value of collective deliberation. (1) To begin with, a significant number of social scientists have been skeptical of the value of collective deliberation for all these years: "Why invite people to argue" – the reasoning goes – "if no one changes their mind." These scholars looked at public life from the point of view of established *interests* and from there, they minimized the role and nature of open deliberation, and therefore resisted the idea vindicated by so many other authors that *deliberation is an appropriate means to favor changing preferences* (Elster 1983, 1986). (2) This point also helps us resist a common and related criticism against citizens assemblies and the like. The objection says that collective assemblies may be appropriate for the task of defining better policies, but not necessarily for "making those that are going

[9] I take this criticism from a reviewer of this work, to whom I am thankful.

[10] In addition, I resist the idea that, under populist and authoritarian leaders, people are feeling included and represented. I think that such worrisome results (people becoming easily seduced by authoritarian leaders) are an endogenous product of our exclusive and impoverished democracies. In fact, I would claim, after decades living under so-called democratic regimes that neither deliver social justice nor favor political participation, people (understandably) begin to demand and accept "favors" and "concessions" from anyone who can make credible promises. This is a pity, but it does not qualify as an argument against deliberative democracy. On the contrary, it offers us additional reasons for fighting in favor of a more deliberative democracy.

to comply with them endorse them and ... identify them with those policies" (in this respect see, particularly, Lafont 2020). In this way – the objection continues – "citizen assemblies substitute the mind of people subjected to them and ask people to blindly defer to their policies."[11] I think that this is an important objection against a very peculiar type of citizen assemblies, namely those that are radically disconnected with the people at large. Perhaps, in the near future, and precisely as a result of the "success" that popular assemblies obtained, many of them will intentionally be designed in such a way – I mean radically separated from the people at large – which would undermine their attractiveness (thus, in particular, by weaking the requirement of "inclusion"). This is a risk that we, advocates of these popular alternatives, should seriously address (I consider the risk of some of these pathological developments below). However, I do not see the described situation (people forced to blindly defer to the assemblies' decisions) as typical – as the most common or distinctive – among the assemblies that I examined here with greater attention and interest. Take, for example, the case of the popular assemblies that discussed the issue of abortion, both formally (like in Ireland, through citizen assemblies) and informally (like in Argentina). In both those situations – I submit – it would have been strange to say that "citizen assemblies substituted the mind of people subjected to them and asked people to blindly defer to their policies." In the mentioned cases, in fact, I did not observe the problems of "substitution" and "blind deference" at all.[12] On the contrary, what I

[11] I take this objection from a reviewer of my work. It is based on Cristina Lafont's important criticism against "mini-publics" (Lafont 2020).

[12] How to think, however, about "mini-publics" directed at discussing "less fundamental" public issues (not abortion, not constitutional reform, not euthanasia) that is, aimed at deciding on less divisive, less controversial and less serious issues? Would it not be justified here to resort to the "mirror" and "filter" mechanisms that James Fishkin typically encouraged (mechanisms like the "mini-publics," which on the one hand want to reflect/reproduce a "picture of society," and on the other hand, can improve public discussion by focusing only and more intensively on certain particular issues)? (i.e., Fishkin 2009). Let me say something about these questions, even though it is not my purpose, at this point, to engage in a discussion about the details of the possible design of mini-publics. First, I understand that different designs could be thought of for different questions. For example, it may make sense, when discussing a change in the electoral system, to exclude from this discussion part of the citizenry – say, the political representatives who may want to manipulate these rules in their favor. At other times, and for similar reasons (i.e., the need to prevent the discussion from being "captured" by traditional political elites and other interest groups) it may also make sense to turn the discussion over to a citizen assembly (a "mini-public") even though, in this way, the rest

did find was a clear continuity between the discussions in the formal institutions (citizen assemblies, parliaments) and the discussions in the streets and public squares, and also a permanent feedback between the two. Nobody was required to defer his/her judgment, or blindly accept the opinions and judgments of their representatives (moreover – I would suggest – nobody would have even accepted to consider such a dishonorable proposal, concerning fundamental issues like that of abortion). People properly recognized that this issue (the discussion about abortion) referred to an open and ongoing debate where they – "We the People" – ought to have the "last word." (3) Even more importantly – I would add – inclusive deliberation processes such as those examined additionally proved untrue that *when faced with issues that involve one's self-identity or deep beliefs, or where changing one's opinion implies turning on powerful institutions (like the Church) people are unable to change their opinions, even after exchanging them with those of others*. The evidence before us shows that even in countries with strong religious convictions, where the Church and other "traditional" institutions have enormous weight, countries with a significant rural population and medium to low levels of education, many people changed their position or qualified their initial positions without major difficulty after processes of broad public debate. We saw this, for example, in the case of two very Catholic countries, Ireland and Argentina, in the discussion over abortion. (4) Moreover, deliberative processes have also enabled us to appreciate that even – if not especially – in situations of economic crisis or deep, bitter rifts between political factions, it makes sense to continue discussing, and investing in the exchange of perspectives, arguments, and reasons.

(iii) At this point, I would highlight another relevant fact of the deliberative assemblies. The organization and results of the deliberative assemblies discusses contrasts starkly with the two most common models of collective decision-making in our countries: *the model of elitist deliberation*, in where the grand social "experts" – judges,

of society becomes somewhat disconnected "from the debate carried out in the micro-assembly." Consider, for example, a discussion about the rates of public services; or a new regulation on fishing zones. In these cases, the "mini-publics" can offer important advantages over traditional representation mechanisms (beyond the fact that – depending on the case – their decisions could then be submitted to ratification by the citizens). Public decisions can in this way gain in diversity and inclusion; and become, at the same time, less vulnerable to interest group pressures. Meanwhile, broader forms of "inclusive discussion" could be reserved to address more fundamental public issues (abortion, etc.).

scientists, or whatever their names are – decide on behalf of everyone else and without consulting the public;[13] and *the model of participation without dialogue* – an increasingly common model in Latin America – where citizens are called to decide, abruptly, either yes or no, on issues of public interest, completely neglecting the entire process of discussion and mutual clarification. We have already examined, in this last respect, the unfortunate "participation without dialogue" plebiscite trend, which the inclusive assemblies directly challenge.

(iv) For the rest, I would underline another fundamental lesson to be learned from these assemblies. Specifically, I am referring to the way in which they invite us *to critically rethink the relationship between democracy and rights.* I am thinking of the following the separation, which we have seen repeated many times throughout this book, between the "sphere of rights" and the "sphere of democracy," which some academics and jurists propose as if they were two distant and untouched realms (Ferrajoli 2008). As we saw, a good part of contemporary legal doctrine, very particularly in the wake of the trauma and atrocities of World War II (Nazism, fascism, genocides, etc.), began to distinguish between both "spheres" in an effort to

[13] Let me use this opportunity to discuss another issue that we may call the problem of *overinclusion*, which was raised by Cristina Lafont (Lafont 2020), in her critical analysis of Helene Landemore's important work on epistemic democracy (particularly, regarding Landemore 2013). Based on the idea of the "wisdom of the crowds" and a particular, "epistemic" approach to democracy, Helene Landemore has advocated for the value of including diverse viewpoints in democratic debates. Through the inclusion of different viewpoints – she argues – a democracy may obtain "cognitive diversity," which would favor the adoption of right, wiser, richer, and more informed decisions. Against Landemore, Lafont wonders what "the proper set of knowers" would be, in such scenario (Lafont 2020, 93). If what matters is *finding out the right answer to difficult political questions* – Lafont argues – then why to constrain the decision to "all those affected"? In other words, why not be "overinclusive," why not consult the opinions of experts from beyond the borders, so as to expand the "diversity of viewpoints"? This objection may be a relevant one, against Landemore's project, but not a critical one against the "conversation among equals" that I defend here. In the "conversation among equals" we have reasons to limit our public discussions to "all those affected" (in other words, we have reasons not to be overinclusive). In this case, we are not looking for the "truth" or "correct" answer to a certain problem (say, regarding the question whether to favor a market-oriented or a more regulated economy; or regarding how to deal with health issues during the pandemic, etc.). Rather, we are looking for the decision that is more impartial among us (among "all those affected," in our community). In our community, we may have to face specific difficulties (say, the lack of potable water; millions of people living in conditions of misery), that do not appear in neighbor communities, and that would be wrong to "balance" or to consider in other contexts, but not in ours.

"shield" rights from majority interference, which it left under the strict control of experts or judges (the philosopher Ernesto Garzón Valdés wrote at the time a beautiful and controversial text, in which he finally alludes to this question, under the title "Don't put your dirty hands on Mozart," Garzón Valdés 1992). Discussions such as those around abortion and gay marriage in Ireland put these issues in a different light that, again, seriously challenges many dogmatic, premature, or unduly conservative statements on the matter. The fact is that *citizens are perfectly capable of respectfully, thoughtfully, and meaningfully discussing basic issues of fundamental rights without jeopardizing the legal construction of rights.* Not only do common citizens have the ability to do it (again, the process – open, inclusive, without stark power asymmetries – of discussion and its organization is critical) but even more – I would add – common citizens have the right to discuss and make decisions on issues that involve rights. Rights are not pre-existing, alien "planets" in a distant orbit that need to be discovered by and entrusted to the "experts" (i.e., the judges).

(v) As a supplementary observation relevant to institutional design, assemblies like the ones reviewed offer some important suggestions and clues about how to avoid some of the major institutional problems of our time. I will point out three very interesting proposals that derive from what we have examined in the previous pages. (1) In the first place, and taking the example of the Canadian assemblies as an illustration, I would call attention to the problem that was decisively recognized: *the problem that arises when the officials ultimately in charge of deciding public issues are the people with the most personal interest invested in them* (Ferejohn 2008). In other words, we have a problem when we give elected officials interested in winning re-election, or extending their mandates, or reinforcing or expanding their competencies, the responsibility (with few or limited controls over them) to set the rules for elections. Hence the wisdom of encouraging – as was done in Ontario or British Columbia – citizens themselves to take part in the decision-making process. (2) Secondly, I would highlight the lesson that the experiences with inclusive assemblies teach us about another important topic that we have already touched on: the politics of *presence*. In this regard, the experiences described reaffirm a postulate that came up in a previous chapter. Even though the real, effective "presence" of certain groups in an assembly – as we now know – may not guarantee adequate representation of the demands of the "represented" groups, it is also true, or it seems very clear, that the "absence" of certain points of view greatly increases the chances that the interests at stake (those of women or indigenous communities, for example) will be neglected, misunderstood, or misrepresented (Phillips 1995, Kymlicka 1996). In my opinion, the inclusion of "ordinary citizens" in the debates made it possible to publicly discuss issues that traditional political authorities (e.g., predominantly conservative, Catholic, male legislators) wanted to protect from public debate (i.e., abortion and gay marriage). (3) Thirdly, I would highlight in a special way the value of random selection as a means of selecting representatives for political decisions. In my opinion, this particular initiative has been enormously successful, on many different levels. In general, I would emphasize that neither the public authorities nor the public found the use of lotteries in constitutional matters unfair or inefficient. In fact, in the evaluation phase after the experience, some of the processes reviewed received significant criticism regarding their design and operation (excessively crowded assemblies, for example, or too short a duration), but this was not the case of the use of lotteries. In particular, when lottery mechanisms were refined to make them more sensitive to geographic, gender, or racial distribution, they were largely deemed fair and efficient systems for the selection of representatives.

19.4 The Problem of "Capture": When the Past Holds Back the Present, and the Old Will Not Let in the New

Before closing this chapter on promising and hopeful experiences, I would like to address a "realistic" note that contrasts with the optimism of the last few pages. The main point is that my emphasis on the potential of "inclusive assemblies" is warranted *despite the clear fact that many (certainly not all) of the experiences were eventually blocked* from achieving their highest goals: the Icelandic Congress, after regaining democratic legitimacy through a recent election, blocked the citizen project for constitutional reform (which also, in a very different framework, occurred in Chile); the Assemblies of Ontario and British Columbia produced remarkable results, in terms of both their technical quality and efficiency, but the referendums to put them into effect were not passed (largely by virtue, of course, to the supermajority requirements established by the government); the Dutch Forum was also "closed from above"; and the debate over abortion in Argentina fizzled after the bill under discussion was rejected by a few votes of senators from the most conservative or "feudal" provinces of the country.

All this reaffirms the concerns expressed centuries ago by Juan Bautista Alberdi. Alberdi, as we know, believed that special attention should be paid to the limitations that the prevailing legal context (and I would add, the distribution of power) tended to impose on the introduction and development of new reforms (Alberdi 1981). This dynamic is perhaps the most worrying element when creating or reforming constitutions in times of crisis. In many of the cases examined, in fact, we have found experiences where: (i) a profound institutional crisis breaks out; (ii) the crisis triggers initiatives favorable to the adoption of ambitious reforms; (iii) the ambitious reforms are launched; (iv) the crisis is slowly brought back under control; (v) the established authorities (including many of those considered responsible for the crisis) reassert themselves and begin to obstruct or undermine the reforms that had been implemented in response to the crisis.

As an additional note, I would add that in certain countries (such as Latin American ones), where the institutional frameworks tend to be fragile and the structure of controls less powerful than in more "legally developed" countries, government authorities have tended to benefit from those changing circumstances. On certain occasions, they have taken advantage of opportunities to make sure that the reforms are unattainable (e.g., by preventing – through the legislative regulations – the effective application of any new constitutional clauses favorable to popular participation that come out of "inclusive" constituent assemblies), and in others they have used the support for reforms for their own benefit (e.g., by expanding the powers of the executive; adding elements to allow their reelection, and so on).

At this point, before concluding this study, I would like to draw attention to a crucial problem that is still pending, one obviously related to the potential of deliberative assemblies. I am referring to the fact that, even if a citizen assembly is convened in the place of the traditional decision-making bodies; even if its deliberations are fruitful; and even if – against the efforts of the established power – the reforms are actually passed (i.e., they are not "vetoed," or rendered null by a lack of legislative implementation, or by any other traditional method for blocking them) the proposed reforms of the inclusive assembly – however powerful and promising – may still be frustrated, in practice, by the old powers. *This is because, alongside the "veto points" controlled by the political branches, lies the possibility of "invalidation" by the traditional judiciary.*

Let me offer a dramatic example of the problem. The widely participatory (and also highly conflictive) constituent process that took place in Ecuador at the beginning of the twenty-first century ended with the promulgation of the 2008 Constitution. That Constitution became particularly known worldwide for its "sumak kawsay" clause. The "sumak kawsay" principle of "good living" is taken from ancestral Quechua knowledge, which "establishes a vision of the cosmos different from the western vision, and that arises from communal, non-capitalist roots" (Salazar 2015, 26). This principle was incorporated into the Constitution on the initiative of indigenous groups and advocates (like, for example, the prominent environmentalist Alberto Acosta, who presided over the Assembly sessions for most of their duration). If the adoption of this principle meant anything, it represented a firm decision to protect nature against the risks of capitalist devastation. However, shortly after the Constitution's promulgation, both the National Congress and the Constitutional Court transformed these radical principles into empty principles by privileging alternative constitutional interpretations which allowed the government to carry out natural resource extraction activities with absolute impunity. In other words, the most "revolutionary" clause of all those incorporated into the Constitution as a result of the direct demand of the most disadvantaged groups in the community was completely subverted as soon as the new Constitution was put into effect.

In the end, we are facing the latest manifestation of the old problem that worried Alberdi: How is the "past" able to hold back the "present," how can the old block the "new"?

20

Conclusion

For a Conversation among Equals

This book has addressed the crisis of democratic constitutionalism, a crisis that is not new, but that has found extreme expression in our time. I have approached the question from a particular perspective – a "regulative ideal" – the ideal of *conversation among equals.*

The route that I followed was meant to demonstrate the nature and dimension of this institutional crisis. I wanted to resist the suggestion – supported by distinguished colleagues – to understand as the cause of this crisis leaders of whom we are ashamed, or the institutions that those same leaders have undermined. If they were the cause, and as many seem to propose, all we would have to do to return to a normal state of public affairs would be to remove the abusive leader through impeachment or to restore, through hard work and care, the old system of institutional checks and balances that in all appearance has been corroded "from the inside." But that would not solve the crisis. I have taken pains to point out how far back the real causes go, how they are structural in nature and are *not only* related to problems of constitutional design, but also not only to problems *fundamentally unrelated to constitutional design.* I readily admit that changing a few legal norms is not and will never be enough, ever, to end or resolve an institutional crisis ("no reform of any constitutional clause will ever enable us to stop a coup," as the political scientist Guillermo O'Donnell once pointed out). At the same time, I tried to emphasize that constitutional organization is a relevant part of the problem, and that our diagnosis of the crisis would be mistaken (and would unnecessarily complicate any attempt to solve it) if we did not realize its relevance. Nor does the analysis or its conclusions mean that all remedies to solve mitigate the institutional debacle require recourse to constitutional reforms. I have been keen to highlight, in previous pages, the value of some very interesting reformist experiences – in Canada or Ireland, for example – that did not perceive a need to undertake the difficult path of constitutional reform.

Having said all that, I would like to emphasize that one of the central axes around which this book revolves refers to the insurmountable deterioration of the constitutional scheme on which our democracies are based. I mean, we are facing a major institutional problem, and if we are genuinely interested in confronting it, we should begin by recognizing its magnitude. It is a problem too big to solve by retightening the nuts and bolts that have become loose. It is a problem that requires radically rethinking what we built the engine for, what the meaning – the first purposes – are of the institutions we have, and whether they are still capable of satisfactorily performing them.

My outlook is skeptical. This is not only because of the inertia and lack of constitutional imagination that we have shown for more than two hundred years, but also based on the capacity for resistance that both the old power structures and the constituted authorities have exhibited. (I could recall here the example of Venezuela and the political leader Nicolás Maduro, who has shown himself capable of staying in power for months amid an unprecedented social disaster, but I prefer to turn to a case I remember better, because it is much more familiar: the demonstrations of 2001 in my country, Argentina. I remember the vibrant militancy when thousands upon thousands of people protested for weeks on end, every day from morning to night, against a degraded system that was falling to pieces. The demand was – like so many other times, from so many different sides, and in hardly any different terms – "may they all leave." However, after all that impressive mobilization that would be enormously difficult to repeat, everything remained as it was: the cast and crew were all the same people. Nobody had really left and, as importantly, the institutions looked just the same as ever too.)

In any case, and for what matters here, one thing seems clear: the old institutions are now a significant part of the problem. Because of their antidemocratic profile; for what they promise and cannot give; by the type and strength of the limits that they impose on us; due to their restrictive nature. The fact is that they have become a tight-fitting suit that starts to split at all the seams, unable to contain the variety and intensity of our expectations and demands. Our constitutional democracies, in this sense, are structurally incapable of serving their best purposes – and that would still be the case if times were good and they were led by "virtuous," altruistic people (angels). In the best of cases, our institutions were born to face problems directly linked to the pressing issues of their time (the "drama" of "factions" in the United States and the "tragedy" of the "desert" and depopulation in Latin America); and they did so starting from a political sociology that is completely incapable of describing the societies that surround us: our "founding fathers" were working with societies with a reduced population that was divided into relatively few, internally homogenous groups and where people were fundamentally motivated by their own self-interest. In this framework, they concluded that incorporating a few representatives of each group into the institutional system would allow the entire society to be represented and the interests of each group to be well protected. This image of society (regardless how well it even reflected the reality at that foundational moment) has been shattered after more than two hundred years of social growth. Today we live in fundamentally multicultural societies that are marked by the "fact of pluralism" – fragmented into countless groups that are themselves internally heterogeneous (and not only the groups, for none of us could define our identity today as essentially that of a "peasant," a "debtor," a "landowner," or a "philosopher"). It is absurd, then, in the present context, to speak of "majorities" and "minorities," as if they were fixed and frozen factions. It is also absurd, therefore, to continue thinking of the institutional system in the same terms that perhaps, but only perhaps, were appropriate two hundred years ago.

Regarding the problems in institutional design, and what explains the choices behind each of its particular pieces, there are also errors and miscalculations. For example, Madison did not recognize in time that the system of "checks and balances" that he designed "does not work well when the different branches of government are controlled by the same party" (Luo & Przeworski 2019, 5); Alberdi did not realize that, by incorporating a "president-king" within the scheme of checks and balances, he irretrievably knocked the entire structure of controls off balance; and in other instances the error had to do with erroneous premises (e.g., the focus on "self-interest" that did not leave adequate space or incentives for the "cultivation of civic virtues").

In any case, at the center of our concerns are *the elitist assumptions that came to shape our institutions* and have been maintained up to this day. These assumptions are still operative in the systems governing societies that have not only undergone deep sociological transformations, but that also appear to have taken on a shared sense of democratic empowerment. This has generated the difficulty that we have called *democratic dissonance*. This refers to the dissonance between past and present conceptions of democracy. The conception of democracy upon which the constitutional institutions were built was restricted (distrust towards majority rule, towards citizen participation, activism, and assembly) and the societies of those times were politically "contained" (which is especially visible in terms of restrictions on political rights). Today, however, those same institutions must govern a completely different social base, one marked by the conviction that public policies must be guided according to our claims and that our public life must be guided by our decisions, the same way that our personal life must depend exclusively on what each one of us decides.

20.1 The Different Pieces of "Institutional Decoupling"

The radical mismatch between our reasonable (and at the same time high) expectations and democratic demands and what the institutions are designed to deliver generates "anguish" or "fatigue," giving rise to mistrust that is now directed toward the institutions and the weary disgust that representatives inspire, which can be seen almost without exception wherever we look, in whatever country we live, at whatever moment.

The original bias of *democratic distrust* that was translated or "injected" into the institutions when they were molded during the "founding moment" has spread deeply, reaching a severe degree. A quick look at each of the central pillars of this old scheme is enough to recognize it. In what follows, allow me to briefly review what we have already examined more extensively.

Representation. The representation system that was chosen at the "founding moment" was not thought of as a "second-best" or "necessary evil" system, but rather as a first option, preferable to its alternative (some form of direct democracy). Representation – in accordance with "democratic distrust" – was to "filter" or "purify" (instead of "recognizing" or "expressing" or "allowing its refinement through debate") the citizens' voice through the sieve of "a chosen group of citizens." This original representative scheme was explicitly chosen because it was thought that, going back to Madison's words, the "public voice, spoken by the representatives of the people, is more in line with the public good, than if it had been pronounced by the people themselves, summoned for that purpose." As we argued, that representative system (as well as its most important alternative) was subject to risks that its own proponents recognized, and that with the passage of time (and the accommodation of the risks with the other parts of the institutional system then put in place) materialized: representatives who were "too removed" from their constituents, who failed to recognize the citizens' demands and needs;

who began to act according to their own interests in disregard for or against the interests of the voters; who formed a "class" or "caste" and began to act primarily for the benefit of that group. Was any of this not presaged by the "founding fathers"? Are any of these recognized risks nowhere to be seen when we examine the way the institutions are working in our own present-day contexts?

External Controls: The Vote. The system of controls on government chosen during the origins of modern constitutionalism also reflected the fear of and resistance against citizen activism. For this reason, of the different control models that were considered, "internal" or "endogenous controls" were chosen over others that emphasized "popular," "external," and "exogenous controls." Of the vast panoply of "external controls" existing or imagined at a time, only the "periodic vote" endured over time, and it was, as we saw, left on its own, that is, unassisted by any of a whole battery of instruments that might accompany the vote in the first (actual or imagined) republican systems: obligatory instructions for representatives; revocation of mandates; rotation in positions; short terms in office; frequent town meetings. In its resulting solitude, the vote would lose much of its meaning and, above all, its power. How to hold accountable dozens of representatives, on hundreds of issues, for so long, with a single vote? And how to do all that (or somehow introduce some rationality into the system) without even a remote possibility of nuanced messaging to convey any message not on the ballot that any individual, sensibly and austerely, may want to transmit to their political officials? These conditions not only reinforced the risks related to the "autonomy," "independence," or "separation" of the rulers of which we were already warned, they also made possible what we called "electoral extortion" or "democratic extortion." Rulers who are aware of the advantages that such a scheme provides are tempted to invite citizens to vote for what they actively desire (e.g., greater rights), while forcing them in exchange to accept, in the same act, something they repudiate (e.g., a rule change to allow the leader to stay in power).

Internal Controls: The System of "Checks and Balances." The system of checks and balances, which was one of the fundamental innovations of modern constitutionalism, was also marked, from the beginning, by a strongly antidemocratic bias. This began with the pretense of balancing the "ambition" of the landowning minorities with the "ambition" of the indebted majorities. The choice was made to value political stability and social balance over democratic principles, which came at a very high cost.

In this way, majority rule lost much of its meaning. This system for the protection of minority rights involved – more than defense, protection, or precautions – a significant surrender of democratic power, as if the only sensible way of defending rights were definitive counter-majoritarian mechanisms. Moreover, this reasoning also relies on a conception of the idea of "minorities" that is at the very least controversial (one with a definition very different from the idea of minorities that we tend to use today, that is, one especially focused on the rights of the most vulnerable members of society). Hence certain inexplicable biases of the system designed then: the preponderance of "indirect elections"; special requirements to run for the Senate; and the peculiar organization and competencies of courts. The system of checks and balances was conceived, moreover, from a logic that is particularly worrying for those of us who defend a "conversational" or "deliberative" approach to democracy. I refer to the fact that the system was much more motivated to "avoid war" between factions than to promote dialogue between them. "Constitutional dialogue" was possible, or at least not prevented by the institutional system erected, but the system certainly did not promote it and did in fact pose obstacles to it. In this way, the "dialogue" possible was dependent on the disposition and character of those in power who valued it. In other words, *in a scheme prepared to pit "demons" against each other for the common good, collaborative dialogue came to depend on the presence of "angels."*

The Political Branches. The proposed constitutional organization of the political sphere, including, in a special way, the design of the executive and legislative branches, also reflected assumptions of democratic distrust. Without repeating the details, I will simply highlight a number of "antidemocratic arrangements" that were implemented, what Roberto Unger called the "dirty little secret" of our institutional system or a "ceaseless identification of restraints upon majority rule." The examples are innumerable, but include the design of the Senate; the disproportionate controls imposed on the Lower House; the use of indirect elections; the President's power to veto congressional decisions; "reserving" the most important appointments – judges, ambassadors, etc. – for the relatively least democratic organs; etc. For my part, I would only additionally emphasize *in a very special way*, given the purposes of this book, the continuing presence of this original conception related to "democratic distrust" even among our most enlightened theorists. This assumption reflects the Federalists' conception that representation is the first-best option, rather than a second-best option made necessary by the practical impossibility of including every citizen in public decision-making.

Judicial Power. The judicial branch, as it was designed at the end of the eighteenth century, was recognized from the start as capable of jeopardizing the entire democratic nature of the incipient government. That risk explains the early attacks on it from the antifederalists and the urgent defense formulated by Alexander Hamilton. Although Hamilton's defense carried the day and quieted his adversaries for decades to come, the "democratic objection" against the judiciary would never go away. As was admitted by one of the most famous defenders of the judges' counter-majoritarian role: it is undeniable that, "When the Supreme Court declares unconstitutional a legislative act or the action of an elected representative, it thwarts the will of representatives of the actual people of the here and now; it exercises control, not on behalf of the prevailing majority, but against it" (Bickel 1962, 17). And as argued by one of the main contemporary critics of this model of institutional organization, it is "offensive" ("it seems something of an insult") for a democratic society, and for the equal dignity of its members, that in the face of profound constitutional disagreements, that a minority of judges, and not the representatives of the people, pronounce the last word on the matter (Waldron 1999).

Rights. The declarations of rights that were incorporated into the modern constitutions also relied on a conception of rights that was hostile to democracy. There were various versions of the idea of "natural rights" to which the "founding fathers" subscribed, but the one that prevailed placed rights and citizenship in separate, distant boxes. A good part of the prevailing doctrine, still today, on the subject (even the most interesting of them all), are derivations of that original paradigm. Both the idea of rights as "trump cards" that "beat" majority decisions (in Ronald Dworkin's terms) and – the riskiest and strongest version – the idea that rights constitute a sphere ("the sphere of the undecidable" in Luigi Ferrajoli's work) separate rights and put them out of reach of democracy. According to this vision, rights are not democratic creations and are thus removed from democratic deliberation: not only can we not "vote" on them but, in the most demanding yet not entirely unusual versions of liberalism, the "sovereign people" cannot even discuss their form or content. Usually, in accordance with this reading, rights must be rigorously left to the technical and exclusive care of the judges.

20.2 What to Do?

We can now move on to a question Lenin posed, if that is allowed nowadays. From all this, in response to the panorama described, is there anything that can be said about what we can do? We have an institutional system that seems old, yes, but even more relevantly, even in its own terms, it is inefficient, not to mention unfair and unjustified. Furthermore, what can be done to change a system that has taken root so deeply that it has remained almost unchanged and unmodified for more than two hundred years? Are we dealing with a system that was designed not to change? Allow me some speculation in light of what we have learned along the way and the tools at our disposition.

The first intuition in this regard is that we must resist urges to revive, recover, or repair what we have or used to have, because, to a large extent, these are "lifeless institutions" that have lost track of the original purpose that was their public justification and that gave them democratic legitimacy at the time they were created. Worse still, these are institutions that have largely begun to contravene their original purposes. This is not uncommon in life, where so many tools that we create with emancipation in mind, with a desire to increase freedom, seem to take on a life of their own, are appropriated by others, and end up being used to control and dominate us. This phenomenon is the alienation Karl Marx spoke of.[1] In our case, we are dealing with legal and constitutional alienation. This is why it is necessary and – given the circumstances – urgent that we resist the temptation to "readjust" the existing institutional framework, but rather, inasmuch as possible, strive to disassemble it so we can put a better one in its place. I am not saying this because I have a soft spot for radicalism, but rather because I genuinely fear for the survival of decent, democratic life. For its sake, we need to lay new institutional foundations.

[1] This is how Marx spoke about alienation, putting the accent on alienation through labor (whereas we are putting the accent on alienation through institutions): "What, then, constitutes the alienation of labor? First, in the fact that labor is external to the worker, that is, that it does not belong to his essential being; that in his work, therefore, he does not affirm himself but denies himself, does not feel well but unhappy, does not freely develop his physical and mental energy but mortifies his body and ruins his mind. The worker, therefore, feels himself only outside his work, and feels beside himself in his work. He is at home when he is not working, and when he is working he is not a home. His work therefore is not voluntary, but coerced; it is forced labor. It is therefore not the satisfaction of a need, but only a means for satisfying needs external to it. Its alien character emerges clearly in the fact that labor is shunned like the plague as soon as there is no physical or other compulsion" (Marx [1843], 1983, 136).

But how should we go about it? Without pretending to have a rescue plan or any neatly wrapped package ready to go, for exploratory purposes I would look to the alternatives raised when the current system was devised. I would therefore begin by having another look at the democratic majoritarian alternatives that we have already encountered in some shape or form.

Establishing a Regulative Ideal. Above all, I would start by reaffirming the regulative ideal that should guide our effort. In this work, the ideal that I have tried to outline is that of a conversation among equals. I have tried to specifically relate this ideal to certain theoretical requirements that are commonly accepted today, mainly those that emphasize the inclusive, deliberative, and egalitarian criteria which should characterize such conversations. From there, the task is conceiving of institutional procedures capable of translating the ideal into effective practices.

Identifying the "Dramas" of Our Time, and Means to Address Them. As did all of our great predecessors – the "fathers of constitutionalism" – from James Madison to Juan Bautista Alberdi, we need to identify the "dramas" of our era and (in light of the ideals we defend) means to remedy them. Clearly, the great problem we face, unlike them, is neither the "drama" of factions nor that of the unpopulated desert. We must therefore consider carefully where we allocate the (little) constitutional energy that we have. My impression is that our current "dramas" have more to do with the "crisis of democracy" than with the "crisis of rights" (which was typical of the post–World War II era), and that the root of this crisis is found in inequality. I would therefore look for ways that institutional design could help us, in this here-and-now, to confront inequality, a problem that has been with us for so long and has been expanding and worsening over time.

Distinguishing the Problems of Constitutionalism from Those of Democracy. In this moment of extreme institutional crisis, it is absolutely crucial that we distinguish between the problems of those two spheres, instead of confusing them or conflating them as if they were practically the same thing. Of course, the problem of political authorities who constantly seek to undermine or "erode" the controls on their power, for example, is also a serious problem of our time. However, we must not lose sight of the fact that while "repairing" these shortcomings (by tightening the nuts and bolts of the system) may help us to get the machinery of the effective "checks and balances" back up and running, it could leave the problems affecting democracy very much intact. As I said before, the "detachment" of citizens from democracy and the widespread sense of "political alienation" are not simply or fundamentally due to the abuses of any particular President or the imperfections of the justice system. Rather, these problems go to the crisis of our democracy (to the idea of "government of the people, by the people, and for the people"), which is independent from the crisis of constitutionalism.

The Lessons of History and Accumulated Knowledge. Much of our most interesting knowledge, in terms of the institutional system, derives from historical and empirical study – from what has been learned from observing effective institutions in practice. Examples of such lessons include: "without limits of any kind, every organism tends to develop abusive behavior"; or "decision-making bodies (even ones based on majority rule) tend to fall under the control of a minority of the members"; or even: "without mechanisms that oblige them otherwise, decision-making bodies tend to make decisions improperly" (related to the "multiplicity," "mutability," and "injustice" of the laws passed by local assemblies that Madison spoke of in *Vices of the Political System*). We have thus already accumulated a significant amount of knowledge on the subject from the analysis of effective practices (historical learning) and also from the reflections of our predecessors. For example, to cite some of these reflections that they left us: "representatives should be able to use think independently," "representatives must be allowed to change their minds," "representatives must not be reduced to mere 'puppets' of their constituents." We also have examples like, "it is important for decision-making bodies to have an opportunity to rethink their decisions"; or "it is best for decision-making bodies to avoid hasty decisions," etc. Then there are time-tested pearls like, "the groups that attain the control of power tend to act against the interests of rivals" (or as Hamilton put it, "give all power to the majorities, they will oppress the minorities; give it to the minorities, they will oppress the majorities").

Recent Experience and Inclusive Deliberation. Also prominent in our institutional knowledge should be the successful execution of certain institutional experiments in our own time. These vanguard experiments have been opening paths that political, social, and management theory largely failed to anticipate or guide. In particular, I would add, there is much to learn from the successes of recent experiences of "deliberative assemblies" (formal ones, as in Canada or Ireland, or more informal ones, as in Argentina) as well as from the limits they have run up against. Given the apparent consistency of "deliberative assemblies" with the regulative ideal of "conversation among equals," it makes sense to reflect on their potential and limitations. We have already identified some of these lessons: the effective dissemination of refined technical knowledge through well-designed procedures and reinvigoration of the rational and reasoned basis of public decisions; their potential to stimulate citizens' civic engagement; and the capacity demonstrated of these procedures to "change minds" even when deep interests or even self-identity are at stake.

20.3 Three Themes and Three Cases

At this point in the book, my hope is that the study presented in the preceding pages will help us to prepare and lay the groundwork for an alternative, more egalitarian institutional framework. As I understand it, the work has enough theoretical density to suggest paths that lead to such an alternative, as well as the reasons for undertaking the project. I have also made reference to certain antecedents from historical and recent experience that support the theoretical conclusions and hopefully shed light on promising ways to convert speculative alternatives into effective practices. In what follows, let me try to express the above aspiration using three issues and three relevant cases. The themes are political representation, constitutional interpretation, and the protection of rights. The selected cases, meanwhile, are, respectively, the inclusive assemblies in Canada, the ones in Ireland that discussed abortion, and the public hearings held in Argentina.

Political Representation. As I have argued above, I believe we have to abandon all expectations regarding the old representative system's ability to cure our ills ("Lasciate ogni speranza, voi ch'entrate," as the sign at the gates of hell reads in Dante's *Inferno*). The best that this system promised us is irretrievable today. That system promised us effective representation, all the time, in all of the countless decisions that come up daily in our community's political life. The extraordinary richness of our public life has overcome the system and is spilling out on all sides, and that which has poured out cannot be forced back into the box. On the contrary, the attempt to force our political aspirations back into the back (the mismatch between the "size of the box" and the "size" of citizens' demands and expectations), reveals something important about the type of problem we are facing.

I understand, however, that some recent practices, such as those offered by the revised "deliberative assemblies," show promise for "getting out of the labyrinth at the top": they have shown themselves capable of dealing in a very interesting way with the representative difficulties in which we were bottled up. Take the discussions in the Canadian assemblies about electoral systems. Beyond their concrete results (whether we agree or not with their specific electoral system recommendations and regardless they were ultimately accepted or not by the voters), those assemblies offer some extraordinary lessons: (i) it is not necessary to use the same predefined, stable body of representatives all the time for every issue and decision; (ii) there are few alternatives more implausible than allowing a public policy to be decided by a minority that is itself highly invested in the policy, especially when it is to make the decision on behalf of all the rest; (iii) collectively discussing relevant and complex public issues can in fact lead to elaborate, concrete, technically virtuous proposals; (iv) ordinary citizens chosen at random can learn in a short time enough about complicated subjects (even the most difficult of all, such as electoral systems) and present valuable alternatives, if the process is organized properly.

Constitutional Interpretation. The predominant practice today in terms of constitutional interpretation – how to interpret our law with regards the public issues most concretely relevant to our lives – has reached scandalous levels that I believe often approach delirium. As Jeremy Waldron argued in one of his latest books in this regard: constitutional interpretation has developed into "sophisticated, but morally distracting, esoteric legalisms" (Waldron 2016). Indeed, it is often literally impossible to predict which way judges will decide constitutionality, in the name of law and their technical knowledge. The protagonists, even (if not above all) in its theoretically most sophisticated body – the high courts of the land – frequently give themselves the freedom to "jump" from one interpretative approach to its opposite, from one ruling to the next one. In doing so, they enthusiastically cite the dictates of the particular interpretative conception that they have, at their whim, decided to apply to the case at hand. They simply feel completely free and authorized to "reach" whatever decision as long as they duly cite the precedents and conducive theory. In reaction to the desperate anguish this situation elicits, we should recognize the practical alternatives that we have theoretically endorsed in this work, ones that are politically possible and yield attractive results. I am thinking, for example, of *the discussions about* *abortion in Ireland and in Argentina.* The strength and value of these examples is, in my opinion, extraordinary, and extends across over various relevant areas. These examples help us to recognize fundamental issues, including: (i) contrary to what much of legal theory has forcefully and long resisted, meaningful "democratic" discussion of our fundamental rights is both possible and desirable; (ii) the spheres of rights and democracy are intimately connected, not separate: there is value in collectively debating issues of public morality and we have the right, the ability, and the practical means to do just that – this we now know; (iii) decisions on issues of public interest can be reached through deliberative, inclusive conversation, as long as we strictly respect the demanding implications of those two adjectives: there must be effective debate, where people criticize each other and change their minds; and inclusive debate, one that is literally open to "all" people and makes genuine effort to include as wide a variety of perspectives as possible.

The Protection of Rights. Our experience and accumulated knowledge also allow us to recognize that protecting rights does not necessarily require emptying, degrading, or diluting the democratic content of our Constitution. As a community, we have every right to define the rights we feel deserve universal protection, by which we understand certain interests as basic (interests that matter to us in a special way; or that we know from historical experience, or can anticipate in the light of our knowledge, may become vulnerable or threatened by our future actions if we do not take concrete steps to prevent it). In these cases, identifying, emphasizing, and making explicit the fundamental interests to which we are most committed is just as important as designing institutional mechanisms that can help us to protect them. The point is that we do not have to throw democracy out with the bathwater. More precisely, many of the mechanisms that we have instituted to protect rights – particularly the presidential veto and judicial review of constitutionality – have proven very costly and difficult to compensate in democratic terms. The good news, again, is that recent practical experience helps us to recognize efficient, consistent, and intimate institutional procedures aligned with the ideal of a "conversation among equals" are available and might be explored to protect the universal, basic rights or interests that we hold dear. Consider *the public hearings held to discuss the pollution of the Matanza and Riachuelo Rivers in Buenos Aires.* This case involved the systematic violation of many fundamental rights (environmental, social, and economic rights), on a massive scale (more than a million people were affected!), for decades without cease, with tragic consequences (including mortalities due to disease and birth defects), throughout which the public powers (both the political branches and the courts), declared their impotence or incompetence, and ended up doing nothing. Then came the extraordinary power of the *Mendoza* decision by the Argentine Supreme Court, which taught us that: (i) the bodies in charge of protecting rights (not merely deciding on a "binary" basis whether a legislative decision is valid or not) are perfectly capable of exploring other alternatives by establishing procedures favorable to a collective solution of the problem, and making use, for this purpose, of reasonable and available remedies that no legal norm proscribes; (ii) the judiciary has the power, as demonstrated in the case, to convoke a forum in which the political bodies and interested citizens and organizations meet and discuss in search of a political solution. The judiciary is capable of monitoring the discussions to ensure that they remain within the bounds permitted by Constitution and providing incentives for the parties to engage in genuine discussion and collaboration (as South African Supreme Court did with its "meaningful engagement" principle); (iii) Such discussions, promoted by the highest body entrusted with the protection of rights, can be duly inclusive and deliberative in line with the dictates of the ideal of "conversation between equals."

20.4 Final Objections

The criticism I have heard of the arguments presented in this book range from familiar, to obvious, to unconvincing. Before concluding the book, I would like to address some of these objections in order to clear – as definitively as possible – a path that leads toward the construction of more egalitarian institutional alternatives in accordance with the ideals subscribed.

"The Practical Results Have Not Amounted to Much." People could object that, in cases such as the Canadian assemblies: "the plebiscites organized after the assemblies turned down the inclusive proposals" or in the case of the hearings in Argentina: "nothing got better, the Riachuelo River is still heavily polluted."[2] I have already briefly addressed this type

[2] Someone could claim that these criticisms are similar to those presented by Ian Shapiro against what he identifies as the "republican" alternative (as presented by Philip Pettit, Quentin Skinner, etc.). For Shapiro, the republican "account of public institutions is a recipe for protecting the status quo" which would imply the "embrace of institutional sclerosis" (Shapiro 2012, 331). I do not agree, however, with his characterization of republicanism (which implies assimilating it to "the American constitutional model");

of objection, but I want to insist here anyways on the basic value of these examples. Their importance lies not in the end results but in what they show us is possible. These are issues that have long been simply considered unthinkable, nonlegal, or utopian. (I remember when Carlos Nino, whom I worked for at the time, proposed deliberative forms of the exercise of the judicial function: the legal community reacted with utter indifference, or by dismissing them as fantastic speculations from the ivory tower, removed from reality, and completely unrelated to the requirements of law – as if, in fact, what we were proposing did not even fall within the legal realm. A few years later – when the Argentine Court recognized in *Mendoza* that the kinds of solutions we had proposed were legally impeccable, and politically productive – the court was actually able to recuperate some of its reputation and democratic legitimacy through the decision.) Among the lessons that I have tried to convey includes one related to preventing the "old system" from smothering with its inertia the potential good that a "new" system can offer. Today, as I said and underlined above, we are still forced to wear the only suit we have. Similarly, we live within a network of institutions that have come to depend, centrally, on the discretionary will of the minority interests that have taken over (or appropriated) the institutions. Much of the exploration carried out up to now has been aimed at raising awareness of the need to disassemble, layer by layer, the institutional structure that has been captured by the elites.

Inclusive Assemblies: Impossible? Undesirable? In a review of my work, which I appreciate, Tom Ginsburg objected to my defense of inclusive and deliberative assemblies (Ginsburg 2021). In his view, "participation is no panacea" (Ginsburg 2021, 22). He adds, then "three reasons not to over-idealize" participatory alternatives such as citizens' assemblies. Firstly – he maintains – it is not clear that such participatory mechanisms

I do not think that the promotion of political participation (which I would associate with the "republican alternative") would imply in any way the protection of the status quo (rather the contrary, as the cases of Chile, Bolivia, Argentina, and so many other countries suggest); and I do not share his proposal favorable to the establishment of a "competitive parliamentary system," for reasons already explored (including the problems affecting political representation and traditional representative institutions). Together with Jeremy Bentham, I would suggest that – precisely – one of the reasons we have for opening the political system to "We the People" resides in the need of breaking the "sinister interests" that – still today – we find dominating our institutional system (for such reason, for example, Bentham proposed annual elections, secret ballot, a substantial extension of the franchise, etc.). See another, partially similar, criticism of Shapiro's approach in Dyzenhaus 2012.

"can become a regular or routine part of democratic government" (Ginsburg 2021, 22). Secondly – he continues – sometimes, the "inputs" of participation "are not particularly attractive," especially "in highly polarized times" (Ginsburg 2021, 23). He illustrates this claim by mentioning some threatening possibilities that include the "revival of death penalty," the risk to "demonize outsiders" or "endanger the planet" or "call into question basic science" (Ginsburg 2021, 23). Thirdly, he mentions that such participatory alternatives "may not easily scale up to the level of an entire country" (Ginsburg 2021, 23). Expectedly, and respectfully, I would say that I disagree. Concerning points one and three: I do not think that a more inclusive and participatory democracy should require citizens to actively participate in politics, on an everyday basis. In my view, that demanding scenario is neither possible nor required. If I had to give a suggestion on the matter, I would propose reserving the more ambitious, large-scale debates, to a few issues a year. The examples of the Chilean constitutional assemblies, or the French *Grand Débat* on Climate Change, suggest that those experiences can "easily scale up to the level of an entire country" and at the same time work in a successful way. My strongest disagreements with Tom Ginsburg concern his critique number two. Following Locke and Jefferson, I would say, trust the people in those rare occasions (constitutional moments?) when they stand up and engage in politics. If the collective discussion refers to a topic the people care about, I would simply say: pay attention to them, listen to them carefully, people will finally get involved in the decision-making process, if they perceive that the political process is genuinely open to their opinions (this, without considering the ways in which a more participatory practice can favor our civic education). Finally, in this work, I have insistently distinguished between (brutal, abrupt) instances of political participation, and formal-institutional instances of inclusive deliberation. My conviction is that the threatening scenarios described by Tom Ginsburg can be related to instances of "participation without deliberation," but not to our "inclusive conversation" (what is worse, I think that what Ginsburg has in mind are neither formal instances of popular participation, nor citizens assemblies, but rather informal opinion polls suggesting that people are only interested in adopting scandalous policies. I would suggest disregarding those informal polls). And I do not think this claim is just a matter of faith (none of the inclusive assemblies that we revised produced anything like the horrendous results that he predicted).

"The Law Requires Authority and Decision!" Many people still discard the legal and political value of alternatives such as those mentioned by emphasizing the need for the law to offer effective decision-making mechanisms for conflict resolution. They say: "We cannot simply rid ourselves of a legitimate source capable of creating and enforcing authoritative decisions. We cannot encourage the mechanisms that lead to endless debate when what we need are decisions that put an end to conflicts." Some well-known authors have also objected to the potential of "new dialogical constitutionalism" by saying: "All these new alternatives to traditional judicial review are ultimately unattractive because they introduce inadequate degrees of uncertainty and instability in conflictive situations. Contrariwise, the traditional system avoids these problems and guarantees the resolution of conflicts through the intervention of authorized bodies" (Alexander & Schauer 1997; Alexander & Schauer 2000; Alexander & Solum, 2005). From my point of view, dialogical constitutionalism has been developing for more than thirty years, both in legally advanced countries and in fragile legal communities. It may be vulnerable to various critiques (of which we mentioned several in previous pages), but those just mentioned have largely been answered by the practice itself. Instead of the predicted legal chaos and uncertainty, the practice of dialogical constitutionalism has raised expectations and revitalized old and unattractive legal systems. Of particular relevance to this type of criticism, we only need note that *the experiences of dialogical constitutionalism have helped to reach decisions in areas that lie completely stagnant for decades while the political and judicial organs remained immobile.* Before the decision in *Mendoza*, politics had shied from taking even a single step towards addressing the problem for decades (perhaps fearful of the very powerful business community responsible for the pollution), while the courts were quick to declare their lack of jurisdiction in the case (perhaps for similar reasons). The result was the worst of all: indecision, inertia, and ongoing massive, serious and continuous violation of rights. To borrow from Mark Tushnet: "the empirical case against non-judicial constitutional review has not yet been established" (Tushnet 2003, 490).[3]

"We Need to Protect Rights!" Another common objection, the last I will deal with for now, insists that serious violations of rights require forceful answers and decisions, a resounding yes or no, the kind courts are good at giving. In such cases, the speculations typical of deliberative politics are

[3] Similarly, as the constitutionalist Keith Whittington has argued, the objection of Alexander and others "exaggerates the value of constitutional stability, while at the same time overestimating the ability of the judiciary to enforce constitutional agreements and underestimating the ability of non-judicial actors to effectively resolve constitutional disputes . . . " (Whittington 2002, 788–789).

considered "excessive." A great example applicable here might be a case like *Brown* v. *Board of Education*. I am referring, of course, to the case that allowed courts to assume a heroic stance against the southern states, ending forever, from one moment to the next centuries-old discrimination and the aberrant constitutional norm of "separate but equal." The force of *Brown*'s example is extraordinary, but now it is common knowledge that there was much more going on than a high-minded court. In the first place, *Brown* would not have been what it was without years of political campaigning, massive demonstrations, and often heroic action by social and political leaders (Cover 1983, 1985; Post & Siegel 2004, 2007). Secondly, in terms of the concrete consequences of the decision, *Brown* might not have achieved nearly as much (as it did, disregarding the fact that serious racial discrimination and inequality remained intact today) without permanent accompaniment and monitoring by the political branches (which authors like Gerald Rosenberg (1991) have shown).

20.5 So Then . . .

The regulative ideal of "conversation among equals" that I have been advocating throughout this work is based on my conviction that *democratic trust requires taking seriously the results of inclusive deliberation, most particularly when the principles of inclusiveness and deliberation are strictly respected and the procedures are properly organized to that end.* We have every reason to do just that.[4]

This ideal seeks – following the principles from which it starts and the historical lessons that have molded it – to help us to construct institutions that are sensitive to the issues and claims that citizens are willing to "stand up for." That is why the ideal urges special attention to social claims that are maintained over time (e.g., through the arduous activism of social movements), and it is also for this reason that the ideal proposes *the right to protest as the first right*. This is so because it understands that citizens do not take on the serious costs and risks that protest implies as a hobby or for fun, but because they feel the need to express something that matters to them, something that they feel they cannot otherwise express through the institutional system (Gargarella 2005, 2012). The

[4] As evidenced by the (narrow and limited) mechanisms of trial by jury: the very people who, when faced with a violent crime, would tend to react viscerally, demanding extreme coercive responses, set to deliberate, in a jury, with the obligation to listen to the parties, to contrast information, to look the accused in the eyes, they tend to make more parsimonious and considerate decisions than the professional judges themselves.

institutions of an egalitarian society must therefore be especially sensitive to such manifestations, trying to recognize and take into account the value of the protestors' demands (even if we do not like the form of expression chosen, even if the messages irritate us, even if our momentary ideological differences place us on opposite sides).

Having said this, I would like to emphasize again and again that the ideal of dialogue between equals does not require large mobilization or thunderous events to be activated; neither social movements nor "constitutional moments" are required for us to recognize others. Vital civic expressions are by all means welcome when they bring together people united by abstract ideals or concrete demands. However, the principles on which the dialogue among equals is built are also, or even above all, open to other types of understanding: these principles start from the idea that the voice that it is most important to listen to is the one complaining, even if it is a single voice that incessantly points out its annoyance with something we are doing. If we stop listening to that voice, we might as well stop listening altogether.

In this sense, and in order to properly take in the whole myriad of demands, we must put aside – once and for all – the hope of reviving or restoring our old institutions. We know that enormous structural difficulties stand in the way of adequately representing the multicultural societies we live in, including the Congress that appears hopelessly rotten from the inside and the unipersonal executive that has, since the beginning of time, embodied an authoritarian leader standing over us from goodness we do not expect. At the same time, to solve what politics does not solve or to address the difficulties that politics creates, we cannot rely on judicial institutions, which continue to act under discretionary schemes and are organized under unnecessarily antidemocratic criteria. Constitutional democracy must be something else. It must be ordered on the basis of other principles – egalitarian principles – and act with purpose to serve better ends – the ends defined through inclusive, deliberative dialogue. Throughout this work, and in the light of the arguments that we have reviewed, I have suggested thinking about constitutional democracy in a way that is different from what we already know. What I mean is, I have been advocating for a sort of democratic constitutionalism that can only be seen in glimpses through the window of what is possible. The truth is that the type of constitutional democracy I advocate does not yet exist, and it may never exist, but I believe it is one worth fighting for, because it is one under whose protection it would make sense to live. In short, I imagine a dignified constitutional democracy aimed at making possible fraternal conversation within the framework of a community of equals.

BIBLIOGRAPHY

Abramovich, V. & Courtis, C. (2002), *Los derechos sociales como derechos exigibles*, Barcelona: Trotta.

Ackerman, B. (1980), *Social Justice in the Liberal State*, New Haven, CT: Yale University Press.

Ackerman, B. (1991), *We the People*, Cambridge, MA: Belknap Press.

Ackerman, B. (2007), *The Failure of the Founding Fathers: Jefferson, Marshall and the Rise of Presidential Democracy*, New York: Belknap Press.

Ackerman, B. (2010), *The Decline and Fall of the American Republic*, Cambridge, MA: Harvard University Press.

Ackerman, B. (2014), *The Civil Rights Revolution*, Cambridge, MA: Harvard University Press,

Alberdi, J. B. (1852) (1981), *Bases y puntos de partida para la organización política de la República Argentina*, Buenos Aires: Plus Ultra.

Alberdi, J. B. (1854) *Sistema económico y rentístico de la confederación argentina*, Valparaíso: Imprenta y Librería del Mercurio.

Alexander, L. & Schauer, F. (1997), "On Extrajudicial Constitutional Interpretation," 110 *Harv. L. Rev.* 1359.

Alexander, L. & Schauer, F. (2000), "Defending Judicial Supremacy: A Reply," 17 *Const. Comment.* 455.

Alexander, L. & Solum, L. (2005), "Popular? Constitutionalism?" 118 *Harvard L. Rev.* 1594.

Allan, T. (2016), "The Rule of Law," in D. Dyzenhaus & M. Thorburn, eds., *Philosophical Foundations of Constitutional Law*, Oxford: Oxford University Press, 201–221.

Arato, A. (2017), *The Adventures of the Constituent Power*, Cambridge, UK: Cambridge University Press.

Arendt, H. (2006), *On Revolution*, London: Penguin Classics.

Atria, F. (2016), *La forma del derecho*, Marcial Pons, Madrid.

Ávila Santamaría, R. (2009), ed., *Desafíos constitucionales. La Constitución ecuatoriana del 2008 en perspectiva*, Tribunal Constitucional del Ecuador.

Bachtiger, A., Dryzek, J., Mansbridge, J., & Warren, M. (2018), *The Oxford Handbook of Deliberative Democracy*, Oxford: Oxford University Press.

Barber, B. (1984), *Strong Democracy*, California: University of California Press.

Basadre, J. (1949), *Historia de la República del Perú*, Lima,Editorial Cultura Antártica.

Bateup, C. (2007), "Expanding the Conversation: American and Canadian Experiences of Constitutional Dialogue in Comparative Perspective," 21 *Temp. Int'l L. J.* 1.

Benedetti, M. & Sáenz, J. (2016), *Las audiencias públicas ante la Corte Suprema*, Buenos Aires, Siglo XXI.

Bentham, J. (1843), *The Works of Jeremy Bentham*, vol. 6, The Online Library of Liberty. Liberty Fund, https://oll-resources.s3.us-east-2.amazonaws.com/oll3/store/titles/1923/Bentham_0872-06_EBk_v6.0.pdf.

Bentham, J. (2002), *The Collected Works of Jeremy Bentham*, ed. by P. Schofield, C. Pease-Watkin, & C. Blamires, Oxford: Oxford University Press.

Bergallo, P., Jaramillo, I. & Vaggione, J. (comps. 2018), *El aborto en América Latina. Estrategias jurídicas para luchar por su legalización y enfrentar las resistencias conservadoras*, Buenos Aires: Siglo XXI.

Bickel, A. (1962), *The Least Dangerous Branch*, Connecticut, CT: Yale University Press.

Bolívar, S. (1951), *Selected Writings of Bolívar*, 2 vols., New York: The Colonial Press.

Bolívar, S. (1976), *Doctrina del Libertador*, Caracas: Biblioteca Ayacucho.

Bonilla, D. (1993), *Constitutionalism on the Global South. The Activist Tribunals of India, South Africa, and Colombia*, Cambridge, UK: Cambridge University Press.

Brinks, D. & Blass, A. (2018), *The DNA of Constitutional Justice in Latin America*, Cambridge, UK: Cambridge University Press.

Buchanan, J. (2000), *Politics as Public Choice*, Indianapolis: Liberty Fund.

Burke, E. [1774] (1999), "Speech to the Electors of Bristol," in *Selected Works of Edmund Burke* (4 vols.), vol. 4, Indianapolis: Liberty Fund, http://oll.libertyfund.org/title/659/20392.

Cepeda, M. (2004), "Judicial Activism in a Violent Context: The Origin, Role, and Impact of the Colombian Constitutional Court," 3 *Washington University Global Studies Law Review* 259.

Chipman, N. (1833), *Principles of Government*, Burlington, IN.

Cohen, G. A. (2009), *Why Not Socialism?* Princeton, NJ: Princeton University Press.

Colon Ríos, J. (2020), *Constituent Power and the Law*, Oxford: Oxford University Press.

Contesse, J. (2015), "Subsidiarity in Inter-American Human Rights Law," *SELA*, manuscript on file with the author.

Courtis, C. (2006), "Judicial Enforcement of Social Rights: Perspectives from Latin America," in R. Gargarella. Siri Gloppen & Elin Skaar, eds., *Courts and Social Transformation in New Democracies*. London: Ashgate.

Cover, R. (1983), "The Supreme Court, 1982 Term – Foreword: Nomos and Narrative" (1983). *Faculty Scholarship Series.* 2705, https://digitalcommons.law.yale.edu/fss_papers/2705
Cover, R. (1985), "Violence and the Word," 95 *Yale L.J.* 1601.
Crozier, M., Huntington, S., & Watanuki, J. (1975), *The Crisis of Democracy: Report on the Governability of Democracies to the Trilateral Commission Paperback*, New York: New York University Press.
Da Silva, V. A. (2011), "Ideas e institucois constitutionais do século xx no Brasil," in D. Valadés et al., eds., *Ideas e instituciones constitucionales en el siglo XX.* México: Siglo XXI.
Dahl, R. (1956), *A Preface to Democratic Theory*, Chicago: The University of Chicago Press.
Dahl, R. (1989), *Democracy and Its Critics*, New Haven, CT: Yale University Press.
Dahl, R. (2003), *How Democratic Is the American Constitution?* Connecticut, CT: Yale University Press.
De Jongh, M. (2013), "Group Dynamics in the Citizens' Assembly on Electoral Reform," Thesis, Grasten (Denmark), Toptryk Grafisk, at Utrecht University Repository, dspace.library.uu.nl/handle/1874/275018.
Dixon, R. (2018), "Constitutional Rights as Bribes," 50 *Connecticut Law Review* 769.
Dworkin, R. (1975), "Hard Cases," 88 *Harvard Law Review* 1057.
Dworkin, R. (1977), *Taking Rights Seriously*, Harvard, MA: Cambridge University Press.
Dworkin, R. (1997), "The Arduous Virtue of Fidelity: Originalism, Scalia, Tribe, and Nerve," 65 *Fordham Law Review.*
Dyzenhaus, D. (2004), "The Left and the Question of Law," 17 *Can. J.L. & Jurisprudence*, 7.
Dyzenhaus, D. (2010), *Hard Cases in Wicked Legal Systems: Pathologies of Legality*, Oxford: Oxford University Press.
Dyzenhaus, D. (2012), "Response to Ian Shapiro, 'On Non-Domination,'" 62 *UTLJ* 337.
Dyzenhaus, D. & Thorburn, M. (2016), *Philosophical Foundations of Constitutional Law*, Oxford: Oxford University Press.
Eberhardt, L. (2017), "La Revocatoria de Mandato en América Latina: una herramienta de participación y control al servicio de los ciudadanos (¿o de los gobernantes?)," Doctoral thesis, on file with author.
Echeverría, J. (2008), "Plenos poderes y democracia en el proceso constituyente ecuatoriano," in J. Echeverría & C. Montúfar, eds., *Plenos poderes y transformación constitucional*, Quito: Ediciones Abya-Yala.
Elster, J. (1983), *Sour Grapes*, Cambridge, UK: Cambridge University Press.

Elster, J. (1986), "The Market and the Forum: Three Varieties of Political Theory," in J. Elster and A. Hylland, eds., *Foundations of Social Choice Theory*, Cambridge, UK: Cambridge University Press, 104–132.

Elster, J. (1988), *Ulysses and the Sirens. Studies in Rationality and Irrationality*, Cambridge, UK: Cambridge University Press.

Elster, J. (2000), *Ulysses Unbound*, Cambridge, UK: Cambridge University Press.

Elster, J. & Slagstad, R. (1988), *Constitutionalism and Democracy*, Cambridge, UK: Cambridge University Press.

Elster, J. et al. (2018), *Constitutional Conventions*, Cambridge, UK: Cambridge University Press.

Farrand, M., ed. (1937), *The Records of the Federal Convention of 1787*, New Haven, CT: Yale University Press.

Farrell, D., Suiter, J. & Harris, C. (2019), "Systematizing Constitutional Deliberation: The 2016–18 Citizens' Assembly in Ireland," 34 (1) *Irish Political Studies* 113–123.

Ferejohn, J. (2008), "Conclusion: The Citizens' Assembly Model," in M. Warren & H. Pearse, eds., *Designing Deliberative Democracy: The British Columbia Citizens' Assembly*, Cambridge, UK: Cambridge University Press.

Ferrajoli, L. (2008), *Democracia y garantismo*, Madrid: Trotta.

Fishkin, J. (1991), *Democracy and Deliberation*, New Haven, CT: Yale University Press.

Fishkin, J. (1997), *The Voice of the People*, New Haven, CT: Yale University Press.

Fishkin, J. (2009), *When the People Speak*, Oxford: Oxford University Press.

Fishkin, J., Kousser, T., Luskin, R. & Siu, A. (2015), "Deliberative Agenda Setting: Piloting Reform of Direct Democracy in California," 13 (4) *Perspectives on Politics* 1030–1042.

Fiss, O. (1976), "Groups and the Equal Protection Clause," 5 (2) *Philosophy and Public Affairs* 107–177.

Fiss, O. (2005), "El carácter indócil de la política," 80 *Lecciones y ensayos* 1–25.

Forst, R. (2013), *Justification and Critique: Towards a Critical Theory of Politics*, New York: Polity Press.

Gardbaum, S. (2013), *The New Commonwealth Model of Constitutionalism*, Cambridge, UK: Cambridge University Press.

Gardbaum, S. (2020), "Comparative Political Process Theory," 18 *International Journal of Constitutional Law* 1429–1457.

Gargarella, R. (1995), *Nos los representantes*, Buenos Aires: Miño y Dávila.

Gargarella, R. (1998), "Full Representation, Deliberation, and Impartiality," in J. Elster, ed., *Deliberative Democracy*, Cambridge, UK: Cambridge University Press.

Gargarella, R. (2005), *El derecho a la protesta. El primer derecho*, Buenos Aires: Ad Hoc.

Gargarella, R. (2010) *The Legal Foundations of Inequality*, Cambridge, UK: Cambridge University Press.

Gargarella, R. (2012), "Law and Social Protests," 6 *Criminal Law and Philosophy* 15–27.

Gargarella, R. (2013), *Latin American Constitutionalism*, Oxford: Oxford University Press.

Gargarella, R. (2014), *La sala de máquinas de la Constitución. Dos siglos de constitucionalismo en América Latina (1810–2010)*, Buenos Aires: Katz ed.

Gargarella, R. (2020), "Constituent Power in 'a Community of Equals'," 41 *Revus. Journal for Constitutional Theory and Philosophy of Law*, https://journals.openedition.org/revus/.

Gargarella, R. (2020a), "Diálogo democrático y emergencia en América Latina" (Democratic Dialogue and Emergency in Latin America) (June 10). *Max Planck Institute for Comparative Public Law & International Law (*MPIL) Research Paper No. 2020-21, c/ Jorge Roa. Available at SSRN: https://ssrn.com/abstract=3623812 or http://dx.doi.org/10.2139/ssrn.3623812.

Gargarella, R. (2020b), "Argentina: Facing Coronavirus in the Shadow of the Rule of Law," *Bill of Health. Harvard Law*, https://blog.petrieflom.law.harvard.edu/2020/06/08/argentina-global-responses-covid19/.

Gargarella, R. (2020c), "The Fight Against COVID-19 in Argentina: Executive vs Legislative Branch," *Verfassungsblog. On Matters Constitutional* (June, 2020), https://verfassungsblog.de/author/roberto-gargarella/.

Gargarella, R. (2021), "From 'Democracy and Distrust' to a Contextually Situated Dialogic Theory," 18(4) *International Journal of Constitutional Law* 1466–1473, https://doi.org/10.1093/icon/moaa094.

Gargarella, R. (2022), "In the Name of the People. Review of Joel Colon Ríos' *Constituent Power*" manuscript, to be published.

Garzón Valdés, E. (1992), "No pongas tus sucias manos sobre Mozart," 19 *Claves de la Razón Práctica* 16–23.

Gilly, A. (1994), *La revolución interrumpida*, México: Ediciones Era.

Ginsburg, T. (2021), "Notes on a Continuing Conversation," 49 *Revista Derecho del Estado* (May–August).

Ginsburg, T. & Huq, A. (2018), *How to Save a Constitutional Democracy*, Chicago, IL: The University of Chicago Press.

Gloppen, S., Wilson, B., et al (2010), *Courts and Power in Latin America and Africa*, London: Palgrave.

Godoy, M. (2017), *Devolver a Constituicao ao povo: critica a supremacia judicial e dialogos interinstitucionais*. Belo Horizonte: Editora Forum.

Graber, M., Levinson, S., & Tushnet, M., eds. (2018), *Constitutional Democracy in Crisis?*, Oxford: Oxford University Press.

Greenberg, M. (2020) "Legal Interpretation and Natural Law," Natural Law Colloquium Special Issue, 89*Fordham Law Review* 109.

Guastini, R. (2017), *Saggi scettici sull'interpretazione*, Roma: Giappichelli.

Guzmán, J. (1979), "El camino político," *Revista Realidad*, 13–23.

Habermas, J. (1996), *Between Facts and Norms: Contributions to a Discourse Theory on Law and Democracy*, Cambridge, MA: MIT Press.

Halperín Donghi, T. (1980), *Proyecto y Construcción de una Nación*, Caracas: Biblioteca Ayacucho.

Hamilton, A., Madison, J. & Jay, J. [1788] (1961), *The Federalist Papers*, London: Penguin Books.

Hart, H. (1961), *The Concept of Law*, Oxford: Oxford University Press.

Holmes, S. (1988), "Precommitment and the Paradox of Democracy," in J. Elster & R. Slagstad, *Constitutionalism and Democracy*, Cambridge, UK: Cambridge University Press.

Huntington, S. (1983), *American Politics: The Promise of Disharmony*, Cambridge, MA: Harvard University Press.

Jaksic, I. (1997), *Andrés Bello. Selected Writings*, Oxford: Oxford University Press.

Jefferson, T. (1999), *Political Writings*, Cambridge, UK: Cambridge University Press.

Kelsen, H. (1967) (2005) *Pure Theory of Law*, New York: The Lawbook Exchange Ltd.

Kramer, L. (2005), *The People Themselves. Popular Constitutionalism and Judicial Review*, Oxford: Oxford University Press.

Kymlicka, W. (1996), *Multicultural Citizenship: A Liberal Theory of Minority Rights*, Oxford: Oxford University Press.

Lafont, C. (2020), *Democracy without Shortcuts. A Participatory Conception of Deliberative Democracy*, Oxford: Oxford University Press.

Landau, D. (2013), "Abusive Constitutionalism," 47 *UC Davis Law Review* 189–260.

Landemore, H. (2013), *Democratic Reason*, Princeton, NJ: Princeton University Press.

Landemore, H. (2014), "Inclusive Constitution-Making, The Icelandic Example," 23(2) *Journal of Political Philosophy*, 166–191.

Landemore, H. (2014a), "We, All of the People. Five Lessons from Iceland's Failed Experiment in Creating a Crowdsourced Constitution," *Slate*, available at https://slate.com/technology/2014/07/five-lessons-from-icelands-failed-crowd sourced-constitution-experiment.html.

Landemore, H. (2020), *Open Democracy. Reinventing Popular Rule for the Twenty-First Century*, Princeton, NJ: Princeton University Press.

Lechner, N. (1991), "A la búsqueda de la comunidad perdida," 129 *Revista Internacional de Ciencias Sociales*, UNESCO, 8.

Lerner, H. (2013), *Making Constitutions in Deeply Divided Societies*, Cambridge, UK: Cambridge University Press.

Lerner, H. (2017), "Constituent Assemblies in Divided Societies," in J. Elster, R. Gargarella et al., *Constituent Assemblies*, Cambridge, UK: Cambridge University Press.

Levinson, S. (2008), *Our Undemocratic Constitution*, Oxford: Oxford University Press.

Levitsky, S. & Ziblatt, D. (2018), *How Democracies Die*, New York: Crown.

Levy, R., Kong, H, Orr, G. & King, J. , eds. (2018), *The Cambridge Handbook of Deliberative Constitutionalism*, Cambridge, UK: Cambridge University Press.

Liebenberg, S. (2012), "Engaging the Paradoxes of the Universal and Particular in Human Rights Adjudication. The Possibilities and Pitfalls of 'Meaningful Engagement'," 12 *African Human Rights Law Journal* 1–29.

Lima Lopes, J. (2008), *O Direito na Historia*, Sao Paulo: Editorial Atlas.

Luo, Z. & Przeworski, A. (2019), "Subversion by Stealth: Dynamics of Democratic Backsliding," manuscript on file with the author.

Lutz, D. (1988), *The Origins of American Constitutionalism*, Baton Rouge: Louisiana University Press.

Manin, B. (1997), *The Principles of* Representative *Government*, Cambridge, UK: Cambridge University Press.

Mansbridge, J. (1983), *Beyond Adversary Democracy*, Chicago, IL: University of Chicago Press.

Molina, G. (1970), *Las ideas liberales en Colombia*, Bogotá: Ediciones Tercer Mundo.

Moyn, S. (2010), *The Last Utopia*, Cambridge, MA: Harvard University Press.

Moyn, S. (2018), "Human Rights Are Not Enough," *The Nation*, www.thenation.com/article/human-rights-are-not-enough/.

Hogg, P. & Bushell, A. (1997), "The Charter Dialogue Between Courts and Legislatures," 35 *Osgoode Hall L. J.* 75.

Manfredi, C. & Kelly, J. (1990), "Six Degrees of Dialogue: A Response to Hogg and Bushell," 37 *Osgoode Hall L. J.* 513.

Manin, B. (1997), *The Principles of Representative Government*, Cambridge, UK: Cambridge University Press.

Marx, K. [1843] (1978), "Contribution to the Critique of Hegel's *Philosophy of Right*," in R. Tucker ed., *The Marx-Engels Reader*, New York: Norton & Company.

Marx, K. [1844] (1983) "Alienated Labor," in *The Portable Karl Marx*, London: Penguin Classics.

Michelman, F. (1969), "On Protecting the Poor Through the Fourteenth Amendment," 83 *Harvard Law Review* 7.

Mill, J. [1859] 2003, *On Liberty*, London: Dover Publications Inc.

Molina, G. (1987), *Las ideas liberales en Colombia*, Bogotá: Tercer Mundo.

Murillo Toro, M. (1979), *Obras Selectas*, Bogotá: Camara de Representantes.

Nino, C. (1987), ed., *Presidencialismo vs. Parlamentarismo*, Buenos Aires: Consejo para la Consolidación de la Democracia.

Nino, C. (1991), *The Ethics of Human Rights*, Oxford: Oxford University Press.

Nino, C. (1997), *The Constitution of Deliberative Democracy*, New Haven, CT: Yale University Press.

O'Donnell, G. (2007), "Las crisis perpetuas de la democracia," 3(1) *Polis* 11–20.

O'Donnell, G. (2010), *Democracia, agencia y Estado. Teoría con intención comparativa*, Buenos Aires: Prometeo.

Parkinson, J. & Mansbridge, J. (2012), Deliberative systems. *Deliberative Democracy at the Large Scale*, Cambridge: Cambridge U.P.

Petter, A. (2003), "Twenty Years of Charter Justification: From Liberal Legalism to Dubious Dialogue," 52 *UNB Law Journal* 187–199.

Pettit, P. (2012), *On the People's Terms*, Cambridge, UK: Cambridge University Press.

Phillips, A. (1995), *The Politics of Presence*, Oxford: Oxford University Press.

Pincione, G. & Tesón, F. (2006), *Rational Choice and Democratic Deliberation*, Cambridge, UK: Cambridge University Press.

Pitkin, H. (1972), *The Concept of Representation*, Berkeley, CA: The University of California Press.

Posner, E. & Vermeule, A. (2010), *The Executive Unbound: After the Madisonian Republic*, Oxford: Oxford University Press.

Post, R. & Siegel, R. (2004), "Popular Constitutionalism, Departmentalism, and Judicial Supremacy," *Faculty Scholarship Series* No. 178. Yale Law School, https://digitalcommons.law.yale.edu/fss_papers/178.

Post, R. & Siegel, R. (2007), "Roe Rage: Democratic Constitutionalism and Backlash," 42 *Harvard Civil Rights-Civil Liberties Law Review* 373–433.

Priestley, J. (1791), Lectures on History and General Policy, Dublin.

Przeworski, A. (2019), *Crisis of Democracy*, Cambridge, UK: Cambridge University Press.

Przeworski, A. & Sprague, J. (1988), *Paper Stones: A History of Electoral Socialism*, Chicago, IL: The University of Chicago Press.

Przeworski, A., Stokes, S., & Manin, M., eds. (1999), *Democracy, Accountability and Representation*, Cambridge, UK: Cambridge University Press.

Rawls, J. (1991), *Political Liberalism*, New York: Columbia University Press.

Roach, K. (2001), "Constitutional and Common Law Dialogues Between the Supreme Court and Canadian Legislatures," 80 *La Revue du Barreau Canadien* 481–533.

Roach, K. (2004), "Dialogic Judicial Review and its Critics," 23 *Supreme Court Law Review*, 49–104.

Rodríguez-Garavito, C. (2011), "Beyond the Courtroom: The Impact of Judicial Activism on Socioeconomic Rights in Latin America," 89 (7) *Texas Law Review* 1669–1698.

Rosenberg, G. (1991), *The Hollow Hope: Can Courts Bring About Social Change?* Chicago, IL: The University of Chicago Press.

Rossi, J. & Filippini, L. (2010), "El derecho internacional en la justiciabilidad de los derechos sociales," in P. Arcidiácono et al., *Derechos sociales: justicia, política y economía en América Latina*, Bogotá: Siglo del Hombre-Universidad de Los Andes.

Sandel, M. (1996), *Democracy's Discontent. America in Search of a Public Philosophy*, Cambridge, MA: Harvard University Press.

Sandel, M. (2020), *The Tyranny of Merit*, New York: Farrar, Straus and Giroux.

Salazar, D. (2015), "My Power in the Constitution: The Perversion of the Rule of Law in Ecuador," SELA, Yale University, at www.law.yale.edu/sites/default/files/documents/pdf/SELA15_Salazar_CV_Eng.pdf.

Scanlon, T. (1984), "Rights, Goals and Fairness," in J. Waldron, ed., *Theories of Rights*, Oxford: Oxford University Press.

Scalia, A. (1996), "Judicial Adherence to The Text of Our Basic Law: A Theory of Constitutional Interpretation." Speech delivered at the Catholic University of America on October 18,www.proconservative.net/PCVol5Is225ScaliaTheoryConst lInterpretation.shtml.

Schumpeter, J. (2008), *Capitalism, Socialism and Democracy*, London: Harper Classics.

Setala, M. (2017), "Connecting Deliberative Mini-Publics to Representative Decision Making," 56(4) *European Journal of Political Research* 846–863.

Shapiro, I. (2012), "On Non-domination," 62 *UTLJ* 293.

Sigalet, G., Webber, G., & Dixon, R. (2019), *Constitutional Dialogue*, Cambridge, UK: Cambridge University Press.

Stone, G. (2018), "It Can't Happen Here. The Lessons of History," in C. Sunstein ed., *Can It Happen Here? Authoritarianism in America*, New York: Library of Congress.

Storing, H. (1981), *The Complete Anti-Federalist*, Chicago, IL: The University of Chicago Press.

Strauss, D. (2018), "Law and the Slow-Motion Emergency," in C. Sunstein ed., *Can it Happen Here? Authoritarianism in America*, New York: Library of Congress.

Sunstein, C. (1985), "Interest Groups in American Public Law," 38 (1) *Stanford Law Review* 29–87.

Sunstein, C. (1993), "Against Positive Rights," 2 *East European Constitutional Review* 35.

Sunstein, C. (1993), *The Partial Constitution*, Cambridge, MA: Harvard University Press.

Sunstein, C. (1996), "The Supreme Court 1995 Term: Foreword: Living Things Undecided," 110 *Harvard Law Review* 6.

Sunstein, C. (2001), "Social and Economic Rights? Lessons from South Africa," *Chicago Unbound*, University of Chicago Law School.

Sunstein, C. (2006), *The Second Bill of Rights*, New York: Basic Books.

Sunstein, C., ed. (2018), *Can It Happen Here? Authoritarianism in America*, New York: Library of Congress.

Sunstein, C., Schkade, D. , & Ellman, L. (2004), "Ideological Voting on Federal Courts of Appeals: A Preliminary Investigation," 90 *Virginia Law Review* 301.

Sunstein, C., Schkade, D. , Ellman, L. , & Sawicki, A. (2006), *Are Judges Political?: An Empirical Analysis of the Federal Judiciary*, New York: Brookings Inst.

Suteu, S. (2015), "Constitutional Conventions in the Digital Era: Lessons from Iceland and Ireland," 38 (2) *Boston College International and Comparative Law Review* 251.

Suteu, S. & Tierney, S. (2018), "Squaring the Circle? Bringing Deliberation and Participation Together in Processes of Constitution-Making," in R. Levy et al., eds., *The Cambridge Handbook of Deliberative Constitutionalism*, Cambridge, UK: Cambridge University Press.

Svampa, M. (2019), "Hacia dónde se mueven las placas tectónicas?" *Brecha*, available at https://brecha.com.uy/hacia-donde-se-mueven-las-placas-tectonicas/?fbclid=IwAR1yj90_22dQzcOmooLIfcx8CGNwE0zA7vhzEQmkCBk4WnarODxPUnBXHAI.

Tullock, G., Seldon, A., & Brady, G. (2002), *Government Failure: A Primer in Public Choice*, Indianapolis: Cato Institute.

Tushnet, M. (2003), "Non-Judicial Review," 40 *Harv. J. on Legisl.* 453–492.

Tushnet, M. (2008), *Weak Courts, Strong Rights*, Princeton, NJ: Princeton University Press.

Tushnet, M. (2009), "Dialogic Judicial Review," 61 *Ark. L. Rev.* 205.

Unger, R. (1996), *What Should Legal Analysis Become?* London: Verso Press.

Valencia Villa, A. (1992), *El pensamiento constitucional de Miguel Antonio Caro*, Bogotá: Instituto Caro y Cuervo.

Van Reybrouck, D. (2017), *Against Elections: The Case for Democracy*, London: Random House.

Vile, M. (1967), *Constitutionalism and the Separation of Powers*, Oxford: Clarendon Press.

Villa, M. A. (2011), *A historia das constituicoes brasileiras*, San Pablo: Leya.

Waldron, J. (1999), *Law and Disagreement*, Oxford: Oxford University Press.

Waldron, J. (1999a), *The Dignity of Legislation*, Oxford: Oxford University Press.

Waldron, J. (1999b), "Deliberation, Disagreement, and Voting," in H. Koh & R. Slye, *Deliberative Democracy and Human Rights*, New Haven, CT: Yale University Press.

Waldron, J. (2009), "The Core of the Case Against Judicial Review," 115 *Yale Law Journal* 1348–1406.

Waldron, J. (2016), *Political Political Theory*, Cambridge, MA: Harvard University Press.

White, M. (1987), *Philosophy, The Federalist, and the Constitution*, Oxford: Oxford University Press.

Whittington, K. (2002), "Extrajudicial Constitutional Interpretation: Three Objections and Responses," 80 *N.C.L. Rev.* 773–783.

Williams, M. (2018), "Book Review: The Adventures of the Constituent Power. Arato, Andrew, Cambridge University Press, 2018," *Constellations* Issue Online, March 20, 2019.

Winterton, G. (1998) "Australia's Constitutional Convention 1998," 5(1) *Agenda* 97–109.

Wood, G. (1966), "A Note on Mobs in the American Revolution," XXIII(4) *William and Mary Quarterly* 635–642.

Wood, G. (1969), *The Creation of the American Republic*, New York: W.W. Norton & Company.

Wood, G. (1991), *The Radicalism of the American Revolution*, New York: Alfred Knopf.

Wood, G. (2002), *The American Revolution. A History*, New York: The Modern Library.

Young, A. (2017), *Democratic Dialogue and the Constitution*, Oxford: Oxford University Press.

INDEX